Claude Francois Meneval, Napoleon Joseph Ernest Méneval

Memoirs Illustrating the History of Napoleon I from 1802 to 1815

Vol. 1

Claude Francois Meneval, Napoleon Joseph Ernest Méneval

Memoirs Illustrating the History of Napoleon I from 1802 to 1815
Vol. 1

ISBN/EAN: 9783337350130

Printed in Europe, USA, Canada, Australia, Japan

Cover: Foto ©ninafisch / pixelio.de

More available books at **www.hansebooks.com**

MEMOIRS

ILLUSTRATING THE

HISTORY OF NAPOLEON I

From 1802 to 1815

BY

Baron CLAUDE-FRANÇOIS DE MÉNEVAL
PRIVATE SECRETARY TO NAPOLEON, FIRST CONSUL AND EMPEROR,
MAÎTRE DES REQUÊTES AT THE COUNCIL OF STATE UNDER THE EMPIRE,
OFFICER OF THE LEGION OF HONOUR AND OF THE ORDER OF THE IRON CROWN
(BORN IN PARIS IN 1778, DIED IN THE SAME CITY IN 1850)

EDITED BY HIS GRANDSON
Baron NAPOLEON JOSEPH DE MÉNEVAL

WITH PORTRAITS AND AUTOGRAPH LETTERS

NEW YORK
D. APPLETON AND COMPANY
1894

EDITOR'S PREFACE.

Les nuages auront passé dans votre gloire,
Rien ne troublera plus son rayonnement pur.
Elle se posera sur toute notre histoire,
   Comme un dôme d'azur!
                              VICTOR HUGO.

MARSHAL CANROBERT did me the honour one day to say, with that courtesy and kindness for which he was famous, "Ah, you will have to work very hard indeed to reach the reputation of a man so universally respected as was your grandfather; to acquire in your turn the qualities which attracted the attention of Napoleon, and which won for him the confidence of the extraordinary genius who, at a glance of the eye, could unfailingly judge a man's character."

It is with grateful pride that I record the flattering words of the glorious soldier—the soldier of the Crimea, of Italy, of Africa, and of Saint Privat—and it is with his permission that I place them at the commencement of this work of mine. All who have had the good fortune to approach him know that sentiment of innate benevolence which forms one of the most striking characteristics of the respected Marshal.

I will admit that these words of his may to some extent have been directed by his benevolence, but still such a eulogy, coming from the mouth of so illustrious and authoritative a man, seemed to me an enviable one. I think I may permit myself to add that these praises of my grandfather seemed to me justified by the qualities ot honour, of truthfulness, and of modesty which all those who knew him in his lifetime, or who formerly read his writings, unanimously agree to have been the leading qualities of the character of the private secretary of the Emperor Napoleon I. Faithful to his master till the grave, he sought always and everywhere, with a complete conviction and the most absolute good faith, to defend the memory of this great man. He was persuaded that time—the great master, as Napoleon himself used to call it—would throw light over this prodigious history, and would dispel no small number of erroneous judgments and prejudices which formerly, like so many clouds, obscured the glory ot the First Empire.

The work which I publish to-day—Memoirs to Serve for the History of Napoleon I.—was written by my grandfather at the end of his life. Indeed it was only very shortly before his death that he had given it the finishing touches. There will be found in it here and there reminiscences and repetitions of his first work, "*Napoleon and Marie Louise*"; but for the greater part the reader will find in this book anecdotes and details which I do not think have been published before. The present generation, moreover, is unacquainted with the first work, the editions of which have long been out of print.

I have religiously respected the opinions of the author of these Memoirs, though here and there I have thought it advisable to cut down passages which seemed to me unnecessarily long, and to carry out certain modifications of pure form; but it did not seem to me that I had any right to change anything, even on certain historical points, where I felt inclined to express, on men or on matters, an opinion different from his.

May the public receive this work with benevolence, and may it find in the perusal of these pages an interest of which I think this book worthy, for it emanates from "an honourable and a truthful man, whose lips were never stained with a lie."*

If this work attains the kind of success which I hope for it I, for my part, shall be sufficiently rewarded for the experiment and for my pains.

  1894.   N. DE MÉNEVAL.

* Public homage rendered to him by M. Thiers in the French Parliament.

AUTHOR'S PREFACE.

THE EMPEROR said to me one day: "In the order of things, I must die before you. When I am no more what will you do? You will write."

I was not prepared for this thought of death, thus unexpectedly expressed, and Napoleon seemed to me immortal. As I did not answer him immediately, he added: "You will not be able to resist the desire to write *Memoirs*."

I vigorously rejected the idea that I should survive him. I could not foresee that the vigorous oak would, in a very few years, be struck down by a terrible storm, and that the humble plant which raised itself under his protection would vegetate after he was gone.

Napoleon, during his last moments at St. Helena, amongst other recommendations which were contained in the instructions which he addressed to his testamentary executors, expressed a desire that certain persons, amongst whom he deigned to include my name, should undertake to direct the ideas of his son on facts and on things, and should bring to his acquaintance communications which would have a special interest for him. The premature death of the direct heir to this great name has not prevented me from fulfilling, as far as I am concerned, this honourable mission.

Since I have had to deplore the loss of the Emperor's son, in comparing the words which his father said to me at another time with the wish which escaped his dying lips at St. Helena, I have often thought that there was no more reason why I should keep silent. I hesitated for a long time before a task which a just want of confidence in my own strength made me fear might be beyond my power to carry out; but age hurries me on to put into shape the souvenirs which my long residence with the Emperor has left me.

However much my pen may be lacking in skill, I shall essay to give a sketch—pale no doubt, but true to nature—of this great man, and at the same time my work will be the homage paid by my gratitude to a memory which will always be dear and sacred to me. "*C'est icy un livre de bonne foy*," as Montaigne said, a book without pretence, whose only merit is that it is the truth. I have tried to show Napoleon just as he was, and as he will inevitably be judged when he is better known, without preoccupying myself about the reproaches of blind partiality which still prejudiced minds will be tempted to address to me.

I have wished to be just—not exclusive.

Whilst judging with severity the conduct of certain men, whom no consideration whatever may absolve, I do not think it necessary to draw fresh attention to other persons who were dragged away by circumstances which were stronger than human nature itself, as Napoleon himself admitted; for, as Christ says, "Let those who are without sin cast the first stone."

I was attached to the person of Napoleon, at that time First Consul, from the month of April, 1802. The great fatigues which I had undergone, and the state of exhaustion in which I came back to Paris after the disasters of the retreat from Moscow, rendered it absolutely necessary that I should take rest. The Emperor, who never forgot old services, understood my need of repose, but not wishing to remove me from his person, appointed me *Secrétaire des commandements* of the Empress, a post which, until then, he had refused to fill. I was, then, placed with this title in the service of this Princess, who just at that time had been proclaimed Regent.

When I saw the Emperor again he made me promise to come back to him as soon as the state of my strength would allow me to do so, and each time that I had the honour of seeing him he did not fail to remind me of my promise. While he was in Paris during the years 1813 and 1814, he received me in private audience in the evening, and during his military campaigns I used to write to him every day.

The stories which I publish are intended to illustrate certain sides of his private history, rather than to depict the conqueror and legislator. However, in a life so largely filled, politics and affairs of government have more or less left their mark on everything. The man, as history knows him, is almost always the principal person. It is therefore impossible to neglect these great pages in the history of Napoleon.

I have also recorded some less known facts which were anterior to my entrance into Napoleon's Cabinet. Initiated—although very young at the time—in the quality of secretary to the principal negotiator to the important transactions of the Congress of Lunéville, of the Concordat, and of the Peace of Amiens; called, after this last treaty, into the Cabinet of the First Consul, my situation has enabled me to throw a retrospective glance on these days of the Consulate and on the first years of the Empire. I shall therefore occasionally speak of personal matters, not indeed for the vain pleasure of putting myself forward, but because, in my opinion, he who undertakes to furnish material for history should make known what are his titles to undertake such a mission. Be it that he obeys a dying request; be it that he lays upon himself the obligation of bearing testimony in the discussions on the solemn cause which posterity shall judge; be it that he yields to the solicitations of his friends, he must make it clear by what means he has learned the things which he relates—how he knows the persons whom he puts forward, and what position occupied by him justifies the confidence which he claims. It has therefore seemed to me necessary to relate as simply as I can the circumstances which brought me into connection with Napoleon, and what share I had in his confidence.

I hope that this narrative may make up for the disadvantage under which I labour of not having been sufficiently before the public to offer my reputation as the guarantee of my truthfulness. I shall relate nothing of which I was not an eyewitness or the direct depositary. It is not my object to relate occurrences which are of public notoriety. Of these I shall only speak where they are necessary to the comprehension of my story. Well-known facts will only be related to serve as connecting links with those which I record. I have not always been able to keep to a methodical classification of facts, but have followed the chronological order as far as possible.

I have to justify myself for having spoken of the Empress Marie Louise without her authorization. The total interruption of the rare communications which up to the year 1830 existed between Paris and Parma, the stubborn silence which ensued, the distance which separates us from the time when the Duchess of Parma shared with Napoleon the most glorious throne in the world, will absolve me for having given publicity to matters which concern this Princess. It is now close upon thirty years, at the moment of writing, that the tomb closed upon the Emperor. The events which illustrated this epoch are to-day matters of history. Barely a few actors in this great drama survive. Changes of opinion or the scythe of time have removed those who played the most important rôles. Those who survive are either lost to the present generation, or have undergone a complete metamorphosis, and are removed from these imposing souvenirs by new interest. The Emperor's wife has become a total stranger to our country. The shortness of her stay in France, the total oblivion of the ties which she formerly contracted here, the death of the only offspring of her union with Napoleon, her abandonment of her adopted Fatherland have barely left any trace of her passage in our midst. Her accession to a sovereignty most Austrian in character, in which the form of government had for its direct object to obliterate all reminiscences of an imperial Italy, the new union which she has contracted have combined to definitely sunder all the ties which bound her to France. What we can say of her, and of the time when a common destiny united her to the Emperor, has also fallen into the domain of history. I have sought to free myself from all prejudices concerning her; I shall be neither her apologist nor her traducer. I describe my impressions with sincerity, just as I received them. Relating facts, it is not my duty to admit extenuating circumstances; it is for the reader to judge. I shall speak of the hopes to which the arrival of the Empress Marie Louise in France gave birth; hopes which seemed to be realizable by the alliance to a new Empire which genius and glory had raised to the highest possible grade of greatness, of one of the most ancient and most powerful Empires in Europe. I shall speak also of all the sinister elements which were contained in the pledge of an apparent reconciliation between the two states, and I shall relate how the blessings with which at first the arrival of the new Empress was saluted, were changed into cries of reprobation.

I desire that my narratives, however imperfect they may be, should give an exact and truthful idea of the great man who was their subject, without diminishing him to satisfy the prejudices of his enemies, and yet without endowing him with supernatural proportions. It is a *juste milieu* which it will be difficult to observe. Nothing is more likely to strike the imagination than the prestige exercised by a man who has probably no equal in history, and in whose person Providence was pleased to unite an incomparable genius, fortune without limits, and an excess of adversity. To this imposing memory are attached imperishable souvenirs of glory, and at the same time of sorrow. All opinions are united in a sentiment of admiration which this memory excites in the highest degree, but it is popular sympathy with which it is especially endowed, a sympathy which bestows itself upon the leader who was animated by a sincere love of his country, who conceived those high ideals of government on which France founded her greatness and her prosperity, and which, surviving their author, have been the rule and the safe guide of the governments which followed the Empire. It is to him that are owing those examples of civic and military virtues, of heroism, of self-sacrifice, of constancy, and above all that vigorous hatred of all foreign domination which keeps alive amongst us the salutary sentiments of nationality. It is thanks to him that France knows all that she is worth. The name of Napoleon is to her a palladium that expresses dignity, grandeur, national honour, immortal sentiments which were inherited by the nation, proud of the man who called her "*La Grande Nation.*"

The infinite number of books published on Napoleon have not been able to satisfy the curiosity of the public. One expects to find in each new publication some new facts, some important revelations. As a matter of fact the history of Napoleon has still to be written. Writers, honourable in intention, have lent him actions, language, and habits which tend to make of this extraordinary man a commonplace personage. A just appreciation of this noble character, the true picture of his public and private life, a strict observation of local colour are wanting in the majority of their books; which are, moreover, disfigured by romantic circumstances. Other writers have believed that Napoleon only walked enshrouded by thick shade, that he had sinister designs—in short, that he only raised himself by the manœuvres of refined hypocrisy. It has been forgotten that the consciousness of his own strength rendered recourse to oblique and mysterious ways unnecessary for him; that in matters of politics at home and abroad he often proceeded with a frankness which was sometimes pushed to the extreme of brutality; that his honour and his sentiments of personal dignity would never allow him to have recourse to deceit or to corruption. If, as a general rule, he took no counsel but his own, on the other hand his ministers carried out all his plans. Nothing was done without their co-operation, and in this respect they have nothing to hide.

It is in the secrecy of the cabinets of our enemies that the light which is still wanting to us must be sought. The writers of the Coalition have raised a corner of the veil, but they have not revealed all. What foreign monarchs would not have been able, and perhaps would not have desired to attempt against their great adversary was accomplished without scruple by their ministers, who had the initiative of the conduct of their masters' policy, and who did not always take them into their confidence. They covered themselves in the eyes of the nation with a responsibility which in absolute governments lies with the monarch. All means were good in their eyes. Success has justified them.

I do not pretend to reveal nothing but secrets; Napoleon's government had fewer secrets than is generally supposed. Some of the things, however, which I relate, are little known, or not known at all. There are questions on which controversy has gone astray. I have sought to explain them. Amongst the facts which I have related, and the resolutions which were their consequence, some are of superior interest. Some of the stories are of value only because they speak of Napoleon's person. It has been my desire above all to make known the heart and the character of a man endowed by Providence with such extraordinary qualities. Anecdotes which have no other merit than to feed malignity without profit to anybody have been suppressed. The principal object which I had in view in collecting my souvenirs was, I repeat, to furnish some materials likely to be useful to the future historian of Napoleon. As to the appreciation of the important resolutions which signalized his reign, and an examination of the causes from which they appear to have proceeded, it is to a more experienced pen than mine—to which fuller and richer documents shall not have been wanting—that it would appertain to retrace them. *

* Thiers.

The epoch which the labours and the genius of Napoleon have immortalized cannot but become well known in the end. The march of truth is slow, but as she casts her beams around clouds are dissipated. The revelations which time will bring will show Napoleon raised on the summit of greatness by means of which morality approves; they will show him free from all baseness, straightforward, magnanimous, exempt from low passions, endowed with every kind of courage, constantly occupied with the care of ameliorating the condition of humanity, and finally moved by the noble ambition to have desired to make of France the most glorious and the most prosperous of nations, ambition too great perhaps, in a worn-out society, for the rejuvenation of which time as well as the constancy of fortune were lacking to him.

TRANSLATOR'S NOTE.

IN translating Baron de Méneval's Memoirs I have endeavoured to follow the original as closely as possible. The style is the man, and in view of the very strong opinions expressed by the Baron on men and politics in general, and on Englishmen and British politics in particular, it seemed to me advisable, by rendering his style as nearly as might be, to present him as he was. This is a model of what is known in France as *"le style administratif,"* which is distinguished by complexity rather than by directness; and I have often found myself wondering, in the course of my work, how, in the constant rush of affairs of Napoleon's cabinet, his private secretary can have found time and occasion to cultivate a style which is the reverse of laconic. It is true that Napoleon himself was a past-master of it, and here again, in its want of plain-speaking and directness, the style was the man.

Historical and other notes have been added, wherever they appeared necessary for the elucidation of the text.

ROBERT H. SHERARD.

Paris, March 1st, 1894.

MEMOIRS

ILLUSTRATING

THE HISTORY OF NAPOLEON I.

From 1802 to 1815.

CHAPTER I.

I leave School—Palissot, and details concerning him—Anecdotes—Men of Letters and Artists who Associated with Him—Mlle. Bourgoin and M. Antoine—Urbain Domergue—I make the Acquaintance of Louis Bonaparte at His House—The Return of General Bonaparte from Egypt—On his Putting into Port in Corsica—Letters of Recall from the Directoire—Testimony of MM. Bourrienne, Amédée Jaubert and Eugène Merlin on This Matter—Letters Received at Acre—General Bonaparte Receives Letters from the Directoire Cancelling his Recall, under way from Fréjus to Lyons—General Lecourbe—Text of Letters from the Directoire, from M. de Talleyrand, and Admiral Bruix—Louis Bonaparte—On the Speech of Artillery Lieutenant Bonaparte, destined for the Competition Opened by the Lyons Academy—Napoleon's Prophecy on His Destiny—His Taste for the Music of "*Le Devin du Village*"—Opinions of Napoleon on J. J. Rousseau—Visit of the First Consul to Ermenonville—Anecdote—Napoleon French, not Italian—Probable Conjectures on the Fate of the Manuscript of Napoleon's Academical Speech—I am Taken by the Conscription—Six Months with the 5th Regiment of Dragoons—Capture and Execution of Frotté at Verneuil—Return to Paris—My Introduction to Joseph Bonaparte—Sedition against His Embassy to Rome—His Story *Moïna*—My Work with this Minister—Negotiations with the United States of America—Conclusion of the Treaty—M. Pichon, Secretary of the Diplomatic Commission is appointed Consul General to the United States—Reasons of his Recall—Fête Given at Mortfontaine on the Occasion of Peace—Description of this Fête—I See Napoleon for the First Time—Ancient Medals found in the Oise Department Presented by the First Consul to the American Ministers—M. de Lafayette—Reflections—Joseph Bonaparte is Appointed Plenipotentiary Minister to the Lunéville Congress—M. de Cobenzl is Austrian Plenipotentiary—His arrival in Paris—His Refusal to Sit unless an English Minister is Admitted to the Congress—Examination of this Claim—Negotiations with the English Cabinet—Two Notes Dictated by Napoleon on this subject—Renewal of Hostilities, and Momentary Suspension of Negotiations—Passage of General Moreau to Lunéville—The Cordial Reception Given Him in Paris by the First Consul—His Instructions for the Campaign—Strange Conduct of General Moreau's Chief Staff Officer at Lunéville—Coldness of General Moreau—The Victory of Hohenlinden Changes the Face of the Negotiations—Armistice of Steyer—Peace Concluded—Principal Conditions—Some

Details about the Negotiations—On the Convention of Lunéville Opposed to the Suspension of Hostilities Concluded at Treviso—News of the Explosion of the Infernal Machine on the 3rd Nivôse—The Horror at this Outrage Expressed by the Austrian General—The *Personnel* of the French Legation—General Clarke Governor of Lunéville—Anecdote—General Hugo and His Sons, Abel and Victor—Anatole de Lawoestyne—Scene at the Café Tortoni—Return of the French and Austrian Plenipotentiaries to Paris—First Conference on the Distribution of the Indemnities due to the Princes dispossessed on the Left Bank of the Rhine—Definite Settlement Concluded at Ratisbon—Part Taken by M. de Talleyrand in this Negotiation—Extortions Committed, and Prosecutions Instituted in Consequence—Summer of 1801 Passed at Mortfontaine—Notes about the *Château*—Count de Cobenzl and M. Hoppé—The Poet Casti—His Continual Quarrels with Mesdames Leclerc and Murat, Sisters of the First Consul—Hospitality at Mortfontaine—Le Plessis-Charmant—Lucien Bonaparte—Dramatic Performances —Excursions from Mortfontaine to La Malmaison—Family Life at La Malmaison—League of the Maritime Powers of the North against England—Agreement of Paul I. and the First Consul—Death of Paul I.—Change in the Policy of this Prince's Successor—Dissolution of the Northern League—Bad Directions given to the Operations of the Army in Egypt—General Menou—Defeats—Evacuation of Egypt—The King of Etruria in Paris—Concordat—Causes which Made France take Part in It—Attachment of the French to the Roman Catholic Religion—Divided Opinions of a Necessity of a Religious Transaction—Its Advantages—National Council—Papal Nuncio to Paris—Cardinal Consalvi—French Plenipotentiaries—Abbé Bernier—Signing the Concordat—Its Publication Adjourned—Purging the Tribunal—Te Deum on the Occasion of the Concordat and the Peace of Lunéville—Court dress Assumed on this Occasion—The "Regent"—Opposition of some Generals—Hostile Conduct of Bernadotte—Reflections on the Concordat—Creation of a Directoire, then of a Ministry of Religious Worship—M. Portalis—Cardinal Caprara sent with the Title of Legate *a Latere*—Cardinal Fesch—M. de Chateaubriand—The Fall of the Pitt Cabinet—Ministry of Haddington and Hawkesbury—Revocation of the Order Given by the preceding Ministry that French Fishermen were to be Treated as Enemies—Tendency of the New Ministers Towards a Reconciliation—Overtures to M. Otto—Words and Notes Exchanged on this Subject—Negotiation and Signature of Preliminaries in London—Note Dictated by Napoleon on the Refusal of the English Government to Listen to the Proposals of Peace made in 1800—Amiens Designated as the Place of Reunion of the Congress for the Conclusion of the Definitive Treaty—Glance at the Results of the Administration of the First Consul—Arrival of Lord Cornwallis in Paris—Preliminary Conferences—Opening of the Amiens Congress—Negotiations—Long Discussion on the Malta Question—Close of the Protocol—Conditions of Peace—Signature of the Treaty at Amiens Town-Hall—Lord Cornwallis's Loyalty—Mr. Merry—M. Dupuy—M. Portalis—Insinuation to Recognize the First Consul as King—Sentiments Expressed by Napoleon on this Occasion—General Sebastiani's Avowal to the Chamber of Deputies—Household State of the Plenipotentiary Ministers—Courtesy of Lord Cornwallis to the Amiens Manufacturers—Reception of the Principal Authorities—An Unpublished Song from the Poem *Vert-Vert*—Reflections—Mlles. Emilie and Hortense de Beauharnais—Marriage of Louis Bonaparte—Small Sympathy between the Spouses—Religious Sanction given to the Marriage of Murat and His Wife—This Consecration of the Church is not Given to the Union of General Bonaparte with Madame de Beauharnais—Reasons Given for This.

I HAD not quite completed my education at Mazarin College, where I was a boarder, when the events of the Revolution, becoming every day more stormy, and threatening to destroy all ancient establishments, at last affected the public schools. I left Mazarin, like the monks, the doors of whose monasteries were violently thrown open. I had no fixed plans. I was moved by a vague desire to profit by my college reminiscences, to exercise myself in different kinds of literature simultaneously, without vocation, *invitâ Minervâ*. I felt, as is trivially, though appropriately said about young people who have just left school, a desire to sow my wild oats. Some boyish attempts at writing drew me to a man who was at that time, it may be said, the *doyen* of littérateurs. I was received by the respectable Palissot with the kindness which he showed to young people whom the pureness of his style had led to seek his advice.

Palissot, naturally good and obliging, about whom a witty woman could say with truth that he had a keen wit and a dull heart, had been drawn on to embrace the most thorny kind of literature, namely satire. The comedy entitled "*Les Philosophes*," written at the instigation of the Duc de Choiseul, had made for him mortal enemies. This Minister, alarmed by the progress of the philosophical sect which numbered Voltaire (a secret enemy), and Diderot and d'Alembert (openly declared adversaries), amongst its leaders, desired to add to his means of repression the powerful arm of ridicule. The mordant hyperboles of Palissot of necessity drew upon him the enmity of the philosophers, who inveighed against him in the most furious manner. A desire of vengeance inspired the author of "*Les Philosophes*" with an imitation of Pope's Dunciad. The stinging darts with which he transfixed his enemies kindled in their hearts an inextinguishable hatred. Their rancour, which they bequeathed to their heirs, pursued him to his extreme old age. Palissot has frequently told me that all the reward he ever obtained, in compensation for the bitter hours with which these quarrels had filled his life, was a smile with which Madame de Pompadour considered him amply repaid. Meeting the favourite one day, accompanied by the Duc de Choiseul, who was driving her carriage, the author of "*Les Philosophes*" was presented to her by the Minister. Madame de Pompadour deigned to stop for a moment, and, without speaking to him, thanked him with a nod of her head, and her most graceful smile, before which the good Palissot lost himself in obeisances.

Palissot had thrice put himself forward for a seat in the Academy. Thrice the cabal, which was got up against him by Naigeon, testamentary executor of Diderot, and by Lalande,[*] the Diogenes of philosophy, succeeding in defeating him. At the last election, General Bonaparte, at the request of Chénier, went to the Institute to give his vote in his favour. Intrigue turned against Palissot a step which should have been decisive in his favour. A rumour was spread that General Bonaparte had come to vote in favour of Abbé Leblanc, Palissot's competitor, the now forgotten author of a translation in verse of "*Lucrèce*", and of a tragedy called "*Manco-Capac*", the fall of which was

[*] Joseph Jérôme François de Lalande, born at Bourg, 11th July, 1732, Professor at the Collège de France in 1761, Director of the Paris observatory in 1768, Died in Paris, April 4th 1807. Wrote *Traité d'Astronomie* (1792), and *Bibliographie Astronomique* (1803.)—R. H. S.

determined by the following line, since become proverbial:
"*Crois-tu d'un tel forfait Manco-Capac capable?*"
Abbé Leblanc, an inoffensive poet who had wounded no man's vanity, was elected. Chénier, referring to this, said to General Bonaparte, who was surprised at the result of the election, "General, you had to come here to be defeated."

Discouraged by the failure of his attempts, Palissot renounced the honours of the Institute. He consoled himself for his misadventures at the Academy in the bosom of his family, and in adding some lines to the Dunciad. The post of perpetual administrator of the Mazarin library, which he owed to the friendship of François de Neuf-Château, and the pensions which were granted to him under the Consulate and the Empire, enabled him to close with honour a career rendered illustrious by intrigues, which should have opened to him the doors of the Institute had it been possible to disarm the old rancour of the philosophers.

I used to meet many more or less distinguished men of letters at Palissot's house. There was Marie Joseph Chénier, whom Palissot had encouraged as a young writer, and whose talent reached the highest summits, when death took him still in the full strength of his age; there was Lebrun,[*] the lyrical poet, and Saint-Ange, the author of a translation in verse of Ovid's Metamorphoses, who had changed, for names which they considered more poetical, their patronymics of Écouchard and Fariau; there was Felix Nogaret, the French Aristenetes, who affected cynicism, but who

---

[*] Ponce Denis Écouchard (1729—1807). His *œuvres* were published in four volumes in 1811. His selected works, in two volumes, were published in 1821.

professed a veritable friendship for Palissot. Legouvé, Talma, and Mademoiselle Contat used sometimes to come and call upon the *doyen* of the authors of the Théâtre Français. The calls of his friends and a modest rubber of whist used to occupy his evenings. He rarely went to the theatre, and deplored its decadence, like all old men in whose eyes the imperfections of the present only increase the illusions and the regrets of the past. Talma and Mademoiselle Contat alone had the privilege of inducing him to return to the theatre. To these exceptional talents was to be added a growing talent which Palissot, who loved to exercise a kind of patronage, protected with the ardour which he placed at the services of his new acquaintances. Mademoiselle Bourgoin, destined herself to play the part of juvenile lead at the Théâtre Français, had been introduced to him by M. Antoine, architect of the Mint, from whom she had received instruction. She was at that time sixteen years of age, and was very pretty, piquant, and giddy, with ingenuous manners. She had no difficulty in winning over an old man, who was only too disposed to let himself be seduced by her affectionate and caressing ways. M. Antoine, her master, had at one time mistaken for a decided vocation an irresistible passion which he had had for the stage. His friend Lekain had combated the mania of his stage-struck friend with all his powers, and had prevented him from abandoning a useful and honourable profession for an uncertain and precarious career, from which he had little to hope for but mediocrity. M. Antoine was grateful for this to his friend, but could not help regretting not to have made his début in the *rôle* of Don Sancho of Aragon, by Corneille. The début of Mademoiselle Bourgoin was the unique object of his solicitude, and he had come to find in his neighbour Palissot one whose influence in the theatrical world might be useful to his favourite pupil. Mademoiselle Bourgoin used to come almost every evening with her professor, and rehearse before Palissot different passages from the parts which she had chosen for her first appearance on the stage, receiving advice and encouragement from the poet.

Amongst other men of letters whom I had occasion to meet at Palissot's house was Urbain Domergue, a Member of the Institute, and an eminent grammarian, who was distinguished for charming simplicity and kindheartedness. He had only one passion, and that was grammar, for which he had a kind of worship. His profound studies and his zeal for the propagation of this art had induced him to introduce into the grammatical system certain new terms and innovations which were not received with favour. A quarrel which he had with Lebrun, most irascible of poets, and his mania for writing in verse, drew down upon him the most biting of epigrams. His happy carelessness was not disturbed by them. Enemy of everything which might disturb his idleness, he had abandoned the entire management of his affairs to a young servant, who displayed but little order and economy at his house, a circumstance which never disturbed him. In this house I made the acquaintance of one of the brothers of General Bonaparte, recently arrived from Egypt, where he had been sent on a mission by the Directoire.

Louis Bonaparte employed his leisure during his stay in Paris in attending lectures. He associated himself with the friends of literature, artists, and professors.

He was preparing himself for the culture of literature, for which he had an innate taste, a taste which was his consolation in the highest rank and in his subsequent retirement. He was good, and of a straightforwardness which made him adopt as his motto : "Do what thou shouldst do, let happen what may", to which he has constantly been true. He treated me with kindness. Although it was at that time impossible to foresee the high estate to which he has since risen, his personal merits, and his near kinship to the illustrious General Bonaparte, already gave him a superiority behind which my youth, and the first steps which I took in the political world of that strange epoch, were sheltered.

It was only a few months after the return of Louis Bonaparte from Egypt, when General Bonaparte unexpectedly landed at Fréjus.

Corsica had seen her illustrious child again during his crossing from Egypt to France. Forced by stress of weather to put into port at Ajaccio, it was of importance to him to avoid the delays imposed by quarantine. As soon as the presence of General Bonaparte before Ajaccio became known, the Treasury paymaster, a M. Barberi, who was a friend of his family, hastened to take boat and row to the frigate on board which the General found himself, to congratulate him on his return. Bonaparte asked for some fruit, and for the newspapers, of which he had been deprived for a long time. He also expressed the pleasure which he should experience in landing in the midst of his fellow townsmen.

Whilst M. Barberi was occupied in sending on board what had been asked for, his father, who was President of the Sanitary Commission, explained to his colleagues the plausible motives for which the General should be permitted to land, so as to satisfy the desire of the population, in whose hearts the news of his presence was exciting the warmest enthusiasm. The Commissioners alleged the rigours of the regulations and the responsibility under which they lay. This refusal might compromise Napoleon's plans. The President, convinced that there were no sick men on board—drawn on, on the other hand, by his zeal and his devotion—proposed to the members of the Commission of Health that they should go in a body alongside the frigate, so as, at least, to offer their congratulations to the General. This suggestion was adopted without difficulty. The members of the Commission embarked on the health boat under the guidance of a man who had secretly been ordered to run into the frigate, under pretext of an accident, so that the members of the Commission would be brought into forced contact with the crew of the ship. The interdiction must then be raised, M. Barberi being convinced that they would not want to undergo quarantine themselves. This plan, carried out with decision, was fully successful. Napoleon, surrounded by Generals Berthier, Murat, Andréossy and others, made haste to reassure the Commissioners. A return was immediately made to land, where the General and his suite were received with enthusiasm by the entire population.

Detained by unfavourable winds, General Bonaparte tried to utilize his enforced stay in Corsica. His first care was to remedy the pitiful state in which he found the troops drawn up to receive him. Learning that for nineteen months past these soldiers had received neither pay nor allowances of any kind, and that the paymaster, to keep them alive, had exhausted every resource, including his private means, he made haste to put at his disposal, towards meeting their most pressing needs, all the money in his possession, (about forty thousand francs,) reserving for himself only just enough to pay his posting expenses to Paris.

Whilst congratulating the paymaster on the disinterestedness which had been shown by his family, he expressed his indignation at the carelessness of the Government, which seemed to attach so little importance to the welfare of its soldiers. These details were communicated to me by M. Barberi himself, who was at that time Treasury Paymaster at Ajaccio.

I may add those which follow, given to me by an eye-witness, M. Amédée Jaubert, secretary to General Bonaparte. Napoleon, impatient to continue his voyage, waited until favourable winds would allow him to sail out of the Bay of Ajaccio. On three different occasions it was thought that the wind had changed. At last, an officer sent by Rear-admiral Ganteaume, came to announce to the General, during a ball given in his honour by the municipality, that the wind had veered to the south, and that not a moment was to be lost in taking advantage of it. Everybody embarked without delay, each in the costume which he had worn at the ball. Sail was set, and the ship headed towards Toulon, near which an English squadron was stationed. Fortunately the frigate was not sighted.

Towards the evening of the 16th Vendémiaire (corresponding to October 7th, 1799), the ship was allowed to drift in the direction of the mountains which rise above Nice, and it was only at a very early hour on the following morning that it was found to be in the neighbourhood of Fréjus. The General-in-chief, in spite of the observations which had been made to him in the course of the night by the Rear-admiral, had decided to embark in a longboat and to gain the coast, when the commander of Saint Rapheau, a small military post, situated about a league's distance from Fréjus, came in a boat to the frigate. He took Napoleon and his suite on board, and landed them at Saint Rapheau, from which they walked to Fréjus. The frigate lay to in the offing. The foot squadron of guides, who had accompanied the General-in-chief, went to finish their quarantine at Toulon and Napoleon set out without delay for Paris.

I will not undertake to describe the enthusiasm which the news of the debarkation of General Bonaparte excited throughout France; it was everywhere received with the presentiment that the liberator expected by the nation had at last arrived. I will tarry over a fact on which sufficient light has not been thrown; some correspondence which remained unpublished till the day on which I printed it in the number of the *Spectateur Militaire* for May 15th, 1850, will determine the opinion of the reader on the value of the generally-accredited assertion that General Bonaparte returned from Egypt against the wishes of the Directoire. When I published this correspondence I expressed the hope that its publication might entail some revelations, which would not leave any doubt on the question whether the letters under consideration had been received by General Bonaparte whilst he was in Egypt, and whether consequently they had authorized his return to France. I have to say how this problem of history, which to-day only possesses an interest of curiosity, has been solved. The letters of which this correspondence is composed are seven in number. The first was already known; it has been quoted in numerous publications. It is dated the 7th Prairial, of the year VII (26th May, 1799) and is signed by three directors, a condition exacted by the constitution of the year III for the validation of all acts emanating from the Directoire. This decision was transmitted the same day by president Merlin de Douai to Admiral Bruix. Published by itself, and unsupported by any testimony, it has been regarded up to our time as supposititious. In his unpublished memoirs Laréveillère-Lepeaux, a former member of the Directoire, one of the three signers of whom I have spoken, declares, it is assured, that he does not remember having signed any letter which had for its purpose the recall of General Bonaparte. This is an error of memory on the part of M. Laréveillère-Lepeaux. The existence of this letter and the signature affixed to it by himself, cannot be doubted any more than the authenticity of the letters which accompanied it, and which are still extant in their original forms.

The assertion contained in the memoirs published under the name of M. de Bourrienne, which disposes of this question by declaring it absurd, has not appeared sufficiently authorized. Very much confidence cannot be accorded to the allegations contained in memoirs published under the name of a man who never wrote them. I will show later on what reasoning this last assertion is based.

The testimony of M. Amédée Jaubert and that of General Eugène Merlin, the former of whom was secretary-interpreter, and the latter aide-de-camp to the commander-in-chief of the army of Egypt, merit a more serious examination. These two witnesses, each in his respective capacity, did not leave the person of the commander-in-chief during the course of the expedition, and embarked with him on his return to France. They were, all things considered, in quite as favourable a position as Bourrienne to know what orders were given by the commander-in-chief, and what was going on about him both before his departure and at the moment when this departure was effected. They heard nothing during the voyage home which could lead them to suspect that orders from the Directoire were recalling General Bonaparte home. They agree in saying that his departure seemed to have been decided by the reception of English newspapers containing detailed news about the reverses suffered by our armies in Italy and in Germany, papers which had been sent to the head-quarters of the French army by the English admirals. This testimony, without being decisive, was a great argument in favour of the opinion that General Bonaparte's letters of recall were not received by him whilst he was in Egypt. Since these letters have been published the words of Napoleon himself have come to throw fresh light on this question.

In the notes dictated by him at St. Helena it is said that during the siege of Acre, on the 27th of Floréal, year VII—(May 13th, 1799) he received letters from France which apprised him of the bad state of our affairs, and that this news was what chiefly impelled him to raise the siege and to retire to Alexandria. These letters could not be those which contained the orders of the Directoire, inasmuch as these are dated the 7th Prairial—(May 26th)—of the same year, and were not sent off until the 23rd of the same month, that is to say, on the 11th of June. It is more than probable that the letters which were received before Acre were the letters sent by Joseph Bonaparte, and carried by the Greek Bourbaki; but what finally dissipates all doubt is the following fact which was communicated to me by General Bertrand, to whom the Emperor related it at St. Helena. To name General Bertrand is to mention a man worthy of all confidence, from the nobility of his character, and the just esteem to which his constant fidelity in misfortune so fully entitled him.

General Bonaparte, who was believed by the Directoire to be still in Egypt, had landed at Fréjus on the 17th Vendémiaire of the year VIII—(October 9th, 1799).—He was on his way to Paris when, between Fréjus and Lyons, he met a courier bearing despatches addressed to the commander-in-chief of the army in Egypt. These letters contained a revocation of the order which recalled him from Egypt, and enjoined upon him to remain there. It was by the perusal of these letters that General Bonaparte learned simultaneously of the order which had recalled him, and the counter-order by which he was to remain in Egypt. The Directoire also informed him of the intention of the Government to place General Lecourbe at the head of the principal army. When we had nearly lost Italy, and the scene of war had been transplanted to the Var, the Directoire had felt the pressing necessity of having recourse to the talents of General Bonaparte and ardently desired his presence. But when the victory of Zurich and the results obtained in Holland had reassured them, like the sailor, who forgets his vow when once the storm is past, they made haste to revoke the order which had been so hastily despatched three months previously, an order which had been torn from them by the imminence of the peril which at that time menaced the Republic. It was accordingly only at Paris that General Bonaparte received the letters from the Directoire which Admiral Bruix had been commissioned to hand to him if he succeeded in landing in Egypt, together with the copy of the letter which the Admiral had sent to him from Carthagena, and the letters of Barras and of Talleyrand.

As to the choice of General Lecourbe, on whom the Directoire had decided, Napoleon did not altogether disapprove of it. He had a high opinion of this general, and acknowledged him to possess the qualities of the soldier. He had formed a favourable opinion about him, in finding amongst the papers seized at the house of General Moreau, who was arrested in 1804, several letters which Lecourbe wrote to this general during the Hohenlinden campaign to urge him on to conquer his scruples, or his want of resolution, and to inspire him with courage.

The Emperor deprived himself with regret of the services of General Lecourbe, having noticed in him so much ill feeling at the time of Moreau's trial that he did not think it possible to employ him. One day, whilst Lecourbe was crossing the Tuileries Gardens he noticed the Emperor at the window of the palace, and cast on him a look so full of hatred that Napoleon could never forget it. When, during the hundred days, Lecourbe came back to him, the Emperor received him with cordiality, and entrusted him with an important command.

Letters relating to the Recall of GENERAL BONAPARTE *to France.*

I.

To GENERAL BONAPARTE,
    Commander-in-Chief
        of the Army in the East.

PARIS, 7th PRAIRIAL, AN VII.

The extraordinary efforts, Citizen General, which Austria and Russia have just been displaying, and the serious and almost alarming turn which the war has taken, demand that the Republic should concentrate her forces. The Directoire has, in consequence, just given orders to Admiral Bruix to use every means in his power to become master of the Mediterranean, and to betake himself to Egypt, in order to bring back the army under your command. He has received instructions to concert with you as to the measures to be taken for the embarking and the transport of the troops.

You will judge, Citizen General, whether you can leave a part of your troops behind with safety, and the Directoire authorizes you in this case to entrust the command of them to the man whom you shall deem best suited for this post.

The Directoire will, with pleasure, see you at the head of the Republican armies, which till now you have so gloriously commanded.

(Signed) THEILHARD.
LARÉVEILLÈRE-LEPEAUX.
BARRAS.

II.

Letter from THE DIRECTOIRE *to* ADMIRAL BRUIX, (*written by the hand of* SECRETARY GENERAL LAGARDE, *and signed by* MERLIN DE DOUAI.)

PARIS, 7th PRAIRIAL, AN VII.

The Executive Directoire, Citizen General, after due reflection on the present state of affairs, has felt the necessity of uniting and concentrating as much as possible the forces of the Republic. In consequence, you are ordered to take the promptest measures to effect a junction with the Spanish fleet. As soon as this has been done you will search for the English fleet, and if, as is probable, you are then superior in force to the enemy, you will attack it. As soon as you have put the English out of the possibility of opposing your operations with success, you will make sail to Egypt with the object of embarking the army there. You will concert with General Bonaparte on the measures to be taken, and, should he deem it necessary, you may leave a portion of his forces behind you in Egypt.

You will hand the annexed letter to General Bonaparte. It communicates the plans of the Directoire to him.

(Signed) MERLIN,
President of Executive Directoire.

LAGARDE,
Secretary General of the Executive Directoire.

By a decree of the Directoire, dated 14th Germinal, An VII, (April 3rd, 1799), Bruix, Minister of Marine, had been appointed Admiral in command of the naval army at Brest, a rank equivalent to that of Captain-General in Spain, so that Admiral Massaredo should have no objection to serving under him.

III.

Autograph Letter of the CITIZEN TALLEYRAND, *Interim Minister of Marine, to* ADMIRAL BRUIX.

PARIS, 7th PRAIRIAL, AN VII.

So now, my dear Bruix, your mission has taken the form that you first desired. I am delighted at this. You are no longer in doubt; you have an object, a prescribed object, an object of the highest importance. The Directoire writes only one word to Bonaparte. I am sending him a letter from Barras to which I have added a few lines. The Directoire relies on you to inform him of our situation at home and abroad. Bring him back. You are asked to keep the strictest silence on your mission. Good-bye, I embrace and love you well. Believe me your friend for ever.

(Signed) CH. MAUR. TALLEYRAND.

P.S.—My opinion is that Belleville, our Consul at Genoa, will be your successor; that is not yet decided, but the Directoire will not make its definite selection until the first days of next decade. Siéyés will arrive here between the 20th and the 24th.

IV.

ADMIRAL BRUIX *to the* CITIZEN BONAPARTE, *Commander-in-Chief of the Army in the East.*

CARTHAGENA, 29th PRAIRIAL, AN VII.

CITIZEN GENERAL,

The Executive Directoire has ordered me to effect a junction with the Spanish Fleet, then to attack the enemy and, having defeated it, to go to Egypt to take and to transport to France the troops under your command.

My junction has already been effected, and the combined army has a strength of forty-two line vessels, but this force does not give us superiority over the English; they have sixty vessels in the Mediterranean. Nevertheless, by well concerted manœuvres, it will be possible to defeat them before they have been able to concentrate their forces. This is what I hope to do, if my constant and pressing applications to the Spanish General, and to the Court of Madrid, are successful.

Once this success obtained, I assure you, Citizen General, that I shall not lose a moment in betaking myself to Alexandria, directly after the engagement. Make your arrangements accordingly, that the fleet be detained the least time possible on the coast of Egypt. You must count, General, on all the efforts of which I am capable, to overthrow every obstacle and to join you as promptly as possible. Nevertheless, it is impossible to exactly fix the date of my arrival, and as nothing is less certain than the result of a naval engagement, nor even that I may be able to succeed in attacking the enemy before they have united their forces, I must ask you, General, not to take final measures for embarking your army until the early arrival of the naval force be announced to you by some frigates which I shall send off immediately after the encounter.

Believe me, Citizen General, that it will be for me the best day of my life, and, for the brave army which I command, a day of glory and of happiness, the day on which we shall be able to give back to the fatherland the heroes who have done so much for its glory.

Receive my fraternal and respectful salutations,
(Signed) E. BRUIX.

P.S.—I promised the Greek who will hand you this letter that you would make him a present of five hundred louis. I do not think, General, that in spite of the enormity of this sum, you will hesitate in doing so.

Letters V and VI were addressed by the Interim Minister of Marine, Talleyrand, to Admiral Bruix, under dates of 13th and 27th Prairial. Amongst other instructions they repeat the orders of the Directoire on the 7th of Prairial, and insist on their execution.

VII.

Rough Draft of a Letter written by ADMIRAL BRUIX, *to the* CITIZEN JOSEPH BONAPARTE.

PARIS, THE 22nd VENDÉMIAIRE, AN VII.

Receive, Citizen, the compliment which my heart addresses to you on the happy return of your brother. The happiness of your family is public happiness. I hear that you leave this night or to-morrow for Fréjus. I send you some papers which may interest you and your brother.

(1) Copy of a letter which I received in the roads of Vado It was in accordance with this letter that I wrote him the one that I showed to you in Paris. You know how, once my junction with the Spanish effected, the superior forces of the enemy prevented the realization of my further projects.

(2) Two letters from the Directoire to your brother, which I was commissioned to hand him myself.

(3) A letter from the Citizen Talleyrand, which had the same destination and which contained a letter from Director Barras.

(4) Copy of a letter in which Talleyrand forwarded me these despatches.

I share your joy and I salute you cordially.

(Signed) E. BRUIX.

Shortly after the 18th Brumaire, the Consuls still occupying the Luxembourg Palace, I was at the house of Colonel Louis Bonaparte, who had been appointed to the command of the 5th regiment of dragoons; he was living at the Hotel La Trémoille, in the Rue de Vaugirard. He showed me a manuscript of about fifteen folio pages, entirely written by Napoleon. It was the draft of a speech composed by him whilst still only an artillery lieutenant, on the subject proposed for a prize essay by the Academy of Lyons: "What are the Truths and the Sentiments which it is Most Important to Inculcate to Men for their Happiness?" Louis Bonaparte had tried to decipher this manuscript, but, rebutted by its difficulties, had given it up. That was the first time that I saw Napoleon's writing. I seemed to have hieroglyphics before my eyes. At the same time I was impelled by a strong feeling of curiosity and interest to ask Louis Bonaparte to trust me with the manuscript. I wanted to see whether I should be more skilful or more fortunate than he had been. I spent eight days in studying the words, and after infinite trouble succeeded in deciphering them, with the exception of five or six words, which I left blank. I carried the manuscript, with the translation, back to Colonel Louis Bonaparte, who, contenting himself with the copy which I had made of it, seized roughly upon the original, and before it was possible for me to interfere, had thrown it into the grate. A bright fire was burning, and this precious relic was destroyed in a moment, nor was I able to save any portion of it. The speech had not been finished, if I may judge by the draft I read. The last part was wanting. This makes me doubt that he can have gained the prize, as was at first announced, and that he even took part in the competition. The impression that remained to me after reading this writing of his, as far as I can remember, was that he had a great deal of imagination, but little art and sequence of ideas in his composition. It contained pleasant thoughts, a somewhat pompous philanthropy, and a dreamy sentimentality, expressed with the exaltation and candour of youth.*

A picturesque definition of sentiment and melancholy,

---

*I have heard the Emperor say that, when he was a young man he could not read Arnauld Bacculard's "*Épreuves du Sentiment*" without crying.

an enthusiasm for the music of "*Le Devin du Village*," to whose author Napoleon would have had a statue raised for this single composition, and the sentence with which his speech ended, were the passages which most struck me. To give a definition of sentiment the author took his reader to the places most favourable to the meditation which he depicted, now in large lines, and now with descriptive details. He transported him from the shepherd's hut to the Church of St. Peter's at Rome, and described the impressions which are felt by the traveller on first entering into this immense fane, lighted by the mysterious light of a lamp. Such is the impression which I have retained of my perusal of this precious manuscript, an impression which would perhaps be modified if I were to read it to-day again.

The taste which Napoleon had at that time for the music of "*Le Devin du Village*" will seem strange to those who know that he preferred Italian music to French, and that he did not like the writing of Jean-Jacques.*

He remembered all the airs of this charming pastoral,

---

*His opinion of the "*Nouvelle Héloïse*" was almost the same as that of Voltaire. As to his political writings, the following remark will show what he thought of them. This is told in the Memoirs of Stanislas Girardin, so that the authenticity of the note cannot be doubted. Here is the article entitled "Visit of the First Consul to Ermenonville." "Arriving before the Île des Peupliers the First Consul paused before the tomb of Jean-Jacques, and said that it would have been better for the repose of France that this man had never existed. 'And why so, Citizen Consul?' said Girardin. 'It was he who prepared the French Revolution.' 'I should not have thought, Citizen Consul, that you had any reason to complain of the Revolution.' 'Well,' answered he, 'the future will show whether it would not have been better for the peace of the world that neither I nor Rousseau had ever lived.' And so saying, he continued his walk with a dreamy air." Girardin, in his lifetime, frequently told this story in my presence, and in that of other people.

and loved to sing them. Not altogether, as Rousseau said of Louis XV., with the most discordant voice in his kingdom, but with a voice of which it could not be said that it was always strictly in tune. To these impressions of youth, which he retained till his maturity, there had succeeded a passionate attachment to Italian music, which he listened to with delight, and which was the most effectual recreation he could enjoy in the midst of his great and arduous labours.*

*This taste of Napoleon for Italian music should not be an argument in favour of the opinions which sought to disinherit him of the name of Frenchman, in attributing to him Italian habits and customs, and an exclusive knowledge of the Italian language. I do not wish gratuitously to renew polemics against pretensions which could not be sustained to-day; but I will take the opportunity of giving an extract from a letter addressed on this subject to the editor of the American newspaper, *Le Courrier des États-Unis*, by the man who best knew the Emperor, and who was united to him by the most tender affection as well as by blood-kinship: "Napoleon was not born in Italy. He was born at Ajaccio on the fifth of August, 1769, in the Island of Corsica, which was occupied by the French troops from the year 1764. The interior of the island was entirely subjected to France in 1716. Napoleon had never been in Italy before the French troops threw open the road before him. He could not, then, have contracted Italian habits. Charles Bonaparte, his father, nominated Deputy of the States of the Province of Corsica to the Court, in 1777, took him to the college of Autun, in Burgundy, and left him there. He afterwards obtained for him a place at the military school at Brienne, in Champagne, from whence he was sent to the military school in Paris, previous to his nomination as Officer of Artillery in 1787. At that time he did not know a single word of the Italian language. His habits and his speech must have been entirely those of a Frenchman of, old France, since it has been seen at what age he came to Burgundy, to Champagne, and to Paris. Whilst in garrison at Valenciennes, and at Grenoble, and at Marseilles he made the acquaintance of Mounier, the ex-constituent, of Abbé Raynal, and other friends of the newly-born liberty, whose principles he embraced with ardour. He passed a few months of his first year in his natal town, in order to make some historical investigations, and to write an essay on the revolutions of Corsica, which was written in good French, and which he sent to Abbé Raynal. This celebrated author answered him, amongst other things: 'This writing is full of features which reveal a genius of the first order.' At that time Napoleon did not know a single word of Italian. He learned some Italian words during his brief visit to Cor-

But the passage in the speech which left upon me the most profound impression, and which since constantly reverts to my memory, is the sentence with which it terminates. It is a kind of prophecy, such a prophecy as was attributed by popular belief to superior genius and to the dying. "Heaven lends prophetic actions to the dying." It was a kind of presentiment of his future destiny which the great, august, and unhappy man had that day. This is the sentence, quoted literally: "Great men are meteors, destined to burn, to light their age."

M. de Las-Cases relates in the "Memorial of St. Helena" that Prince de Talleyrand, either to pay court to the Emperor, or perhaps by his express command, had had the speech sought for in Lyons, and had it presented to him. Napoleon read a few pages of it and threw it into the fire. I have since learned that, as a matter of fact, the essay was handed in for competition. What I saw of it, then, must have been a rough draft, a composition written in the first flood of thought, the colour and originality of which were weakened and destroyed by a certain number of corrections. This rough draft of the speech remaining amongst Napoleon's papers would thus later on have fallen into the hands of his brother. I did not recognize in the speech which was printed in 1826, and which forms a part of a collection published under the name of General

---

sica, and a few in his campaigns in Italy, like a good many officers of the French army. But in spite of what Professor V—— has said, Napoleon never knew perfectly any other language than French." We may add that he was all that he wished to be, and added to the variety of his accomplishments the talents of a great writer.

Gourgaud,* the one which I had read in 1800.†

There remained the hope that the Comte du Saint-Leu might have preserved the copy which I gave him; but a letter, written by this Prince from Florence on the 31st of March, 1840, showed me the inanity of this hope. It is not on account of its literary merit that we may regret the loss of the original document. Its interest would be very small to-day did it not prove by what a serious course of study the faculties with which nature had endowed the man called to such great labours were developed. The author himself attached but little importance to it. Finding the rough draft ten years later, he wanted to throw it into the fire. He only gave it to his brother on his pressing request, and on condition he should burn it, a condition which Louis Bonaparte, to my great regret, only too loyally fulfilled.

I was taken in the conscription of the year VII. I felt no vocation for a military life. A constitution far from robust, and a state of health which, without being feeble rendered me unfit for the fatigues of war, disinclined me for a military career. However, every citizen had to pay his tribute to the fatherland. None were exempt from this duty. The various applications which I made to obtain an exemption had the effect of delaying a decision being taken about me for a whole year. This application of mine, which put me in communication with various kinds of people, brought me at last into the presence of the First Consul. Thus

* *Mémoires de Napoléon à Ste.-Hélène* (8 vols. 1823) by Gaspard, Báron de Gourgaud, and Montholon.—R. H. S.

† The one which has been published was extracted from the archives of the Lyons Academy. It obtained no mention. The first prize was given to the speech composed by M. Daunau.

does Providence guide man toward the goal it has marked out for him by ways which he cannot suspect. My efforts to escape the application of the law on conscription were the obscure routes which led me to the protection of a man who was reputed to be inflexible in its execution, and to have carried its rigour to the extreme limit.

Louis Bonaparte had been appointed Colonel of the 5th regiment of dragoons. His regiment was sent to the Vendée. He invited me to meet him in Verneuil, in the Perch district, where he was quartered. I went there in the last days of June. The pacification of the Vendée was just on the eve of accomplishment. Barely had he assumed the reins of Government when the First Consul turned his attention to this unhappy country, and took measures to put an end to the discord by which it was torn. All efforts made by preceding governments to effect this purpose had been practically fruitless. It was reserved to the First Consul to put an end to this cruel war, in which the victor had always reason to deplore his victory. He succeeded in his object by the use and skilful mixture of rigour and of indulgence, and by the firmness of his will. The leaders of the Chouans, divided amongst themselves, discouraged by their reverses, and incapable of resistance to the forces which were directed against them, had finally to submit. One only, Frotté, still resisted. Taken by surprise he wished to parley, at the same time encouraging his lieutenants to wait for better days. The letters which he wrote to them were intercepted, and served as proofs of his want of good faith. He was brought before a court martial, and shot, together with some of his comrades.

The death of Frotté was the last scene in this bloody war. The public feeling was still such at that time that on the day when Frotté and his accomplices were executed the inhabitants shut themselves up in their houses, and the streets of the town were entirely deserted. Frotté was seized at the house of the General in command at Alençon with whom he had taken refuge, and who gave him up. It was that same Guidal who was afterward implicated in a revolutionary plot in the south, and who ended miserably in the Mallet* affair.

After having passed six months in the 5th dragoons, where my name only figured on the list as a matter of form, I was able to leave this mockery of military service without attracting any attention. Colonel Louis Bonaparte, who knew how little I was anxious to serve my apprenticeship for the *bâton* of a Marshal of France, introduced me to his brother, Joseph Bonaparte, who had recently arrived from the Embassy at Rome, after the outrage which had forced him to leave that city in the month of December, 1797. His rank as Ambassador had not protected him from the outrage to public liberty which was committed on his person. Some partisans of the revolution had claimed the protection of the French Embassy. They had been pursued by the Papal troops, who massacred a number of these refugees. In this attack the life of the French Ambassador had been menaced, and he

---

*Claude François de Mallet, French general, born 1754, brigade-general in 1799, became Governor of Pavia in 1805. Dismissed as a Republican he engaged in conspiracies against Napoleon, and was arrested. Confined in the state prison he plotted with fellow-prisoners, including Guidal, to overthrow Napoleon during his absence in 1812, escaped October 23rd, spread the report of Napoleon's death in the barracks, was overpowered with his accomplices and shot with them on October 29th, 1812. See *Lafon* (1814.)—R. H. S.

had seen killed by his side General Duphot, who was engaged to marry the sister of his wife, who afterwards became Madame Bernadotte, and who is to-day Queen of Sweden. Victim of his generous devotion, this general was mortally wounded whilst he was seconding the efforts of Joseph Bonaparte to induce the malcontents to withdraw, and the Papal troops to cease firing. The Ambassador only owed his life to the intrepidity and to the calmness which he displayed during this terrible event. More fortunate than the French officer Basseville, who was cruelly murdered by the Roman mob four years previously, he was allowed to escape the dangers to which he was exposed, and found a refuge in the house of the Spanish Ambassador, Chevalier d'Azzara.

Joseph Bonaparte was at that time writing his story "*Moïna*", a work of little importance; but which can be commended for the simplicity of the subject, the gentleness of the sentiments expressed, and for the graces of its style. These various circumstances put me in relationship with this worthy Mæcenas, who received me with the greatest kindness, and showed an interest in me from which he never departed, and for which, all my life long, I shall be profoundly grateful to him.

When he was commissioned to negotiate for peace with the American envoys he was good enough to appoint me his secretary. These peace negotiations were happily brought to a close by a treaty which was signed on the 30th of September, 1800, by the Councillors of State, Joseph Bonaparte, Roederer, and Fleurieu, on behalf of France, and by Messrs. Ellsworth, Davy, and Murray, for the United States. By this agreement, which was to last over a period of eight years, the rights of the neutrals were solemnly established. It was a victory over England. The great principle that a ship is under the protection of the nation whose flag it flies, a principle which has since been maintained and defined with such rigour, was expressly recognized. Munitions of war alone were to be considered contraband. The right of passage of neutral ships was regulated, and the right of blockade was restricted to places really blockaded. The Secretary of the Commission charged to treat with the Ambassador was M. Pichon, a young man full of ardour, whose special knowledge was very useful in the various stages of these negotiations. M. Pichon, as a reward for the services which he then rendered, was nominated Consul General and Chargé d'Affaires to the United States. At the time of the expedition to San Domingo he was commissioned to provide for the revictualling of the military and naval forces, and was unfortunate enough to sign certain contracts which were exceedingly unprofitable to the State. A commission of the State Council was appointed to examine the management and the books of the Consul General. The result of this commission was that he was absolved as a bookkeeper, but condemned for his negligence. In consequence of this report M. Pichon was dismissed, and the various sums of which he had unduly ordered payment were put to his charge. M. Pichon, in his misfortune, deserved public sympathy. This just, but severe sentence, filled him with a resentment which prompted him to publish, in 1814, a very bitter pamphlet full of unjust attacks against the fallen government. The government of the king was grateful to him for having placed his personal resentment at the service of the restored dynasty, and rewarded him for it by appointing him Councillor of State.

The treaty with the United States was celebrated by a fête given at Mortfontaine two days later. The First Consul was present with his family. The Second and Third Consuls, with the ministers, the presidents and various members of the Council of State, of the Senate, of the Legislative Body, and of the Tribunate,* were also present. The diplomatic corps was also invited. Various persons who had formerly served in America in various capacities met together on that occasion. M. de Lafayette, and M. de la Rochefoucauld-Liancourt were present at the fête, and were good enough to undertake to invite the Americans who happened to be in Paris, and also to act as interpreters between Joseph Bonaparte and those who did not speak French. It was these two gentlemen who suggested the subjects of the emblematic devices and inscriptions which served to recall the most glorious feats in the American War of Independence. There were a number of pretty women present, at the head of which figured the two youngest sisters of the First Consul, Mesdames Leclerc and Murat.

The fête of Mortfontaine was very brilliant. The beauty of the site lent its aid to the taste and the magnificence which were displayed there. Mortfontaine was already at that time one of the most beautiful places in France. To-day it is almost without a rival, thanks to the improvements and the embellish-

* Created by the Constitution of 1799 the Tribunate was composed of one hundred members. Shared the legislative power with the legislative bodies, and discussed and advised upon the Government bills. Became quite dependent on the Emperor after 1804 and was abolished by a senatus-consultum in 1807.—R. H. S.

ments which the taste of its illustrious proprietor added to it. There is nothing particularly remarkable either about the park or the *château*, but the lakes spotted with wooded isles, and animated with the movement of boats and skiffs of elegant forms, surrounded with shrubberies and shady avenues, offer a delightful aspect. These lakes are immense sheets of water separated by roadways, and communicating with each other by locks, over a distance of nearly two leagues. The hill sides are covered with a large number of green trees and are crowned with fine timber. On their slopes are to be seen sandstone rocks, some of colossal height. One of them fully warrants the inscription which may be read upon it:—

"*Sa masse indestructible a fatigué le temps.*"—
DELILLE.

Every kind of site is to be found in this little valley of lakes, and here living nature contrasts with dead nature. Hamlets and mills, grouped picturesquely, fill it with movement and with life, whilst at the other end is to be found a long extent of arid sand worthy of the desert, the illusion of which is completed by some ruins in the Moorish style.

A concert was given on the first day of the fête, at which Garat and the most distinguished artists in Paris were heard. On the following day a great hunt was given. In the evening there was a display of fireworks on the first lake, in front of the *château*. A flaming obelisk—on the pedestal of which were seen allegories consecrating the union of the French and American Republics—illuminated its approaches. At the moment when the bouquet exploded a small flotilla appeared on the water, illuminated with coloured globes, carrying the flags of the United States and of France interlaced.

The fireworks were followed by theatricals. Two little comedies were performed by Fleury, Dazincourt, Mlles. Contat, Devienne and Mézeray, on a stage, the back of which opened out on to the park. Through this opening at the back could be seen a little wood, which was lighted by fires, producing a fairylike effect, thanks to a skilful juxtaposition of light and shade. The actors of the Théâtre Français played with their usual skill. Fleury and Mlle. Contat, invited to the fête, distinguished themselves by their good manners and their amiability. The proprietors of Mortfontaine greatly appreciated these two artists, so signally worthy of that name. They invited them sometimes to dinner during the following winter, at their fine house in the Rue du Rocher.

Between the two pieces, *couplets* alluding to the re-establishment of cordial relations between the two States, were sung by Garat and by Mlles. Contat and Devienne.

The fête terminated with a magnificent ball, to which more than twelve hundred persons had been invited. The First Consul and Madame Bonaparte withdrew at one o'clock, being obliged to return to Paris.

It was at Mortfontaine that I saw Napoleon for the first time. No occasion presented itself by which his attention could have been drawn to me. Seeing him surrounded with that prestige of grandeur, which imposed respect on all those who approached him, I did not suspect that one day I should be his familiar. He was very affable to everybody. He neglected his affairs to give himself up to the pleasures of the fête. The library of the *château* in which he worked was almost entirely deserted during those days. He conversed with each on his speciality; he even spoke of music with Garat.

During the short stay which the First Consul made at Mortfontaine some gold medals, dating from the days of the Roman Empire, had been presented to him by M. Cambry, Prefect of the Oise department. These medals had been found on the borders of the department, in a little plain surrounded by hills, where the remains of an encampment could be traced. The First Consul presented these to the American Envoys, asking them to carry them back to America.

The First Consul conversed at length with M. de Lafayette, a general for whom he had a particular esteem. If his conduct during the terrible crises of the Revolution, where so many men lost their lives or their honour, did not seem to the First Consul to have always been worthy of the occasion, he considered, nevertheless, that he had always acted in an honourable manner, and gave him full credit for his good intentions.

The fame of M. de Lafayette rested entirely on his unyielding perseverance in one order of ideas. He had not moved since the fall of the Bastille. He had not made one step in advance since 1789, nor alighted from the white horse on which he rode at the head of the national guards. He had dreamed for France an American form of Government, and, full of this Utopian idea, would never admit the difference between the two countries, nor the necessities of the times, nor the bent of men's minds. The results of the 18th of Brumaire upset all his past. Immovable—when all around him was changing, either by conviction or by policy—he remained faithful to his maxims at a time when everybody held his personal convictions cheap, and when oaths were current coin, the stamp on which constantly changed. The situation of M. de Lafayette was a novelty which, in the eyes of some was original and piquant, and which inspired others with a feeling of respect.

Whatever may have been Napoleon's private opinion about him, such a man was, in his eyes, a man of real value. He must have hoped to make use of him, for he was an instrument the use of which he could not neglect. He accordingly expressed his desire to place him in the Senate. M. de Lafayette thanked the First Consul for his kind intentions, and begged him to transfer them to his son, alleging his desire for retirement and the disinclination that he felt to re-enter public life. Napoleon understood him. He had need of the father, not of the son; he did not press him. Nevertheless he continued to receive him, and remained on friendly terms with him. Till then M. de Lafayette had been consistent, and his scruples, whatever may have been their motive, were worthy of respect. Afterwards, either because he was dissatisfied with the indifference with which his resistance had been received, or because he grew tired of the obscurity into which he had entered, or be it that the strength of his convictions drew him on, the voting on the question of the creation of a Life-Consulate seemed to him a favourable opportunity for once again drawing public attention to himself. He could have abstained from voting, but not only did he vote, but sent his vote to the First Consul, with a letter which is too well known to need reproduction here. This act did not produce the effect that its author had expected. Its natural result was to estrange the First Consul from M. de Lafayette who ceased to take any further interest in him.

Less than a month after the events which I have related above, the brother of the First Consul was appointed plenipotentiary Minister to the Congress at Lunéville. The Austrian plenipotentiary was Count Louis de Cobenzl, formerly ambassador at St. Petersburg, the same who signed the treaty of Campo-Formio* with General Bonaparte. The arrival of this minister at Strasburg having been announced by telegraph, Joseph Bonaparte left Paris without delay, leaving his wife behind him, and arranging for her to join him later on. But Count Cobenzl had only stayed a short time in Strasburg, and hearing at Lunéville that the French Minister had not yet arrived, continued his route to Paris. The French and Austrian plenipotentiaries met half-way. The latter desired to continue on to Paris. I accordingly gave him my place in Joseph Bonaparte's carriage, and took his place in his carriage, with M. Hoppé, his secretary, for the return to Paris.

M. de Talleyrand lent his house in the Rue d'Anjou to the Austrian minister, with whom he was already acquainted. On the following day M. de Cobenzl was presented to the First Consul. They had several conversations together.

---

* Signed Oct. 17th, 1797. Austria surrendered Milan, Mantua, the left bank of the Rhine, and the Belgian provinces, receiving in exchange Istria, Dalmatia and Venice.—R. H. S.

After spending a week in Paris the two negotiators started off for Lunéville, which they reached in the first days of November. The Austrian Minister declared at the very outset that he could not treat without the presence and co-operation of an English Minister, his Court being bound by a treaty to England. The First Consul had done everything in his power to effect a reconciliation with this State. Negotiations had been opened in London through M. Otto, a French agent, for the exchange of prisoners, with the object of bringing about the signature of a naval armistice, on the same basis as the one which had been concluded with Austria.*

England had asked to be admitted to the Congress as a contracting party; this demand had appeared suspicious. If this power was sincere in her desire for peace it was open to her to negotiate separately without combining with Austria. The relative positions of France and England were very different from those of France and Austria. Everything was subject for discussion with England; for twenty years no treaty had been signed between the two powers. Since then the Revolution of 1789 and the wars of the Republic had entirely changed the face of Europe. England had considerably increased her possessions beyond seas at the expense of France and of her allies, and had extended her power in India

*The narration of the diplomatic transactions directed by Joseph Bonaparte at the Congress of Lunéville, at the conferences on the Concordat, and at the Congress of Amiens, contains developments taken from official sources. Some details have been added relative to the negotiations for the admission of an English representative to the Lunéville Congress, for the distribution of the indemnities stipulated by treaty amongst the dispossessed princes on the left bank of the Rhine, and for the London Preliminaries which preceded the Peace of Amiens.

beyond all measure. All matters of negotiation had to be approached for the first time. With Austria the basis of the negotiations already existed; only a renewal of treaties was in question. The negotiations could with difficulty be simultaneous; obstacles were certain to arise at each step; and for this reason the French Government was disposed to suspect the English Cabinet of a lack of sincerity. To assure itself of this fact, and to expose the secret designs of England, it made the following proposals:—

(1) To admit an English representative to the Lunéville Congress, on the understanding that hostilities should be suspended on sea as they were on land, so that the contracting powers should, as far as possible, be in the same situation. [This demand was a just one. France could not be at war with one of the powers and in suspension of hostilities with the other. If the naval armistice gave France the advantage of being able to re-establish commercial relations between her ports and her colonies, and of allowing her to re-victual and to recruit her army in Egypt, the continental armistice gave Austria the means to reorganize her armies, to fortify her strong places with English money, and to prepare to resume the contest with advantage to herself. In reply the English Cabinet refused to allow munitions of war of any kind to enter any of the blockaded ports and towns, but only provisions for a fortnight, at a time when, with the exception of Malta, almost all the blockaded places were well supplied with victuals. This proposal tended to render the armistice illusory.]

(2) The First Consul then offered to negotiate whilst continuing hostilities on sea and on land, as in

many previous negotiations had been the case. It was a means for accelerating the conclusion of peace, because the two allied powers, pressed by the probable successes of the French forces, would be interested in the termination of the negotiations, so as not to render the conditions of peace every day more onerous. [This proposal was not considered acceptable by the English Cabinet.]

(3) A further proposal was made. France offered to accept the armistice proposed by the British Cabinet, in spite of its great disadvantages, if England would agree to separate negotiations. [In this expectation the renewal of hostilities against Austria was delayed for eight days. The English Cabinet refused.]

(4) As a final proposal the French Government asked to be allowed to send six frigates under a flag of truce into Alexandria, it being specially stipulated that these frigates should not carry more arms than form the usual equipment of storeships. [This was a practical acceptance of the principle of the armistice proposed by the English Government. The reinforcements—of about four thousand men—which this expedition could have conveyed to the army in Egypt was by no means an equivalent to the advantages which Austria would derive from English subsidies during the prolongation of the continental armistice, which would enable her to increase her military resources. It was, moreover, a means of forcing the English to finish the negotiations rapidly, so as to prevent the arrival of the frigates in Egypt; for more than a month would have had to elapse before they could be got under sail. These different proposals were rejected. They could only be acceptable in the eyes of a Ministry really

anxious to conclude peace, for where a real desire to agree exists, an arrangement is soon come to.]

These repeated refusals clearly showed how little disposed England was for peace. In presenting herself at the Lunéville Congress as having a common interest with Austria, England, no doubt, had not any intention of sacrificing herself to her ally, nor of winning for her at the price of her own conquests any restitutions of territory. All that she then desired was to gain time, and to intervene in the Lunéville negotiations for the purpose of delaying their progress and of provoking some cause of rupture. "To admit an English representative to Lunéville," said Napoleon, "would be to put into his hands the spindle and the thread with which to weave some new coalition." As a matter of fact these ruses on the part of the English Government had no other result than to delay for the space of one year the peace which England so contemptuously refused in January, 1800, after the 18th Brumaire, and which she solicited in 1801, March 21st.

At the end of the third note, referring to General Mathieu Dumas's work, entitled "*Précis des événements militaires,*" which the Emperor dictated whilst at St. Helena, are to be found the following reflections:—

"The spectacle of the changes which were brought about in so short a time was sufficiently gratifying to a true Frenchman. In January, 1800, France solicited peace. Lord Grenville replied with a torrent of abuse, allowing himself to make the strangest insinuations. He desired that a prince of that race of kings who, during so many centuries had known how to maintain the prosperity of the nation at home and to ensure consideration and respect abroad, should remount the throne of France. He exhorted the First Consul to establish with proofs the legitimacy of his government; and to-day it was this same Lord Grenville who begged as a favour to be allowed to treat with the Republic, offering even to pay for this grace with new concessions.

"The negotiations for a naval armistice were broken off. The towns of Ingolstadt, Ulm, and Philipsburg were ceded by the Emperor to France, as the price of a six weeks' prolongation of the armistice. A few months later the Peace of Lunéville saved the house of Austria, and re-established peace on the continent. And finally, shortly afterwards, the Cabinet of St. James's signed the Preliminaries of London, by which the humiliated English oligarchy recognized the French Republic, aggrandized, not only by the Belgian provinces, but by Piedmont, by Genoa, and by the whole of Italy. In the meanwhile how many millions had been added to the English national debt? Such was the result of Pitt's passionate policy."

What follows was also dictated by the Emperor, but was not printed in the memoirs published under his name:—

"Pitt, who did not desire peace until Belgium should have been ceded to Austria, was not sincere in asking to be admitted to the Lunéville Congress. If during the pourparlers between M. Otto and Lord Grenville on the question of a naval armistice, which lasted six weeks, the latter had really been anxious for the conclusion of peace he would have made his desire clear, and would have proved it in his confidential conversations. He said nothing which could remove an impression to the contrary. Lord Hawkesbury's very first words, at the time of the negotiation of the Preliminaries of London, showed the sincerity of the English Cabinet. M. Mathieu Dumas shows little experience in imagining that the rupture of negotiations between the two countries depended on the admission, or the refusal of admission, of six frigates into the port of Alexandria. It would have been as mad on the part of England as on the part of France. It sometimes happens in war that an army of one hundred thousand men retreats after losing thirty or forty hussars in a reconnoitring expedition under the command of the commander-in-chief. Is so slight a loss the cause of the retreat? No, the retreat is the result of the reconnoitring expedition."

England refusing all proposals, and Count Cobenzl, on his side, persisting in his refusal to treat without the assistance of an English *envoyé*, hostilities recommenced, in spite of the presence of the French and Austrian plenipotentiaries at Lunéville. General Moreau, who was in Paris, whither he had betaken himself after the prolongation of the armistice, left it on the 19th of November to put himself at the head of the army of the Rhine. He had been received with unwonted cordiality and marked favour by the First Consul, who presented him with a pair of beautifully worked pistols, embellished with diamonds. As he handed him these pistols he remarked that if he had not had the names of the General's victories engraved on them it was because these were so numerous that there was not room for such an inscription. Moreau received these advances and this present with an indifference which was noticed by all.

The resumption of hostilities having been declared,

the First Consul drew up his plan of campaign for the ensuing winter. He was forced to abstain from taking personal command of the troops, as the state of affairs at home rendered it impossible for him to absent himself from the seat of Government. The army of the Rhine was destined to play the most important part in this campaign. The First Consul, remembering no doubt with what coldness Moreau had received his suggestion of a bold plan at the opening of the previous campaign, ordered him simply to act on the offensive, leaving to him the care of directing his operations as circumstances might dictate. The army of the Rhine was the finest of our armies; it was composed of more than one hundred thousand men, all veteran soldiers, under the command of experienced officers. To confide such an army to General Moreau, giving him at the same time a free hand, was to refute in advance the frivolous reproach that Bonaparte was jealous of Moreau's glory.

General Lahorie, General Moreau's chief staff-officer, who had preceded him, had arrived in Lunéville two days before him. Instead of putting up at the house of the French Minister, he went directly to the Austrian Minister's. When Moreau arrived in Lunéville the French Minister, without awaiting his visit, called on him at the inn at which he had alighted. I accompanied Joseph Bonaparte to see Moreau, who received us in a low room, lighted by a lamp. He was dressed in a blue frock-coat, which bore no distinctive marks of his rank, and he was smoking a pipe. Our call was short and without importance. The want of attention on the part of Moreau, and the prank played by Lahorie, showed us sufficiently plainly that the relations between the chief and his *entourage* were not of the friendliest. Before continuing his journey, General Moreau returned Joseph Bonaparte's call, meeting Count Cobenzl at his house. After some general conversation, which did not last more than half-an-hour, he re-entered his travelling carriage, which was waiting for him outside.

The preliminaries of a peace advantageous to Austria had been signed in Paris on the 28th of July, 1800, but had not been ratified by the Emperor of Germany.

Six weeks later the Austrian Goverment asked for a resumption of the negotiations, at the cost of conceding Ingolstadt, Ulm, and Philipsburg. If Austria, abandoning her dilatory policy, had frankly entered upon the negotiations without again risking the hazards of war, she would have saved Mantua and Tuscany, and could have re-established the King of Sardinia in Piedmont. Such an offer was made to the Austrian plenipotentiary. France's moderation encouraged Austria to increase her demands, and to insist on the admission of an English plenipotentiary. Meanwhile the armistice was coming to a close. Austria preferred to run the risk of war, but the return of General Bonaparte had brought victory back to our flag. The hopes of the Cabinet of Vienna were deceived; our victories at Hohenlinden* and elsewhere in bringing our troops forward to the gates of Vienna put an end to Austria's hesitation. A new armistice—to last thirty days—had been agreed upon at Steyer, between Moreau and Arch-duke Charles, one month after the renewal of hostilities. Count Cobenzl then resigned himself to treat without the co-operation of England, but the fa-

---

* Village in Upper Bavaria, in the Ebersberg district, scene of Moreau's victory over Arch-duke John, Dec. 3rd, 1800.—R. H. S.

vourable opportunity had been lost. The conditions of peace could no longer be the same after the victory of Hohenlinden. Thus did the enemies of France conspire together for her greatness and lead Napoleon by the hand to the summit of power. Already three times had they refused peace under unhoped-for conditions. The more moderate the French Government showed itself, the more their pretensions increased; experience seemed to teach them nothing.

The point of the negotiation which the Austrian Minister defended with the most obstinacy was the preservation of the German ecclesiastical States. It was his wish that the ecclesiastical electors and princes should obtain on the right bank the equivalent of what they had to abandon on the left. Austria felt that their suppression was a death-stroke to her influence, and, later on, to her domination over Germany. But the compensation which Austria asked in their favour would have absorbed the greater part of the lands available on the right bank, and certain princes whose inheritance belonged to their families would have been deprived of a compensation, which the losses they had suffered gave them the right to claim. Besides, the abuse of preserving to the ecclesiastical authority temporalities to defend, and the inconvenience of leaving Germany split up into thousands of little princedoms or lordships, exercising sovereign rights, had long stood in need of reform. One, only, of the four ecclesiastical electors was maintained; his seat was transferred from Mayence to Ratisbon.

Austria also ardently desired the maintenance of the Grand-Duke of Tuscany in Italy. At the opening of the Congress this prince would have been able to retain his states. Austria later on limited her demands on his behalf to the three legations which at first she had desired for herself; but she was to lose Italy as she had lost Germany. The Duchy of Salzburg was the indemnity awarded to the Grand-Duke. The maritime interests of France, the safety of the new Italian States, and the necessity of removing the inimical influence of Austria from this country, decided the First Consul to take advantage of his victories. Personal overtures made by M. de Cobenzl to Joseph Bonaparte were, for the French plenipotentiary, only one reason the more to insist on the cession of Tuscany, which was granted. An ultimatum was notified to the Austrian Minister. In spite of all its efforts, and the threat of desperate measures, the Vienna Cabinet was forced to yield, regretting bitterly not having listened to the first proposals made by France. Peace was signed on the 9th of February, 1801. The Treaty of Lunéville assured the possession of Belgium and Mantua to France, and gave her as frontiers the Rhine, and the line of the Adige in Italy. It overthrew the Gothic edifice of the German Empire in suppressing the ecclesiastical sovereignties; in reducing to a small number of real sovereignties the crowd of helpless and defenceless little feudal principalities, it finally established the basis of the confederation of the Rhine.

The course of the Lunéville negotiations was marked by a notable occurrence. A suspension of arms had been concluded on the 16th of January, between Generals Brune and Bellegarde, commanding the hostile armies in Italy. By this convention the important fortified town of Mantua remained in the possession of

Austria, blockaded only at a distance of eight hundred *toises* * by the French troops. By a convention signed at Lunéville, eight days later, Mantua, together with the forts of Peschiera, Sermione, Ferrare, Ancona, and the castles of Verona and Legnano, were handed over to us. Our diplomacy might well be proud of having succeeded better than our armies.

The skilful, firm, and unselfish conduct of Joseph Bonaparte seconded the genius and the power of the First Consul. The Tribunate accordingly expressed the wish that a testimonial of the nation's satisfaction should be offered to the French plenipotentiary.

During the momentary interruption of the negotiations there arrived at Lunéville Moustache, the courier, bringing the news of the explosion of the infernal machine of the Rue St. Nicaise. The stupor into which the whole town was thrown by the news of this abominable outrage can easily be imagined. Count Cobenzl made haste to come and express his horror to the French Minister, and to congratulate him on the good fortune with which his brother had escaped so great a danger. The same sentiments were expressed by the civil and military authorities.

The sons of Councillors of State Portalis, Siméon, and Roederer were attached to the French legation. The first two, after the fall of the Imperial Government, went over to the service of the Government which succeeded to it. The third, faithful to the cause which he had embraced, after having honourably served the State in prefectorial offices, voluntarily retired. He applied part of his activity and of his talents to directing the glassworks, which were the foundation of the

---

* A *toise* equals a fathom.

fortune of his family, and beguiled his leisure hours with the study of letters.

M. de Laforêt, Secretary to the Legation, brought M. de Moustier, son of the former minister of Louis XVI.,—under whom he had been consul in the United States--to Lunéville. He treated this young man, who afterwards married his daughter, as a son. Moustier was appointed Secretary of Legation in Saxony, at the end of the congress. He then and afterwards served in the embassies with the greatest zeal. His father, one of the most devoted agents of the Comte de Lille, sought in vain to draw him over into the enemy's camp. The Restoration came, but then Moustier, whose fidelity had resisted a threat of disinheritance, did not resist his father, who returned high in credit with the new sovereign. It must be added, however, that he made use of his favour only in the service of old friends. He closed his career as a diplomat with the mission to the Court of Spain, which he carried out in 1827.

General Clarke was sent to Lunéville as governor of the town and commander of the department. He celebrated the anniversary of the 18th Brumaire, the day on which the conference opened, with a splendid dinner, which was followed by a ball. During the course of the Congress, there was a dance at his house almost every week. The plenipotentiaries dined alternately at each other's houses. The local authorities and leading citizens were usually invited. Mild gambling was indulged in, or an hour was spent at the theatre, where a fair troupe was performing. In the intervals of the negotiations we made several excursions in the neighbourhood of Lunéville, visiting the glassworks, the paper mills, and the various factories of the Vosges, the Rosières studfarms and the salt-pits of Dieuze and Moyenvic.

The former castle of King Stanislas had been decided upon for the habitation of the plenipotentiaries, but as it was recognized that it would be some time before it could be put into a proper state of repair, and that this would also cost a considerable sum of money, two private houses were hired for them instead. The minister of France lived at the house of a M. de Fresnel, whose son, like the majority of Lorraine officers, was in the service of Austria.

There were a number of retired generals at Lunéville, who were frequently invited to the houses of the plenipotentiaries. During our stay, there arrived in Lunéville a general who seemed to have been prompted to come by the desire by show off his gold embroideries. It was apparently by the mistake of one of the representatives of the people that he had been promoted to such high rank. The naïveté of his *fanfaronades* was for a time the delight of the town. People used to get him to relate how, in a battle, his bravery and excellent appearance had attracted the attention of Souwaroff,* who cried out: "Who is this young Frenchman, who brings terror and death into our ranks?" "Marshal, it is General Liébaut!" "I thought so!"†

---

* Count Alexander Wassiljevitch Suworow-Rimnikski (1729—1800) commanded the Russian and Austrian troops in Italy in 1799. Defeated the French in the space of three months in Northern Italy, taking all the towns and fortresses in their possession. In consequence of this campaign was created Prince Italijski and commander-in-chief of all Russian armies.—R. H. S.

† The French is: "Je m'en *avais* douté," a sentence containing a gross grammatical error, from which it would appear that General Liébaut's grammar was not as remarkable as his courage.—R. H. S.

M. Hugo, major of the 20th demi-brigade, a young officer full of fire and activity, who had served during the previous campaign on the staff of General Moreau, was charged with the command of the garrison of Lunéville under the orders of General Clarke. When Joseph Bonaparte became King of Naples he summoned this officer, whom he had learned to know and to appreciate during the Congress, to his army. General Hugo followed the king to Spain, where he rendered important services, and returned to France with him in 1813. He has published some memoirs, preceded by a very interesting preface written by his eldest son, Abel Hugo, author of several highly appreciated works, on his campaigns, and chiefly about the military events in Spain. The youngest son of the General, Victor Hugo, has won a European reputation, and is the author of a large number of prose and poetical works, in which the beauties and the defects of a brilliant imagination, to which the study of good models has not been wanting, but which has enfranchised itself from the old paths to open out for itself a new road, may be noticed.

Brought up by a mother who was hostile to the principles of the Revolution, Victor and his two brothers acquired, from the education she gave them, prejudices which soon yielded to their maturer judgment. Since the death of his mother, Victor Hugo has returned to a more just appreciation of the genius of Napoleon. He is to-day one of the greatest admirers of the benefits of his rule, and of the military glory of France, in which General Hugo participated.

I must not omit to mention the arrival of young Anatole de Lawoestyne in Lunéville, who was brought there by his father to be introduced to his uncle, Count de Cobenzl. Anatole was twelve or thirteen years of age at the time of his visit to Lunéville, and was a charming child.

The events of the Revolution of 1789, which brought about the suppression of feudal rights, and caused losses of every kind to the Lawoestyne family, were the principal causes which destroyed the fortune to which Anatole had a claim. He had had the prospect of still being rich. The Sillery estate had been intended for him by the first husband of his grandmother, Madame de Genlis, M. Brulart de Sillery, who fell a victim under the Revolution. Count Louis de Cobenzl had appeared to have an affection for his young nephew. He had proposed to his father to take the lad with him to Austria to finish his education, and that he should enter the military service. But the French instincts of the child, and the preference which he showed for the French uniform, so glorious by victory, discouraged the Austrian diplomat in his good intentions, and easily absolved him from any further responsibility in his nephew's future.

On leaving Paris to return to Vienna, Count Cobenzl made the most splendid promises to Anatole's father; the interest he professed remained, however, without fruit. Knowing my friendship both for the father and the son, he particularly recommended his young nephew to me, thinking that my position with the brother of the Head of the Government would give me opportunities of being useful to him. Lawoestyne did not follow M. de Cobenzl, and remained with us. This child, to whom I attached myself, became dearer and dearer to me, a real brother. He entered the military school at Fontainebleau at an early age. On leaving the school he entered a cavalry regiment where his bravery and brilliant qualities secured him rapid promotion. He was colonel at the age of twenty-six, and commanded the 3rd regiment of chasseurs at the disastrous battle of Waterloo. The fall of the Empire interrupted the career which he was following with such success.

All great and heroic ideas marked this ever-memorable epoch. What impression must the overthrow of so many hopes have produced on the ardent and generous mind of Lawoestyne. To an era of grandeur and glory succeeded a return to Gothic ideas and the reign of a prince strengthened by the misfortunes of his family in the hatred of our institutions. The indignation and contempt of Lawoestyne burst out in a scene concerted with his friends Jacqueminot and Durand, who were both distinguished by a gay and original turn of mind. They went one after the other to the Café Tortoni and met together there, dressed up in the grotesque costumes of those old caricatures of the ancient regime which they humorously styled voltigeurs of Louis XIV., obtuse minds which the great events which had occurred had been unable to lighten, and which, like Epimenides, seemed to have fallen asleep in 1788 only to awake in 1814. Anatole and his friends played so true a scene in this café that the effect it produced was immense. The sensation produced in Paris was such that the authorities thought fit to proceed against the principal culprit. Anatole took flight to Belgium, from which his family had sprung. He settled down in the country near Brussels and lived there faithful to his souvenirs until the time of the revolution of July.

He then returned to France, and once more entered the army. He commanded for some years the department of Seine-et-Oise, with the rank of major general and has since become lieutenant-general.

After peace had been signed the plenipotentiaries left Lunéville to return to Paris. I remember that Siméon and myself wished to celebrate this great event by some scenes which were to be performed by the troupe of actors at Lunéville. With this object in view we shut ourselves up for the best part of the night which followed on the signing of the peace, but Thalia was rebellious to our wooings. We only brought forth a few couplets, for the larger part of which my brother in Apollo was responsible.

Count Cobenzl and Joseph Bonaparte returned to Paris together. Conferences took place on the execution of the article of the treaty relative to the distribution of indemnities to the princes who had been ousted from their possessions on the left bank of the Rhine by the cession of these territories to France. Article 7 of the Treaty of Lunéville had stipulated that the German Empire should compensate the hereditary princes who had been dispossessed on the left bank of the Rhine with grants of land in the centre of its territories, according to arrangements to be ulteriorly determined. The First Consul, satisfied with having secured to those of the secular princes who were in this situation a compensation and the hope of an increase of territory, which would attach those interested to him, did not greatly hurry on the settlement of the indemnities. This was delayed for more than a year by German dilatoriness and the pretensions of Austria. The French Government decided not to give way, and, determined to profit by all the advantages which were secured to it by the Treaty of Lunéville, took measures to baffle the intrigues and underhand practices which had for their object to keep France aloof from any participation in the distribution of the indemnities. The Russian Cabinet was pressed to join France in urging on the settlement of this business. In consequence M. de Buhler, Russian Ambassador to Munich, and M. de Laforêt, who had been appointed French ambassador to the same place, after the signature of the treaty of Lunéville, were sent to Ratisbon to present to the Diet a general scheme of indemnification.

After seven months' discussion the allotment and the definitive distribution of the indemnities were effected. The supremacy which France exercised in the new arrangements began to establish her influence in Germany. This affair was conducted by the First Consul with a skill which the school of M. de Talleyrand attributes largely to this Minister, who without any doubt was a valuable agent in the execution of this great political idea. The co-operation of Russia in the operations at Ratisbon, conferred upon this power the rôle of witness alone, France having entire preponderance in the matter. Her high influence and the exaggerated nature of the claims of the interested parties served her purpose marvellously. The distribution of the indemnities gave rise to a number of abuses. The claims of justice were but little heeded, and it is no exaggeration to say that the territories which were to be allotted were put up to auction. But the timid complaints which arose were soon silenced and hushed up. The princes who had profited by the abuses committed made no boast of the fact, whilst those who had been wronged did not dare to raise their voices to reach the ear of the First Consul. He, however, had suspicions as to the real state of affairs, suspicions which were not confirmed until many years later. The French Ambassador at one of the secondary German courts, was at last able to procure a list of the extortions committed, with the names of their authors. Napoleon sent this list to Count Mollien, Minister of the Public Treasury, with orders to have all sums unduly received paid over to the sinking fund. The cares of war and various other considerations prevented him from rigorously pursuing the execution of this order. The Restoration saved the purses of the guilty, who had the double advantage of remaining unpunished and of securing the favour of the new Government by claiming to be the enemies and the victims of the Government which had just fallen.

Joseph Bonaparte spent most of the summer of 1801 on his fine estate of Mortfontaine. All that, in more than one way, was most distinguished in Paris, was assembled there. Mesdames Bacciochi, Leclerc and Murat, sisters of the First Consul; Lucien Bonaparte, Count Cobenzl, who took up his abode there for the best part of the summer; the poet Casti, author of the poem "*Les Animaux Parlants*" and of so many clever productions, *naïf* and witty, and the most independent of men; Madame de Staël, who was then protecting Chateaubriand, and who charmed the evenings with reading "*Atala*" and "*René*" aloud; Stanislas Girardin, proprietor of the estate of Ermenonville, whose death in 1827 was mourned by all men of heart, and by the friends of enlightened liberty; M. Miot, distinguished by the variety of his accomplishments and by his administrative talents; Roederer, journalist, writer, and witty conversationalist,—these last three the constant and devoted friends of Joseph Bonaparte;—Regnauld de Saint-Jean-d'Angély, whose wonderful ability and clear-headedness rendered him capable of anything; M. de Jaucourt, a model of urbanity, who had raised the affections of his heart to heroism, and whose attachment to the Bourbon family awoke in 1814, but who seemed attached to his hosts by a sincere devotion; the poets Arnault, Andrieux, Boufflers, Fontanes; Madame de Boufflers, *ci-devant* Madame de Sabran, amiable and witty; Marmont, Chauvelin, Mathieu de Montmorency, who on account of a former liaison with Madame de Staël frequently came to Mortfontaine; and finally many other French and foreign politicians and litterateurs found an abode of delight in this beautiful place.

The days were spent in shooting, fishing, walking, and in games; in the evenings there was music or reading aloud; sometimes a proverb or charade was acted. M. de Cobenzl knew our poets and chiefly our dramatists by heart, and would repeat comic scenes with a verve that was nearly buffoonery; he used to organize little games, charades, or *tableaux vivants*, in which he always had a part, and in which the sisters of the First Consul always played the principal rôles. Count Cobenzl spoke French without any accent and had nothing German about him but his name. Although clumsy, big, fat, and short, his manners were easy and graceful. His conversation, as a general rule, was superficial, and abounded in witticisms; his wit was ingenious rather than profound. He affected a vivacity and an evenness of temper which was sometimes modified by a sudden preoccupation. Sometimes in the midst of some gay anecdote, such as he delighted in telling, his features would become set, a grave expression would take the place of a smile, and his wandering eyes become fixed like a machine of which the movements cease suddenly without apparent cause. His affectation of appearing delighted with everything, and of finding that everything that was proposed to him was just what he had been wishing for, was vexation of soul to excellent Madame Bonaparte, who was never able to detect in him a preference for anything whatever.

M. Hoppé, his only secretary, was the type of a German embassy employé. He was a little man already past the middle age, with large wrinkled eyes, fatigued by the assiduity with which he had deciphered old charts and written out diplomatic notes. He was so short-sighted that his nose played as great a part in his work as his eyes. A minute observer of forms, he delighted in parading his knowledge of the little particularities of his profession, the high importance of which he never tired of proclaiming; insisting at the same time on his long experience. He had lived for many years in Paris, as attaché to the embassy of Count de Mercy d'Argenteau. He was a very good man, and devoted to Count Cobenzl, who in return treated him with much affection. Madame de Staël, twirling in her fingers a flower, or a spray of heather, would carry on with our wits a conversation which was now humorous, now serious, but which at all times was lighted up with flashes of wit.

Joseph Bonaparte was kind enough to ask my old friend Palissot to Mortfontaine. I brought him there for some days. This veteran of the great wits of the age of Louis XV., whose life had been spent in drawing-rooms, witnesses of his triumphs, found himself out of his sphere at Mortfontaine. Each epoch has its ideas, its tastes, and its particular character. Palissot was received with distinction and was treated with the deference due to his age. But though sensible of the regard which was shown him, and though he made an effort to raise himself to the diapason of a society which was new to him, it was evident that he felt himself entirely out of his element. He ere long returned with pleasure to the solitude which he had left for a world which was not in accordance with his habits, and which disagreed with his remembrances.

The poet Casti used to recite at nights what he had composed during the day. He wrote a part of his poem "*Les Animaux Parlants*" at Mortfontaine. He was frequently to be seen sitting at the foot of one of the century-old trees, which shaded the rocks scattered here and there on the slopes of the lakes, seeking the inspiration which never refused itself to his facile genius. Casti was the "poet laureate" of Vienna. He succeeded Metastasio in this post of poet to the imperial court, which died with him. He had been presented at Mortfontaine by M. de Cobenzl. At that time he was nearly eighty years of age, but had preserved all the verdure and vivacity of his younger days. Endowed with an iron constitution, he had victoriously triumphed over a disease which can be cured only by the most violent remedies, and the only trace of it which remained was a kind of snuffling, which interfered to some extent with his pronunciation. He was in continual warfare with Mesdames Leclerc and Murat, who had selected him as their victim. Now they would snatch off his wig whilst he was sitting in grave meditation in his arm-chair, now they would come and mix up the figures on the chess-board just as he was absorbed over some difficult move. And so it was that he bore them a grudge, and refused to address any of the verses which cost him so little trouble to either of them. He was better disposed towards Madame Bacciochi, and made a madrigal on her name, which was found one morning fastened to the mirror on the mantelpiece of the drawing-room. This madrigal played on the words "*baccio*" and "*occhi*" and was in honour of Madame Elisa's' eyes, which were very beautiful.

The good and witty Andrieux, author of charming comedies, and poems which Voltaire would not have disavowed, was one of the habitués of Mortfontaine. He had abandoned literature for Parliament, but had returned to it after the suppression of the Tribunate. He was anxious to translate Casti's "*Animaux Parlants*" into verse, but never carried out his plan. He satisfied himself with translating one of this poet's stories, a story called "*La Bulle d'Alexandre VI.*"

Frequent parties of coursing and shooting were given at Mortfontaine under the direction of General Berthier and M. d'Haneucourt, who were rehearsing—the former for the post of Master of the Hounds, and the other for that of Captain of the Hunts.

The hospitality of the proprietors of Mortfontaine was noble and honourable. They charmed their guests by a natural politeness and by their simple and affectionate manners.

The vicinity of the estate of Plessis-Charmant, which belonged to Lucien Bonaparte, rendered communications with Mortfontaine frequent, and did much to enhance the charm of the two residences. There was nothing pompous about either place, but they were the rendezvous of men of varied merits. In this respect Plessis was the rival of Mortfontaine. The presiding taste at Plessis was for the performance of tragedies; these performances were given under the direction of the actor Lafond.

Lucien had lost his first wife, Christine Boyer, who had left him two daughters. One of them has married the Roman Prince Gabrielli, the other, after the death of her first husband, married Lord Dudley Stuart. Madame Bacciochi, who was tenderly attached to her brother, spent the summer at Plessis, warmly protecting the poet Fontanes. The Marquise de Santa-Cruz, a Spanish lady whose acquaintance Lucien had made whilst ambassador to Madrid, helped Madame Bacciochi to do the honours of the house, and was supposed to have a very great influence over him.

Joseph Bonaparte used to make frequent excursions from Mortfontaine to La Malmaison, in which I had the honour of accompanying him. We used to spend part of the day there, coming back to Mortfontaine after dinner. Dinner was served at La Malmaison at one table only, where often a family reunion might be seen. The First Consul sat on one side, having Madame Louis Bonaparte next to him, and Madame Bonaparte opposite. The aides-de-camp of the First Consul were admitted to his table, and generally one of the

Consuls, a minister, and one or two ladies were amongst the guests. Strangers were rarely seen there.

I will mention, in a summary manner, the events which took place in the interval which elapsed between the signing of the Treaty of Lunéville and the conclusion of the Concordat—events which were brought about by the accession to power of the mighty genius who already exercised such a great influence on the destinies of Europe.

The abuse which England made of her maritime supremacy, the tyranny which she exercised over the shipping of other maritime powers, our victories, the treaties which had been their consequence, the wisdom and the skill of the government of the First Consul, had produced a revolution in the minds of men throughout Europe. The influence which England had enjoyed was rapidly declining. Her despotism had revolted the powers of the North, who had united in a convention the direct object of which was to enforce the respect of neutrals. The Emperor Paul I. had put himself at the head of his league with his customary ardour. The general embargo under which England laid the ships of the countries which had signed this convention and her treacherous attack upon Copenhagen only tightened the bonds of the coalition against her. The First Consul had spared no effort to bring about an understanding with the Emperor Paul. There were seven thousand Russian prisoners in France, whom the First Consul fitted out with clothes and sent back home ransom-free. This action finally won the heart of Paul I. He had contracted a close alliance with France and was vigorously pursuing the execution of the plans agreed upon in concert with her, when he was ruthlessly assassinated. The particulars of the murder of this prince are well-known to-day, and there is no necessity for me to repeat them. * The *Moniteur* announced this event in the following terms: " Paul I. died in the night of the 24th—25th March. The English fleet passed the Sound on the 31st." History will teach us what connection may exist between these two occurrences.

The effect of this catastrophe was the dissolution of the league of which Paul I. had been the most ardent promoter. Before long a total change in the policy of Russia took place. General Duroc had been sent to St. Petersburg to compliment the new Emperor on his accession, and to endeavour to continue the relations which had existed between his father and the First Consul. Duroc had been received with kindness and with protestations of a desire to continue on friendly terms with France. But, about six weeks later, the Emperor Alexander signed a treaty with England, by which he abandoned all his father's projects and submitted to the exactions of that power.

The death of General Kléber had let the command of the French army fall into the hands of General Menou, who was invested therewith by right of seniority. He was a brave officer and a good administrator, but lacked in military qualities. He was devoted to French political interests in Egypt; in this interest he had become a Mussulman and had married a Turkish girl. The generals of the army of the East,

* Petrovitch Paul I., son of Peter III. and Catherine II., was born Oct. 1st, 1754, was strangled, March 23rd, 1801, by the conspirators Pahlen, von Suboff, Bennigsen, and Uvaroff.—R. H. S.

either from a want of confidence in their commander-in-chief, or from a spirit of rivalry with him, only yielded him a constrained obedience, and the divisions which ensued therefrom contributed to the ruin of the expedition. The English profited by this to send a picked army to Egypt which combined its operations with an Ottoman army. The First Consul had made useless efforts to send reinforcements of troops and provisions to Egypt. Menou committed the error of not marching with his army to oppose the debarkation of the English troops and to drive them back into the sea. He divided his troops, and was everywhere outnumbered. It was thus that he lost the important battle of Nicopolis, where he succumbed to greatly superior numbers. General Abercromby lost his life there. General Belliard, in Cairo, and General Menou, in Alexandria, were forced to capitulate and to accept the conditions of the enemy, who accorded the transport of the French army with arms and baggage back to France.

It was about this time that the Infant of Parma, in whose favour the Treaty of Lunéville had created the kingdom of Etruria, came to Paris with the Queen, under the names of Count and Countess of Leghorn. They spent a month there in a series of fêtes. It had seemed to the First Consul that it would be a good stroke of policy to exhibit a Bourbon in Paris—a Bourbon, created king by his omnipotence, by the omnipotence of him who made men kings without wishing to be a king himself—and to admit to the Tuileries a prince who sprang from the blood which had reigned over France, at a time when his presence did not create the least sensation in Paris but when on the contrary his entire worthlessness was patent to all who saw him.

The conferences about the Concordat followed on the negotiations for the treaty of Lunéville. It was a fixed idea in the mind of the First Consul that religion should be re-established in France. He was firmly convinced of the importance of religion to a nation. Catholicism seemed at its last gasp. Most of the men who had any influence in public affairs seemed disposed to embrace the Protestant religion, but on the other hand the large majority of Frenchmen were disposed to the Roman Catholic faith. This attachment is indestructible in the larger number of departments. In spite of the immense confidence which the First Consul inspired, his influence did not extend to the point of being able to make a selection between the two forms of religion.

From an adoption of Protestantism dissensions were to be expected, all the more violent because the remembrance of the religious wars had not yet been effaced. Could a schism then be created at a time when the progress of civilization and the personal inclinations of the Head of the State prescribed the union and conciliation of all parties? But apart from the motive that, born a Roman Catholic, it was distasteful to him to abandon this religion for any other, other motives also impelled him to give his preference to Roman Catholicism. France being surrounded by Roman Catholic States needed all her advantages. A repudiation of her ancient faith would have weakened her prestige, and at the same time would have aroused in Europe the anxieties which the errors of the Revolution had justified.

In maintaining the Roman Catholic religion the First Consul secured the Pope to his interests and profited by an influence which at that time could not fail to be of service to his government. Italy remained attached to France. Napoleon's mental reservation was to bring the Catholic faith back to Evangelical purity and to effect the separation of the spiritual and temporal power, a separation which in his eyes seemed destined to assure religious peace.

This immense result, which later on was very nearly secured, would perhaps have exercised a great influence on the tranquillity of Europe, and have set at rest much religious discord, without fear of any return. In this, as in many other things, the First Consul was before his time. Some day, no doubt, the future will realize his plans. In matters of religion, however, progress must be slow and gradual. Reforms of this nature cannot be combined in ministries. They are the work of circumstances and of time; they must come at the right moment; nor does it appertain to any human power to hurry on their accomplishment. It was a matter of primary importance to reunite people divided by religious discords, and in so doing to satisfy the almost general wish of the French people. Some of these considerations were developed by the Councillors of State, who exposed the motives of the Concordat negotiations to the Tribunate and the Legislative Body.

Full of these lofty plans the First Consul resolved to attempt a reconciliation with the Holy See. He had much resistance to overcome on the part of his ministers. Monseigneur Spina, Archbishop of Corinth, was sent to Paris to open negotiations. The preliminary articles proposed by the French Government having been agreed to, with some modifications, by the Council of Cardinals, the Holy Father, to invest this act with more solemnity, and to assure its prompt accomplishment, sent his Secretary of State, Cardinal Consalvi, who arrived in Paris at the beginning of June. He had several conferences with the First Consul, and the consequence was that negotiations were opened between the Papal envoys, Cardinal Consalvi, the Archbishop of Corinth, and Father Caselli, His Holiness's consulting theologian, and the French plenipotentiary, Joseph Bonaparte, to whom the First Consul adjoined the Councillor of State, Cretet, and Abbé Bernier, a former curé at Saint-Laud d'Angers. This priest, after having been the soul of the insurrectional government in La Vendée, had seconded General Hédouville's work of conciliation in that district to the entire satisfaction of the First Consul.

A national Council was convened eight days after Cardinal Consalvi's arrival in Paris. Forty-five archbishops and bishops and eighty ecclesiastical deputies of the second order met together at Notre-Dame. In a new declaration of the principles of the Gallican Church, this assembly declared that the Church of France recognized the Pope as its head, but denied him any right in the temporal affairs of the State. This declaration seemed destined to lay the basis of the projected convention and to support the impending negotiations. These were long drawn out, and it was only the fear lest the First Consul might yield to the persuasions of the Councillors of State, the majority of whom were in favour of Protestantism, and the threatened establishment of a Gallican

Church, that decided Cardinal Consalvi to conclude.

The preliminary articles, which had been agreed upon with Monseigneur Spina, Archbishop of Corinth, were converted into a definitive treaty, which was signed on the 15th of July, and was ratified by a Papal Bull dated the 15th August following. Abbé Bernier was rewarded for his participation in these negotiations with the See of Orleans.

When the Concordat agreement was made public the Republican party and the ideologists, as Napoleon used to call them, severely blamed this arrangement with the Court of Rome, asserting that it was a return to Gothic ideas, to introduce a foreign power into the State, and to accord a privilege to the Roman Catholic clergy in a country where the equality of all religious creeds had been proclaimed. Others, less passionate, whilst admitting that this arrangement had some advantages, expressed the wish that the marriage of priests should have been permitted by the new law. But the most regrettable omission was that of a clause fixing the time in which the Pope should canonically institute the bishops.* This matter had been discussed in the conferences at the time of the Concordat negotiations. It was thought, however, that sufficiently large concessions had already been obtained from the Pope, and that it was not just to insist on that one. This omission has become a terrible weapon in the hands of the Head of the Church. Those who blamed the French Government for not having secured liberty for priests to marry, and having omitted to establish a Gallican Church, forgot that such reforms cannot be

* Modified by the Council convened by the Emperor in Paris, June 17th, 1811, under the presidence of Cardinal Fesch—R. H. S.

improvised, that for the time being considerable advantages had been obtained, and that ameliorations which time alone can bring to maturity must be hoped for from the march of events.

However this may be, the Concordat was productive of great good. It was a pledge of reconciliation to the large majority of Frenchmen. Whilst abolishing the distinctions which existed between unsworn and sworn priests, it at the same time dissipated the scruples which were felt by those who had acquired national property.* Morality found once more the powerful sanction of religion, for it is the respect for religious opinions which assures the empire of law. On the other hand the Concordat was a step in the direction of the reforms rendered necessary by the progress of human enlightenment, which Napoleon had in preparation. The clergy ceased to be a body in the State, it was salaried and subjected to discipline, a discipline to which for many years it submitted in conformity with the law, restricting itself to the limits of its attributions. Restrained by the strong hand of the chief of the State, it would never have attempted to emancipate itself had not the difficulties which were later on thrown in the path of the government encouraged its pretensions, and given rise to cavils which grew as the times became worse. It cannot be denied that the encroachments of the Court of Rome sorely tested the Emperor's patience, and often rendered vain the precautions which at the dictates of his foresight he had taken to protect the rights of the State against

* Property belonging to the exiles and other victims of the Revolution, *confiscated* by the State, or what represented the State, and sold, at the price of stinking mackerel, to honest Republicans.—R. H. S.

the enterprise of the priests. The troubles caused by the influential party of the clergy, encouraged in their hostilities by the reverses which our armies have suffered have gained the cause of the traducers of the Concordat and justified, in appearance at least, the censures passed upon this great act.* The French Government, without doubt, has reaped a bitter harvest from a treaty which was inspired by the desire to bring back peace to the Church, and was accorded to the desires of the representative of a God of peace and charity on earth; but Napoleon would have triumphed over all the embarrassments which it caused him, if the pacification of Europe had allowed him to do so.

A pastoral letter, which was issued from Rome simultaneously with the ratification of the Concordat, exhorted the French bishops to resign their sees, a delay of three months being granted them in which to pronounce themselves. Almost all the old incumbents made haste to accede to the wishes of the Pope, and sent in their patents. A very small number of former prelates, who had retired to England, showed themselves recalcitrant, and formed a centre of opposition which received the name of Little Church. Their resistance passed unnoticed. The bull, which suppressed the archbishoprics and bishoprics which had existed at the time of the Revolution, was none the less put into execution. In the place of the twenty-three archbishoprics, and the hundred and thirty-four bishoprics which were abolished, only ten archbishoprics and fifty bishoprics were created.

* The Concordat still governs the relations between the State and the Church in France.—R. H. S.

The articles of the Concordat were not published. No communication of this act was made to the Tribunate, nor to the Legislative Body, after its conclusion. The apparent reason of this delay was the necessity of awaiting the resignation of the incumbents of the ancient sees, amongst whom were a certain number of *émigrés* who might be expected to refuse to resign. But the principal reason was the fear of brusquely making matters which concerned the peace of men's consciences the subject of the discussions of the umbrageous and speculative minds who dominated in the National Tribune. The publication of the Concordat was postponed to the opening of the second session of the Legislative Body. This interval was made use of in preparing, in the Council of State, various regulations which were necessary for the co-ordination of the religious system of the State with the needs of the nation and the progress of enlightenment.

I must speak, in connection with the Concordat, of a measure which to a great extent decided the early communication of this convention to the Legislature and the Tribunate. The sessions of these two assemblies, and notably that of the Tribunate, had been marked by violent opposition. The majority of the laws presented to them had been unfavourably received; two even had been rejected. Hostile words had been pronounced in the Tribune. These convinced the First Consul that he could not count in this direction on any sincere co-operation, and that the presence of these orators, whom he considered evilly-disposed or led astray by an ill-timed zeal for public liberty, would be fatal to the introduction of the ameliorations which he had conceived. The renewal of the fifths both of the Tribunate and of the Legislative Body, which by the terms of the constitution had to be effected annually, seemed to him a favourable opportunity for ridding himself of the members who had the most opposed the laws proposed by the government. The method of the renewal of these fifths of the members both of the Tribunate and of the Legislative Body, never having been defined by a constitutional act, the Senate was free to effect it either by election or by drawing lots. The first method was adopted. At the re-election of four-fifths of the two bodies the twenty most recalcitrant tribunes were eliminated. The influence of the Government was seen in this act of the Senate, in which, it had to be recognized, the law had not been materially violated. This purification, for so it must be called, provoked and still provokes the reprobation of honourable and independent men, familiar rather with theory than enlightened by practice, and who for the most part profess the motto: "Let the State perish rather than principles." This measure was, however, one of urgent necessity. The firm desire to obtain good laws had either to be persisted in or to be abandoned under pressure of men who, for the most part, thought the young government weak, and who wanted to render themselves indispensable by means of systematic opposition. There could be no doubt which of these two alternatives the First Consul would choose.

The Concordat was the first law presented at the extraordinary session convened on the 5th of April. It was adopted by a very large majority. On the 18th of April, Easter Sunday, a Te Deum was sung in the church of Notre Dame to celebrate the re-establishment of religious worship, and the Peace of Amiens.

The First Consul assumed, on this occasion, a green court-dress with gold embroideries; he wore the Regent, a diamond of great beauty, in the guard of his sword. This diamond was called the Regent, after the Duc d'Orléans, who had bought it during the minority of Louis XV. to adorn the royal crown. Stolen from the *garde-meuble* during the Revolution, and afterwards discovered, this diamond had been pledged by the Government. It was for sale at much less than its value when the First Consul bought it in.

Mass was said by Cardinal Caprara, in the presence of the diplomatic body. The bishops who had been nominated took the oath. In the evening the city was illuminated throughout. The opposition of the free-thinking party manifested itself, on the part of some of the generals, in quibbles which only provoked smiles of contempt. Their first impressions had suggested the very worst designs against the person of the First Consul, who was by no means in ignorance of the fact; but reflection brought wiser counsels. Many leading generals met together to discuss the matter. Some wildly excited men carried their madness to the point of suggesting that the First Consul should share the fate of Romulus. Bernadotte was amongst their number. Napoleon, who was always indifferent to his personal safety, refused to act on the reports which he received concerning this matter. His stoicism remained unshaken. He contented himself with roughly scolding the principal leaders. Some he sent away. Bernadotte was sent off to the army in the West, which he had left to come to Paris. His attitude towards the Head of the State became, from that time, so equivocal and strange that his chief staff-officer, the general of brigade, Simon, was removed from the army. I have seen Napoleon, at the time that I am speaking of, so incensed against Bernadotte, that he spoke of having him tried by court-martial. It was only thanks to the intervention of Joseph Bonaparte, Bernadotte's brother-in-law, that the General escaped this jurisdiction.

Of the three prelates sent from Rome to negotiate the Concordat, Cardinal Consalvi and Monseigneur Spina were very enlightened men. Father Caselli, who acted with them in the capacity of adviser on all matters of form, cases of conscience, and pontifical protocol, was a simple and loyal man, wrapped up in the theological questions which had been the study of his life. Cardinal Consalvi, without openly blaming the decree of the Council of Trent, which enforces celibacy on the priests, did not in conversation reject the idea of allowing them to marry. He did not proscribe theatrical performances and, as he himself said, would have had no objection to be present at the representation of a moral play on the stage. These remarks of his, which in no way bound him, were a trifling concession to the free-thinking spirit with which he was besieged in Paris. Whilst speaking as a man free from prejudices, he could only act in accordance with the spirit of the Church. He only spoke so freely of the marriage of priests because the question had been eliminated, either in deference to the views of the First Consul, or because the latter did not wish to complicate negotiations which were sufficiently thorny without it.

The Concordat is perhaps the most important act of Napoleon's government. After having considered it in its relation to politics, and in its general effect, there would be something wanting to the appreciation of this great work if the part played in it by the personal feeling of the Head of the State were to be passed over in silence. Some people have thought that, in the eyes of Napoleon, religious belief was but a superstition consecrated by time, and that in re-establishing the Catholic religion he only made use of it as the tool of his ambition, without in any way considering the social influence of religion. Those who spoke thus were ignorant of the fact that Bonaparte was sincerely religious—I may add, a true Catholic. His detestation of the free-thinking cynicism which preaches contempt for religion—which was considered by him, on the contrary, as the basis of morality and decency—was as great as his horror for the bigotry which fetters human intelligence. If, in the course of private conversation, or in the discussions into which he was drawn by his active brain, and in considering the history of the Catholic Church in its various vicissitudes he has expressed certain opinions blaming the excesses committed in the name of religion by its ministers, what a mistake it is to conclude that he was blind to the civilizing influence of Christianity, or that he was an unbelieving and sceptical philosopher. His respect for the doctrines of the Gospel was the outcome of his convictions and his early training; witness the religious thoughts which the church-bell of Rueil, heard in the garden of La Malmaison, awoke within him; and his recourse, during his last moments at St. Helena, to the consolations and succour of religion. In re-establishing the Roman Catholic religion in France he filled the void which its absence left in the State, but at the same time he obeyed the dictates of his religious instincts.

The first measure was the creation of a Ministry of

Public Worship. The direction of this ministry was entrusted to Portalis, who at first assumed the title of Councillor of State charged with matters concerning public worship, and shortly afterwards that of Minister. Portalis was a learned lawyer and a flowery orator, gentle and conciliatory in character. He has been accused, and perhaps with reason, of too great flexibility. But in the functions which it was his to perform this quality was an advantage rather than a drawback; he was a good man of the kind defined by Cicero as: "*Vir bonus et dicendi peritus.*" His philanthropy was as great as his learning and his eloquence.

Monseigneur Spina, who had been created Cardinal after the signing of the Concordat, remained in Paris as *chargé d'affaires*. He was replaced by Cardinal Caprara, who had been appointed Legate *a Latere*. The Cardinal, who arrived in Paris in the month of September, was not presented to the First Consul until the 9th of April following.

The Archbishop of Lyons was sent to Rome with the title of ambassador. He was the uncle of the First Consul, the maternal grandmother of Napoleon having married M. Fesch, on her second marriage. M. Fesch was captain of one of the Swiss regiments which the Republic of Genoa maintained in Corsica at the time of her domination. Cardinal Caprara was the issue of this second marriage. Abbé Fesch had left Holy Orders at the commencement of the Revolution and had performed laical functions in Italy. He resumed the priest's gown after the 18th Brumaire. Patronized by his nephew he rapidly rose to the highest dignities in the Church. He was appointed Archbishop of Lyons in 1801, and promoted to the cardinalate two years later. He went to Rome to replace M. Cacault, French *chargé d'affaires*, when the Concordat was signed. M. de Chateaubriand, author of "The Genius of Christianity," who had returned from the emigration before the amnesty, had been presented by M. de Fontanes, his intimate friend, to Madame Bacciochi, sister of the First Consul, and to his brother Lucien Bonaparte. Brother and sister declared M. de Chateaubriand under their protection. The publication of "The Genius of Christianity" at the moment when Catholicism had been re-established in France, produced a great sensation. Religious ideas were spreading all the more rapidly that for so long they had been repressed. No more favourable opportunity could have been found for the publication of this work, and it was received with favour by the First Consul. The protection of Madame Bacciochi, but more especially the satisfaction felt by the First Consul at the publication of a work which seconded his opinions, and gave assistance to the Concordat, decided him to give the author a mark of his favour, in appointing him Secretary of Legation at the Holy See.

The evacuation of Egypt was keenly felt by the First Consul. The tragical death of Kléber was a disaster,* for if he had lived France might have retained this important conquest. The signature of the Preliminaries of London was a powerful diversion from the unfortunate issue of the Egyptian campaign. The object pursued by the First Consul since his accession to power was realized. His first step had been an

* Jean Baptiste Kléber born 1753, General of Division in 1793, was murdered in Cairo by a Turk on June 14th, 1800.

appeal to the King of England to assist in a pacification which should be satisfactory to the interests of the two countries; this appeal had not been listened to. A second negotiation had been attempted, but the British Ministry did not think the new Government sufficiently well-established, and these negotiations had come to nothing.

Whilst the continental peace was being signed at Lunéville Messrs. Pitt, Dundas, and Granville,* fiery partisans of war, believing peace with France to be inevitable, had retired to make way for a new Ministry. They did not wish to incur the responsibility, in the eyes of the aristocracy and commerce of England, of an experiment which would show whether peace was more advantageous to these two important classes than war.

The ministers, who were succeeded by Addington and Hawkesbury, had ordered that French fishing-boats should be pursued and captured like ships of war. In answer to the communication made to M. Otto, discharging the functions of French commissioner in London, for the exchange of prisoners, communication of an order which violated every usage and every rule of war, M. Otto declared that he had received instructions to leave England, where his stay had become useless, but that his government would not take reprisals, and that the French cruisers would abstain from any interference with fishing-boats. In answer to the French commissioner's note the new Ministry repealed the order concerning the French fishermen. This abandonment of a measure which had given the war a character of savagery, quite unworthy

* Lord Grenville?

of a civilized nation, bespoke less hostile dispositions. In the discussions which this matter provoked the English Ministry held out the prospect of a reconciliation. As a matter of fact, one month later M. Otto received a note which contained an offer to send a plenipotentiary to Paris with authority to negotiate for peace. This overture was cordially responded to by the First Consul, who accredited M. Otto to receive the proposals of the English Ministers and to treat preliminarily. M. Otto was instructed that it was no ostentatious negotiations that were desired, but that the preliminary articles of a treaty of pacification should be secured. In consequence, Lord Hawkesbury handed to M. Otto a synopsis, written by his own hand, of the terms on which England would sign the peace. These terms exacted that France and her allies should cede to England her most important colonies, Egypt and Malta. The First Consul having refused these proposals, which already previously had not been considered acceptable, Lord Hawkesbury asked the French Government on what basis it was disposed to treat. M. Otto made the following proposals:—

Egypt to be restored to the Porte.

Malta to be dismantled and restored to the Order.

The island of Ceylon to be ceded to England.

The Cape of Good Hope and all other establishments to be restored to France and her allies.

Portugal to be maintained in her integrity.

The English Government haggled over these conditions, though, at the same time, it declared itself ready to agree as to Malta. It renounced its claim to Martinique, but desired to retain possession of Trinidad, which was a Spanish possession, and of

Tobago, a French possession, and in this case proposed that the Dutch possessions of Demerara, Essequibo, and Berbice should be declared free ports; or as an alternative it offered to abandon Trinidad, but to retain the French islands of Tobago, Sainte-Lucie, together with Demerara, Essequibo, and Berbice.

These alternatives were embarrassing to the French Government, for either Spain or Holland had to be sacrificed. To save these powers from the loss of the important colonies which England demanded, the First Consul consented to give up Tobago, but the English Government refused to be satisfied with this concession, even though M. Otto offered to add Curaçoa.

At last, after six months of negotiations, the preliminaries of peace were signed. The principal conditions were that all possessions which had belonged to France and her allies should be restored to them, with the exception of Ceylon and Trinidad; that the Cape of Good Hope should be opened to the trade of both nations; that Egypt should be handed over to the Porte; that the Republic of the Ionian Islands should be recognized; that Portugal should be maintained in her integrity; and, finally, that Malta should be evacuated by the English and restored to the Order; and that the power guaranteeing the independence of this island should be designated later. It was agreed upon that a Congress should be held at Amiens for the settlement of a definitive treaty, in which certain points which had not been settled should be decided upon.

The following reflections of Napoleon on the refusal of England to accept the peace which he had offered her in 1800 will be considered of great interest:

"(1) Could the English Cabinet refuse the overtures attempted by the First Consul without rendering itself responsible for the miseries of war?

"(2) Was this refusal good policy, and was it in conformity with the interests of England?

"(3) Was war then to be desired for France?

"(4) What were Napoleon's interests under these circumstances?

"(1) Pitt refused to enter upon negotiations in the hope that by continuing the war he would force France to recall the House of Bourbon and to give Belgium back again to Austria. If these two pretensions were legitimate and just, he could with justice refuse peace; but if the one as well as the other were illegitimate and unjust, he rendered his country responsible for the horrors of war. Now, the Republic had been recognized by the whole of Europe; England herself had recognized it when in 1796 she invested Lord Malmesbury with full powers to treat with the Directoire. This plenipotentiary had visited Paris and Lille in turn, and had negotiated with Charles Lacroix, Letourneur, and Maret, ministers of the Directoire. Besides, the war had not the return of the Bourbons as its object. The Belgian provinces had been ceded by the Emperor of Austria by the treaty of Campo-Formio, in 1797, and England had recognized their union to France by the negotiations of Lord Malmesbury at Lille. They formed a legitimate part of the territory of the Republic. To wish to separate them from her was to usurp, to rend, to dismember a recognized State.

"(2) Was Pitt's policy in this matter in conformity with the interests of England? Could he reasonably hope to obtain Belgium by continuing the war? Would it not have been wiser to restore peace to the world in securing real and lasting advantages? The Kings of Sardinia and of Naples, the Grand-Duke of Tuscany, and the Pope, would have been re-established and consolidated on their thrones; Milan would have been assured to Austria; Holland, together with Switzerland and Genoa, would have been evacuated by the French. English influence might have extended in these countries. Egypt would have been restored to the Porte, and Malta to the Order. Ceylon, the Cape of Good Hope, and Trinidad would have assured the power of England in the two Indies. What a magnificent result for the campaign of 1799! These advantages were certain; the hopes to which they were sacrificed were less likely of realization. The coalition had been victorious in 1799, in Italy, but had been defeated in Switzerland, Holland, and the East. France had just changed governments. A man whose military talents and knowledge had been tested had succeeded five persons who were in feud amongst themselves, and who were less than skilful. This man had been raised to power by the wish of the nation. At the mere sound of his name the Vendée submitted and the Russians marched to recross the Vistula. Lord Grenville himself admitted that even if the First Consul wished to give up Belgium, the French people would oppose any such cession. The object of the war was, then, popular in France. Berlin, Vienna, and London might deceive themselves in 1799, the circumstances were then so new. Could English statesmen be excused for falling into the same error in 1800? It was probable that the campaign of

1800 would be favourable to France, that she would reconquer Italy and, in fine, that even if her success were problematic, England would none the less be obliged to pay immense subsidies for many years; for, in order to tear Belgium from France, the reunion of Austria, Russia, and Prussia would be needed, or at least the union of one of these powers to the coalition. Now no such result could be obtained by the campaign of 1800. The risks, then, of this campaign were not to be incurred.

"(3) The interest of the Republic was opposed to the interest of England. Had she signed peace then, she would have done so after having lost Italy. She would have retrograded as the result of one doubtful campaign. That would have been dishonouring, and would have prompted all the kings to league themselves against her. All the chances of the campaign of 1800 were in her favour. The Russians had left, the Vendée was pacified, the interior factions were under restraint, and there was absolute confidence in the head of the government. The Republic could only, and should only, make peace after having re-established the equilibrium of Italy. She could only play herself false and compromise her future by signing peace on any terms less advantageous than those secured at Campo-Formio. War was at that time necessary to her for the maintenance of the energy and the unity of the State then badly organized. The nation would have insisted upon a great reduction of taxation and the disbandment of a large portion of the army, so that, two years after the war, France would have come on to the battle-field under great disadvantages.

"(4) Napoleon needed war. The campaigns of Italy,

the peace of Campo-Formio, the Egyptian expedition, the 18th Brumaire, the unanimous desire of the people to raise him to the highest post in the state had no doubt placed him very high. A treaty of peace inferior in advantages to France to the one secured at Campo-Formio—which would have ruined all his creations in Italy—would have blasted the imagination of the French nation, and would have deprived him of the force necessary for the termination of the Revolution, and the possibility of establishing a definitive and permanent system of government. He saw this, and awaited the answer from London with impatience. The answer filled him with secret joy. The more the English oligarchy insulted the Republic, the more it was serving Napoleon's private interests, and he said to his minister: "We could not have had a more favourable answer." From that moment he saw that having to deal with politicians so swayed by passion, there would be but few obstacles in the path towards the fulfilment of his destinies. Pitt, so distinguished by his parliamentary talents, and his knowledge of affairs at home, was completely ignorant of what is called politics. As a general rule England knows nothing about continental affairs, and especially about French affairs. The glory of France was carried to the highest point, all Europe was subjected to her, and Lord Grenville was obliged, in a very few months after his insulting declamations against the nation, to sign a treaty of peace which was more advantageous to us than the peace of Campo-Formio, inasmuch as it gave us Piedmont and Tuscany.

"But for the assassin's dagger which threw the command of the army of the East into the hands of a man* who no doubt distinguished in many ways, was without military genius, Egypt would have been united to France for ever; for both the English and the French agree that Abercromby would have been beaten if Kléber had lived. The Porte had already shown herself favourably disposed towards France in abandoning Egypt to her. How heavily a fanatic of twenty years of age weighed in the balance of the world!" †

It is impossible not to tarry a moment over this brilliant epoch. Napoleon had been at the head of the government for barely two years, and already the wounds of the Republic were everywhere cicatrized. Finance was re-established, public instruction had been reorganized, the civil code had been drafted, the Vendée pacified, union restored to the Church, immense projects for the improvement and embellishment of Paris and the provinces by the construction of roads and canals were already in execution, peace had been re-established with the United States, with Austria, with Prussia, with Russia, Bavaria, the Porte, and with the Barbary Regencies, with Naples, Spain and Portugal, and all these treaties were crowned by the preliminaries signed with England. In consequence a solemn fête throughout the whole territory of the Republic was ordained, to be celebrated on the 18th Brumaire following, the anniversary of the happy day from which so many benefactions dated.

During the first eight days which followed the signature of the preliminary clauses of peace with England, the respective plenipotentiaries were nominated: Joseph Bonaparte, negotiator of the treaty of

---

* General Menou.   † Kléber's murderer.

Lunéville, and of the Concordat, for France, and Lord Cornwallis for England.

The English plenipotentiary arrived in Paris a month later. Some preliminary conferences took place. It could be seen from these pourparlers that the question which would give the most trouble, and which, as a matter of fact, was the pretext of a rupture a year later, was that of Malta. The only point which seemed a matter for discussion was the designation of the third power which should guarantee the independence of this island, this question was frequently transformed during the progress of the Amiens Congress.

The first conferences opened at the beginning of December 1801. Spain and the Batavian Republic* intervened in the negotiations. Spain was represented by Chevalier d'Azzara, Spanish ambassador, and the Batavian Republic by M. Schimmelpenninck, plenipotentiary minister, both accredited to Paris. These two ministers were witnesses rather than principals. Chevalier d'Azzara did not come to Amiens nor take any part in the discussions until towards the end of January 1802. The English Cabinet, which had wished to force the admission of an English plenipotentiary on the Congress at Lunéville, protested against the intervention of the Dutch and Spanish representatives in the Amiens negotiations, alleging the influence exercised by the French Cabinet over Holland and Spain. This pretension, which appears to have been put forward only for what it was worth, was not maintained by Lord Cornwallis. The protocol of the conferences was held alternately at the houses of the French and the English Minister, and in the French language.

* Holland.

The first pourparlers turned on the question of Malta, and it seemed as if the English Ministry regretted having simplified it. The British plenipotentiary appeared to be strongly interested in the future fate of this island. He desired that its protection should be assured by a large foreign garrison. He asked that if the French language were maintained in Malta, English should also be spoken. The French plenipotentiary asked that the Order of Malta should be converted into a hospitable Order, instead of being re-established as a religious and military Order, that the fortifications of the island should be levelled, and that it should become a great lazaretto, open to all nations trading in the East and on the Mediterranean. The English plenipotentiary refused to consent to the destruction of the fortifications, because one clause of the preliminaries stipulated that the island should be restored in its existing state.

Since the discussion was not limited to the one point in the preliminary articles which remained to be settled, that is to say the designation of the power to which the protection of Malta should be assigned, the scruples which the English Cabinet affected, and its respect for the letter of the preliminaries, in so far as this island was concerned, were in contradiction with the tricks of every kind which it imagined for the purpose of misrepresenting its spirit. But the English Government had secret motives, afterwards unmasked by the rupture of the Peace of Amiens, for refusing to allow the dismantling of Malta. This question was turned about in every direction and discussed with a care and a minuteness which ought to have brought about an immediate understanding. But instead of that, difficulties kept cropping up, not only on this particular article but on some other points in the treaty under consideration.

At last, after long and laborious negotiations, in the course of which the shrewdness and the moderation of the French plenipotentiary were more than once put to the test, the treaty was signed. The same hand which had so judiciously directed the conferences of the peace of Lunéville, signed the maritime pacification at Amiens.

The definitive treaty confirmed the stipulations of which the preliminaries had laid down the basis. There was a derogation in favour of Holland, who obtained the restitution of the Cape of Good Hope.

The Maltese question, so obstinately discussed, was evaded rather than resolved. Malta was to be handed over to the order of St. John of Jerusalem. Neither French nor English was to be the insular language; there was to be a Maltese tongue. The British troops were to evacuate the island in the space of three months. Half the garrison was to be composed of Maltese. The King of Naples was to be invited to furnish two thousand men to complete it. Malta was to be placed under the protection and under the warranty of France, England, Austria, Spain, Russia, and Prussia. Its neutrality was to be proclaimed.

M. Dupuy, former intendant of the Isle of France, who had governed this colony during nine years, in troubled times, and had succeeded in preserving it to France, was secretary to the French legation. His co-operation on the treaty was rewarded with a place as Councillor of State, and afterwards by his admission to the Senate. His wife was one of the ladies of the

Queen of Naples, and his eldest daughter was afterwards married by the Emperor to M. d'Audenarde, one of the Empress's equerries.

The son of Minister Portalis was attached to the legation of Amiens, as he had been to that of Lunéville. In the interval between the two treaties he had married a young lady of Holstein, in whose house his father had found refuge during the proscription under which he fell on the 18th Fructidor.

Lord Cornwallis, Minister of England at the Congress, was a fine old man of about sixty-eight, tall, with a noble face, and with open and kindly manners. He fully justified his reputation for fair-dealing at Amiens. His first secretary of legation was a Mr. Merry, who appears to have been attached to him by the office in Downing Street to attenuate the effects of his very military frankness. This secretary was a man difficult to deal with, full of English reserve. His troublesome carriage contrasted with the frank and conciliating ways of the English plenipotentiary. In spite of quibbles over words, the old routine of English diplomacy, the length and obscurity of the notes, and the multiplicity of the incidents created, the two ministers agreed very well together. That was not always Mr. Merry's fault, and Lord Cornwallis had more than once to impose his authority.

The following act of fair play was the worthy termination of this estimable minister's mission. The protocol of the last sitting had been closed, the definitive treaty had been agreed upon, and parole had been exchanged for the signature, a ceremony which was to be solemnly carried out at the Town-hall on the following day. In the night which preceded the day of signing, a courier from London brought Lord Cornwallis orders to modify in favour of England certain provisions of the treaty relating to the balance of sums due for the subsistence and maintenance of the prisoners. Lord Cornwallis had declared to Joseph Bonaparte that nothing that might happen should interfere with the signing of the peace. And though at the moment of signing he received from his government orders to claim a balance in favour of England, he considered his honour pledged, and declared that he would not go back on what he had promised.

At eleven o'clock on the morning of the 15th of March, detachments of infantry and cavalry marched to the houses of the plenipotentiaries and escorted their carriages to the Town-hall, to the sound of military music, and amidst the acclamations of a large crowd. The plenipotentiaries were received by the mayor and his deputies, and were congratulated by the prefect and the authorities. At last, when, on the order of the French Minister, it was announced that peace was about to be signed, the doors were thrown open, and an orderly crowd streamed in. The plenipotentiaries then signed with due solemnity and embraced each other with such an effusion of cordiality that the rooms of the Town-hall re-echoed with applause, and more than one looker-on was moved with emotion. In the evening the town was illuminated, and a theatrical performance was given in aid of the poor.

It fell to M. Dupuy to carry the treaty to Paris. A half-hour after his arrival the cannon of the Invalides announced the news. Peace was proclaimed on the squares and *places* with the customary solemnities.

It was during the negotiations of Amiens that, at

one of the conferences, the English Minister hinted at a proposal to recognize the First Consul as King of France. This was no longer what Lord Grenville had said in 1800. The new English Minister had understood that the recall of the princes of the ancient dynasty was an easy matter, but that, as to restoring them to their thrones, that would have been fraught with as much difficulty to their auxiliaries as to the man who should recall them, and that by its very nature such a service would have rendered them suspicious of him. The prejudices as well as the pretensions of those around them, the new interests which had arisen, the revolution that had taken place in men's minds, the new forms of government, the military system, did not all these things conspire against a durable re-establishment of the House of Bourbon on the throne of France?

Napoleon, however, paid no attention to this hint. He did not wish to reign by the grace of a foreign nation and by no means stood in need of such permission. When, two years later, the throne was once more raised in France, he was made emperor, and not king; this reign could not be a continuation of the reign of the Bourbons. A new era had dawned, the face of Europe was changed. It was not a royal monarchy that Napoleon proposed to restore, it was a constitutional monarchy that he desired to found.

General peace, that peace which the coalition had steadily refused to grant to his desire, could not do otherwise than bring with it a completion of institutions which had only been temporary. The times rendered a dictatorship necessary, and allowed only of temporary measures destined to make way for a system of government adapted to the requirements of the epoch, and which no man better than Napoleon could define and establish. I take a real pleasure in mentioning, in this connection, that in a sitting of the Chamber of Deputies, on the 3rd of March, 1827, General Sebastiani, speaking on a petition relating to the re-establishment of the jury-system in Corsica, gave the Imperial Government the credit of having suspended, not destroyed, the institution of trial by jury in this department, and added that in general it had only taken temporary measures which it was one day to abolish.

The English and French ministers kept house splendidly. We were invited to the houses of both in turns. M. Schimmelpenninck gave tea-parties, of which his wife and eldest daughter did the honours. Madame Schimmelpenninck had left a certain reputation for beauty in Paris. She knew how to unite the domestic virtues and the duties of a good mother with her worldly successes. Her daughter was then sixteen years old. She had a charming face, and attracted all the young men of the legation by her candour and her modesty. All in this family breathed the spirit of patriarchal simplicity.

It was sometimes necessary to send couriers to Paris and to London to procure additional information on important points in the negotiations. During the short intervals between their departure and return we made several excursions in the Somme department. We visited the sea at Saint-Valéry, and inspected the cloth and carpet factories at Abbeville.

Lord Cornwallis used to take horse-exercise every day on the Paris road. He was usually accompanied by his natural son, Captain Nightingale, whom he had introduced by this name. His son, Lord Brome, and his son-in-law, Colonel Singleton, came to stay with him for some time. After dinner Lord Cornwallis and Captain Nightingale used to retire to his lordship's chamber, and spend the rest of the evening in drinking, according to the English custom.

Lord Cornwallis returned to London two days after the treaty had been signed. Before leaving Amiens he paid a compliment to the industries of this town, purchasing some pieces of velveteen at different factories there, to take back to England as a proof of our superiority. He left behind him the reputation of a man worthy of all respect by the probity and elevation of his character. He looked on his participation in the treaty as the last act of a long and honourable career, and congratulated himself on having closed his public life with a pacific mission. Nevertheless, some time later, he accepted the government of India, where he died shortly after his arrival.

The French Minister had taken up his abode in the house of M. de Folleville, formerly member of the constituent assembly, where he had drawn attention to himself, amongst the members of the Right, by his extreme views. Madame de Folleville, who was then in middle life, had been remarkably beautiful. Having lost a son whom she idolized, she placed his embalmed body under her bed, in the extremity of her regret. Her daughter married General Musnier, who commanded the Somme department. Madame de Folleville had received a man's education. She rode, fenced, and swam with the greatest courage. This masculine education had not, however, made her lose the distinctive qualities of her sex, gentleness and modesty.

M. Quinette, the Prefect of the department, used to give evening parties, at which a large and brilliant company assembled. The mayor, M. Debray, used also to do the honours of his house with considerable good grace. We were invited one day to hear the reading of an unpublished song, called "*L'Ouvroir,*" taken from the poem, "*Vert-Vert.*" This song, which had been found amongst the author's papers, was recited by one of his relations, whose snuffling voice by no means enhanced its beauties. It seemed inferior to other songs in Gresset's * poem, though it also bore the impress of his flow of language and of his facility of style. No doubt this song had been suppressed by its author, who was the best judge and the one least open to suspicion. I believe that since then it has been published. † This episode reminded us that we were in the land of a man to whom Amiens is justly proud to have given birth.

It was during the course of the Congress, in the month of January, 1802, that we heard of the marriage of Mademoiselle Hortense de Beauharnais, daughter of Madame Bonaparte, to Louis Bonaparte, afterwards King of Holland. This marriage was against the wishes of both parties, whose affections were placed elsewhere. Shortly before the expedition to Egypt, Louis Bonaparte at that time aide-de-camp to his brother, being on a visit to his sister Caroline, at Madame Campan's *pension*, at St. Germain, frequently met there one of his sister's friends Mlle. E. de Beauharnais, and fell

---

* Jean Baptiste Louis de Gresset, born in Amiens Aug. 29th, 1709, died there June 16th, 1777. Author of the comic epic "*Vert-Vert*" which is the story of a parrot. Also wrote a comedy "*Le Méchant*".—R. H. S.

† Gresset's works were published in 3 volumes in 1811.

deeply in love with her. When he received orders to leave for Toulon, there to await the departure of the expedition, he was filled with deep regret at being torn from the person he loved. Bernadotte's prank, in hoisting the tricolour flag over the house which he occupied as French ambassador, which aroused the whole population of Vienna, delayed the departure of General Bonaparte, the Directoire fearing that this incident might rekindle war on the Continent. It was in the meanwhile that Mademoiselle E. de Beauharnais allowed herself to be married to Lavalette, aide-de-camp to the commander-in-chief, on the eve of Napoleon's departure to Egypt.

On his return from the Marengo campaign, Mademoiselle Hortense de Beauharnais was proposed to Louis Bonaparte, who, filled with his first love, at first refused this union. To avoid it, he asked to go to Prussia, with the intention of following the manœuvres at Potsdam. He afterwards followed at the head of the 5th regiment of dragoons, to which he had been appointed colonel, the army corps which General Beauclerc, his brother-in-law, had been ordered to lead into Portugal. An affection, which afterwards degenerated into an incurable disease, obliged him to take the waters at Barèges. On his return he gave his consent to his marriage with Hortense de Beauharnais, who on her side only entered in upon it with reluctance.

Malevolence found in this union the pretext for a black calumny. Madame Louis Bonaparte gave birth to a son ten months after her marriage. The partiality of the First Consul for this child strengthened the lying rumours, which in spite of their proved absurdity, may have contributed to trouble the union of the two spouses, as much, perhaps, as their want of sympathy and the divergence of their tastes.

Madame Bonaparte had anxiously desired this marriage. She hoped by increasing the number of bonds which attached her to Napoleon to render more difficult a divorce which her sterility constantly prompted her to fear. The churches not yet having been reopened, the nuptial ceremony was celebrated in the drawing-room of the house in the Rue de la Victoire, Cardinal Caprara giving the religious benediction to the two spouses. The marriage of the Murats, which had not been consecrated by the Church, was blessed at the same time. It is said that the First Consul would not take advantage of this opportunity to sanctify his union with Josephine, to whom he had only been civilly married. His subsequent divorce drew attention to an incident which passed unnoticed at the time of its occurrence.

CHAPTER II.

JOSEPH BONAPARTE informs me of my Admission into the First Consul's Cabinet—My Anxiety on Hearing this News—Admiration expressed by General Bernadotte for Napoleon—I am Summoned to the Tuileries—Friendly Reception from Madame Bonaparte—Family Dinner—Audience in the Evening in the First Consul's Cabinet—First Day—Second Day—The Moral and Physical Properties of Napoleon—His Malady—Consequences of Skin Disease caught at the Siege of Toulon—On His Early Education—On the Attempts of Poetry attributed to Him—On an Alleged Discovery at Lyons of Manuscript in His Own Writing—His Respect for His Parents—Death of His Father—Vote for the Erection of a Monument to His Father by the Municipal Council of Montpellier—Napoleon's Refusal—Affection of Napoleon for His Great-Uncle—Description of the First Consul's Cabinet—The Map Office—His Librarians—His Secretary-Interpreter—Father Dupuis—Souvenirs of His Youth with which Napoleon Surrounded Himself—The First Consul's Household Arrangements—The Changes which were Made in Them—Conspiracy Against His Person—Retrospective Souvenir of the Criminal Attempt of 3rd Nivôse—Secret of the 18th Brumaire, Year VIII. —Félix Lepelletier—Napoleon's Indifference about His Personal Safety— Quiet Life which he Led at the Beginning of the Consulate—Family Theatricals at La Malmaison—Advances Made to Literary Men and Rejected—Ducis and Lemercier—His Opinions on Poets—Napoleon's Simplicity and Kindheartedness—Souvenirs of the Egyptian Campaign—Orders of the Day in the Army of the East—Count D'Orsay—M. De Bourrienne— His Position with the First Consul—Reasons of His Disgrace—Its Consequences—Bulletin of the Sitting of the Court of Assizes During the Georges Trial—How His Memoirs, full of False or Inexact Assertions, were not Written by Him—His Mission to Hamburg—My Position with the First Consul, and How it was Almost Unknown—The Second and Third Consuls —The Ministers—The Secretary of State—The State Council—First Labours of the Cabinet—Amnesty of the Émigrés—Origin and Motives of the Senatus Consultum—MM. de Breteuil and de Calonne—Mesdames de Damas and de Champcenetz—La Harpe—Law on Public Instruction—Foundation of the Public Schools—Scholarship Awarded to Young Thiers—Foundation of Houses of Education for Girls—Institution of the Legion of Honour— Opposition which it Encountered—The Consulate for Life—On Popular Suffrage—"Edward in Scotland"—"*L'Antichambre*"—Mademoiselle Chevigny—Duel between Generals Destaing and Reynier—Bichat and Desault— Numerous Arrivals of English in France—Lord Henry Petty and M. Dumont— Mr. Fox—Moreau—The Memel Interview—The First Consul sends an Officer of His Guard There—Repression of Algerian Piracies—Hulin at Algiers—On the Different Anniversaries of the 14th of July.

THE reader will pardon me for having spoken at such length on my first initiation to a knowledge of a period of history which occupied my entire attention, and the magnificent commencement of which, marked by the most important transactions of this new era—the continental peace, the Concordat, and the maritime peace—was amongst my most interesting memories, for the special reason that I had been directly connected with it. The proclamation of the general peace coincided with the date of my admission into the confidence of Napoleon, and the day from which my lot began to be bound up with his destiny. Like so many others of the same period I experienced the magnetic influence which this powerful genius exercised over all those who approached him. As a satellite I was faithful to the impulse I had received, and the sun in whose sphere of attraction I have never ceased to revolve had for its device "*Nec pluribus impar*," a device which, in this case, was no flatterer, but the strictest expression of truth.

I returned to Paris with Joseph Bonaparte towards the end of March, 1802. He took me aside one day, and told me that the First Consul wished to see me, and would receive me at the Tuileries on the morrow. He confided to me that the head of the State had decided to attach me to his Cabinet; that he was dissatisfied with Bourrienne, and that as soon as I had familiarized myself with his work he would dismiss him, and that I should occupy his place.

I saw in this proposal the fresh proof of the assiduous kindness of Joseph Bonaparte, and his desire to promote my welfare, but at the same time I was perplexed. I begged him to dissuade the First Consul from this project, alleging that I did not feel myself at all capable of filling the post for which he intended me, and confessed that I feared the loss of my independence.

Joseph Bonaparte said everything that the affection with which he honoured me could suggest to him, persuading me not to throw away the opportunity of advancement and fortune which his friendship had procured for me. I remember that General Bernadotte, who was present, added his persuasions to those of Joseph Bonaparte, to make me change my mind, pointing out to me the happiness of a life with so great a man, where I should be the constant witness of the inspirations of his genius. He seemed to lack words to express the admiration and devotion which he appeared to feel for the First Consul.

On the morning of the second of April Joseph Bonaparte gave me a letter from General Duroc, who wrote to tell me that the First Consul could receive me at five o'clock in the afternoon of that day. I was obliged to accept an invitation which was really a command. General Duroc conducted me to Madame Bonaparte, who received me with exquisite grace and politeness. She was kind enough to talk to me of the business which had brought me to the Tuileries. I was encouraged by her kindness to tell her the objections I felt to a gilded chain. She succeeded in making me agree to remain three years only with the First Consul. I should be free to retire at the end of that time, and she assured me that the First Consul would reward me with an honourable post, and further undertook to gain his consent to this arrangement.

I mention this circumstance to show with what cleverness she could enter into the sentiments of others, and appear to share their illusions. On reflection I had no reason to hope that the First Consul would agree to a transaction of this kind, or would, indeed, approve of my dictating terms. Madame Bonaparte did me the honour to say that I must be her guest at dinner that night. A moment after, Madame Louis Bonaparte entered the drawing-room, and the conversation became general. In the meanwhile time was passing. At last, at about seven o'clock, the sound of hurried steps on the staircase, which led to the room in which we were sitting, announced the arrival of the First Consul. Madame Bonaparte introduced me to him. He condescended to receive me with a kindness which at once dissipated the respectful awe in which I stood. He walked rapidly into the dining-room, whither I followed Madame Bonaparte and her daughter. Madame Bonaparte made me sit next her. The First Consul spoke to me several times during dinner, which only lasted twenty minutes. He spoke of my studies, and of Palissot, with a kindness and a simplicity which put me entirely at my ease, and showed me how gentle and simple this man, who bore on his forehead and in his eyes the mark of such imposing superiority, was in his private life.

When I returned to the drawing-room we found General Davout. The First Consul walked up and down the room with him, conversing, and a quarter of an hour later disappeared in the staircase from which he had come, without having spoken to me on the matter for which he had ordered my attendance.

I remained with Madame Bonaparte until eleven o'clock. I had asked her to be so good as to tell me whether I should go away, thinking that I had been forgotten. She told me to remain, and assured me that the First Consul would send for me. True enough, a footman came to fetch me. I followed him down a long passage to a staircase by which we reached a little door, at which he knocked. There was a wicket in this door which I examined with curiosity. My state of mind was such that I seemed to be outside the place of eternal imprisonment, and involuntarily I raised my eyes, to see whether I could not read over the door that inscription of Dante's, "*Lasciate ogni speranza voi che entrate...*"

An usher, who had looked through the wicket, opened the door after some words with the footman, and I was shown into a small drawing-room, poorly lighted. Whilst I was being announced I cast a rapid glance around the room, being anxious to acquaint myself with what was to be my prison. The furniture consisted of some chairs covered with green morocco, and a very luxurious roll-top writing table, which was loaded with gilt bronze ornaments, and inlaid with rose-wood mosaics representing various musical instruments. I afterwards learned that these pieces of furniture had belonged to Louis XVI. It was subsequently sent to the *garde-meuble* as useless. A low book-case ran round one side of the room. Some papers were scattered on the top.

I was announced, and immediately afterwards was ushered into a room, where I saw the First Consul seated behind a writing-table. A three-branched flambeau, covered with a shade, cast a strong light on the table. The rest of the room was in the shade, broken only by the light from the fire on the hearth.

The First Consul's back was toward me, and he was occupied in reading a paper, and finished reading it without taking notice of my entrance. He then turned round on his chair toward me. I had remained standing at the door of his cabinet, and on seeing him turn round I approached him. After having examined me for a moment with a piercing glance, which would have greatly intimidated me if I had seen it there for the first time, he told me that he wished to attach me to his service, and asked me if I felt myself strong enough to undertake the task which he proposed to confide to me.

I answered him with some embarrassment, with the commonplace remark that I was not very sure of myself, but that I would do all in my power to justify his confidence. I kept my objections to myself, because I knew that he would not like them, and, besides, the way in which he had received me at dinner had considerably weakened them.

He did not seem dissatisfied with my answer, for he rose from his seat and came up to me smiling, rather sardonically, it is true, and pulled my ear, which I knew to be a sign of favour. He then said to me, "Very well, come back to-morrow morning at seven, and come straight here."

That was all the conversation which preceded my admission into this sanctuary, which I imagined as a sort of place from which nothing but invisible oracles proceeded, accompanied by lightning and thunder.

Such was the very simple investiture which I received for a post, the responsibility of which seemed so terrible that, when it was proposed to me, I could only think of it with terror. After this short audience, and this laconic dialogue, the First Consul made a sign with his hand which I took for an order to withdraw, and left me, to go into an adjoining drawing-room, where, no doubt, some business awaited him. Slightly reassured by the simplicity of this commencement I went back the way I had come, preceded by my guide, who had waited for me outside the door. Nothing but solitude and silence reigned in the dimly-lighted corridors through which I passed. I met nobody on my way out, except a sentry placed at the gate of the inner court.

I went back to the Hôtel Marbeuf, where Joseph Bonaparte was then living. He had gone to bed, but I sent my card up to him, and told him what had happened. He gave me fresh encouragement, and I returned to the apartment which I occupied in the house. I was in a very anxious state of mind, and felt little disposed for sleep. I stood in need of the calm of the night to reflect on what had happened to me that day, so fruitful to me in unexpected events. I went over in my mind my introduction to Madame Bonaparte and to the First Consul, the simplicity of their home life, that simple and familiar dinner, and my reception in the evening. My ideas were confused in my head. I could not accustom myself to the thought that I was irresistibly led on towards the goal which I had desired, and that I found myself destined for a future the perspective of which was so different from the one I had imagined.

I was then twenty-four years of age. What did fortune want with me, who asked nothing of her? No doubt this change of condition was advantageous, but should I be fitted for my new position? Was I not putting my neck into an iron yoke, which I should not be able to bear? I was in that state of perplexity which always besets a man in his passage from the known to the unknown. These reflections kept me awake.

I got up before daybreak, and made my way to the Tuileries, arriving there before the appointed hour. I rather feared that I should not be able to find my way in the intricacies of the palace, and that I should have difficulty in explaining to the sentries who I was, and was very much surprised at the ease with which I made my way to the door through which I had passed the previous evening, and which I recognized by the wicket in it. As soon as he saw me the usher showed me into the Cabinet, which was empty.

The First Consul was in his drawing-room with the Minister of Finance, M. Gaudin, who afterwards became Duc de Gaëte. I sat down at a table which stood in the embrasure of a window, and waited for nearly two hours for the return of the First Consul. He arrived at last, holding a paper in his hand. Without appearing to pay any attention to my presence in his study, just as if I had always been there, and had always occupied the same place, he dictated a note for the Minister of Finance, with such volubility that I could hardly understand or take down half of what he was dictating. Without asking me whether I had heard him or whether I had finished writing, he took the paper away from me, and would not let me read it over, and, on my remarking it was an unintelligible scribble, he said it was on a matter well known to the Minister, who would easily be able to make it out, and, so saying, he went back to the drawing-room.

I never knew if M. Gaudin was able to decipher my writing. I feared that the paper might be sent back to me, and that I might be asked to explain what I had written, which would have been quite impossible. I never heard any more about it.

The First Consul returned almost immediately. He sent for General Duroc, and ordered him to have rooms prepared for me in the palace, and to invite me to the table of the ladies and aides-de-camp in service, over which the General presided.

Just then Bourrienne entered the room, and seemed surprised to find me there. It was the first time that I had seen him in the First Consul's study. The First Consul told him to have a table arranged for himself in the outside room, and to give the table in the window, where I had written the note from dictation, up to me. Bourrienne had been in ignorance of my introduction into the First Consul's cabinet. At first he examined me with curiosity, giving me a cold salute, but his manner soon became more friendly. General Duroc took me away to lunch, and we separated from Bourrienne. I afterwards learned that he was accustomed to take his meals in his private rooms. I returned to the study after lunch.

The First Consul came back late, and spent almost the whole day receiving people in his drawing-room, so that I had plenty of time to think over my new position, and to occupy myself with Bourrienne's arrangements and my own.

Before continuing my story, I will trace the portrait of Napoleon as I saw him at this time.

He was then in the enjoyment of vigorous health. He had recently been cured of an internal disease, from which he had begun to suffer greatly during the second year of the Consulate. This suffering was caused by an inveterate cutaneous affection, which had been driven into the system by the remedies he had taken, and of which the skilful doctor, Corvisart, had just relieved him.

I have heard it said that during the siege of Toulon one of the gunners of a battery where Napoleon was, was killed. It was important that the firing should not slacken. Napoleon took the rammer and loaded the cannon several times. Some days later he was covered with a very malignant itching skin disease. He tried to remember when and where he could have caught this disease. It was then discovered that the artilleryman, from whose burning hand Napoleon had taken the rammer, was infected. In the carelessness of youth, and being entirely absorbed in his work, he had neglected to undergo any treatment. He contented himself with some remedies which only caused the outward signs of the disease to disappear, but the poison had been driven into his system, and caused great damage. This was the reason, it was added, of the extreme thinness and poor, weak look of Napoleon during the campaigns in Italy and Egypt. *

In the second year of the Consulate, as his health grew worse and worse each day, he thought it necessary to undergo serious treatment. General Lannes urged him to consult Doctor Corvisart. The General's father-in-law brought Corvisart, who was his doctor and friend, to La Malmaison. Napoleon entrusted his case to the doctor. Corvisart treated him with blisters, and prescribed a regimen which, in conjunction with the treatment, produced the best results. The more Napoleon got to know Corvisart the more highly he esteemed him, and when he became Emperor he attached him

---

* A lady who met Napoleon several times in April and May, 1795, speaks of him, according to Stendhal, as "the thinnest and queerest being I ever met," and elsewhere as "so thin that he inspired pity."— R. H. S.

to his person, as his first and only medical adviser.

Napoleon was at that time moderately stout. His stoutness was increased later on by the frequent use of baths, which he took to refresh himself after his fatigues. It may be mentioned that he had taken the habit of bathing himself every day at irregular hours, a practice which he considerably modified when it was pointed out by his doctor that the frequent use of hot baths, and the time he spent in them, were weakening, and would predispose to obesity.

Napoleon was of mediocre stature, (about five feet two inches), and well built, though the bust was rather long. His head was big and the skull largely developed. His neck was short and his shoulders broad. The size of his chest bespoke a robust constitution, less robust, however, than his mind. His legs were well shaped, his foot was small and well formed. His hand, and he was rather proud of it, was delicate, and plump, with tapering fingers. His forehead was high and broad, his eyes gray, penetrating and wonderfully mobile; his nose was straight and well shaped. His teeth were fairly good, the mouth perfectly modelled, the upper lip slightly drawn down toward the corner of the mouth, and the chin slightly prominent. His skin was smooth and his complexion pale, but of a pallor which denoted a good circulation of the blood. His very fine chestnut hair, which, until the time of the expedition to Egypt, he had worn long, cut square and covering his ears, was clipped short. The hair was thin on the upper part of the head, and left bare his forehead, the seat of such lofty thoughts. The shape of his face and the *ensemble* of his features were remarkably regular. In one word, his head and his bust were in no way inferior in nobility and dignity to the most beautiful bust which antiquity has bequeathed to us.

Of this portrait, which in its principal features underwent little alteration in the last years of his reign, I will add some particulars furnished by my long intimacy with him. When excited by any violent passion his face assumed an even terrible expression. A sort of rotary movement very visibly produced itself on his forehead and between his eyebrows; his eyes flashed fire; his nostrils dilated, swollen with the inner storm. But these transient movements, whatever their cause may have been, in no way brought disorder to his mind. He seemed to be able to control at will these explosions, which, by the way, as time went on, became less and less frequent. His head remained cool. The blood never went to it, flowing back to the heart. In ordinary life his expression was calm, meditative, and gently grave. When in a good humour, or when anxious to please, his expression was sweet and caressing, and his face was lighted up by a most beautiful smile. Amongst familiars his laugh was loud and mocking.

The stoutness, which grew upon him in the last years of his reign, developed his trunk more than the lower part of his body, a circumstance which made people say after his fall that his bust gave the idea of an imposing and majestic monument, the pedestal of which was not at all proportioned to its greatness.

My portrait of Napoleon would be incomplete did I not mention the hat, without trimming or lace, which was ornamented by a little tricolour cockade, fastened with a black silk cord, and the gray surtout which covered the simple uniform of colonel of his guard. This hat and this surtout, which became historical with him, shone in the midst of the coats covered with gold and silver embroidery which were worn by his generals, and the civil and military officers of his household.

The contradictory opinions pronounced by Napoleon's schoolmasters, or school inspectors, go to prove that as a boy he gave no signs of what he was to be one day. As a matter of fact, it was not until he left the military school that he gave himself up with ardour to study. He has often told me that since that date he has constantly worked sixteen hours a day. Nevertheless he already had within him the germs of the qualities which were brought out by education, and which, under the influence of events, developed to the highest degree. These dominating qualities were pride, and a sentiment of his dignity, a warlike instinct, a genius for form, the love of order and of discipline. As a child an unjust and humiliating punishment distressed him to the point of injuring his health. A gratuitous insult to his father's name provoked him to demand a reparation by arms, even at the cost of the loss of his career. He was then about fourteen years old. At the same age, during the winter of 1783—1784, at the head of his comrades, he collected the snow which had fallen abundantly in the court of the school at Brienne, and used it to construct forts and redouts, which were then besieged under his orders—snowballs and cannon-balls of ice being used as projectiles—he was at one and the same time engineer and general.

Arriving at the Paris Military School at the age of sixteen, he found this school used to a system of prodigality and laxity which shocked his precocious mind. On this occasion he addressed a memorandum to the sub-principal, in which he indicated a plan of reform, the principal points of which he afterwards applied to the schools of Fontainebleau, Saint-Cyr, and Saint-Germain. One holiday at Brienne, being charged with the direction of a performance of the tragedy of Cæsar's death, he endeavoured to keep order at the theatre. The wife of the college porter, who had no ticket of admission, thinking herself authorized by her position of servant of the house, made a disturbance at the door, trying to push in in spite of the order given. She drew down on her head a sharp rebuke from the officer Bonaparte, which at once re-established order: " Remove this woman, who brings into our midst the licence of the camp."

Those who knew Napoleon in his youth agree in saying that his nature was gentle, reserved, and pensive; that he had little taste for noisy pleasures, and more inclination for the sciences than for accomplishments. He did, however, it is said, sacrifice to the muses. There are, we are assured, some pieces of poetry of his in existence, but these are only short, and are mere attempts. I have never heard that he admitted writing them.

On this point, I may add that I have more than once had the opportunity of hearing him express himself on the art of poetry in general. With the exception of true poetry, in which he recognized the elevation of ideas united to a brilliancy of style, he looked on versification as a frivolous occupation, which caused a great and useless waste of time. The mechanism of poetry, the restraint of the hemistich and the rhyme, were not at all suited to the *abandon* and vivacity of his ideas. Napoleon was a born poet. His vast thoughts, the originality of his speech and his style, his proclamations, testify to a strong and fruitful imagination. As with Plato, there was more poetry in his prose than in the verses of many poets, and like Plato also, he would have been disposed to conduct, crowned with flowers, every poet over the frontier of the Republic.

I have had in my hands a little pocket-book, the keeping of which he had entrusted to me. This pocket-book contained his principal papers. His certificate of baptism, his contract of marriage, some letters, and a few sheets of paper, on which thoughts and short compositions, all in prose, were written. No traces of any attempt at poetry existed. This, however, is not a proof that he never wrote poetry. This makes me speak of an article which appeared some years ago in the "*Revue des Deux-Mondes,*" which announced the discovery of papers containing the youthful productions of Napoleon, partly in his handwriting.

The story of this discovery seems to me to resemble a good deal the trick of the novelist who tries to excite public curiosity by stating that his manuscript was found in some old ruin, or in some vault, which had not been entered for centuries. I may recall that according to this story the papers had been confided to Cardinal Fesch, (who was certainly not the confidant that Napoleon would have chosen), that the cardinal handed them over to a priest of his diocese when he left Lyons, that this priest abandoned the box in which they were locked up, that a grocer bought this box, and so on. It is a highly improbable tale.

Having thus digressed on the childhood and early youth of Napoleon, I must not let the occasion pass to mention what was one of the leading traits of his moral character. I mean the respect which he always showed for his parents and for his great-uncle, the archdeacon Lucien, who became, after the death of his nephew, Charles Bonaparte, the head of the family. Napoleon was fifteen years old when his father, who had brought him to France at the age of ten, died at Montpellier. The letters which he wrote to his mother and to his great-uncle on that occasion show the sorrow which he felt at this loss.*

Napoleon had almost always been separated from his father, and knew him but little. Charles Bonaparte had not been able to look after the education of his children. He had entrusted that duty to Madame Bonaparte, a woman of strong character, who had fulfilled her maternal duties with a tender and severe solicitude. She had inspired her children with no sentiments but such as were elevated and generous, and whilst developing their good natural characters had been careful to remove from them all examples which might have tainted their innocence.

It was in 1787,† whilst at the Paris Military School, that Napoleon lost his father, who died in the arms of his son Joseph. Abbé Fesch, who afterwards became a cardinal, and Madame de Permon, mother of the Duchesse d'Abrantès, were present. Charles Bonaparte told his son that he wished him to give up the military career which kept him separated from his family, and would be pleased to see him return to Corsica to take his place. He recommended his six other sons to his care, mentioning each one by name,

---

* These letters, together with the letter addressed to Doctor Tissot, of which I speak later, have been published in a work entitled "Biography of the First Years of Napoleon Bonaparte," by Baron Coston.
† 1785?

and made him promise that he would be a father to them as far as his age would allow. Joseph was then seventeen years old.

In 1802 the municipal councillors of Montpellier voted the erection of a monument to the memory of Charles Bonaparte. Napoleon thanked the councillors for their good intentions, but, considering that his father's death had taken place eighteen years before, replied to their proposal with the words, "If I had lost my father yesterday it would be proper and natural that I should accompany my regrets with some high mark of respect, but this occurrence took place nearly twenty years ago, and is therefore not one of public interest." If he refused this homage it was chiefly because he saw it was intended rather for his personal glory than in honour of the memory of his father. Louis Bonaparte has since had the body of his father exhumed and transported to his Saint-Leu estate, where a monument has been erected.

Napoleon went to see his family in Corsica at the time he was artillery lieutenant at Valence. It was then long since his uncle, the archdeacon Lucien, crippled with gout, had been forced to take to his bed. Touched by the sight of his suffering, young Bonaparte, who was then barely eighteen years old, wrote to Doctor Tissot* in secret, carefully describing in his letter the state of the invalid, and imploring him, with touching solicitude, appealing to his science and humanity for advice as to the cure, or at least, as to the relief of his uncle. This letter was never answered. It was no doubt lost amongst the number

* Andrew Tissot, celebrated Swiss Doctor (1728—1797).—R. H. S.

of letters asking for consultations and signed by strangers which the great doctor received.

Five years later Napoleon obtained a fresh leave of absence, and without delay took advantage of it to return to Corsica, where he found his great-uncle on his death-bed. This sad sight recalled to him vividly the kindness with which this worthy man had always treated his nephews, and himself, Napoleon, in particular. The version of the words which archdeacon Lucien addressed to them, which is generally accredited to him, was incorrect. He was bitterly regretted by his nephews, to whom he had been a second father, and his family lost in him a guide and a protector. Napoleon united in the same gratitude the memories of this good kinsman and of his father.

I could never weary of examining the room in which I found myself since my admission to the Tuileries, and I kept looking at the papers which covered Napoleon's bureau, but had scruples to touch them as I could not imagine that from the first day he had accorded me a confidence of which I knew him to be chary, and of which I did not fancy myself worthy.

The room which he had made his study was moderately large, and was lighted by a single window, constructed in an angle, and looking out on the garden. The principal object of furniture was a magnificent writing table, placed in the middle of the room, and covered with gilt bronze, the legs being in the form of griffins. The table was a sort of square box, and the lid was a sliding one, so that it could be closed without disturbing the papers. The chair was antique in form, the back being covered with a drapery of green kerseymere, pleated and fitted with silk cords. The arms ended in griffin heads.

The First Consul, as a rule, never sat down to his writing-table except to sign. His usual place was on a settee covered with green taffeta, beside which stood a small table on which the day's post was laid. Every morning the letters of the previous day were removed from this little table and laid on the writing-table, to make room for the day's letters. A screen of many folds shielded him from the heat of the fire. My writing table was placed within reach of his. This arrangement of the interior of his workroom was followed in all the palaces and residences which Napoleon occupied. There was never any back cabinet. But when space allowed it the maps which he was constantly using were placed in an adjoining room, to which the head of the topographical bureau only came when he was summoned. When it was necessary for Napoleon to follow the subject with which he was dealing, on the map, I used to go into this room to write from his dictation. At the far end of the study were two large bookcases placed in the corners, and between them was one of those large clocks which are called regulators. A long glazed cupboard was against one of the walls. It was of breast height, and had a marble top, and contained some cardboard cases. There were also some chairs in the room, and a bronze equestrian statuette of Frederick the Great of Prussia. Such was the simple furniture of the Consul's workroom. The only luxurious object was the writing-table, which had been bought at the Industrial Exhibition as a masterpiece of the skilful manufacturer Biennais. The simplicity of Napoleon's tastes were shown here as clearly as in everything touching his person. The only dependency of the Consul's cabinet was a topographical bureau or map room, which was under the charge of an officer who had been formerly attached to the staff of General Clarke, and whose son, M. Cuvillier-Fleury, a distinguished man of letters, after studying brilliantly and carrying off the prize of honour at Louis-le-Grand, directed the education of his Royal Highness the Duc d'Aumale, and became his secretary of commands.

The librarian was M. Ripault, who had followed General Bonaparte in the Egyptian campaign. He was an erudite littérateur and a learned bookman, and had been a member of the Commission of Science and Arts at Cairo, and secretary to General Kléber. In 1807 he suddenly became disgusted with his post, without giving any reason for the same. It was suspected that he was offended at his subordination to Abbé Denina. This *savant*, author of "Revolutions in Italy" and many other valuable works, and formerly librarian to Frederick the Great, had been presented to the Emperor at Mayence. Napoleon wished to give him a proof of his admiration, and to show him how highly he esteemed his talents, and nominated him his first librarian, a title which was, however, purely honorary. The Emperor ordered me to invite M. Ripault to come back to his post which he had abandoned, retiring to live in the country near Orleans. I wrote him several urgent letters, which he left without an answer. The Emperor was then obliged to arrange for a substitute. I drew his attention to M. Barbier, who in the literary world held the sceptre of bibliography. I had had occasion to appreciate the extent of his knowledge of this science, for I had been under his orders for a short time after I left school, when he had been commissioned to form the libraries of the Directoire and of the Legislative Council. Every voice being in his favour, the learned bibliographer was appointed the Emperor's librarian. M. Barbier is the author of the "*Dictionnaire des Anonymes*," and of many bibliographical and philological works, which are distinguished by scientific research and a judicious critical spirit.

M. Amédée Jaubert, who has since become peer of France, and a member of the Academy of Inscriptions and Belles-Lettres, was secretary-interpreter of Oriental languages to the Government. In this capacity he undertook a great number of translations for the Cabinet. He enjoyed the entire confidence of the First Consul as a translator, many of the translations with which he was entrusted being of the highest importance. M. Lelorgne d'Ideville, who has since become *Maître des Requêtes* to the Council of State, and a member of the Chamber of Deputies, was some years later attached to the Cabinet as secretary-interpreter of northern languages. M. d'Ideville had lived many years in Germany, Poland, Russia, Sweden, and Denmark, as attaché to different French legations in those countries. He was charged in the Cabinet with an important work, which consisted of extracting from the despatches of our diplomatic agents and from foreign publications information as to the composition and movements of the enemy's armies; and to give a résumé of this information in a detailed report. M. d'Ideville's reports were drawn up with such clearness and exactness that the Emperor knew the condition of foreign armies as well as he knew that of the French armies. During his campaigns in Russia and Germany M. d'Ideville constantly followed the Emperor on horseback. It was his duty to question prisoners and the inhabitants of the country through which they were passing, and to translate contents of letters or reports which might come into his hands. The Emperor, thanks to the zeal and penetration of M. d'Ideville, thus obtained information which was often of the highest interest to him.

Napoleon was surrounded by living reminders of his youth. He had with him, besides Bourrienne, Colonel Lauriston, who had also been at school with him at Brienne. Father Dupuis, formerly schoolmaster in his town, was living in peaceful and honourable retirement at La Malmaison. Although there were very few books there, and these were in Napoleon's study, which M. Dupuis never entered, he enjoyed the title of librarian. He was an excellent man, and literally worshipped his former pupil. He had retained from his management of the Brienne school the practice of domestic economy rather than a taste for books and study. He had principally occupied himself there with the cultivation of vineyards. At Malmaison there were no longer the precious vines of Champagne to be inspected, but M. Dupuis bought plots of standing vines at Garches, and at Suresnes, and by means of a certain process removed the greenness and acidity of the grapes for which Suresnes wine has been proverbially notorious, and was able to produce sweet and sparkling Champagne wine. The house-porter at La Malmaison was a man called Hauté, who had formerly been porter at the Brienne school. This excellent man and his wife had found pleasant quarters here also. The two brothers Desmazis, who had been with Napoleon at the Military School were not forgotten. The elder was appointed director of the State Lottery in 1806, and the younger, who had been Napoleon's particular friend, was provided with the place of Director of the Crown Furniture. During the Hundred Days he filled the office of chamberlain.

On my arrival at the Tuileries in 1802 I found the following arrangements in force: The First Consul no longer kept common table. He dined with Madame Bonaparte and with some persons of his family. On Wednesdays, which were the days of the council, he kept the Consuls and the Ministers to dinner. He lunched alone, the simplest dishes being served, whilst for drink he contented himself with Chambertin wine diluted with water, and a single cup of coffee. All his time being occupied he profited by the lunch hour to receive the people with whom he liked to converse. These were generally men of letters, or artists. General Duroc was Governor of the Palace. Amongst the General's functions were the regulating of expenditure, and the order and supervision of the palace. He presided at the table at which the ladies and officers in waiting and the aides-de-camp dined. The military household at that time was composed of four generals commanding the consular guard, Generals Lannes, Bessières, Davout, and Soult; of eight aides-de-camp, Colonels Lemarois, Caffarelli, Lauriston, Caulaincourt, Savary, Rapp, Fontanelli, (the latter an Italian officer,) and Captain Lebrun, son of the Third Consul. There were four prefects of the palace: Messieurs de Luçay, Rémusat, Didelot, and

Cramayel; and four ladies, Mesdames de Luçay, Talhouet, Rémusat, and Lauriston. One of the generals of the guard was on service with the First Consul each week, as was also an aide-de-camp and a prefect of the palace.

The prefects of the palace were charged with the service of the interior of the palace, the regulation of etiquette, and the inspection of the theatres. The ladies were charged with accompanying Madame Bonaparte, and it was by them that the wives of foreign ambassadors and others were presented. One lady was on duty with Madame Bonaparte each week. At ceremonies, or on extraordinary occasions, all the ladies and the prefects of the palace were present. A general of the guard, who was on duty, presided at the table of the officers of the guard. Already at that time the house of the First Consul resembled a court.

With the exception of these changes in the house of the Head of the Government, changes which had been necessitated by the increase of power and honour accorded his position, by the increase of personnel which surrounded him, by the extent and the importance of the transactions in which he was engaged, by his multifarious relations with the high functionaries of state, and the representatives of foreign powers, the private life of Napoleon had remained the same. During the first year of the Consulate several plots had been made against the life of the First Consul, all inspired by men belonging to the party which was vanquished on the 18th Brumaire. Some of these plots had been stopped before they could be carried into effect, others had failed. The one which attracted the most attention was the plot to stab the First Consul at the Opera.

Napoleon's conviction of the impotence of the conspirators, a conviction produced either by his confidence in his destiny, or by his contempt for danger, and his indifference for these attacks against his person, had until then prevented the prosecution of the accused. The criminal attempt of the 3rd Nivôse interrupted this feeling of security, and made him see the necessity of repressing, by a sharp example, the audacity of the turbulent Jacobins, to whom this bloody catastrophe was attributed. The consequence was an extraordinary measure which has been severely condemned by some of Napoleon's historians. Without entering into the details of the conception of this infernal machine, let me say that the result of the explosion which took place only a few seconds after the carriage of the First Consul had passed was that nearly eighty people were wounded, and a whole quarter of Paris was shaken, and several houses were severely damaged. This unjustifiable crime excited general indignation, and irritated the First Consul to the highest degree. This new attack upon his life, and upon the lives of some of the population of Paris, hurried on the condemnation of the Opera conspirators, and occasioned the arrest of one hundred and thirty persons who had stained themselves with crime under The Terror, or who were considered dangerous from their fanaticism. The list of their names was drawn up by Fouché. Police investigations brought about, more than a month later, the discovery of the real authors of the infernal machine. They were Royalists under the direction of Georges, an ardent and indefatigable enemy of the First Consul. No doubt that proscription without trial is an arbitrary act. But if one remembers the times, it would be easily understood how inconvenient and how difficult it would be to proceed against these men in a judicial way. It will be admitted that these sanguinary men, justly abhorred, were marked out for punishment by the public voice, which is also a tribunal; that it was necessary to put a stop to the agitation which was caused by the impunity of these odious and dreaded men; that their transportation beyond the frontier of the fatherland which they had covered with blood and ruins, was a satisfaction given to public opinion and a pledge to public peace; that the First Consul, dominated no doubt by sentiments of generosity, had to defend himself against the reactionary spirit of the majority of his advisers; that he restored their liberty to many Jacobins who had been arrested, and diminished the sentences passed upon the least implicated. Some, as a matter of fact, were detained in France, and later on subjected to a simple police supervision. Those whose ferocity and callousness rendered them dangerous to the public peace suffered the penalty of transportation. One of those who was affected by the senatus consultum, and whose acquaintance I made, admitted that this measure had been comminatory, rather than rigorously carried into effect. This man was Félix Lepelletier, who had been inscribed on the list of persons to be transported, but was pardoned by the First Consul, *proprio motu*. He was a man of exaggerated ideas, but of honourable sentiments. As mayor of his village, the only post which he would accept under the Empire, he distinguished himself by his skilful and beneficent management of affairs. He had refused the decoration of the Legion of Honour from a desire to be consistent with his principles. A member of the Chamber of Deputies during the Hundred Days, he understood that the time had come to rally to Napoleon as the only man capable of saving France from a foreign yoke. His patriotic conduct made him the mark of the animadversion of the Government of the Second Restoration, and this time he was sentenced to banishment.

Since the occurrence of this event Napoleon had fallen back into his usual feeling of security, ceasing to trouble himself about the danger which might menace his person. He listened even with impatience to the reports on this subject which were transmitted to him by the police or by the persons around him; he needed all his calm; he made no change in his habits, and continued his work without allowing himself to be turned aside from his path. When I entered the Consular palace I did not see any of those precautions which denote suspicion or fear. He lived in a very homely manner, especially when at La Malmaison. He used to spend the hours which were not taken up by work, exercise, or shooting, with Josephine. He used to lunch alone, and during this repast, which was a relaxation for him, he received the persons with whom he liked to converse on science, art, and literature. He dined with his family, and after dinner would look in at his cabinet, and then, unless kept there by some work, would return to the drawing-room and play chess. As a general rule he liked to talk in a familiar way. He was fond of discussions, but did not impose his opinions, and made no pretention of superiority, either of intelligence or of rank. When only ladies were present he liked to criticize their dresses, or tell them tragical or satirical stories—ghost stories for the most part. When bed-time came, Madame Bonaparte followed him to his room. Napoleon wasted very little time in preparing for the night, and used to say that he got back to bed with pleasure. He said that statues ought to be erected to the men who invented beds and carriages. However, this bed into which he threw himself with delight, being often crushed with fatigue, was quitted more than once during the course of the night. He used to get up, after an hour's sleep, as wide awake and as clear in his head as if he had slept quietly the whole night. As soon as he had lain down his wife would place herself on the foot of the bed, and begin reading aloud. As she read very well he took pleasure in listening to her. At La Malmaison Napoleon used to spend the moments which were not taken up in his work-room in the park, and there again his time was not wasted.

Josephine spent her time as she chose. She received numerous callers during the day. She used to lunch with some friends, and with new and old acquaintances. She had no accomplishments, did not draw, and was not a musician. There was a harp in her apartment on which she used to play for want of anything better to do, and it was always the same tune that she played. She used to work at tapestry, and would get her ladies or her visitors to help her. In this way she had made the covering for the furniture in the drawing-room at La Malmaison. Napoleon approved of this busy life. The re-establishment of peace with England had allowed Josephine to correspond with some English botanists and the principal London nursery-men, from whom she received rare and new plants and shrubs to add to her collections. She used to give me the letters from England, written in connection with this business, to translate into French. At La Malmaison Josephine used to visit her fine hothouses regularly, and took great interest in them. In the evening she would take the back-gammon board, a game she was very fond of, and which she played well and quickly. Family theatricals were also played at La Malmaison, in a little theatre which accommodated about two hundred spectators. Eugène Beauharnais, who excelled in footmen's parts, and his sister Hortense were the principal actors, not only by rank but by talent. Next to them came Bourrienne, Lauriston, Denon and some ladies and officers of the First Consul's household. Michot, an excellent comedian, and shareholder in the Théâtre-Français, was stage manager, and directed the rehearsals. Napoleon was regularly present at the performances, which consisted of little comedies, and thoroughly amused himself. He took pleasure in praising or criticizing the actors' performances. His remarks, which were often words of praise, and which were always interesting, showed what an interest he took in these spectacles. On Sundays there were little balls given, at which Napoleon used to dance. He found a charm in this patriarchal life.

In his retreat at La Malmaison Napoleon appeared like a father in the midst of his family. This abnegation of his grandeur, his simple and dignified manners, the pleasing ways and gracious familiarity of Madame Bonaparte had a great charm for me. In our leisure moments the First Consul used to go over his bookcases with me, telling me what books I ought to read. He spoke of poetry as a frivolous occupation, and advised me not to waste any time over it. He had heard that, like all young men fresh from school, I had paid my tribute of verse—some attempts at tragedy. When he saw me unoccupied, he thought I was dreaming of poetry, and when I told him that I had found that I had no vocation for this art, he said: "You are right. It's a hollow science."

Napoleon had not always had this opinion of poetry; or rather, I should say, he looked on the poets in renown at the time about which I am speaking, as the buglers of his fame. On his accession to the Consulate he had made frequent advances not only to the scientists but also to the poets and littérateurs. He had treated Lemercier with respect and affability. Ducis, and Bernardin de St. Pierre had had no reason to complain of his treatment. He attached particular importance to the talents which both Ducis and Lemercier possessed in tragedy. He had, it is said, offered the former an honourable retreat in the Senate, and later on the decoration of the Legion of Honour. This offer was, it appears, brutally refused. However this may be, Ducis accepted, in 1814, from the hands of Louis XVIII., the same decoration which he is said to have considered as a badge of slavery in 1800, and with it a pension of six thousand francs.

The boldness of thought and expression which characterized Lemercier's talent, the variety of his conceptions, and his fertility had attracted the attention of the First Consul, although by no means fascinated by him. He was disposed to give him a mark of his goodwill and of the esteem which he had for his talent.

The distinctions and the favours of the First Consul were equally rejected. After the second year of the Consulate, when, by the way, Napoleon's glory, to make use of the expression of those who after the fall of the Empire sought an excuse for their defection, was still "innocent", Lemercier, wounded no doubt in his Republican sentiments by the show of power, suddenly withdrew from La Malmaison. No steps were taken to call him back. This indifference provoked him to systematic opposition. From that day forth he professed hatred for Napoleon, and declared this openly in his " *Cours de Littérature,* " published in 1817. Poets, however, must not be too severely judged. Their nervous organization, produced by the perpetual state of excitement in which they live, their indifference to the material interests of life, an indifference which was clearly marked both in Ducis and in Lemercier, plead in their favour and prevent a too severe judgment. The experience which Napoleon had made of their susceptibility, of the mobility of their imagination, of their exclusiveness, had shown him how unfitted they were for affairs of any kind. He seemed to have learned to his cost what the illustrious Béranger thought about them. I have often heard Béranger say, with his habitual modesty and unselfishness, that poets were really good for nothing but writing poetry.

I could not master my surprise at finding such simplicity of habits in a man like Napoleon, who from afar seemed so imposing. I had expected to find him brusque, and of uncertain temper, instead of which I found him patient, indulgent, easy to please, by no means exacting, merry with a merriness which was often noisy and mocking, and sometimes of a charming *bonhomie*. This familiarity on his part did not, however, awake any ideas of reciprocity. Napoleon played with men without mixing with them. He desired to put me entirely at my ease with him, from the very first days of my service, and, in consequence, from the very first I felt no embarrassment in his presence. Doubtless he impressed me to some extent, but I was no longer afraid of him. I was maintained in this state of mind by all that I saw of his pleasant and affectionate ways with Josephine, the assiduous devotion of his officers, the kindliness of his relations with the consuls and the ministers, and his familiarity with the soldiers.

The Egyptian campaign was at that time a matter of recent occurrence, and the memory of it still fresh in the minds of men. I heard it related, amongst other instances of his solicitude for the needs of his army, that at the raising of the siege of Acre, having given orders that all horses, without distinction, should be used for removing the wounded, he flew into a violent passion with his equerry Vigogne, who had thought that the horses of the commander-in-chief were to be exempted from this general order. M. Amédée Jaubert, who had been General Bonaparte's interpreter, said that one day seeing the General returning from the trenches, harassed with fatigue and dying with thirst, he had told him that a Christian had just brought a skin of wine as a present, and that Bonaparte ordered it to be immediately carried to the ambulance.

And apropos of this I wish to give in this place a curious document, which seems to have been overlooked by Napoleon's historians. I owe my knowledge of it to the kindness of a man, remarkable from his aptitude for the arts, which he has cultivated with great success, adopted by the fashionable world as the type of elegance and *bon ton*, and who to these brilliant advantages has added a philanthropy which will always recommend him to the gratitude of his fellow-citizens. He is the founder of the *Société de Bienfaisance* of London, an institution destined for the relief of indigent Frenchmen. Numerous subscribers, amongst whom are kings, have endowed the asylum, thrown open by his care to all the unfortunate of his nation.

M. d'Orsay copied the document to which I am referring from the order book of the 2nd company of the 3rd battalion of the 2nd brigade of light French Infantry. This book of orders, found at Cairo, after the departure of the French army, was given to the Rev. Mr. Moore—who lent it to the Duke of Wellington—by the son of General Moncrieff.

RÉPUBLIQUE FRANÇAISE,
Liberté—Égalité.

At Head-Quarters at Cairo,
1st Nivôse, Year VII.

"Every day at noon, on the squares opposite the hospitals, will be played by the regimental bands, various national airs, which inspire the sick with gaiety, and recall to their memory the most beautiful moments of their past campaigns.

"The commanding officers will in consequence give orders that the bands of the various corps shall perform in turn of service.

"For the Commander-in-Chief,
"ALEXANDER BERTHIER."

This mark of interest given to poor sick men, to unhappy wounded soldiers, sad and discouraged at the thought of their distant homes, reveals a delicate attention, a maternal solicitude, as Comte d'Orsay expressed it, and that provident goodness which was the basis of Napoleon's character.

The partiality which the First Consul retained for his memorable Egyptian campaign was shown even in the taste which he had retained for the produce of that country. For a long time his favourite dishes were pillau and dates. He had in his private gardens both at La Malmaison and at St. Cloud, gazelles which he had brought back from Egypt, and which he loved to feed with his own hands. Sometimes he would offer them his snuff-box. They were very fond of tobacco, and would empty the snuff-box in a minute, without appearing any the worse for it. There were also for some time, in the little park at St. Cloud, some muffions which had been sent from Corsica. Their natural wildness was, however, such that it was impossible to keep them.

M. de Bourrienne,* whom as a matter of fact I had succeeded, though not titularly so, had been Napoleon's schoolmate at the Military School. They had commenced their military careers together, and Bourrienne had followed Napoleon to Italy and to Egypt. These associations, these habits and the perfect tact of his conduct towards the First Consul had created him a position of confidence and intimacy which seemed

---

* Louis Antoine Fauvelet de Bourrienne was born at Sens, July 9th, 1769. After the events related by Méneval was appointed Prefect of Police in Paris, and afterwards Cabinet Minister, by Louis XVIII. As Deputy from 1815—1821 opposed all Liberal reforms. Died mad at Caen on Feb. 7th, 1834. His "*Mémoires sur Napoléon, le Directoire, le Consulat, l'Empire et la Restauration*" were published, in ten volumes, in 1829.—R. H. S.

BARON CLAUDE-FRANÇOIS DE MÉNEVAL,
PRIVATE SECRETARY TO NAPOLEON I.

destined to last for ever. The First Consul had appointed Bourrienne Councillor of State on special duty, and had accorded to him rights and prerogatives which rendered him an important person in the State. He corresponded directly with the Ministers on certain details of their service. Napoleon treated Bourrienne with familiarity, and often went out with him into the park of St. Cloud, either on foot or in a buggy. Mme. Bourrienne was almost independent, and neither ate nor slept in the palace. He had just bought a charming house at St. Cloud, had furnished it richly, and used to give dinners there to which the ministers, and particularly Fouché, the senators, councillors of State, and so on, were invited. His expenses and his purchases were out of proportion with the private fortune which the First Consul knew him to possess. Although their mutual relations did not appear changed the First Consul's vexation, which he still concealed from Bourrienne, sometimes showed itself in things which he said in my presence. He seemed to me to have some private grievance against him, which he had not sufficiently investigated. The unfortunate affair of the brothers Coulon put a stop to his hesitation, and was the drop which made the vase overflow. One Wednesday, being the day of the Cabinet Council, I was busy in the First Consul's study, when I saw him enter hurriedly. He asked me if Bourrienne was in his office, and on my affirmative answer he called him to the threshold of the door. Bourrienne came, somewhat troubled by the Consul's excited appearance. The Consul said to him in a severe tone of voice: "Give any papers and keys which you have of mine to Méneval, and withdraw.

And never let me see you again." After these few words he went back to the council, slamming the door violently behind him.

M. de Bourrienne, at first dumbfounded by this violent tirade, gave way to extreme despair. I did all I could to calm him. I tried to comfort him with hopes which I knew to be fallacious, for what hope could there be after a decision so laconically and so severely formulated? During the first two or three days which followed this painful scene, we exchanged some letters, but after that all relations between us ceased on the express command of the First Consul. This is what had caused this explosion. About the same time as I was called to Napoleon's cabinet Bourrienne, thanks to his standing with the Ministry of War, had obtained a contract for the supply of military equipments and harness. As his name could not figure in this transaction, it was with the Brothers Coulon that the contract was made. Bourrienne supplied the funds necessary to the enterprise. A banking firm advanced a sum of 800,000 francs on a mortgage furnished by the Coulons but exacted that M. de Bourrienne should be surety for the loan. The Brothers Coulon having failed shortly after, the bank proceeded against Bourrienne as bondsman. Bourrienne denied all responsibility for the Coulons' debts, but as the guarantee consisted of private deeds, defeasances, memoranda, and other papers, all in Bourrienne's writing, a lawsuit ensued, which he lost before the Lower Court, won before the Court of Appeal, and definitely lost when his adversaries carried it up to the Court of Cassation.

This speculation, in which Bourrienne had participated as described, strongly disgusted Napoleon, who had an invincible repulsion for what is called "doing business." The object of the lawsuit and the scandal which resulted therefrom revolted him. He never pardoned his old schoolfellow and secretary. He spoke to me of him for a long time, and often in real pain which used always to end in bitter complaint against him.

It would be distasteful to me to enumerate the various grievances which Napoleon had against Bourrienne, and to repeat the reproaches which he used to make against the man whom I had replaced. The revelations which invariably pour in torrents on a sinking man, revelations many of which were of a very serious nature, increased the displeasure of the First Consul. He gave orders to General Duroc to ask Bourrienne for the keys of the apartment which he had placed at his disposal in the Tuileries, and which he had kept, hoping by a moment's conversation to win back the friendship which he had lost. The First Consul refused to see him. He sent him word to return to the national *garde-meuble* the furniture of his apartment, as well as that of his house at Rueil. Before purchasing the house at St. Cloud, which he occupied at the moment of his disgrace, Bourrienne had acquired another house at Rueil, where he had established himself with his family. He objected that he had thought himself authorized to consider this furniture as a gift, and to keep it as his property. General Duroc took back this answer to the First Consul, who replied that his command must be obeyed without any delay, adding irritably that he gave money and not chairs.

However, in remembrance of their old friendship,

and of services rendered, Napoleon gave Bourrienne the mission to assist each day at the Court of Assizes, during the trial of the individuals implicated in the Georges and Moreau plot, and to send him a report of each sitting. After the First Consul had finished reading these reports, which were handed to him by me, they were deposited at the Archives. If they still be there, they might be compared with the accounts of the sittings of the tribunal and of the circumstances of the trial given in the memoirs published under M. de Bourrienne's name. The difference between the thoughts and the language of these two versions could be established. As I have said higher up, I do not think that Bourrienne was the author of the memoirs published under his name. I met him, in 1825, in Paris, and he told me that he had been asked to write against the Emperor: "In spite of all the wrong he did me," he added, "I could never make up my mind to do so. My hand would wither rather."

The ever-growing enfeeblement of his faculties, the state of financial embarrassment to which he found himself reduced, added to the deep resentment with which he remembered his disgrace, rendered him accessible to the pecuniary offers which were afterwards made to him. It is stated that the publisher of Bourrienne's Memoirs offered him, at the time when he had fled to Holstein to escape his creditors, a sum, said to be thirty thousand francs, for his signature to the work. M. de Bourrienne, already seized with the disease of which he died a few years later in the hospital at Caen, consented to allow these memoirs to be published under his name. His entire co-operation in this book consisted in some stray incomplete notes which were worked out by certain professional writers. These writers, whose names are mentioned, had to make up for the insufficiency of these notes by their own researches, and with the help of materials supplied by the publisher. If M. de Bourrienne had written these memoirs himself, he would not have stated that, when he was minister from the Emperor to Hamburg, he assisted the agents of the Comte de Lille in drawing up a proclamation in favour of this prince, nor that in 1814 he received the thanks of Louis XVIII. He would not have said that Napoleon had confided to him, in 1805, that he had never had any serious intentions of an expedition against England, and that the project of a landing, the preparations of which were made with so much noise, was only a trick to amuse fools. M. de Bourrienne would have spoken neither of his private conversations with Napoleon nor of the alleged confidences which had been made to him, seeing that Napoleon never saw him again after the 20th of October, 1802.* When, in 1805, the Emperor, forgetting his offences, appointed him plenipotentiary Minister to Hamburg, he granted him the usual audience, but did not add to this favour any return of his old friendship. He constantly refused, both before and afterwards, either to receive him or to correspond with him. I have had occasion to say elsewhere that during his mission to Hamburg, when special information outside the ministerial correspondence was needed by the Emperor, it was I who was charged to ask it of M. de Bourrienne, just as I was charged to get similar information from the worthy

* This is incorrect, as Méneval himself shows in the following sentence.—R. H. S.

M. Otto, French ambassador to Munich, the Emperor wishing to neglect no means of being informed as to what was going on before and behind the great army.

I wanted to say here all that I have to say about M. de Bourrienne so as not to have to revert to this subject.

The First Consul ended by resigning himself to his grievances against his old schoolfellow, and even congratulated himself on having shaken off this yoke. He did—without wishing to make any comparison—what Louis XIV. had done on the death of Mazarin. In this connection he said to me one day: "I have abolished the title of confidential secretary. It has too many disadvantages, and I am forced to admit the fact. I do not wish you to call yourself anything but attaché to the First Consul. You are young, you have a long career before you; later on we will see." This title of attaché, which was imposed on me by no regulation, was the résumé of the reasons which prevented the First Consul from according to me the privileges and personal preferences which Bourrienne owed to the length of their relations and the kind of familiarity which had reigned between them. As a matter of fact routine prevailed. I was constantly being styled secretary to the First Consul or Emperor, sometimes even, confidential secretary. In the course of business I was constantly writing to the ministers on behalf of the Emperor and receiving their replies. It sometimes even happened that he did not sign his letters, because just at that moment he might be setting out on horseback, or was prevented by some reason, and he would then authorize me to send the letters on accompanied by a letter signed by me. Moderation has always kept me aloof from the encroachments which a more enterprising mind than mine might have been tempted to essay. When, after his work was done, the First Consul went to spend an hour in Madame Bonaparte's drawing-room, he would bid me take my hat and follow him. I went sometimes. Often I preferred to employ my rare hours of leisure on my own behalf. Later on it often happened that I had to remain in his study to expedite some urgent piece of business, and that I had only a few brief moments left to devote to my family and to my friends. I ended by contenting myself with the almost obscure position which I occupied in the confidence and familiarity of the Consul and Emperor without boasting about it or drawing attention to myself. This reserve, by the way, did not at all displease him; not indeed that he was suspicious, for I never saw any traces of this in his character. He liked to chaff me about my reserve. He used to tell me, which was quite true, that I was totally unknown to several persons amongst his ladies and gentlemen in attendance. As a matter of fact there were several chamberlains who had heard my name mentioned, but who did not know me by sight. In the notes written in his writing on Fleury de Chaboulon's "*Mémoires du règne de Napoléon*" in 1815, at St. Helena, the Emperor says: "Méneval and Fain lived in such a retired way that there were chamberlains who, after four years' service in the palace, had never seen them." However, he accorded me his entire confidence, and made no change in the custom that his secretary should open all his letters.

Before speaking of the labours with which the First

Consul was occupied at the time of my entry into his service, I should say a word about the men whom he had called to help him in the government of the state.

His two colleagues were, as everybody knows, Cambacérès* and Lebrun.† The former, a learned lawyer, had passed unscathed through the stormiest periods of the Revolution, thanks to his prudence and his skill. The Revolution of the 18th Brumaire had found him Minister of Justice under the Directorial Government. His reputation for learning and tact had attracted the attention of General Bonaparte. Cambacérès showed himself a skilful politician in all circumstances. He was the faithful counsellor of Napoleon, who had entire confidence in his judgment, and who used to consult him on every point. Little eccentricities of his, which somewhat lent themselves to jesting, by no means diminished the respect in which he was held.

The Third Consul was Lebrun. Formerly attached to Chancellor Maupeou he wrote the speeches and the writings of this magistrate, which, at the time of the reform of the Parliamentary system in France, had rendered their author famous for their nobility of thought and brilliancy of style. A pure and elegant writer, he had consecrated to the cultivation of letters the leisure that business had left him. Financial matters and social economy had equally been the subject of his studies. He had drawn attention to himself in the various assemblies of which he formed part, from the States-General to the Council of the Ancients, by his particular knowledge of finance, and by his zeal for wise

---

* Banished as regicide under the Restoration. Died in Paris, March 5th, 1824.

† Created a peer under the Restoration. Died June 16th, 1824.

reforms. His knowledge, and his fine literary talent, promised a useful collaborator to Bonaparte, whilst the sweetness of his character dispelled any fear lest he might prove an unmanageable censor.

The choice of these two men proved Bonaparte's tact, and this triumvirate united the best conditions of association that could be desired.

The Ministry was composed of eight members. I put at the head Talleyrand, who was Minister of Foreign Affairs. He is too well known to need speaking about at any length. His relations with General Bonaparte dated from the treaty of Campo-Formio. His perspicacity had made him see that sooner or later the general's superiority would place him at the head of affairs, and, provident man that he was, he attached himself to his fortunes. Familiar with the course of business, he had brought to his work real talents, a spirit of intrigue, and a high capacity. He was at one and the same time a man of the court, and a man of the Revolution, and it was to this dualism that he owed the favour of Napoleon. Endowed with a shrewd and conciliating spirit, he had rendered himself agreeable to foreign diplomacy. These qualities rendered him fitter than anybody else to direct foreign affairs, and designated him to the choice of the First Consul.

The Minister of Police was Fouché. The colleagues of the First Consul had rejected him, and justly so, because of his immorality, and the sanguinary part which he had played during the revolutionary period. His knowledge of the plans and the secrets of all the parties to which he was initiated, a mind fruitful in resources, a false air of frankness and independence, the art with which he knew how to persuade that he was the indispensable man had prevailed over this repugnance, and he was maintained in the post which he had already filled under the Directoire. In appearance he reminded me of Marat, whom I had frequently seen in my early youth. Fouché was taller, very thin; his hair and eyebrows were pale, his eyes were bloodshot, and his complexion was livid. He spoke with a volubility which made one think that he was unburdening the whole of his thoughts. He affected a limitless devotion to the First Consul. It would sometimes happen that he would come to La Malmaison when Napoleon was away. He would then come to me, and take me out with him into the park, and speak to me at length on the vigilance with which he performed his duties, of the intimidation which he practised on the malcontents of every class, of the zeal which devoured him, and the help which he would always be ready to give the First Consul in whatever he might wish to undertake, invariably finishing with the words: "Be sure to tell the First Consul all I have said."

One of the most important ministries, that of Finance, was occupied by M. Gaudin. Formerly first clerk of Finances, specially charged with the management of taxation, then commissioner of the Treasury, and Director-General of the post, M. Gaudin had twice refused the Ministry of Finance which was offered him by the Directoire. He accepted it at the hands of the First Consul after the 18th Brumaire. When he took possession of his portfolio, credit was destroyed; the collection of taxation was irregular, and hampered on every side; the treasury was empty; in one word national bankruptcy was imminent. At the time of which we are speaking the vigilance and the probity of the new minister had restored confidence, the public services were reorganized, the financial administrations had been re-established, and new ones had been created; chaos had made way for order, and treasury bonds were negotiated with as much favour as the paper of the best banking and commercial firms. Napoleon used to say that everything that it was possible to do to efface the evil results of a bad and abusive system, and to restore to honour the principles of credit and of moderation, had been done by M. Gaudin in a few months; that he considered this minister an honourable and talented administrator, who advanced slowly but surely. He used to add, later, that what M. Gaudin had done during the first moments, had been maintained and perfected during the fifteen years of his wise management, and that he had had no need to reverse any one of the measures taken, because his knowledge was certain and the result of a long experience.

General Berthier was at that time Minister of War. Napoleon, accustomed to the regularity and precision with which he had always executed his orders when attached to him as chief of his staff, both in Italy and in Egypt, had confided this department to him. As a Minister Berthier always remained General Bonaparte's chief staff-officer. Nature had intended him for this part; he never raised himself above it. He was considered to be weak of mind and wavering in character. The First Consul had entrusted him with various missions in which he had acquitted himself well under his direction. Napoleon, who held him in true affection, loaded him with gifts and honours till the end of his reign.

The portfolio of the Admiralty was in the hands of

Admiral Decrés. He owed his advance to his hardy bravery, and to the skill which he had displayed in the various commands which had been entrusted to him. He had plenty of wit and knowledge, and his conversation abounded in sallies. He was industrious, and an upright administrator, but he did not quite suit Napoleon, who blamed him for having no initiative, and for being hostile to all active operations. Decrés did not like to absent himself. It was said that he feared that he might be supplanted in his absence. Nevertheless, in a moment of ill-temper and of discouragement, he sent in his resignation. Napoleon desired to keep him, wrote to him, and sent him Cambacérès, his usual confidant, to invite him to withdraw his resignation.

Decrés is said to have protected men who did not merit his preferences, and to have neglected a number of good sailors whom he did not like, a line of conduct which created him numerous enemies. Napoleon saw France's need of a strong and powerful navy, but his plans of maritime expeditions, on which he exhausted the resources of his genius, were not crowned with the success that he had hoped for. He saw himself forced to postpone to a more favourable opportunity his projects of developing this important branch of our national defence, an instrument indispensable for combating the supremacy of England, and for dictating peace to a government which fomented and financed all the coalitions against France. Decrés, it may be added, was devoted to the head of the government, and remained faithful to him to the last.

The Minister of the Interior was at that time M. Chaptal. He was not only a very distinguished *savant*. His varied knowledge of agricultural and commercial matters, his application of chemistry to the industries and the arts, his talents as administrator, and his studies on public education, had pointed him out as the right man to direct a ministry so wide and so varied in its duties.

M. Abrial, formerly a lawyer, who had honourably fulfilled various missions during the Revolution, of which he had been a temperate partisan, and not long before had occupied the post of public prosecutor at the Court of Cassation, conducted with zeal and probity the reorganization of the magistracy, in the important post of Minister of Justice. He was replaced, only a few months later, by Régnier, the Councillor of State, who afterwards became Duc de Massa, when, after the suppression of the ministry of police the duties of this department were united to those of the Grand-Judge, Minister of Justice.

The Public Treasury was administered by M. Barbé-Marbois. At one time Governor of San Domingo, he had rendered important services in the administration of this colony, effecting useful reforms, repressing abuses, and ameliorating its financial position. Appointed member of the *Conseil des Anciens,* he had been proscribed as a Royalist on the 18th Fructidor, condemned to transportation, and sent out to Guiana. Accustomed to the climate of San Domingo, he remained untouched by the diseases which proved fatal to most of his companions in misfortune. At the time of the Revolution of the 18th Brumaire he was on the island of Oléron, whither he had gained permission to transport himself. The First Consul had recalled him from exile. He had appointed him Councillor of State, and then, after the death of M. Dufresne, director of the Public

Treasury, a post which had just been raised to cabinet rank. M. de Marbois's reputation as a strict and upright administrator, and the spirit of order with which he was endowed, were a guarantee of a sure and vigilant guardian to the public purse.

M. Portalis, one of the chief writers of the civil code, a man endowed with irresistible eloquence and vast erudition, had, at this time, the management of ecclesiastical affairs. He was later on promoted to the rank of Minister of Religious Worship. His conciliating spirit, his great knowledge of law, and his rare qualities as a convincing and florid orator, were very useful in his relations with the clergy.

There was a Secretary of State whose duty it was to hold the pen at the Council of Ministers, presided over by the Consuls, to communicate the decisions and decrees to the heads of the various departments, to countersign them, and to hold in his keeping all private papers and secrets of State. Although at that time he did not enjoy the title of minister, the Secretary of State filled an analogous post, his functions consisting in completing the work of the other departments and even of supplementing them in certain of their duties. This post had been confided to M. Maret, afterwards Duc de Bassano. The scrupulous assiduity with which he had followed the great discussions of the National Assembly had initiated him into the business of the Home Government. He had been the first writer of the reports of the sittings of that Assembly, reports which were the foundation of the *Moniteur*, over whose creation he had presided. He had gathered his knowledge of foreign affairs in the diplomatic negotiations with which he had been frequently charged in London, and at Lille, with Lord Malmesbury as well as in the direction of a political division at the Ministry for Foreign Affairs. M. Maret was a man of a conciliating character, and possessed a cultured mind, a trustworthy memory, and unshaken probity and delicacy. Napoleon found him one of the most pleasant of his fellow-workers, and most frequently employed him.

The Council of State, divided into five sections: Legislation, Home Affairs, Finance, War, and Naval Affairs, drafted the laws, which members of the same council were charged to support in their discussion before the Legislative Body. Regulations of public administration, public affairs in litigation, the conflicts between the law courts and the administration, the inner conflicts between different public bodies, all questions of government, and sometimes of foreign politics were deliberated upon and decided.

The Council of State was the pivot of the new government and the workshop in which all the important acts which emanated from it were elaborated. The various sections were presided over by Councillors of State and had special duties, according to their department. The united sections were presided over several times in the week by the First Consul, and in his absence by Cambacérès, rarely by the Third Consul. Discussion was perfectly free; each Councillor of State had the right to express his opinion, whatever it might be. The First Consul even provoked contradiction, protesting that all he desired was to be enlightened. It sometimes occurred that he yielded to the opinion of the majority, whilst declaring himself, however, unconvinced. He had summoned to the Council of State all kinds of capable men, Revolutionaries and

Royalists, without distinction of opinion, demanding of them only good faith and a desire to assist him in the task which he had assumed. The Council was in consequence a rare composition of eminent and varied talents, all combining with equal zeal towards a common object.

There was no limit to the number of Councillors of State. At the time of which I am speaking there were about twenty-five exclusively employed at the Council of State. There were about twelve employed on extraordinary services, that is to say, fulfilling various functions with the title of Councillor of State. Amongst the Councillors on ordinary services MM. Boulay de la Meurthe, Regnauld de Saint-Jean-d'Angély, Defermon, and Berlier were perhaps the only ones who did not leave their labours in this capacity, and who remained exclusively attached to the Council of State until the end of the Empire. The others were detached either for temporary missions, or for permanent employment, or else were promoted with functions incompatible with those of Councillor of State. The extraordinary Councillors of State were called, as occasion presented itself, to give their opinions and to deliberate on the questions which were related to the services with which they were charged. Other men of proved talents, but especially those who were distinguished by their knowledge of special subjects, would come and assist the Councillors of State with their opinions, called by a chief who summoned merit wherever he could find it.

The most important projects with which the First Consul was occupied at the time at which I entered his service were the amnesty of the exiles, the creation of public schools,—prelude of the vast University organization—a modification of the clause of the constitution which limited the First Consul's term of office to ten years, and finally the institution of the Legion of Honour.

As a matter of fact, before a fortnight had elapsed the decree which recalled the exiles was promulgated. An amnesty was accorded to them in virtue of a senatus consultum. Exception was only made in the case of exiles who had commanded troops against the Republic, of those who had served in foreign armies, of those who had remained in the employment of the princes of the family of Bourbon, of the generals and representatives of the people who had conspired with the enemy, and finally of the prelates who had refused to resign their sees. It was ordained that the number excluded from the amnesty should not exceed one thousand, and that this number should be reduced to five hundred in the course of the year. Nine-tenths of the one hundred and fifty thousand Frenchmen who had emigrated and who formed an anti-national population abroad, had emigrated by fear, under compulsion, or with chimerical hopes which were soon dispelled. Little danger was to be feared from their return home. More important was the question of giving back estates which had not been sold, because this question, above all, interested the most important and the most hostile families. To retain their estates was to throw them into violent opposition to the government. To give them back in totality was to destroy all feeling of gratitude. Forest lands constituted an immense wealth in the hands of the principal exiles. A middle course was adopted by which estates of forest land exceeding three hundred arpents* were not restored to their former owners. By this decision the government alienated families whose possessions consisted mainly of forest land. But the individual restitution which the Emperor made won him back these families. It was thanks to this restoration of their estates, and in particular to that of the forest lands, although this latter restitution was a limited one, that the aristocracy, with the aid of the Restoration, was able to constitute those large landed estates which have become the appanage of what it is conventional to call the Faubourg Saint-Germain, and to concentrate very large fortunes upon them.

Be it said that this act of policy, at one and the same time both hardy and generous, due entirely to the position of the First Consul, which enabled him to defy any evil consequences which it might have had, showed the strength of the new government. It was generally approved of, and was only blamed by a small number of Republicans, and by some of the generals. It pained them to see the vanquished, whom they could not help considering as enemies, sharing the spoils with the victors.

This law was promulgated in the form of a senatus consultum. Napoleon had felt, on his accession to power, that it was necessary for him to surround the indispensable reforms which he was meditating, with formality sufficiently important to disguise their arbitrary nature, and to give them greater guarantee of stability. He had in consequence resolved to associate the first body in the state with the great operations of the government in certain cases, which, as it happened, were

* An arpent is equal to one and a quarter English acres.

very rare. As time went on he extended this participation in the sovereign authority. This interference of the senate in the principal political acts might have its objections. It was, however, thought that the principal danger arising from the new powers with which this body was endowed, could be avoided by granting it the privilege of pronouncing senatus consulta only on the proposal of the Head of the Government. The senate respected this initiative during the prosperous days of the Empire, but seized upon it as soon as it could do so with impunity, and turned against the man who had created, honoured, and aggrandized it, the weapon which he himself had placed in its hands.

By favour of the amnesty two men—who had enjoyed the entire confidence of the princes of the former House of France, asked for and obtained authorization to re-enter the French territory. One of them, the Baron de Breteuil, was introduced to the First Consul, who was very glad to converse with him, hearing from this important witness curious details on his diplomatic mission, and acquiring particular information on the councils held by the princes. M. de Breteuil had asked permission to present his nephew to the First Consul, whom he begged to employ him in his administration. Young Breteuil was favourably received, appointed auditor at the Council of State, afterwards nominated to the stewardship of the Austrian provinces ceded by the Peace of Presburg, and later on nominated to various prefectures in the interior of the Empire, and beyond the Rhine. He served with zeal till 1814, at which epoch old remembrances resumed all their empire over him. I must add, to be just, that the nephew of Baron de Breteuil always preserved great gratitude for the way in which Napoleon received him in his youth.

The other exile who had returned home was M. de Calonne.* He did not long enjoy the benefits of the amnesty, for he died one month after his return to France. His struggles against the nobility and the parliaments, a series of difficult intrigues, his unfulfilled ambition, and his lost illusions, all shortened his days. He had not, however, given up all hope of being able to impose his financial schemes. He relied upon his brilliant intelligence and his facility of argument to win over the First Consul. One of his friends, with whom I had some relations, pressed me to get him admitted to an audience, convinced that if M. de Calonne could once be heard by the First Consul his cause would be won. The First Consul, however, refused to see him, his mind being fully made up on the value of the financial resources of this minister, and on the want of stability of his principles. He was not, moreover, in the least inclined to change his Minister of Finance for anybody else. One of his brothers having asked him to put M. Roederer— Councillor of State and a man of much talent and intelligence—at the head of the Ministry of Finance, Napoleon had answered him: "I fully acknowledge

* Charles Alexander de Calonne, French financier, and author of "*Tableau de l'Europe en Novembre, 1787*" born at Douai Jan. 20th, 1734, became Comptroller General of the Treasury in 1783, greatly increased the deficit, induced the King to convene the notables (Feb. 2, 1787), failed in securing the acceptance of his scheme of an equitable distribution of taxation, was dismissed, fled to England during the Revolution, attacked Necker in numerous pamphlets, died on Oct. 30th, 1802.—R. H. S.

all that your protégé is worth, but it might very easily happen that, with all his intelligence, he would give me nothing but fresh water, whilst with my good Gaudin I can always rely on having good crown pieces."

Whilst the First Consul was preparing to re-open the doors of France to the exiles, he was closing them to the individuals whose enmity was not to be diminished by all the indulgence of the government. Mesdames de Damas and de Champcenetz were in correspondence with the enemies of the State. Madame de Damas, who had drawn attention on herself by her extreme opinions, and by her unceasing attacks against the government, had sheltered Hyde and Limoëlan, who had taken part in the conspiracy of the infernal machine of the 3rd Nivôse. She was conducted to the frontier by the police, and sent to join her husband, the exile, abroad. Madame de Champcenetz, who was the daughter of a Dutchman called Poter, received orders to return to her own country. She corresponded regularly with M. de Vaudreuil, who was one of the members of the Comte d'Artois's council to which the Bishop of Arras, Dutheil, Willot, the Swiss Colonel Baron de Roll and others also belonged.

La Harpe, who was under supervision in Paris, where he made a show of almost fanatical devoutness, after having professed atheism, was removed to a distance of twenty leagues from Paris. The reason of his expulsion was the scandal caused by his furious declamations against philosophy and the new institutions. His intolerance and his excessive conceit were excited by the coteries in which he was oracle. Towards the end of 1802 he obtained permission to return to Paris, and died there some months later.

The law which followed closely upon the amnesty of the exiles had relation to the organization of public instruction, and was the draft of the institution of the University. Lyceums were created in each district in the jurisdiction of a Court of Appeal. These public schools were directed by professors appointed by the State, and paid out of the public treasury. To ensure the success of these establishments, six thousand four hundred scholarships were created, of which two thousand four hundred were reserved to the sons of soldiers, or of judiciary, administrative and municipal functionaries. The other four thousand were given by competitive examination to scholars of the secondary schools. Special schools for the study of law, natural science, physics, mathematics and drawing, and a military school were instituted by the same law.

It was thanks to this law that there was educated at the Lyceum of Marseilles, a man whose natural gifts, rare talents, and wide range of knowledge have raised him to the first rank of literature and of politics. M. Thiers descends from a family of merchants who were engaged in the Levant trade. He remained from his childhood in the care of his mother, (who was a cousin-german of Marie Joseph Chénier,) and of his grandmother, who had both been reduced to a state bordering on poverty. These two ladies, who belonged to royalist families of the south of France, had conceived for the First Consul an admiration which the news of the execution of the unhappy Duc d'Enghien transformed into hatred. Their feeling was so strong in this matter that although their poverty was such that they could by no means be indifferent to the advantages offered them by the law, they at first refused the offer made them by the municipal authorities of Marseilles to recommend their child, who gave the greatest promise, for a scholarship at the Lyceum of this town. It was not until some friends had added their persuasions that they agreed to profit by the benevolence of the government. Young Thiers was placed on the list of recommended candidates, and obtained one of the scholarships which the First Consul had reserved for distribution by himself, and to which a sum of twelve hundred francs was added for the young scholar's outfit. It would seem as if a sort of prescience had revealed to Napoleon what marvellous fruits this boy's education would produce. M. Thiers, in relating this anecdote with his witty good nature, added, "Napoleon no doubt did not foresee when he accorded me this favour, that he was working on the formation of his future historian."

Whilst securing the benefits of education to the sons of soldiers, civil functionaries and others, Napoleon had to provide later for the education of their daughters, in whose future he was no less interested. Houses of education were successively created. I anticipate the period when these establishments were founded because I shall not have occasion to speak of them in their proper place. In 1806 three houses were constructed for the reception of three hundred pupils. In 1809 six hundred pupils were received into schools established in the castle of Écouen, and in the ancient abbey of St. Denis. Some of these pupils were admitted gratuitously, whilst others only paid half fees. These schools were intended to form women for a position in life equivalent to that which had been occupied by their fathers. The terms were forty pounds per annum. The revenues of these establishments were applied to defraying, in part, their expenses. And finally, in 1810, six new schools were opened for the reception of six hundred pupils, orphans of members of the Legion of Honour. The course of education there was less ambitious. The fees were four hundred francs a year. These establishments were managed on the same principles as the schools at Écouen and St. Denis. The rules there were much stricter, indeed almost claustral. Pupils were admitted from the age of four to the age of twelve, and could remain until their twenty-first year.

The Emperor put these establishments under the patronage of Queen Hortense. He drafted their regulations, occupied himself with the choice of the lady superiors, appointed the places where the schools should be built, entered into all details of order and economy connected with them, and supervised the execution of the instructions which he had given with a paternal solicitude.

The Order of the Legion of Honour was instituted at the same time. When the law concerning it was laid before the Council of State it was violently opposed. The First Consul defended it victoriously, by the force of reason alone, for he allowed it to be discussed quite freely. The Tribunate and the Legislative Body at last voted this law, but with a very much smaller majority than the government had counted upon. The eloquence of the First Consul, the lofty range of his views, the arguments employed by the expounder and the promoter of the law before the Legislative Body and the Tribunate could not convince some men, still imbued with the levelling ideas of the Revolution, who persisted in considering the creation of a distinction of this kind, albeit without privileges, a blow struck at the spirit and the principles of the Revolution. The great thought of a unique decoration which accorded no prerogative, which was a type of equality—inasmuch as the soldier equally with the field-marshal, the simple citizen equally with the prince or the highest dignitary, were accessible to it—and which has done wonders, has no need of any justification from me. It defends itself.

The project of a modification of the article of the constitution, which limited to ten years the First Consul's tenure of office, gave rise to numerous discussions between him, his two colleagues, and some of the principal senators and members of Parliament. Cambacérès was his principal intermediary in this delicate negotiation. A deliberation of the Senate had extended to a period of ten years the authority of the Chief of the State. This addition only feebly remedied the precariousness of the post. On a notification from the Council of State, to which the senatus consultum was submitted, this temporary prolongation was converted into a nomination for life. The First Consul desired that this wish should be submitted to the sanction of the people. In consequence a decree of the Consuls ordained that the French nation should be consulted on this question: "Shall Napoleon Bonaparte be Consul for life?" Three million, five hundred and sixty-eight thousand, five hundred and eighty-five votes out of three million, five hundred and seventy thousand, two hundred and fifty-nine citizens who took part in the election, replied in the affirmative. I was charged to carry the draft of the message to the

Senate, to Lebrun, the Third Consul, to receive from him such observations as a fresh reading might suggest.

What has not been said against the almost complete unanimity of votes in favour of the life consulate and the Empire! Some have alleged that the public functionaries who held the registers of votes, had influenced the electors. Others have called the veracity of the lists into question; others, in fine, have pointed out that since constitutions have been made, none have ever been presented for acceptance to the people and have been rejected by it, implying thereby that governments which try this experiment know what measures to take to obtain the necessary majority. Those who were living at the time know very well that the consular government had no need to take recourse to seduction, to threats, or to fraud. The nation's good sense, the instinct which never deceived it, showed in Napoleon the protector of its dearest interests, the man who really loved it, and who was working to bring back to France the reign of justice, order, and equality. Its gratitude for the great services which General Bonaparte had rendered was inseparable from the hope of a happy future which it expected from the First Consul. Napoleon could demand a national vote with confidence. Nations never refuse it to governments which feel themselves sufficiently popular to ask it.

About six weeks before my first entry into the First Consul's cabinet, the performance of two plays had been given. I only speak of this incident because the kind of disgrace which the authors had incurred created some sensation at La Malmaison, and was still being talked about when I arrived there. The first play, "*Edward in Scotland*," was by Alexander Duval. The author had been very well received by Madame Bonaparte, and by the First Consul. His play had succeeded at its public reading, and had also been received with great favour at the first performance; but it had been noticed that persons who were known for their ardent royalism had applauded to excess certain passages in which they wanted the public to find allusions.

The First Consul, hearing of this matter, and not knowing the piece, went to see it. He found it interesting, but his attention having been attracted by a volley of significant applause, at the passages indicated, which burst from the neighbouring boxes, and recognizing that these boxes were occupied by recently amnestied exiles, he was naturally irritated, and considered it his duty to forbid the performance of the piece. Amongst the exiles who on this occasion made themselves noticed by the manifestation of their applause, was the Duc de Richelieu, who afterwards became minister under the Restoration. Although he had remained in the service of Russia, he had, by special favour, obtained the authorization to come to Paris. He received orders to leave Paris and the French territory without delay. M. Duval, fearing to be compromised by this imprudence on the part of the exiles, had taken refuge with his family at Rennes. The First Consul, however, sen t him word that he might come back to Paris, and added that he had no reason for displeasure against him.

The title of the second piece was "*L'Antichambre*". It had been written without offensive intention, but it contained situations and phrases the application of which to the political situation was made with such transparent malignity by the enemies of the government that its performance could not be tolerated. The author, M. Dupaty, fell into disgrace with the First Consul, who had already been offended by the spitefulness of the imaginary allusions in "*Edward in Scotland.*"

M. Dupaty, at that time officer of engineers, was in Paris without regular leave of absence. He received orders to leave for Brest, and to embark with the expedition to San Domingo, but he only remained at Brest a very short time. He obtained permission to return to Paris before the expedition started, and continued his literary work. Amongst a number of very witty comedies which he wrote were several which were consecrated to Napoleon's glory. It was he who arranged the allegorical ballet, "The Hours", which was performed at the Tuileries on the occasion of the Emperor's marriage with Arch-duchess Marie Louise. He is the author of a rondo written in 1814 for the band of the National Guard, which was composed on the occasion of the farewell taken by the Emperor from the chiefs of this Guard, when he confided the Empress and his son to their care before his departure to the army.

Since I have spoken of plays, this may be the place to relate a service which about this time I had occasion to render to one of the most agreeable of the Opera *danseuses*. This theatre was under the direction of M. de Luçay, as prefect of the Palace. He governed this republic of song and dance with severity. Mademoiselle Chevigny, who was not one of the youngest performers, injured her knee during the performance of a ballet, and remained a considerable time away from the theatre. M. de Luçay, getting tired of her prolonged absence, ordered a medical inquiry to be made. The doctors reported that the *danseuse* had a stiffened knee, and that it was impossible to say when she would be able to reappear on the stage. In consequence of this report she was at once put on the retired list. Mademoiselle Chevigny, who knew that she would be very well able to continue her work if two or three weeks' rest were granted to her, was in despair at an exclusion which she considered most unjust. Accompanied by her husband, M. Cellerier, a celebrated architect, she applied to everybody of any influence who could help her to have this decision altered. Amongst others she applied to me, and I was able to obtain three months' holiday for her, which was very much more than she wanted. Her reappearance on the stage showed that doctors' opinions are not always infallible. She had lost none of her powers, and for many years, both as a light-footed dancer and a consummate actress, she contributed to the enjoyment of the Opera public.

About this time the First Consul was exceedingly irritated against General Reynier, who had just killed General Destaing in a duel. These two generals, who had recently returned from Egypt, had quarrelled violently at the time when General Menou took over the command of the army, after the death of General Kléber. Napoleon, greatly affected by the unhappy termination of a campaign which should have been so profitable to France, and so useful to his personal glory, had ordered that all faults committed under these circumstances should be forgotten, as well as everything which would recall attention to an evil for which there was no remedy. He was much incensed, and rightly so, at this duel. He exiled General Reynier to his estate in the Nièvre department, strongly defended the memory of General Destaing, and awarded a pension to his widow. This disgrace of one of our most distinguished generals was also prompted by the opposition which General Reynier had manifested to General Menou, who was far from being his equal in military capacity, but who, thanks to his seniority, had been appointed commander-in-chief of the army in Egypt. This unhappy rivalry had contributed to the ruin of our affairs in this country.

The favour which the First Consul showed to General Menou, whose administrative talents, by the way, he esteemed, was prompted by his desire to protect the General against the excitement caused by the recent events in Egypt, to check its development, and to wipe it out.

Doctor Corvisart, being present one morning with me, at the levee of the First Consul, told him of the death of Bichat (who had died the night before) not then thirty years old. This young doctor, a *savant* of the greatest promise, had enriched science with works of physiology, full of new and fruitful ideas, which have largely extended its domain. This death recalled the remembrance of Desault, his master, who had been the glory of surgery. The First Consul ordered the Minister of the Interior to report on the best means of honouring the memory of these two *savants*. On the report of the Minister, he ordered that a marble tablet perpetuating their memory and recording the services which they had rendered to humanity, should be placed in one of the wards of the Hôtel-Dieu.

The cessation of hostilities between England and France having reopened the French territory to the English, a large number came to Paris. Amongst persons distinguished by their rank or by their birth, who came in the train of Lord Cornwallis, was the son of a Minister of State, famous for his patriotism and his energy, and a friend of Pitt, whose principles he shared. This was young Lord Henry Petty, son of the Marquis of Lansdowne, heir to the titles and to the political opinions and qualities of his father, who himself succeeded Pitt, in 1806, as Chancellor of the Exchequer. Lord H. Petty was accompanied by his tutor, the celebrated Genevese writer Dumont, the former friend and collaborator of Mirabeau, and author of an interesting book on this celebrated and learned man. Both these gentlemen were presented to the First Consul, who received them with marked favour.

It was especially after the Peace of Amiens that the English came in numbers to Paris. A great number of English Members of Parliament, lawyers, officers, and other persons of position, attracted to Paris by the fame of the First Consul, were presented by Mr. Merry, the English Ambassador, who, as I have already said, was formerly secretary to the English Legation at the Amiens Congress. Mr. Fox should be mentioned first of all. This illustrious foreigner came to Paris, less for the purpose of searching among our archives for documents concerning the history of the last two Stuart kings, which he was writing, than to make the acquaintance of the extraordinary man who enjoyed his entire sympathy. Napoleon, on his side, was drawn to Fox by a natural inclination. He received him with marked preference and, admitting him from the first to his intimacy, enjoyed numerous familiar conversations with him. The two did not always, it is said, agree on matters of politics, but the result of their conversations was that they left each other full of mutual esteem. The First Consul ordered all the archives and public establishments to be thrown open to Mr. Fox. He used to accompany him sometimes, notably to the second exhibition of industrial productions, which took place towards the end of the English statesman's stay in Paris.

During the year which preceded the discovery of the Georges plot, I had not once occasion to see General Moreau at the Tuileries. I have accordingly nothing to say about this general, whose peculiarities are, however, well-known. I learned that he had rejected all the First Consul's advances, and refused his numerous invitations. From the time of his marriage with Madame Hulot, to which Madame Bonaparte had contributed, his mother-in-law, a jealous and troublesome woman, did all she could to foment discord between these two rivals in military glory. Madame Hulot had complained of having to wait to be received by Madame Bonaparte, when she called upon her, and said that she had no inclination at all for the antechamber of an equal. General Moreau used to speak with affected frivolity of the hostile attempts against the person of the First Consul, or against the acts of his government. This coolness, in short, degenerated into an enmity which led Moreau to contract an alliance unworthy of his glory, with the enemies of the State, an alliance in which he found his death—wounded, in the midst of the adversaries of France, by a French cannonball.

An interview, which attracted but little attention at the time, took place in the middle of 1802, between the Emperor of Russia and the King of Prussia, at Memel, the eastern port of the Prussian States. The latter sovereign had been reigning five years. The Emperor Alexander had just succeeded his father, the unfortunate Paul I., who had been assassinated three months previously in his St. Petersburg palace. These princes, both young men, desired to make the acquaintance of each other. The Emperor of Russia proposed a friendly meeting, which the King readily accepted. The Queen of Prussia, in all the splendour of her youth and beauty, accompanied the King, and contributed greatly to the close friendship which bound the two sovereigns together. The result of this friendship was that from thenceforward Prussia was attracted into Russia's sphere of action.

The First Consul, anxious not to appear hostile to this meeting although absent from it, and curious to know what would happen there, sent an officer of the palace, a shrewd observer, to attend. Major Dumoustier, who afterwards became general, an officer of great distinction and of really antique virtue, was charged to convey the Consul's compliments to the two kings. He carried a letter from the First Consul to the King of Prussia, which expressed Napoleon's satisfaction at the arrangement which had been concluded for the settlement of the indemnity due to Prussia by the provisions of the Treaty of Lunéville, which had largely increased the territories of the King of Prussia. The indemnity of the Prince of Nassau-Orange, the king's father-in-law, had been settled at the same time in accordance with his wishes. Large indemnities had been stipulated in favour of the houses of Bavaria, Würtemberg, and Baden, which were united to the Russian imperial house by family ties. This news, coming at so favourable a moment, was received with great pleasure by the two princes, and disposed the Emperor of Russia to join with the First Consul in the apportionment of the lands for the indemnification of the small kings who had been dispossessed on the left bank of the Rhine.

This journey of the Emperor of Russia and of the King of Prussia, far from their capitals, was the prelude to those meetings of the monarchs of Germany and of the North, and of those nomadic congresses which became so frequent twelve years later.

Another officer of the palace was sent at about the same time to Algiers on another kind of mission. In spite of the peace concluded with the Barbary States, the corsairs of the regency, yielding to their habits of piracy, were recommencing their raids on our coasts, and had even dared to attack our flag. The First Consul sent a naval division before Algiers, under the command of Admiral Leissègues. He was accompanied on board by Adjutant Hulin, who was commissioned to demand reparation for these insults, and for the injuries caused to our trade from the Dey. The impression which Hulin's lofty stature, his martial attitude, and the richness of his embroideries made upon these savages, completed what had been commenced by the First Consul's letter, and the appearance of the French fleet. The Dey submitted on every point, released all prisoners of French or of allied nationality, and sent an ambassador loaded with presents to Paris.

I witnessed the last Republican celebration of the anniversary of the 14th of July at the Tuileries Palace. A grand parade took place that day in the Carrousel court, at which the First Consul presented flags to the light infantry regiments, represented for the occasion by the colonel and three officers of each regiment.

Just before the parade, the Prefect of the Seine department, accompanied by two of the mayors of Paris, presented the First Consul with a horse of the French breed, richly caparisoned.

The diplomatic body was received in solemn audience. Strangers of distinction were presented by the ambassadors or plenipotentiary ministers of their courts. Marriages were celebrated at the cost of the government in each of the twelve arrondissements of Paris. Banquets, illuminations, and fireworks crowned this fête.

There was no ceremony at the Tuileries on the 14th July of the following year. The First Consul and Madame Bonaparte were away, on a three weeks' journey in the Seine-Inférieure and Oise departments.

On the same day in the year 1804, Napoleon, then Emperor, rode to the Invalides, through a line formed by the troops of the garrison, preceded by the marshals and the great officers of the Empire, by the colonels of the guard, and by his aides-de-camp. The Empress, accompanied by the sisters and sisters-in-law of the Emperor, her ladies, her chamberlains, and her equerries, had preceded him at noon to the Invalides. A mass was celebrated by the Cardinal Legate. After the religious ceremony a distribution of decorations took place, handed by Napoleon in person to each legionary, as he took them from the hands of the Grand Chancellor of the Order. A *Te Deum* terminated the ceremony. In the evening all public buildings were illuminated, a concert was given on the terrace of the Tuileries Palace, and fireworks were displayed on the Pont-Neuf.

CHAPTER III.

Retreat of General Lannes from Lisbon—Curious Particulars—Madame Souza—Return of the General to Lisbon—Plan to Expel the Barbary Pirates from the Coast of Africa—Letter from Napoleon to the Minister of Marine on this Subject—Taking Possession of the Castle of Saint-Cloud—The First Consul's Private Study and Rooms—Portraits of Charles XII. and Gustavus Adolphus—Paisiello's Arrival in Paris—He is appointed Chapel Master—He is Succeeded by Lesueur—Canova at Paris—He Makes Napoleon's Bust—He Executes his Colossal Statue after this Bust—Profanation of This Statue—Madame Fanny Beauharnais—Napoleon's Kindness to the Beauharnais Family—A Dwarf—Piedmont United to France—The Duc de Parma's Death—He Instituted the Dowager Duchess Queen Regent of His States in the Name of His Son—The Duchies United to France—The Island of Elba United to France—Reflections—The Journey of the First Consul and of Madame Bonaparte in the Seine-Inférieure and Oise Departments—Visit to the Saint-Cyr Military Schools—Inspection of the Battle-field of Ivry—Excursion to the Ourcq Canal—Suppression of the Ministry of Police—Letter from the Comte de Survilliers on This Matter—Fouché's Retirement—Napoleon's Police—The Violation of Postal Secrecy—Madame Leclerc's Return from San Domingo—Particulars about General Leclerc—Napoleon Godfather to Bernadotte's Son—Toussaint L'Ouverture—Publication of Colonel Sebastiani's Report on His Mission to the Levant—It Becomes One of the Pretexts for War—Conferences with the Swiss Deputies—Negotiations with the Margrave of Baden—Commission Charged to Come to an Understanding with the Swiss Deputies—The First Consul Grants Long Audiences to ten of the Deputies—Conclusion of the Mediation—Creation of the Auditors—Application of the Prussian Cabinet to the Comte de Lille at Warsaw—Letter from this Prince to the First Consul and His Answer—Alteration of a Letter from the Emperor to King Joachim—The Comte de Lille sent away from Mittau—Flight of this Prince from Verona—Instinctive Feeling of Legitimacy—Louis XVIII.'s Return to the Tuileries—A Portrait of this Prince—Louisiana Ceded to the United States—Particulars on this Matter—Displeasure felt by the English at this Cession—A War Imminent—Violence of the English Newspapers and Certain Members of Parliament During the Peace—Napoleon's Apostrophe to Lord Whitworth—Complaints of the French Government—The Peltier Trial—*La Napoléone*—Charles Nodier—His Hostile and Turbulent Conduct—Nonexistence of Secret Societies in the Army—Napoleon Thrown Out of His Carriage at St. Cloud—Rupture of Peace—Napoleon's Profound Resentment—Arrest of English People Travelling in France at the Time of the Declaration of War—Invasion and Conquest of Hanover—The King of England Refuses to Ratify the Capitulation—Activity in Arming against England—Enthusiasm of the French People—Formation of Camps on the Seashore—Preparations for the Formation of a Flotilla at Boulogne—The First Consul's Opinion on Admiral Latouche-Tréville—His Letters to the Admiral—The First Consul's First Journey Along the Coast—The Enthusiastic Reception Accorded Him—M. de Roquelaure—Audience Given to M. Lombard at Brussels—Napoleon's Friendly Feelings towards Prussia—Cardinal Caprara—The Bishop of Namur—Return to St. Cloud—A Two

Months' Stay in this Residence—A Fortnight's Journey to Boulogne for the Second Time—A Third Ten Days' Journey There—The Consul Travels Incognito Both Times—Marriage of Madame Leclerc with Prince Borghese—Convocation of the Legislature—First Indications of the Conspiracy—Napoleon's Anxiety and Vigilance—The Plots of English Diplomatic Agents on our Frontiers—How They Were Duped—Arrest of the English Resident at Hamburg—He is Restored to Liberty by the Intervention of Prussia—The Diplomatic Body in Paris Protests Against the Conduct of the English Agents—M. de Montgaillard—His Intrigues on the Intrigues of the French Princes—The Abbé de Montgaillard—His Chronological Summary of the History of France—General Foy's Approbation—M. de Vauban—His Memoirs on the Vendée.

ONE night, during one of the First Consul's stays at La Malmaison, in 1802, he was awaked by a courier from Spain, who brought some very urgent despatches from General Lannes, French Ambassador at Lisbon. As soon as Napoleon had read these despatches he gave orders that the courier should hold himself in readiness to start on the return-journey at a moment's notice. I am obliged to go back in my story to explain what precedes.

In the course of November 1801, General Lannes, who was sole commander of the consular guard, had been forced to resign in consequence of some irregularities which had occurred in the regimental treasury. This was the truth of the matter. The First Consul had promised to pay the General's house-furnishing expenses. When the bills were submitted to him he refused to pay them, as they far exceeded what he had expected. General Lannes—who was accustomed to give and spend without counting, and had no idea at all of business, and who had never applied to Bonaparte in vain, when in want of money—considered that the First Consul was so bound by the promise he had made, that he could think of no better plan to make him pay his furniture bills than to get the treasurer of the regiment of guards to hand him over the amount. Such conduct could not be tolerated, and General Lannes lost his command. The consular guard was reorganized more in accordance with its requirements, and the sole command which had till then existed was broken up into four, each vested in a colonel-general. To punish General Lannes for his unbusinesslike proceedings, and anxious to put a stop to a familiarity which had in some way prompted him to act as he had done, the First Consul sent him away for a time, ordering him on a mission to Lisbon. I remember dining with him about this time, at Joseph Bonaparte's table, and hearing with what sarcasm he betrayed his displeasure at the way in which he had been treated. M. de Champagny, who had just been appointed ambassador to Vienna, was present at this dinner.

General Lannes, little acquainted as he was with diplomatic forms, did not at first succeed in his new post. The Portuguese Ministry, and more especially the Minister of Foreign Affairs, Don Joaô d' Almeida, was devoted to England. All diplomatic documents handed in by the French ambassador were passed on to Lord Fitzgerald, the English ambassador, and the answers concocted with him. The Prince Regent of Portugal, either deceived or dominated by his minister, was also not favourably disposed towards the French representative. General Lannes soon felt his military pride, his self-esteem, and his patience flouted beyond endurance. Without warning either the Portuguese or his own Government, he left Lisbon suddenly, giving orders to his household to follow him. He presented himself at the first posting-establishment and demanded horses. The postmaster informs him that an order is necessary, and that without it he must refuse to accommodate him. General Lannes imperiously orders him to have horses put to, and laying his hand on his sword threatens to strike him, unless his order is immediately obeyed. The postmaster is forced to submit. General Lannes crosses through Portugal and Spain post-haste, and, just before arriving at Bayonne, sends his valet de chambre on with a letter to the First Consul, announcing his arrival. The valet, sent back with an answer to his letter, finds his master at Orleans. The First Consul's orders were that the General should remain where the courier found him. He had calculated that General Lannes would not have passed Bayonne. Lannes, however, receiving this order at Orleans, thought himself justified from his proximity to Paris in pushing on to the capital. The First Consul refused to receive him.

In the meanwhile the greatest anxiety was felt by the Portuguese Government. It was a matter of importance that General Lannes's conduct should be disapproved of, and that Portugal should not incur the resentment of France. The General had Talleyrand against him, and Talleyrand, insisting on the violation of diplomatic forms which had been committed, demanded the revocation of our ambassador to Lisbon. The First Consul would not have tolerated such conduct from anybody else, but he knew that though General Lannes was no diplomat, he was an honest man, who had too much judgment to allow himself to be made a dupe of. He finally agreed to see him, and was satisfied with his explanations, although he blamed his conduct.

Don Joaô scattered gold by handfuls in Paris to

prevent the return of General Lannes to Lisbon. The Prince Regent, acting on information which had reached him, sent two men in whom he had confidence to Paris; and this without the knowledge of his minister. One of them was a Frenchman, whom I was acquainted with, and who had been living in Portugal for many years. Whilst Almeida was assuring the Prince Regent that General Lannes had fallen into complete disgrace, the prince's agents reported that a reconciliation had taken place, and that the ambassador had altogether been restored to the First Consul's good graces. The Prince Regent then thought it right—for something decisive had to be done—to ask for his return. Whilst the Portuguese Ministers were flattering themselves that they would make good their escape from the scrape in which they had involved themselves, the First Consul notified to the Prince Regent that he would consent to the return of his ambassador to Lisbon, and that he would forget the reasons for displeasure which the Portuguese Government had given him; but that, in return for this concession, he expected a concession on the prince's part, namely the dismissal of the Minister of Foreign Affairs, whose partiality for the English, and whose bad faith, had been the causes of what had happened. The Prince Regent was only too glad to accept this settlement of the affair. Don Joaô d'Almeida was dismissed, and General Lannes returned to Lisbon. His triumph was complete. The Prince Regent received him at first with a cordiality which was more affected than real, but growing to like him eventually became on terms of great intimacy with him. General Lannes, who had plenty of natural shrewdness, understood his position. The Portuguese nobility of that time, proud and poor, held aloof, and hesitated to make the first advances. General Lannes gave a sumptuous ball, and invited everybody whose names had been inscribed on the embassy register. He did the honours of this ball with all possible refinement, and nothing else was talked about in Lisbon. Those of the aristocracy who were not present, complained at not having been invited. They were informed, in answer, that if the ambassador had thought that an invitation would have been agreeable to them, he would have sent it, and that he should be delighted and honoured if they would call upon him. The hidalgos crowded to leave their names at his house. General Lannes gave another ball to which they were all invited. The invitations were accepted with eagerness, and from that time forward the aristocracy frequented the French embassy. Thanks to his intimacy with the Prince Regent the French *envoyé* was able to assist some of these needy noblemen. His credit at Court was great, and his recommendations were always favourably listened to. The jurisdiction of his embassy, accordingly, was unlimited, nor did the Portuguese Government in any way try to restrict it. No such tolerance was shown to the ambassadors of other powers. Our ambassador's influence in Lisbon was so well established, that when he returned to France he was in a position to dispose of Portugal as Napoleon might desire.

It is calculated that the sum spent in Paris to prevent the return of General Lannes amounted to four millions of francs. Where the greater part of this money went to can easily be guessed.* When the General

* Méneval means Talleyrand.—R. H. S.

heard of this he remarked jocularly: "What clumsy fellows! If they had only offered me half that amount I wouldn't have gone back to Lisbon."

And so it happened that the cause of France was better served by our ambassador's impetuous susceptibility than it would have been by the skill of the most consummate diplomat. The First Consul understood, better than his Minister of Foreign Affairs, to what advantage he could turn it. It is true that Napoleon, at least, saw everything in the light of national interest, and in that light alone.

It is so ordained here below that, side by side with any success there is always a jealous desire to diminish its merit. And so it was that when the money-sacrifices made by the Portuguese ministers to prevent the return of General Lannes to Lisbon were heard of, it was stated, in face of the General's spontaneous exclamation, that M. de Binau, ambassador from Saxony to France, had been commissioned by him to carry a proposal to M. de Souza, Portuguese ambassador to Paris. This proposal, it was said, was to the effect that if a million francs were given to the General he would undertake to refuse to return to Lisbon, in spite of any pressure from the First Consul.

This is what Madame de Souza,* the wife of the Portuguese ambassador told me on this subject. Madame de Souza being one day at La Malmaison, met the First Consul as he was going to Madame Bonaparte. He led her aside by the arm: "What does M. de Souza mean," he asked irritably, "by offering money to my ambassador to prevent his returning to Lisbon?"

* Madame de Flahaut, by her first marriage, and in this way grandmother of the Duc de Morny.

Madame de Souza protested that, on the contrary, it was to M. de Souza that the proposal was made.

"And what is there to prove that?" said the First Consul.

"The treasury of the Consular Guard!" cried Madame de Souza, her excitement getting the better of her reflection, in allusion to the deficit in the accounts of this regiment when it was under General Lannes's command.

The First Consul, knowing the general's honesty, never said a word, but turned his back on Madame de Souza.

Slightly disturbed by this silence, and the tacit disapproval which the Consul's manner implied, Madame de Souza went to Josephine and told her what had just passed between the First Consul and herself.

Josephine advised her to return to Paris at once, to shut herself up and not to see anybody for eight days, so that the First Consul might see that she had communicated with nobody.

Madame de Souza followed this advice, pretended to be ill, and took to her bed, refusing to receive anybody.

It is rather difficult to understand what was the object of all these manœuvres. They were so much trouble thrown away. The First Consul very soon forgot his quarrel with Madame de Souza, and never alluded to it again in her presence.

During the first six months that followed the Peace of Amiens, the first Consul led an almost idle life at La Malmaison, dreaming of the improvements which he could introduce into the various departments of his government; of the encouragements which might be given to agriculture, to industries; of the various works which might be carried out for the improvement and embellishment of Paris and the departments, which he proposed to visit in turn; and finally of the arts of peace.

During this pause in the midst of a life so busy and so fully occupied, he had projected a league of the maritime powers for driving the Barbary people from the coast of Africa, their lands to be afterwards used for planting sugar, coffee, cotton, and produce which had to be drawn from remote colonies. If the plan of this league could have been carried through, it would have diverted him from the expedition intended for the reconquest of the island of San Domingo. The idea had been proposed by Joseph Bonaparte, and was highly approved of by the First Consul. Joseph Bonaparte was anxious that the four powers who had signed the Amiens treaty should take part in this league. It was indeed shameful that Europe should tolerate, opposite to her, a nest of pirates, who levied blackmail on her with insolence, and who each year carried off into the cruellest slavery the prisoners they had captured on sea or on land—pirates to whom nothing was sacred, and who rejected our arts and our civilization. It was useless to hope to bring them to accept the relations and the conventions by which international rights are established between civilized States.

The loss of Egypt enhanced the value of the resources which a colonization of the Barbary States, so conveniently close at hand, and a naturalization of the produce of the islands of America, would have placed in the hands of the various powers. The plan of a conquest of this vast region was carefully examined in the cabinet of the Minister of Marine. A first step towards carrying it into effect was indeed made, by a mission with which the Spanish Government entrusted Badia, a clever and adventurous traveller. The *Moniteur* of 14th Thermidor, Year X, reported that two Spanish *savants*, charged with exploration of these countries, had passed through Paris. This plan of an expedition was perhaps one of the reasons of the rupture of the Peace of Amiens, and the renewal of hostilities which ensued prevented the First Consul from carrying it out. The great events which were played out on the stage of Europe obliged him to renounce his scheme for the time being, but he did not lose sight of a plan which, from the time of the renewal of hostilities with England, was one of the chief subjects of his thoughts.

On April 18th, 1808, Napoleon, being then at the Château de Marrac, near Bayonne, whither he had been summoned by affairs in Spain, wrote the following letter to the Minister of Marine:—

"Monsieur Decrés.—Think over the Algiers expedition both as a military and a naval campaign. If France could get a foot down on this part of the coast of Africa, England would have cause to reflect.

"Is there any port on this coast where a squadron of ships would be under cover from a superior force?

"What are the ports by which the army, once landed, could be revictualled?

"How many ports could the enemy blockade simultaneously?

"In Egypt there was, after all, only the port of Alexandria. Rosetta was a very dangerous harbour; still it was counted. I think that there are a dozen here.

"How many frigates, brigs, and storeships could they hold?

"Could Admiral Ganteaume's squadron enter the port of Algiers, and be sheltered against a superior force?

"At what time of the year is the air good, and pest no

longer to be feared? I imagine that it is in October.

"After having studied the Algiers expedition give your careful attention to the Tunis campaign. Write a confidential letter about it to Ganteaume, who, before coming to Paris, could get the necessary information. His inquiries should extend as far as Oran and should bear on the land, as well as the maritime, aspects of the proposed expedition. What he must find out about the inland is whether there are roads and water. I calculate that twenty thousand men will be necessary for this expedition. You will understand that the enemy is to be led to believe that Sicily is the object of this expedition, and that they will be nicely foiled when, instead, it proves to be Algiers. You need not answer me before a month. In the meanwhile get your information so that when you do answer me there shall be no 'buts', no 'ifs', and no 'becauses'.

"Send one of your engineers, a man who knows how to hold his tongue, on a brig. Let him talk with M. Thainville, but be sure to select a man of tact and of talent. This engineer should have some military as well as some naval knowledge. He must walk about both on the inside and on the outside of the fortifications, and as soon as he gets back home write down what he has noticed, so that he can bring us back plain facts and not merely his own dreams. Consult with Sanson as to the best man to choose. You will be able to find exact information in the archives of the Foreign Office and of the Ministry of War. Have these archives, as well as your own, looked through. Information about these countries has always been asked for in France."

Several Frenchmen who had exercised civil or diplomatic functions in the Algiers Regency, heads of French establishments in that country, engineers and naval officers who had discharged special duties there, were all consulted. M. Jean Bon-Saint-André, who had been commissioner of the government at

Algiers, under the Directoire, handed a detailed memorandum, in which all the questions put to him were answered, to the Minister of Marine.

Napoleon's attention was also taken up with the scheme for re-organizing the Academies. The term "Academy" was suppressed. The Institute was divided into four sections. The first was termed "Class of Physical and Mathematical Sciences". The second, styled "Class of the French Language and Literature", answered to the French Academy, formerly so-called. The third was the "Class of Ancient History and Literature", and the fourth that of "The Fine Arts". The "Class of Moral and Political Sciences", created by the law of Year IV, was suppressed and merged in that of *belles-lettres*. It seemed superfluous to the First Consul. He supported his opinion on this matter with reasons which I do not think it necessary to examine. His principal motive was not, as has been said, his dislike for philosophy. He has often expressed himself on this matter, but he was then convinced that the discussion of political matters had still, at that time, its disadvantages.

The eight or nine months which followed the Peace of Amiens were divided between La Malmaison and St. Cloud, which the First Consul went to inhabit in the spring of that year. This palace, although not vast, afforded a beautiful and comfortable abode, well suited to Napoleon's habits and requirements, and provided with magnificent gardens. His workroom was very large, and its walls were literally covered with books, from the floor to the ceiling. He had himself designed his writing-table, which was in the shape of a bass.

Numerous papers were spread out on its wings. His usual place was on a settee covered with green taffeta, which stood near the mantelpiece, on which were two fine bronze busts of Scipio and of Hannibal. Behind the settee, in the corner, was my writing-table. His study was reached through a bedroom, which he did not occupy. His apartment was on the floor above, and communicated with this room by means of a private staircase. It consisted of three plainly furnished rooms. The only ornament of the bedroom on the ground floor, which looked out on the garden, was an antique bust of Cæsar, which stood on the mantelpiece. Beyond the First Consul's workroom was a small drawing-room, where he used to receive the Minister of Foreign Affairs, who, by reason of the nature of the business of his department, had no reports to address to the Council of State. This drawing-room was also used for private audiences; it was decorated with a fine portrait of Charles XII. The First Consul was dissatisfied that this portrait had been selected, and had it replaced by a portrait of Gustavus Adolphus, for whom he had a particular esteem.

Paisiello came to Paris in the spring of this year, summoned by the First Consul, whose intention it was to entrust him with the direction of the Opera and of the Conservatory of Music. Napoleon admired this celebrated composer's talents. He used to be so delighted with Nina's pastorale: "*Gia il sol si ciela dietro alla montagna,*"—that he said he could listen to it with pleasure every evening. Paisiello was then over sixty. He had hesitated about coming to Paris, fearing to expose his gray hairs to the criticisms of his rivals, and dreading to compromise his great musical reputation. He was received with great honour by Napoleon, and with deference by the artists. He refused to accept any other post than that of chapel-master; and restricted himself to the composition of masses and motets. The only opera which he composed in Paris was "*Proserpine.*" It was only moderately successful; a slight reverse which somewhat grieved him.

After residing three years in France his desire to see his country again, and to take his wife home to a milder climate, induced him to return to Italy. He went home with a pension from the Emperor, and loaded with presents. M. Lesueur, whose talents he admired, succeeded him as chapel-master. Paisiello used to send Napoleon a sacred composition each year, for the anniversary of the Emperor's fête. He also paraphrased the "*Stabat Mater*" of Pergolesi, which was performed in the Imperial Chapel. I have preserved many letters from this excellent man, which he wrote in sending his compositions, and in which he expressed his gratitude to and admiration for the Emperor. I am convinced that these professions, allowance being made for Italian emphasis, were quite sincere.

Canova was sent for to Paris at about the same time. He came to St. Cloud to execute the bust of Napoleon, and devoted himself to this piece of work for several days with a veritable predilection. The First Consul used to lunch in the large drawing-room, which led in to his apartment, so that the celebrated sculptor might work more at his ease during this meal. This drawing-room was afterwards ornamented with portraits of the Bonaparte family. When Napoleon became Emperor he used to receive all the members of his family who happened to be in Paris at dinner every Sunday, and spent the evening with them in this drawing-room. A large balcony, on to which this drawing-room opened, communicated between the private apartment of Napoleon and that of Josephine, afterwards occupied by Marie Louise.

I used sometimes to remain with Canova after the sittings, and to accompany him into the gardens. He spoke bitterly of the statues he saw there, and pointed out to me the decadence of good taste which they proved. He regretted that the artists of the time of Louis XV., and especially Boucher, should have applied their great talents to works which he considered pitiful. A reproach of another kind might be levelled against Canova himself. He carried off the model of Napoleon's bust, a model most true to nature, and most noble in resemblance, and which, on this account, had been generally admired. I do not know why, renouncing this resemblance, which ought to be the first merit of a bust or of a portrait, he made an idealized head. However grand a character he may have wished to bestow on his work, he could not hope to make a more heroic face than the original.

It was after this bust that Canova executed the colossal statue of Napoleon which he sent to Paris in 1811. This statue may be admired as a work of art, but the want of resemblance in the head, and its nudity, displeased the Emperor. It was placed at the Louvre without having been previously exhibited. It was this same statue which either was bought by the Duke of Wellington, or was given to him by the government, in 1815. It was carried off to England as a trophy, and placed in a spot very unworthy of it, and in a way which does little honour to the delicacy of feeling of the victor. One of our sculptors, as remarkable for his great talents as for his national feeling, as he was returning from a walk in London, saw a number of people stopping before the partly-opened door of a mansion—the mansion of the Duke of Wellington. Prompted by curiosity to approach, his astonishment can be imagined in recognizing, in the object which was attracting the eyes of the curious, Canova's beautiful statue of Napoleon, placed at the foot of a stair-case, and being used to hang cloaks and hats on.

I remember that one day the First Consul brought back a quatrain, on his return from Josephine's apartment, where he had been spending an hour. He threw this poem on his writing-table, and said that it had been composed by Madame Fanny de Beauharnais. It was a play of words on the word Bonaparte, and the last line, which is all of it that I remember, ran as follows: "*La bonne part sera la nôtre.*"

The First Consul, whilst doing justice to the authoress's intentions, which he considered better than their execution, took pleasure in speaking of the good qualities of Madame de Beauharnais, Josephine's aunt. He praised the gentleness and the goodness of her character. Even if he was then under the first impression of this lady's innocent flatteries, this impression was a lasting one, as he never ceased his protection of her son and granddaughter. The son was appointed senator in 1804, the senatorship of Amiens being granted to him. When the Emperor married the

Arch-duchess Marie Louise, he placed him in her service as gentleman-in-waiting. In 1806, he married Stéphanie de Beauharnais, the senator's daughter, born of a first marriage, to Prince Charles, the grandson of the Duke of Baden, whom he succeeded in 1811.

Some days later, Madame Bonaparte came and knocked at the door of the cabinet. She immediately entered, followed by the usher, who without a word placed a basket covered over with a cloth in the centre of the room and withdrew. Whilst Napoleon was waiting for the explanation of this enigma Madame Bonaparte drew away the cloth which covered the basket. A little man, not more than eighteen inches high, who was lying down in the basket, raised himself with difficulty and, leaning with his two hands on the handle of the basket, turned a pair of dark and shining, but lustreless, eyes upon us. This dwarf was dressed in complete hussar uniform, with the red shako, vest, and dolman, regulation boots, and was girt with a sabre which kept entangling itself in his little legs. There was nothing monstrous about him except his extreme smallness. His limbs were well-made, his features, if inert, were regular. Nevertheless the evident insensibility of this misconception, whose life seemed merely mechanical, and whose intelligence seemed destined never to develop—for he was said to be then seventeen years old—his debility, the pale and bilious colour of his skin, and his weazened and sickly *ensemble*, excited disgust.

The sight of this poor disinherited creature, nature's cruel sport, placed face to face with a full-grown being, in whom the same nature had been pleased to unite a majesty of features to a superiority of genius, would have offered a singular contrast to the eyes of an observer. The fine and impressionable organism of Napoleon evidently suffered from so painful a sight, and without one word of comment, he prayed his wife to remove the dwarf from his eyes.

The union of Piedmont to France took place in the month of September, 1802. This occurrence gave rise to no recriminations; it had been expected for a long time. Piedmont, the throne of which remained untenanted after the retirement of the king to the island of Sardinia, was in pawn in the hands of France as a stepping-stone, either to serve as an indemnity, or to be used in other diplomatic combinations. The fate of this country having been passed over in silence in the Treaties of Amiens and Lunéville, and Russia not having asked for its restitution to the House of Savoy, its incorporation with the French territory was consummated by a senatus consultum. General Jourdan, who combined the functions of military governor of these provinces with those of general administrator, was replaced by General Menou. The First Consul had certain prejudices against Jourdan, which he afterwards discarded. When at St. Helena he expressed his regret for having misunderstood him, and spoke of him in terms which do honour to them both.

Another event, which occurred about a month later, and which caused no more sensation, was the union with France of the duchies of Parma and Piacenza, brought about by the death of the sovereign of these states. By the Treaty of Lunéville, Austria had lost Tuscany, which was given to the Infant of Parma, who was married to a daughter of Charles IV., King of Spain. The French Government had immediately put the Infant in possession of his kingdom, and he had assumed the title of King of Etruria. In exchange for the life-crown, with which the preponderating influence of the First Consul had endowed this prince, the duchies of Parma and Piacenza had been ceded to France, but Napoleon had desired that the old Duke should finish his days there in peace.

The latter, encouraged by the King of Spain in the hope that after his death his states would be added to the Kingdom of Etruria, had appointed the dowager-duchess Queen Regent in the name of his son, by his last will and testament. This testament, which was without value, was set aside. French officials came to take possession of the country, and M. Moreau de Saint-Méry, who was protected by Madame Bonaparte, was sent there as general administrator.

The island of Elba, which had been retroceded to France by the King of Etruria, was united to France at the same time as Piedmont.

Thus did the power of Napoleon bestow on France two states, reserved to strange destinies. The sovereignty of the one was to devolve on a daughter of Austria, illusory pledge of an ephemeral alliance*; the other was to provide the founder of the most powerful empire in the world with a modest refuge, a harbour of shelter between two shipwrecks.

The monotony of Napoleon's sedentary life in his study was interrupted about this time by a fortnight's journey, which he undertook towards the end of October, going to visit the manufactories of the Seine-Inférieure and Oise departments. Napoleon was accompanied on

* Empress Marie Louise became Duchess of Parma, after Napoleon's banishment to St. Helena.—R. H. S.

this short journey by Madame Bonaparte. He left after having given General Andréossy—appointed ambassador to London—his farewell audience.

The First Consul visited the St. Cyr Military School and examined into every detail. At Ivry he visited the battle-field made famous by Henry the Fourth's victory, and, accompanied by the mayor and numerous citizens of the town, examined the various positions which had been occupied by the two armies, rectifying with his martial instinct the indications which were given to him, and judging with his eagle eye the faults or the skill of the tactics both of vanquished and victors.

Twenty young girls presented Josephine with flowers and verses at Evreux. The cloth-manufactories of Louviers and Elbeuf, and the copper foundries of Romilly, attracted the attention of the Consul, and won his solicitude. Two days after his departure from Paris, the First Consul arrived at Rouen, followed by the entire population. The three days which he spent there were devoted to reconnoitring the heights with which the town is surrounded—which was always the first thing he did when visiting any large town—and afterwards to visiting the factories. In his careful examination of these establishments he displayed the same spirit of investigation which always characterized him, and which was inspired by his desire to increase the national prosperity. He received the archbishop, the prefect, the mayors, the courts of Justice and Commerce, the military and civil authorities, the scientific societies, and the principal functionaries, conversing at length with each on his speciality, and with all on the questions which in general interested the welfare of the department. He was present at the theatre, where he was received with acclamation, and afterwards at some fêtes which were given in his honour. All the corporations were presented to Josephine, who received them with her usual good grace and tact.

From Rouen, the first Consul went to Havre. He stopped at Caudebec, at Bolbec, and at Yvetot. He embarked on a lugger at five in the morning to visit Honfleur, accompanied by M. de Montcabrié, who was in command of the boat. On his return, he visited Dieppe, Tréport, Forges, and Beauvais. Exhibitions of the local industries were prepared for his inspection in the various manufacturing towns through which he passed.

It is superfluous to add that this excursion, undertaken for the purpose of benefiting the various regions visited, was not a mere fruitless pleasure-trip. This journey had a political object also, namely, to show our eternal rivals what perfect harmony existed between the nation and its chief, and to what advantage the latter could turn the resources of the country. The First Consul and Madame Bonaparte were everywhere received with veritable enthusiasm. Companies of mounted men acted as their escort and guard of honour in each town through which they passed.

Shortly afterwards Napoleon went to visit the works of the Ourcq Canal, which had recently been begun. With this in view he left Paris at six o'clock on a fine morning towards the end of January, accompanied by several generals and three aides-de-camp. He rode over the eighteen leagues which form the extent of the canal in five hours. He slept at Lisy, at the house of General d'Harville, uncle of Colonel Caulaincourt, his aide-de-camp, Madame Bonaparte having gone to Lisy the previous day. On the morrow, at daybreak, the First Consul rode to Mareuil, where the water for the canal is taken. He found the Prefect of Paris there, and with him the engineer-in-chief, Gérard, who was charged with the direction of the works. On his way back he stayed at Meaux for two hours. He received the subprefect there, the mayor, and the principal authorities, in the big room of the Town-hall. He returned to Paris the same evening. I accompanied him on this journey on horseback, and it was a pleasant change from the stay-at-home life, which I only grew to like when I was no longer compelled to live it.

The year 1802 brought with it the retirement of Fouché, and the suppression of the Ministry of Police. M. Regnier, who afterwards became Duc de Massa, the Grand Judge, was put at the head of the Ministries of Police and of Justice, united into one single department. A justifiable dislike for Fouché prompted Napoleon to remove him. The way in which this turbulent man managed his ministry was a cause of anxiety to the First Consul. It offended him to see Fouché, in spite of his express commands, interfering in his home, in his private domestic affairs, under the pretence of exercising a necessary supervision. He was delighted to escape from the guardianship of such a man. Fouché was always a suspicious person in his eyes, on account of his crooked ways and his meddlesome mind; nevertheless he was seen back again at the ministry within two years of his dismissal. Napoleon dismissed him again in 1810, acting by the same instinct, but once more took him on in 1815. Clear reason rejects any belief in fatality, and yet who will not be struck by the sight of this evil genius, the object of Napoleon's just dislike and repugnance, twice removed from his post with an advancement in honours, and twice returning to boldly take his place at the council, dominating the destinies of the Emperor by his cunning and his spirit of intrigue, and finally leading him to his overthrow.

Napoleon used to compare the reports of the Minister of Police with those of the prefects, in what concerned provincial matters; and with the reports of the prefect of police, who was never in accordance with the Minister, in matters concerning Paris.

His other police services, which might be styled official, to distinguish them from the private police, were the service under the command of the first inspector of gendarmerie, and that of the commander of the Paris garrison. There were one or two other police services of little importance, the reports of which he frequently neglected to read. A retired major, who was as honest as a man can be in such a profession, and who was not intriguing, was charged with the subaltern military police of Paris.

Count de Survilliers—Joseph Bonaparte—has set forth in the following brief remarks, the motives which prompted the First Consul first to abolish the Ministry of Police and afterwards to re-establish it:

"The Ministry of Police was an institution founded by the Directoire, and not by the Convention. It dates from 1796. The Revolution had the Committee of Public Safety. Napoleon found the Ministry of Police established. He preserved it until he thought that he could dispense with it. He united it, in 1802, after the signing of general peace, to the Ministry of Justice, so as to replace the ardent, rapid, and arbitrary action of a special administration, by the slow and methodical procedure of the magistrates and the *procureurs-généraux*. But conspiracies arose. The slow steps of justice no longer sufficed under the circumstances. A return had to be made to police measures. Réal was charged with their execution, under the orders of the Grand Judge. That was insufficient for the realization of the object in view, and the Ministry of Police was re-established. It was suppressed, as a matter of principle, in Napoleon's mind. Such were the evident causes of the re-establishment of this ministry."

One of Napoleon's methods of government, a method in favour in almost every country, was to open letters in the post.* If this method can be tolerated at all, it is only in the hands of the head of a government whose morality and prudence eliminate its danger. But this guarantee does not always exist in the man at the head of affairs, and when such a man does exist he is not immortal.

On his accession to power, the First Consul had found, at the General Post-Office, a department which was known by the name of the Black Cabinet. Several clerks who had grown gray in this work, were appointed to open such letters as were indicated to them by the Postmaster-General, at that time M. Laforêt, who afterwards became ambassador, senator, and peer of France. This department was at that time made use of by nearly everybody. The civil and

---

* A method still in practice in France. Only quite recently during the anarchist scare in Paris it was announced that letters to and from suspected persons would be handed to the *juge d'instruction*. The "Cabinet Noir" flourishes as in the past.—R. H. S.

military authorities in the provinces had the right to intercept letters, to open them, to make use of their contents, to send copies or even the originals to Paris, where they were read by the members of the Directoire, the ministers, and their friends. The First Consul, in appointing his former aide-de-camp Lavalette, Postmaster-General, forbade that any letters should be intercepted or communicated to any authorities whatsoever, and he made the various postmasters responsible for the commission of any such offence. These precautions prove that Napoleon had it at heart to attenuate what was arbitrary in this system. The majority of the numerous agents kept in Paris by foreign ministries, a few people mixed up in political intrigues, some officials in various branches of the public service, who did not yet enjoy the complete confidence of the new government, or who, for one reason or another, were objects of suspicion, were named to the department, with the object of having their correspondence subjected to particular scrutiny. In this way some important information was obtained, but no letter, whether written by a person or addressed to him, no matter how grave its contents might be, was considered sufficient by Napoleon for his definite conviction. Until his suspicions had been confirmed, the letter was held in reserve.

Sometimes use was made of this means for the furtherance of private interests, in support of some denunciation, or to assist friends. The sagacity and moderation of Napoleon, and the numberless sources of information which he possessed, foiled all these manœuvres. This violation of postal secrecy, which I shall not attempt to defend from a moral point of view, because of the grave disadvantages which such a system might have presented in the hands of those of Napoleon's successors who possessed neither his discretion nor his perspicacity, was in his hands an instrument without danger, and often of great use. On an indication furnished by a letter, the Emperor got at the truth, by investigation, research, and contradictory reports, which never failed to enlighten him. Often, like a tutelary Providence, he was able, thanks to this system, to make reparation for injustice committed, to redress grievances, and to dispense benefits and assistance at the time when those who were the objects of his justice or of his benevolence expected it the least.

Although it was well-known that those who did not want their letters to be read, did not send them by post, it rarely happened that some valuable information was not gathered in this way. I remember that one day the Emperor, forgetting that since the re-organization of the post-office the Minister of Finance had no connection with the Black Cabinet, said to this Minister, pointing through the half-opened door to Fouché, who was in the adjoining room: "See that that fellow's letters are looked into." It is probable that Fouché would not have let himself be taken in this trap, and that if he had sent any letter by the post, it would have been written so as to put the government, to which he then no longer belonged, on a wrong scent. The most absolute secrecy, moreover, enveloped the small number of letters which the Postmaster-General communicated to the sovereign. None but he himself was allowed to read them. The copies, which were handed to the Emperor under seals, were burned as soon as they had been read, no trace of them ever remaining. If the Black Cabinet had allowed itself to send on any letters containing family matters, or had exhumed any scandalous anecdote of the kind which so deeply interested Louis XV., it would at once have been ordered to confine itself within its prescribed limits. I must make haste to add that the Postmaster-General never exposed himself to reprimands of this kind. *

In the first days of the month of January 1803, it was learned that General Leclerc, Captain-General of the Colony of San Domingo, after the unfortunate issue of the expedition which had been sent out to reduce this island to submission, had died of yellow fever at the Cape. The First Consul was deeply grieved by this loss. On the following day letters from Toulouse announced the arrival of the *Swiftsure* in that port, the remains of the general being on board this ship. Madame Leclerc, sister of the First Consul, and her young son accompanied the body.

Madame Leclerc, then in all the splendour of her youth and beauty, had torn herself away from the seductions of a world in which she held the first rank, to accompany her husband, and to accomplish her duties as mother and as wife. Pauline, although surrounded with adulation and homage, to which she was not altogether insensible, felt that the blood of Bonaparte was in her veins. She had resisted the order sent by the commander-in-chief, at the time of the insurrection of the Cape, to take ship home with her son. She wished to share

* A very interesting description of the Black Cabinet and its working is to be found in Count d'Hérisson's "LE CABINET NOIR—Louis XVII.—Napoléon—Marie Louise" published by Ollendorff in Paris. An English translation exists.—R. H. S.

his dangers. During the short sickness which preceded his death she had not left his bedside, and had cared for him with tender solicitude. She came back to France with broken health which was never entirely re-established. She lost her son, still a child, a year later. This child's name was Dermide, a name given him by his godfather, Napoleon, who at the time had been greatly impressed with the original and poetical genius of Ossian.

Bernadotte's son, who was of about the same age as General Leclerc's son, received the name of Oscar. Napoleon was his godfather, and the christening was delayed until he returned from Egypt. Bernadotte, so obsequious towards Napoleon, did not cease conspiring against him, afterwards having recourse to everything and everybody to get his offences pardoned. Joseph Bonaparte and his wife were as persevering in their efforts to obtain his pardon, as Bernadotte was in alternating offences and submissions.

The First Consul wore mourning for General Leclerc for ten days. He was much affected by this loss, not only of a brother-in-law, on whose devotion he could count, but of an officer of the highest merit, who was as useful in the study as on the field of battle. A cultured education and brilliant services had procured him advancement which would have seemed very rapid in ordinary times. He was general at the age of twenty-one, having risen step by step in Italy, at Toulon—where he was on active service with Bonaparte—at Fleurus, and with the army of the Alps. Appointed commander of Marseilles by the Directoire, he made the acquaintance of the young sister of the Toulon artillery commander, the Bonapartes having then retired to Marseilles. General Bonaparte, on his promotion to the supreme command of the army in Italy, called him to his side at Milan. Leclerc was at that time general of brigade. Bonaparte gave him his sister in marriage. This charming lady, one of the most beautiful women of her age, had been ardently courted by Fréron. Fréron, who after the 9th Thermidor became the chief of the *jeunesse dorée*, had not at that time yet distinguished himself by the sanguinary acts which won for him the name of Saviour of the South from the society of Jacobins.

General Leclerc had not taken part in Napoleon's expedition to Egypt. During this time he served in Italy and in the West. He was afterwards sent to Lyons with extraordinary powers. He re-established discipline in the army, which had been disorganized by the evacuation of Italy and dispersed over Lyons and the neighbouring cantons. On the 18th Brumaire General Leclerc vigorously seconded General Bonaparte. After having fulfilled to the First Consul's satisfaction the mission of leading an army of twenty thousand French soldiers into Spain, for action against Portugal, he was appointed to command the San Domingo expedition.

The First Consul, on his accession to power, had invested Toussaint-L'Ouverture with the government of this island, in the name of France. Toussaint, general of division, was a former slave, whom nature had made a deep politician and a skilful administrator. His absolute influence over the blacks had commended him to the French government. The ambitious Toussaint, fostering at heart a secret plan to render himself master of the island, and to expel the French troops, recognized the supremacy of the metropolis during the period of one year. When it seemed to him that the right time had come, he threw off the mask, raised the flag of insurrection and proclaimed the independence of San Domingo. The honour and the interests of France rendered it necessary that he should be forced to return to the path of duty. An expedition to San Domingo was accordingly decided upon. The Creoles who had taken refuge in France urged on this resolution. The fatal issue of this expedition is well-known. The neglect of measures of prudence; the retention of black generals and officers in their posts; the outbreak of yellow fever, which decimated the pick of the French army; the cunning and the activity of Toussaint; all these causes contributed to the failure of the expedition. The seizure of some private letters from Toussaint was followed by his arrest and his transportation to France. He was confined in the fortress of Joux, and died there two years later.

The First Consul, who was fully aware of the ambitious object pursued by Toussaint, and who could not believe in the least sincerity on his side, would have preferred his removal at the very beginning from the island. He would have preferred to receive him in France as an exile, rather than as a captive, but he could in no case allow him his liberty when once his treachery had been unmasked.

The unhealthiness of the climate of San Domingo, and the fatigues and vexations which beset General Leclerc, had rapidly led him to his grave. He was replaced in the chief command by General Rochambeau, who brought about the definite loss of the island by his severity, just as his predecessor had weakened its loyalty by too much indulgence. It was in accordance with the wishes of the First Consul that his sister had accompanied her husband to San Domingo together with her son. When he heard of her arrival at Toulon he immediately sent off his aide-de-camp Lauriston to bring the widow and her child back to Paris.

One of the principal grievances alleged against us by the English Ministry was the mission of Colonel Sebastiani to Egypt. The splendour with which the French envoy had surrounded his mission, the assurance given to the sheiks and the chiefs of the Mamelukes that General Bonaparte, as head of the French Government, had not forgotten them, and that his protection should not be wanting, and the marks of interest lavished in his name, excited the suspicions of England.

In his report to the First Consul, Colonel Sebastiani accused the London Cabinet, and with reason, of working in an underhand way to turn away the chiefs of the country from their fidelity to the Porte, but he omitted to mention the friendly reception accorded to him by the English commander. Napoleon, irritated at the want of good faith shown by the British Cabinet in the relations which, since the signing of the Peace of Amiens, had been established between the two powers, published the report of Colonel Sebastiani, although this had been intended as a strictly confidential document. At the same time, just before it was printed in the *Moniteur*, the idea came to him to show it to M. Amédée Jaubert, who had accompanied the colonel in his voyage, and who was perfectly acquainted with Oriental countries. M. Jaubert was called in the night to the house of M. Maret, Secretary of State, who showed him a proof of the report. Jaubert advised the Minister to suppress several passages, which in his opinion could not fail to produce a regrettable impression, and provoke great irritation. But as this report had to appear in the *Moniteur* of the following morning, these modifications could not be submitted to Napoleon's approval. M. Maret declined to assume the responsibility of these rectifications, or of postponing the publication of the document. The report accordingly appeared in the *Moniteur*, with some slight modifications, which did not in any way affect its essential points, and thus became the starting point of the series of reciprocated antagonisms, which finally resulted, at no distant date, in the rupture of peace between England and France.

Towards the end of 1802 some deputies of various Swiss cantons arrived in Paris, on the summons of the First Consul, to discuss their respective interests before him, and to bring about a reconciliation of the different factions which for five years past had divided the Helvetic Confederation. Several attempts in this direction had been made by Napoleon since his accession to power. He had imposed the recognition of the independence of this Republic at Lunéville, but the revolutions caused by the struggle of the various parties for power, the appeals to arms, and the intervention of European Cabinets called for by the aristocracy, had kept this unhappy country in a series of internecine wars and in a state of anarchy which it behoved the French Government to terminate. The withdrawal of the French troops, which had been effected in accordance with the wishes of the Helvetic Government, had only given a freer field to the passions of the adversaries.

Before taking this decision, the object of which was to ascertain what use Switzerland would make of her restored independence, it had been proposed to vest the supreme authority in this country in a hereditary chief, or *Landamman*. Negotiations to this effect were commenced with the Margrave of Baden. Baron Dalberg, at that time minister of this little State, who afterwards became Duc Dalberg, and a naturalized Frenchman, was the intermediary in these negotiations, which were carried so far, indeed, that the court of Baden thought to indemnify the minister for his trouble who at that time directed foreign affairs in France. The troubles which broke out after the withdrawal of the French troops contributed to the failure of this arrangement.

The federalist faction, led by Aloys Reding, was triumphing, when the vanquished party decided to appeal to the French Government, and to demand its interference. The First Consul had several conferences, one of which lasted more than six hours, with ten deputies, selected amongst the Federalists and the *Unitaires*. He listened to the arguments of the rival factions with attention, and discussed them with the greatest impartiality. He spoke to them like a Swiss citizen, and, as the head of two such great countries as France and Italy, gave them wise advice, and constantly manifested a moderation and a logic which convinced the Swiss deputies. He commissioned four French senators, MM. Barthélemy, Roederer, Fouché, and Desmeuniers to come to an understanding with the Swiss deputies, and to draw up the draft of an act of conciliation, the basis of which should be entire equality between all the cantons, a voluntary renunciation of their privileges by the aristocracy, the division of the national debt in just proportions, and the federative organization of the eighteen cantons * by which their religious creeds, their habits, their languages, and their interests should be conciliated.

This wise and disinterested policy calmed all spirit of faction, and, thanks to our mediation, Switzerland was promptly pacified. The various parties agreed to it, and Aloys Reding himself, who had declared himself one of the most ardent champions of the oligarchy, was present at the first Diet, and admitted the benefit due to the intervention of the powerful peacemaker. All the cantons expressed their gratitude to the First Consul in numerous addresses.

The auditors were instituted by a decree of April 9th, 1803. At first they were only sixteen in number, and were charged with the functions of reporters to the various sections of the Council of State. They were for the most part young men of talent, who had received a good education, and who belonged for the most part to old families. Almost all the reporters of this first nomination attained high positions in the State. Their number was, later on, considerably increased, experience having proved the advantages of this institution. The auditors, it may be said, formed a kind of nursery-garden of adminis-

* Méneval is in error here. There were *nineteen* cantons under the new constitution, owing to the addition of the cantons St. Gallen, Graubuenden, Aargau, Thurgau, Ticino, and Waadtland. This constitution was modified in favour of the Federalist faction on Dec. 13th, 1813.—R. H. S.

trators trained in the school of the Empire, and intended, when once familiar with the direction of affairs, to occupy the highest posts in the government. With this purpose in view they were distributed over the various ministries, occupied in the prefectures and subprefectures, in the offices of the public prosecutors at the various courts, and in the financial administrations. They were later on commissioned to carry the portfolio containing the results of the labours of the ministers during the preceding week to the Emperor, either to headquarters, or during his journeys in the interior of France. In time of war the auditors remained at the disposal of the Secretary of State, but most often were employed by the general intendant of the army, who used them on extraordinary missions. The majority of them were employed at the headquarters of those who superintended the conquered countries. In reward for services rendered in the course of these missions they often received, on their return to France, advancement which had not always been won by long experience. Nevertheless, and with very few exceptions, they justified the Emperor's confidence. No complaint was ever made against their management of affairs, especially with regard to their honesty and loyalty. Almost all the families who had formerly had representatives in the departments of justice, of finance, and in the management of the principal affairs of State, were drawn upon for auditors who rendered useful services. Napoleon often congratulated himself on the advantages which he had derived from this institution.

I think it necessary to speak of a proposal which was made in the month of February, 1803, by the King of Prussia, to the chief of the House of Bourbon, at that time in retirement at Warsaw, that he should renounce his rights to the French crown in exchange for territorial and pecuniary advantages. The friendly relations which existed between the First Consul and the Prussian monarch, the answer made by Napoleon to the Comte de Lille *, on the 20th Fructidor, Year VIII,—7th September, 1800—and the terms of the instructions given by the King to the President of the Regency of Warsaw,

* Almost immediately after the revolution of Brumaire 18th, the Comte de Lille had caused overtures to be made on many sides to the First Consul, to engage him to act as the agent of a Restoration. About nine months later this prince made a last appeal to the Head of the Government in the following letter:

"You must have known for a long time past, General, that my esteem is yours. Should you doubt that I be not susceptible to the claims of gratitude, fix the place you wish to occupy, and dispose of the fortunes of your friends. As to my principles, I am a Frenchman; clement by character, my reason will render me still more so. No; the victor of Lodi, of Castiglione, and of Arcola, the conqueror of Italy, cannot prefer a vain celebrity to glory. Nevertheless you are losing precious time; we can assure the glory of France. I say 'we', because I shall need Bonaparte for that, and because he could not accomplish it without me. General, Europe is watching you; glory awaits you; and I am impatient to restore peace to my country."

The First Consul answered:

"I have received your letter, Sir. I thank you for the agreeable things which you say in it. You should not desire your return to France; you would have to walk over a hundred thousand corpses. Sacrifice your interests to the peace and happiness of France. History will take this into consideration. I am by no means indifferent to the misfortunes of your family. I shall hear with pleasure that you are at peace in your retirement, and will gladly contribute to assure this tranquillity."

The autograph letter of the Pretender, at the foot of which the Emperor's answer was written in Bourrienne's hand, was for a long time in my keeping, in the Emperor's portfolio, together with the Emperor Alexander's famous pencil note. This prince, separated from his followers after the disaster of Austerlitz, wrote this note at the foot of a tree, to persuade Marshal Davout that a suspension of hostilities, which, as a matter of fact, was only agreed upon on the following day, had just been concluded between the Emperor of Austria and the Emperor Napoleon, and assured the retreat of himself and his troops.

These papers were destroyed at Orcha, with several other documents, during the retreat from Moscow.

have led to the belief that this proposal was inspired by the head of the French Government.

These instructions of the King of Prussia to M. Meyer are known by the copy which Louis XVIII. made of them, in his own writing, and which was witnessed by the Archbishop of Rheims, M. de Talleyrand's uncle, and by Abbé Edgeworth. If such an insinuation was made to the King of Prussia I never heard of it. Whatever interest Napoleon may have taken in the misfortunes of the fallen house, he did not think that the initiative ought to come from him. It is more than probable that the first idea of such a proposal was mooted in Prussia, because it was felt that the prolonged stay of the Pretender in the Prussian States might one day lead to difficulties, and that the feelings of the First Consul with regard to the Bourbons were known.

Napoleon did not oppose the making of this proposal by the King of Prussia, but declared that he would in no way participate in it. The future Emperor was so particularly interested in this proposal that one had very good reasons to think that he was not foreign to it. Napoleon was, however, very circumspect, and much too shrewd not to understand that it required only a very little common sense to see that to ask the Bourbons to relinquish their rights, was a practical acknowledgment that the rights conferred by the vote of the nation had to be confirmed by the sanction of the family which had reigned before him.

It is natural to think that Louis XVIII. thought it useful to his interests to attribute this proposal to his adversary, to draw attention to it as an indirect acknowledgment of his rights, and to take advantage of this opportunity to bring himself once more before the eyes of Europe by means of a declaration, which came so exactly at the right time, and which there have been people found to style heroic. Without being unjust to this prince, it may be said that he was lacking in all the qualities which make a hero. Heroism above all implies the idea of danger, whilst Louis XVIII. ran no risk whatever. He was a shrewd and crafty man, very selfish, and penetrated with an instinctive sentiment of his legitimacy, which always prevented him from despairing of his cause. His only arms were intrigues so carefully planned that their source could never be attributed to him, and certain proclamations, in which he also sought after literary renown. And as to these crooked manœuvres, and the proclamations which he hurled forth from the depths of his retreat at times when it was impossible for him to be silent, it may be said that the former were not worthy of his cause, and that the latter, on the other hand, were more in accordance with the duties which his position laid upon him.

I am not in a position to contest the authenticity of the documents published by the Restoration. I will not base any such denial on the instance when the Government of the Restoration published a letter written by the Emperor Napoleon to King Joachim Murat, having previously altered it. M. de Blacas, having found the draft of this letter in the archives of the Emperor's cabinet, deemed it right to publish it in the *Moniteur*, after having arranged it to suit the object which he desired to obtain by its publication. During the Hundred Days, I saw the copy of this letter written by the hand of Abbé Fleuriot, one of M. de Blacas's secretaries, with the alterations noted on the margin in red ink.

But without seeking to base any denial on the want of good faith, which certain governments do not hesitate to employ when it is to their interest to do so, it is simpler to say that these negotiations with the Bourbons, having been transacted between them and the agents of Prussia without Napoleon's expression of any desire to be informed as to their progress, the zeal of these agents, and the doctrines of the Berlin Ministry, gave the form that suited them to their proposals. This is Napoleon's own remark on the subject.

I have omitted to say how the Pretender happened to be at Warsaw. When the Emperor Paul I. had reconciled himself to the Consular Government towards the end of 1800, his attitude towards the Comte de Lille, to whom two years previously he had showed hospitality at Mittau, suddenly changed. He ordered him to leave the Russian territory, although it was then the middle of a very severe winter. In his distress the Comte de Lille asked shelter of the King of Prussia, who allowed him to establish himself at Warsaw. The King of Prussia, however, not wishing to displease the French Government, notified the matter to the First Consul, who did not make the least objection to the Pretender's presence in a city in the Prussian States, and tolerated it with good grace.

In support of my statement that King Louis XVIII. was not a man of heroic character, I may mention the following fact: When, in the month of April, 1796, the Comte de Lille left Verona, at the request of the Venetian Government, he asked, with the pride and the dignity which befitted his rank, that his name should be erased from the Golden Book, and that the armour of Henri IV. should be restored to him. But, fearing to be given up by the Venetians, or to fall in with the French troops on his way, he got the Duc de la Vauguyon to drive in his carriage and to pretend to be the king, whilst he, disguising himself in humble attire, made good his escape out of the district occupied by the French troops. This fact is mentioned in a report from the podesta of Verona to the Senate of Venice. The report in question was amongst the archives which were carried away to France, after the French conquest of Venice.

The instinctive sentiment of his legitimacy never left this prince. M. Beugnot, who in 1814 received the portfolio of the Ministry of the Interior at the hands of the Provisional Government, was commissioned, in this capacity, to establish Louis XVIII. in the apartments of the Tuileries palace, on his return from England. The Minister has since told me that the King walked through the various rooms with an air of the most profound indifference, without paying the least attention to M. Beugnot's explanation of the use to which each of the rooms was to be put. After reaching the room which used to serve as Napoleon's study, and in which had been placed the writing-table on which the prince used to write at Hartwell, Louis XVIII. refused to go any further. He ordered an armchair to be brought up, and sat down to his writing-table as quietly as if he had only left the palace an hour previously to take a walk. *

* The following is the portrait which M. de Montgaillard, who was in constant relations with Louis XVIII., drew of this prince: "The prince possesses much intelligence; his mind is cultivated, and his manners are affable; but he is essentially false and perfidious. He has all the pedantry of the rhetorician, and his ambition is to be considered a man of wit. I think him incapable either of a generous impulse or of a strong resolution. He has never forgotten, he will never pardon an

Louisiana, which had formerly belonged to France, had been ceded to Spain in virtue of a secret clause of the treaty of 1763, to the great discontentment of the inhabitants, and also to the regret of the Versailles Cabinet, which for a long time continued to be in communication with this country, but finally forgot it. England had never ceased to covet this province, which adjoined her American possessions. Our maritime and commercial cities, in the interests of our shipping to the Antilles, hoped that an opportunity of regaining this colony might present itself. The First Consul, having been made acquainted with this wish, and with the future in view, began negotiations with the Court of Madrid tending to its retrocession. By a treaty between France and Spain, towards the end of 1800, we were once more put in possession of Louisiana. When the rupture of the Peace of Amiens became imminent, Napoleon considered, and rightly so, that

injury, a wrong, a reproach. He fears truth, and he fears death. Surrounded by ruins and by flatterers, he has preserved of his old estate only the pride and the vices which brought about its forfeiture. No matter how heavily misfortune may weigh upon him, he dares not look it in the face. And so, however rigorous adversity may be towards him, he will be justified only in the minds of mean and cowardly men. He will be seen to die in the bed of the outlaw, after having worn out the pity and exhausted the generosity of every king. This prince trembles at the sight of a bundle of pikes, or of a sheaf of arrows, yet he has always the name of Henri IV. on his lips. Full of intrigue in times of peace, unskilful in times of war, jealous of literary triumphs, and not less greedy for riches than anxious to parade his person, the enemy of his true friends and the slave of his courtiers, umbrageous and distrustful, superstitious and revengeful, double-faced at all times in his politics, and false even in the affections of his heart, such is the Comte de Lille, that prince whom fortune placed so near to the first throne in the world, without bestowing upon him any one of the qualities which command respect or which win the hearts of the people. Doubtless, even in the happiest times, he would have let the reins of power slip from his hands. His reign would have been a reign of favourites, and France would have had to support all the pettiness of King James, all the profusion of Henri III."

our naval forces would not be able to protect all our colonies against the superior English fleet, and that the conquest of Louisiana, especially, would be a matter of little difficulty to England. Foreseeing even that the first operation of the campaign would be an attack on this colony, he wished to put it beyond England's reach, and at the same time to destroy all England's hopes of ever gaining possession of it, by ceding it in its integrity to the United States. In consequence he caused proposals to be made to the Americans to the effect that Louisiana should be handed over to them, in return for a money indemnity. These funds, he considered, would help to pay the cost of the war which he was about to wage with England.

An American ambassador had been sent to Paris to demand indemnities for seizures which had been made on American ships during peace. The United States Government did not expect the acquisition of the entire colony, limiting their hopes to the possession of New Orleans, and the American ambassador listened to these proposals with a certain amount of distrust, supposing that they might cloak some desire to evade giving him the satisfaction which he claimed. In the meanwhile a new envoy, a Mr. Monroe, arrived in Paris, vested with full powers. M. Barbé-Marbois, the French negotiator, immediately approached him. Mr. Livingstone, the first envoy, had offered thirty millions as the price of Louisiana, M. de Marbois demanding eighty millions. In the end the American envoys agreed to the price of eighty millions, but stipulated that of this sum twenty millions should be applied in indemnifying the American citizens for their losses, so that the purchase-money would be reduced to sixty millions.

Napoleon, who at first would have been satisfied with fifty millions, now desired that the twenty millions reserved for the settlement of indemnities, should also be paid into the treasury. But the news which he received of the English armaments, and the impossible claims which the English Government kept putting forward, rendered him less exacting, and induced him to hurry on the termination of the convention. He feared lest the rupture might break out before the cession had been accomplished, in which case he would only have had an empty title-deed to offer the Americans. Two conventions were signed on April 13th, 1803, the first relating to the payment of the price of the cession, so as not to mix up the abandonment of France's sovereignty with a question of a money sale. Another deed stipulated the conditions of the cession. Napoleon caused an express clause to be inserted in this deed, to the effect that the inhabitants of Louisiana should be maintained and protected in the enjoyment of their liberties and of their properties, and in the exercise of the religion which they professed.

The English Government was profoundly irritated on seeing the Americans become masters of Louisiana. Our adversaries lost, in this way, all hope of ever regaining their preponderance in America. Napoleon's foresight was thus entirely justified. Only a few days had elapsed since the signing of the convention when war was declared. But Louisiana had become American property, and England could undertake nothing against this colony.

England hastened on the rupture. Ten thousand fresh sailors were enrolled. The militia was called out, under the lying pretext that formidable armaments were being prepared against England in the ports of France and Holland. In vain were the most convincing explanations given to the English ambassador; the minds of the English Ministers had been made up. It was evident that in signing the Peace of Amiens the English Government had only wished for an armistice with the mental reservation of breaking the peace as soon as it suited its interests to do so.

The unexpected retirement of Mr. Pitt had given reason for the hope that England wished for reconciliation with France. As a matter of fact Pitt had recognized that the man who had declared eternal war with France could not sign a treaty of peace with her. His self-esteem would have suffered too greatly at being forced to accept conditions so different from those for which he had once hoped. He had accordingly thought it his duty to retire, his successor being one of his adherents, Mr. Addington, son of the doctor of Lord Chatham (Pitt's father). Mr. Addington had been Pitt's schoolfellow, and had remained his friend. Pitt, although absent, continued to direct the English Ministry. The experiment which he had tried had succeeded. Shortly after the Treaty of Amiens, England, which at first had accepted peace favourably, found it onerous. She had enjoyed the sole monopoly of commerce; she alone during the war had drawn profit from the sea and the colonies, peace gave her competitors and reduced her profits. The First Consul had sent his aide-de-camp, Lauriston, to London, as the bearer of the ratification of the treaty. He had been received in London with enthusiasm. The horses in his carriage had been unyoked, and he had been drawn in triumph to the house in Downing Street;

but neither the Government nor the big traders shared these sentiments with the people.

France had scrupulously fulfilled all the engagements which she had assumed on signing the peace. The kingdom of Naples, and the Roman States, had been evacuated in less than three months, whilst in England no arrangements whatever had been made for the evacuation of the island of Malta; the intention of prolonging the occupation was even hinted at. The English newspapers insulted the Head of the French Government with the most spiteful articles, and scattered broadcast the most lying reports. The hatred of France burst out even in the Houses of Parliament. Articles in the *Moniteur*, almost all dictated by the First Consul, replied with dignity and indignation to these venomous attacks. Napoleon was too susceptible to the libels of the journalists. Offences from a hostile country and government could have been explained. But the tolerance, the protection even, which the English pamphleteers found in a country which had recently been reconciled to France, showed him how little anxious the English Government was to maintain friendly relations with him. They denoted very hostile feelings towards France. Napoleon has been blamed for the words which he addressed to Lord Whitworth during the audience at which he received the diplomatic corps. It had not indeed been admitted till then, that the Head of the Government should treat with foreign ambassadors, otherwise than in private audiences. Sovereigns indeed only treated with the governments of other countries through their ambassadors. This violation of a constant practice could not but profoundly offend a government whose conscience could not bear the public exposure of its politics. The bitter indignation which the iniquitous proceedings of the English Government excited in Napoleon's mind justified such an attack to a certain extent. It is none the less true that this scene produced, and could not but produce, a deplorable effect, and that it would have been much better for a man of Napoleon's greatness to have abstained from it.

The French Government complained bitterly of the tolerance accorded to these indecent attacks and vile calumnies. The London Cabinet replied that owing to the liberty of the press in England it was impossible to do justice to these well-founded grievances. A French newspaper written by Peltier, and the organ of the riff-raff amongst the exiles, gained notoriety by the violence and the atrocity of its provocations. At the request of the French ambassador, Peltier was prosecuted for incitation to murder. The pamphleteer was defended by Mr. Mackintosh, M.P., and a small fine only was inflicted, which was never paid. This celebrated barrister was, the same year, appointed to one of the most important posts in the law-courts in British India.

Amongst the pamphlets which Peltier's sheet—*L'Ambigu*—published, the one which provoked the most serious objection on the part of the French Government, was an ode entitled "*La Napoléone*", written in his youth by Charles Nodier. This circumstance prompts me to point out how greatly the persecution, to which it is pretended that this writer was subjected by Napoleon, has been exaggerated. I even believe that he greatly exaggerated its importance himself, and that he sought after emotions in the imaginary persecutions, of which, in all good faith, he imagined himself to be the hero. I know of no measure taken against him which emanated from the First Consul's cabinet. Nodier was a man of imagination, and full of chivalrous ideas, which prompted him to take sides against the victor, no matter who the vanquished might be,—republicans, exiles, Chouans, or friends of the fallen government. His youthful attachments and affections mixed him up in Royalist intrigues. The overthrow of his hopes inspired him with a hatred against the First Consul, on Napoleon's accession to power, which the establishment of the imperial government by no means helped to assuage. This antipathy of his he betrayed in "*La Napoléone*", a virulent philippic, which was reproduced by the newspapers of all the hostile governments, and which naturally attracted the attention of the police to its author. But it would be attaching too much importance to the attacks of a man, who had talents no doubt, but who was certainly obscure, to admit any possibility of a personal and continued struggle between so feeble an adversary and the head of a powerful state. Napoleon had something else to do besides wasting his time over the impotent hatreds which his person inspired. He could but commit them to the vigilance of the authorities, which is what he did in this case.

The persecution of which Nodier complained, was not, moreover, a very violent one, seeing that after a detention of a few months at Sainte-Pelagie he was sent back home to Besançon. The exaltation of his ideas led him on to commit fresh acts of provocation, which exposed him to further disgrace. His perseverance in his hostility, his relations with angry men, his love of independence, and a poetical imagination, made him quit his retreat to indulge his vague reveries in the mountains of the Jura and of Switzerland. After leading this wandering life for some time, he was allowed to return freely to Besançon, where he was even taken under the protection of the Prefect, Jean de Bry. He obtained an authorization to open a class of literature, and was allowed to live, thanks to the indulgence of the authorities, without molestation. He afterwards went to Illyria, where he became the secretary of his former persecutor, Fouché, formerly Minister of Police, who was at that time governor of these provinces. He occupied various lucrative posts, at that time, in the imperial government, and even edited a paper under the protection of the various governors who succeeded each other in the Illyrian provinces. The events of 1814 brought him back to France. I have perhaps spoken at too great length about M. Nodier, but, in entering into all these particulars, I wanted to show, how in reality the rigours, of which he pretended himself to be the victim, will not bear investigation.

I take this opportunity of saying that the existence of the alleged secret societies in the army, the history of which this same Nodier published in 1815, is entirely imaginary, and may be attributed alone to his love of romance and to his craze for conspiracies. The Emperor, in spite of all his sources of information, who was never ignorant of anything that went on in the army, was never able to find any traces of mysterious associations, of hidden compacts, of sects of Philadelphians, or others, under the direction of a single chief or of a secret council. Napoleon's powerful hand, which energetically restrained all those inclinations for trouble and disorder which are hidden under the words liberty, or independence, and his vigilant eye prevented the formation of secret associations. If certain hidden attempts in this direction attained some semblance of execution, it is not until he had gone, or towards the end of his reign, when the elements of his force and his power were dissolving under the baneful influence of his reverses, and when he was no longer served with the same zeal. It is only, therefore, by a propensity natural to romantic minds, that the attempt has been made to connect—as proceeding from a common starting-point—rare and isolated facts, or solitary attempts, which bore absolutely no relation to one another.

This digression on Charles Nodier must not lead me to forget an event which occurred in the midst of the grave preoccupations of the time; an event which might have had fatal consequences. In the beginning of 1803, the First Consul, being then at St. Cloud, wanted to drive a carriage with four young horses. Madame Bonaparte and her daughter Hortense were in the carriage. Napoleon mounted the box, in front of the steps of the St. Cloud parterre. On arriving at the railings which separate this parterre from the private park he lost control over the horses, which were young and fiery. They dashed up against the railings with such violence that Napoleon was thrown from his seat and hurled ten paces away, on to the gravel. I had watched his departure with some slight anxiety, but had been re-assured as I saw him driving quietly away. A sudden cry and the sight of the stoppage of the carriage made me fear that some accident had happened. I ran up, and arrived in time to see the First Consul seated on the ground trying to collect his thoughts. Fortunately this fall had no bad consequences; no bones were broken, or sprained; and there was no reason to fear any internal injury. Napoleon came off with a sprain and a few scratches, and was obliged to carry his right arm in a sling, which prevented him from signing any papers for a few days afterwards.

Lord Whitworth, who was appointed English ambassador to France in the month of June, did not arrive in Paris till the middle of November. General Andréossy, who was only awaiting the departure of the English ambassador from London, set out at once as soon as he heard that Lord Whitworth had started. The latter's mission, to all appearance, was to bring about a rupture of the peace. After the hostile proceedings and the entirely unwarranted recriminations, particulars of which are known, the English Government crowned the series of its aggressions with a very clumsy manifesto, which was based on pretexts of transparent falseness. This declaration of war had, according to the British custom, been preceded by an order that not only French warships, but the French merchant service and ports were to be treated as hostile.

Open hostilities had thus preceded the rupture of peace. French vessels had been captured in our ports and on the ocean, and a general embargo had been laid on all ships belonging to France and to Holland, as well as on their crews and cargoes, even before the declaration of war was made public. It was to retort on these illegal and unjust seizures of men and ships, carried out in violation of all international law by command of the British Government, that the First

Consul ordered the arrest of all Englishmen, both civil and military, who were found on French territory at the time of the declaration of war.

Parleys, however, continued with the English ambassador, who had remained in Paris. The First Consul made every effort to maintain peace, and declared that whilst he could not consent to any derogation from the Treaty of Amiens, he would give England any guarantees of safety which might be considered necessary. The English Ministry only replied with proposals which were contrary to the formal text of the treaty. The First Consul, taking his stand on the terms of the Treaty alone, had appealed to the arbitration of the powers which had signed it. He had specially insisted that the island of Malta should be handed over, to the keeping of the Emperor of Russia. The Emperor had answered the proposal of arbitration with an offer to act as mediator. He agreed to accept the charge of the island for a period of ten years, and asked that its government, which was to have been vested in the Grand Master of the Order, should be placed under the control of the commander of the Russian garrison.

On the 25th of April, Lord Whitworth presented as the ultimatum of his government—this ultimatum being communicated not in writing but by word of mouth—that England should continue to occupy Malta for ten years, and further that Lampedusa, a small island in the Mediterranean, which belonged to the kingdom of Naples, should be handed over. The ambassador declared at the same time, that, unless this ultimatum were accepted in seven days, he was ordered to demand his passports. The First Consul, opposing to these high-handed manners his constant desire to maintain peace, proposed to entrust the care of Malta to Russia, until the final settlement of the various differences between France and England. Lord Whitworth replied that the refusal of Russia to accept the charge of the island rendered any such step impossible; which was false, seeing that the Emperor had consented to take charge of it. The English Ministry, thinking no doubt that Napoleon only demanded the evacuation of Malta to save his dignity, then proposed that he should consent, by a secret clause to be added to the treaty, to allow the English troops to remain in Malta. This subterfuge was rejected by the First Consul as impracticable, and as unworthy of France. At last, wishing to exhaust every means of conciliation, he devised a last expedient which consisted in allowing the English to retain Malta for an indefinite period, on condition that the French troops should occupy the Gulf of Taranto. Napoleon considered Taranto, as regards its position in the Mediterranean, the equivalent of Malta. It seemed to him that a French occupation of Taranto, accorded by treaty, would prompt the powers to interfere with a view to force the English to evacuate Egypt, so that the French might leave the kingdom of Naples. But England would make no concessions on this point, and refused at any price to allow her soldiers to leave the island of Malta. France, on the other hand, was determined to go to war rather than abandon to the English so important a position in the very heart of the Mediterranean. Lord Whitworth refused to even listen to the statement of the arrangement proposed by the First Consul, and said that, since the *sine quâ non* conditions of his government were refused, he must imperatively demand the return of his passports. And, in effect, he left Paris and went to Calais, to await the arrival of General Andréossy at Dover.

The Russian government, in accepting the care of Malta, had asked, in its plan of conciliation, that Lampedusa should be ceded to England. To have agreed to this would have been to have given this power, if by any means Malta again came under her domination, two impregnable positions in the Mediterranean; for Lampedusa would have become, in a very short time, impregnable in England's hands. Now Napoleon had always declared that France would not suffer England to have the mastery of the Mediterranean. Russia demanded—besides the evacuation of Switzerland and Italy by the French, conditions which had not been stipulated in the Treaty of Amiens—an establishment in Italy which should compensate the King of Sardinia for the loss of Piedmont, etc., etc. Russia's partiality for England was made clear by these proposals. As a matter of fact the Chancellor Woronzoff was the declared partisan of England, as was also Count Marcoff, the Russian ambassador to France, who professed the most anti-French sentiments. He used to pay professional libellers to bedaub the government and the person of the First Consul with insults and calumnies. He was moreover the censor of his own master, and used to say: "The Emperor has his will, but the Russian nation has her will also." The First Consul, who had suffered the antagonistic attitude of the Russian envoy during the peace, considered that his presence in Paris after war had been declared, the termination of which could not be foreseen, was not only disagreeable but dangerous. The recall of this agent was consequently demanded, and he was replaced in Paris by a *chargé d'affaires*. At the same time the French Government recalled General Hédouville, who left behind him at St. Petersburg, M. de Rayneval, also a *chargé d'affaires*.

The First Consul, who was on the best terms with Prussia, thought it well to strengthen the bonds which united the two countries. He felt that, in the presence of so bitter an enemy as England, he stood in need of a close and stable alliance, which could be made use of both offensively and defensively. What, above all, to use his own words, was desired by him, was "an evident, powerful, and complete association, the mere announcement of which should be to Europe a pledge of the stability of peace, and of the permanence of the *status quo* of the contracting parties, and which should anew warn England to look beyond the present war." Napoleon had to choose between Austria and Prussia, but his preference was for the latter. It was accordingly to the Prussian Government that he proposed an offensive and defensive alliance.

The rupture of the Peace of Amiens disturbed Napoleon in the midst of the calm of a peaceful life, to which he was unfortunately not destined by fate. Had his indefatigable activity not been turned aside to another object, what prodigies might not have been effected during the time of peace, by the creative power of his genius, and the ascendency which he owed to the splendour of an incomparable fame. He had bound together the olive-branch of peace and the laurels of war. The whole of Europe had been pacified. What glory remained for his hands to gather? To encourage agriculture, industries, the sciences and the arts, and to render France as happy by her pacific development as he had made her powerful and feared by his victories. But these dreams of peace and prosperity, in which he loved to indulge, were destined to fade away before the vast and stormy career which he was called upon to follow. If any illusion as to his future had ever entered his strong and penetrating mind, it was from that day forth banished for ever. The treacherous conduct of England made a profound impression on this susceptible mind, so sensitive alike to reciprocate straightforwardness of conduct, and so full of the feelings of national pride and honour. The odious machinations directed by the English Ministry, or paid for with its gold, against the power and the life of the First Consul; the irruption of sixty assassins, vomited out on to our shores—foul remnants of our civil wars—to consummate a cowardly and criminal attempt; the hidden intrigues carried on with a view to suborning French generals who had distinguished themselves by their victories; falsehood and corruption entering at every door, filled him with the loftiest indignation. He was forced to acknowledge that there was neither armistice nor peace to be hoped for from this irreconcilable enemy, and he had nothing further to rely on than the superiority of his power and unusual means, for it was war to the death. It became, from that moment forward, his sole occupation to throw back on England all the harm that she essayed to inflict upon us. His habits changed; his genius, which had appeared to slumber, awoke, full of courage and daring. He raised himself to the height of the formidable circumstances which our eternal enemies had created, and indeed rose superior to them. His activity became prodigious, and was all-sufficient. From that time forward a new life began for him, a life of action, of combat; a life given up to the hardest labours, to dangers of every kind, to the most fruitful and the most audacious of conceptions; a life from which no diversions of any kind were even for a moment allowed to turn him aside. Like an intrepid athlete, he entered upon this gigantic struggle, which was to produce such marvels—to raise him so high, and to cast him down so low.

The arrest of Englishmen travelling in France at the time of the declaration of war, was an energetic measure which can only be justified by the necessity of taking reprisals on a power which had committed a monstrous and intolerable violation of international law. This first act was speedily followed by the conquest of the Electorate of Hanover.

Orders were given to a French army assembled in Holland to enter Germany. It marched with forced marches, under the command of Marshal Mortier, against the Electorate of Hanover. Leaving Nimeguen on May 26th, this army entered the capital of the Electorate on June 5th. A convention was concluded at Subligen in virtue of which the French troops occupied Hanover as far as the Elbe. The Hanoverian army withdrew to Lauenburg, with the undertaking not to fight against France during the war. All forts, artillery, munitions of all kinds, and all treasure-chests, and other property belonging to the King of England, were handed over to the French army. The King having refused to ratify the convention, our army pursued the Hanoverian troops into their retreat in Lauenburg, and disarmed them. The English Government had sent transport ships over to embark these troops, which formed an army of sixteen thousand men, but the transport ships arrived too late.

The University of Göttingen, alarmed by the menacing approach of war, had applied for protection to the First Consul through the celebrated Heine,* begging that measures might be taken for the safety of the people, and the property of the University, and that orders might be given to prevent any occurrences which might trouble the calm and quiet so necessary to study. The First Consul ordered the Minister of War to reply favourably, and to instruct Marshal Mortier to protect the universities in general, and the University of Göttingen in particular.

Napoleon had made up his mind to attempt a descent upon England, so as to dictate terms of peace in London itself. He applied himself to combine the best means whereby an army of one hundred and fifty thousand men could be shipped across the channel, that being the number of men which he considered necessary for such an expedition. He decided upon the use of small ships suitable for navigation, fitted as was requisite, and adapted to the ports at which they were to land. These ships were divided into gun-boats, sloops carrying guns, and barges. Some vessels of larger dimensions were added for the transport of horses, artillery, and provisions. A certain number of large fishing-smacks scattered along the

* What "celebrated Heine" does Baron de Méneval mean? The poet Heine (born Dec. 13th, 1799,) was barely three years old at the time, and too young, in spite even of his great precocity, to act as intermediary in such a matter.—R. H. S.

coast were purchased. All the ports, and even the river-basins, were used as docks, for the construction of the necessary boats. In a spontaneous glow of enthusiasm, the departments, the townships, and the corporations presented the government with gunboats, flat-bottomed boats, sloops, and frigates. The merchants of Paris set the example by voting funds for the construction of a vessel of one hundred and twenty guns, which bore the name of *Commerce de Paris*. The principal corporations, and even private individuals, paid for the construction of vessels of all sizes, destined to make up the national flotilla.

The First Consul made the necessary arrangements for the organization of six camps, to be formed on the sea coast. These camps were intended to supply the troops to be embarked on board the flotilla, whose mission it was to carry into English territory the implacable war which the English Government was waging against us.

Wishing to attack England from various points at one and the same time, Napoleon gave orders for an expedition into Ireland. He appointed for this purpose eighteen thousand men, who formed the camp at Brest. General Marmont, who was in command of an army of from twenty-two to twenty-five thousand men in Holland, was to embark his troops with the same destination in view. The First Consul had decided to place these two armies under the command of Marshal Augereau. An understanding had been come to with Irish refugees in France, and also with Irishmen in Ireland. Augereau was to march straight upon Dublin. In case there was any delay on the part of the Irish insurrectionists, he was to take his stand, and, after having rallied General Marmont, to wait for the landing of the main army. After having prescribed the necessary arrangements for assuring the defence and safety of France both within and without, in the new situation in which we were placed by the unjust aggression of England, the First Consul, accompanied by Madame Bonaparte, left for the northern departments, one month after the proclamation of hostilities. He visited all the ports on our shore of the English Channel and of the German Ocean, the manufacturing towns of Picardy, Belgium, and the Liége district, stayed several days at Brussels and at Antwerp, and returned home to St. Cloud, on August 10th, by way of Rheims and Soissons. This six weeks' journey was employed in preparations for the organization of the flotilla, and in assembling the invading army at Boulogne. The men and the materials of this expedition were the objects of Napoleon's greatest care. Everywhere in the course of his journey he found an exasperation against the English, which rendered the war a national war, and he urged on the populations of the various districts to assist the government in the construction and the equipment of the fleet. This glow of patriotic enthusiasm had spread over the whole of France. Apart from the vessels for which funds had been voted, and the number of which, had they all been built, would have exceeded the requirements of the expedition, patriotic gifts and voluntary subscriptions supplied a great part of the funds necessary for the arming and maintenance of the flotilla. More than two thousand vessels of every kind were collected together in the harbour of Boulogne and in the auxiliary ports or basins, and the beds of neighbouring rivers were dug out and enlarged, establishments were formed, and the necessary works carried out to adapt them to the purpose for which they were intended. Considerable works of every kind were executed to protect the divisions of the flotilla which were scattered along the coast. In a word, no precaution was neglected to render the execution of this memorable enterprise, in which the genius of Napoleon reached its full development, worthy of its conception.

The assembling at one and the same place, of so large a number of ships armed for war, gave rise to the belief that it was with the flotilla alone that the invasion of England was to be attempted. In order to put the enemy on a wrong scent, Napoleon conceived the idea of assembling in distant waters, by combined operations, the French and Spanish squadrons of Toulon, Rochefort, Cadiz, Ferrol and Brest—in number sixty line vessels—to make them return suddenly at the right time to Boulogne, and to hold the sea during a space of fourteen days. Thanks to the presence of these squadrons, masters of the sea by their numerical superiority, in the waters of the Channel, the flotilla would be able to cross and effect the landing in England of the army of one hundred and sixty thousand men which had been collected in our ports, and notably at Boulogne. The First Consul had decided upon this plan, after having discussed various alternatives with his Minister of Marine.

Napoleon considered Admiral Latouche-Tréville, as the right man to carry out an enterprise which demanded, on the part of the man who should engage in it, great resolution and skill. In the letters which he wrote to him on the subject, he asked him to think over the great work which he was to attempt, and to let him hear his opinion, before signing final orders on the subject, as to what would be the best way to carry it out. He informed him that he had appointed him inspector-general of the Mediterranean littoral, and added that he ardently hoped that the success of the great expedition against England would put him in a position to raise the admiral to such a degree of honour and title, that the admiral could have nothing further to wish for.

Napoleon at the same time communicated to him the number and the positions of the vessels which the commander-in-chief of the naval forces would have to rally under his command, and informed him of the position of the English cruisers and squadrons. The First Consul drew this information from the reports of his bureau of foreign statistics, an office which was so well organized that he knew the exact state of the English navy, as well as it was known at the Admiralty in London. "We possess, at this moment," he added, "between Étaples, Boulogne, Wimereux and Ambleteuse, two thousand gunboats, sloops, barges, etc., able to transport one hundred and forty thousand men and ten thousand horses. Let us be masters of the Channel for six hours, and we shall be the masters of the world."

Napoleon desired that the entire operation should be carried out before the winter. "Supposing that the Admiral can start before July 30th, it is probable that he would not reach Boulogne before the middle of September, at a time when the night is sufficiently long, and when the weather is rarely bad for any length of time."

Whilst planning this great expedition, the First Consul arranged with the Minister of Marine for a series of other maritime expeditions to engage the attention of the enemy, to reinforce and to revictual our colonies, to seize upon insular positions which could serve as putting-into ports for our ships, and to do all the harm possible to English commerce. The organization of these different maritime campaigns was the subject of almost daily correspondence between Napoleon and the Minister of Marine.

These expeditions were carried out with varying results; but, to tell the truth, they did not realize the object that Napoleon had in view.

I shall speak but briefly of the homage that was paid to Napoleon during his journey in the northern departments of France; of the flattering and magnificent receptions accorded to him, and to his wife, who accompanied him; of the triumphal arches under which they passed; of the guards of honour, selected from amongst the most notable families in the towns through which they travelled; of the richness of their uniforms; of the young girls, dressed in white, who presented flowers; of the speeches made by the civil, military, and ecclesiastical authorities; of the *Te Deums* which were chanted; of the illuminations, balls, and concerts; of the triumphal procession, so dear to the people of Antwerp, in which were figured historical, mystical, profane, or fantastic personages, in a series of strange tableaux; in one word, of the extraordinary enthusiasm of the town and country people, crowding together to hail with their cries and their wishes for success, the energetic adversary of England. The newspapers of the time have reported these occurrences, and in no way have they exaggerated the truth.

Napoleon's principal object was to satisfy himself *de visu* of the maritime resources offered by the departments adjoining the coast, and to stimulate with fresh vigour the armament against England. With this object in view he visited, as was his custom, the ports, dockyards, arsenals, and batteries, giving long audiences to the civil, maritime, and military authorities, occupying himself with improvements, and the reform of abuses, and sparing neither encouragements nor rewards. This part of the First Consul's journey was described by the *Moniteur*, and this description is, in every sense of the word, historically trustworthy.

M. de Roquelaure, * who was at that time Archbishop of Mechlin, came to Antwerp to present his respects to the First Consul and Madame Bonaparte. I often saw this prelate again in 1813, in Archchancellor Cambacérès's drawing-room. He was a straight and sturdy old man, who bore with the vigour of middle age the weight of his eighty-two years. He was received and treated with particular distinction. M. de Roquelaure owed this flattering reception to the wise way in which he administered his diocese, and to the spirit of concord and union which he fostered there. He was a man of great intelligence, and had been a member of the French Academy. He resigned his see four or five years after Napoleon's visit to Antwerp, and was appointed Canon of the Chapter of St. Denis. Abbé de Pradt, at that time Bishop of Poitiers, succeeded him at Mechlin. When I saw M. de Roquelaure again

* Son of the Duc de Roquelaure who set the fashion of and gave his name to a kind of coat, known as the "*roquelaure*".—R. H. S.

at the Archchancellor's he was more than ninety-two years old. Age had but little changed him. His sight had weakened, but his legs were as strong as ever. He was always seen standing. His memory had become curiously impaired. It broke off at the time when he was Bishop of Senlis, and first almoner to King Louis XV., high in favour with this king, and honoured with the patronage of the king's sisters. He had no recollection whatever of the events of the Revolution. Comte Siméon was an even more remarkable man, for at a greater age than that of M. de Roquelaure he remained in the enjoyment of all his faculties.

It was at Brussels, on the eve of his departure from that city, that the First Consul received M. Lombard, privy councillor to the King of Prussia, who brought him a letter from his sovereign. The purport of this letter was to compliment the head of the consular government on the occasion of his arrival in Brussels, and to express the wish that steps might be taken to relieve the townships in Lower Saxony of the charges caused by the presence of the French troops there. Nor was M. Lombard's mission confined to furthering Prussian interests alone. He was to endeavour to find out what were Napoleon's intentions as to the limits which he proposed to give to his occupation of Hanover and some other portions of the German States. These matters had been suggested to the Prussian Government by Russia. Napoleon, who had at that time one only interest, namely an alliance with Prussia, received M. Lombard in the friendliest fashion, conversed with him at great length, and showed him real confidence. He spoke of the value which he attached to the friendship of the King of Prussia; he expressed his sincere desire to ally himself closely with this monarch, and to advance the interests of Prussia; and, with this in view, to do whatever might please the king. His interest, equally with that of the powers of the north, was to put an end to the maritime tyranny of England, and the only means of accomplishing this object was to close all the ports of Germany against her. He asked that Prussia should definitely agree with France, so that their mutual alliance might be genuine and effective. These explanations, made with that winning charm which was so irresistible in Napoleon, produced a great impression on the mind of the Prussian envoy. His report of their conversation delighted the King of Prussia, but, with his usual want of decision, and yielding disposition, the king feared to engage himself too far with France. He replied by making insufficient offers, and proposals of neutrality, and in the end declined the alliance, whilst proposing to postpone its completion.

M. Lombard was a French refugee of the French colony in Berlin. A distinguished littérateur and statesman, he had been brought up in the doctrine of neutrality. Faithful to this doctrine he made use of the credit in which he stood with his sovereign to preach neutrality in the king's council; his political sentiments and his inclination for France, from which he had sprung, have very unjustly caused him to be accused of having sold himself to the French Government. His retirement, in 1806, on the eve of Prussia's call to arms, was a disaster for his country.

Whenever the First Consul wrote to the king he used to say to me, laughing: "We must be careful about the style of our letters. The King of Prussia has men in his cabinet who know how to speak and to write French very well." He referred to M. Lombard.

Cardinal Caprara, Legate *a Latere* from the Papal See, accompanied the First Consul on this journey. The presence of this prelate, distinguished as he was for his piety, his spirit of toleration, and his lofty character, had been deemed necessary in a country troubled with religious quarrels, which his conciliatory spirit was eminently qualified to appease. At Namur the Cardinal should have been lodged at the house of the bishop of the diocese, and, as a matter of fact, the episcopal palace had been got ready for his reception. But from reports received on the irregular life led by the bishop, and on his gallant adventures, it was feared lest the legate should find himself, in such an abode, in strange company. This occurrence brought forth a number of satirical verses, and allusions which, till then, had only been whispered in Namur. In consequence of the discredit which was thus thrown on the bishop, he was asked to resign his see. This he did, but only after expressly stipulating that his episcopal revenues should be paid to him during his lifetime.

On his return from this journey Napoleon spent the months of September and October at St. Cloud, occupying himself with his accustomed ardour on the details of the Boulogne expedition, on internal affairs, and on the solution of the various negotiations which had been commenced with the different European ministries, in consequence of the renewal of hostilities with England.

In the first days of the month of November of this same year, 1803, the First Consul made a second journey, which lasted a fortnight, to Boulogne. The object of this journey was to visit the ports of Boulogne and of Wimereux, and to inspect the works which he had ordered to facilitate the assembling of the various divisions of the flotilla. He spent a day and a night in the Roads on board a gunboat, and was present, always in the front line, at an engagement between the frigates of the English cruisers, under the command of Admiral Keith, and a division of the French flotilla. The fire from our sloops, and that of the mortars on our coast batteries, forced the enemy to retire. Six weeks later Napoleon left Paris suddenly, to undertake a new journey along the French coast, which lasted ten days. Only two hours notice was given of this journey, the horses being ordered in the name of General Bessières. The preceding journey had been as secretly prepared, that time under the name of General Duroc. These precautions were taken in consequence of a suspected plot to kidnap the person of Napoleon.

Whilst Napoleon was occupied with these preparations, whilst all the efforts of France were employed on the naval war, and her frontiers on the Adige and the Rhine were defenceless, Austria was marching her troops, under false pretences, towards Bavaria, Swabia, and Switzerland, reinforcing her army in Italy at the same time. The Russians, on their side, were assembling armies in Podolia, behind the Vistula, and in Lithuania; camps were being formed in Livonia, ready to descend on Pomerania, to act in concert with the Swedes and the English. Four men out of every five hundred in Russia were called to arms. And, finally, in England bodies of troops were being formed on the downs, to be shipped to Cuxhaven to join the Russian and Swedish troops. The Court of Naples was also preparing to assemble its army. Napoleon had his eye on all these movements. He took his precautions for the defence of Italy, and spared no pains to enlighten Austria on the pacific nature of his intentions towards her, and to point out to her where her real interests lay.

Marshal Mortier, having assured the submission of Hanover, returned to Paris, where he was appointed one of the four generals of the guards. He was replaced in the command of the army in Hanover by General Bernadotte.

During the First Consul's absence, his sister Pauline, widow of General Leclerc, who had died at San Domingo in 1802, married Prince Camille Borghese, a member of one of the most illustrious and richest families in Rome. This prince, who at a very early age had embraced the principles of the French Revolution, had served in the ranks of our army in Italy during the memorable campaigns of General Bonaparte. He had attached himself to the commander-in-chief, who in his turn had taken him into his affections. The union of his sister with Prince Borghese was accordingly entirely to Napoleon's taste. He received the overtures made to him on this subject with the greatest satisfaction. The marriage was celebrated at Mortfontaine, at the house of Joseph Bonaparte. Pauline followed her new husband to Rome, where, a few months later, she lost her son Dermide, who was

General Bonaparte's godson. On Napoleon's accession to the Empire, a senatus consultum conferred on Prince Borghese the rights of a French citizen and prince.

On the same day on which the First Consul returned from his ten days' journey to Boulogne, the Legislative Body was convoked. The session had been opened, according to the usual custom, by the Minister of the Interior. Apart from the new laws which had to be submitted to the sanction of Parliament, it was necessary that the two chambers should be ready for any emergency. A vast conspiracy, of which the threads had not yet been gathered together, was suspected. It was vaguely known that Georges and his gang had entered, or were about to enter France, and that some of the conspirators had slipped into Paris, where they were lying in hiding. The investigations of the police to discover their hiding-places had so far remained unsuccessful, and general anxiety prevailed.

It would be difficult to imagine the anxieties, resulting in sleepless nights, which assailed the First Consul, as I myself can testify, during the month of January, 1804, when plots, of which he knew nothing definite, were being woven around him, and against which he fought in the dark; when he felt the earth trembling beneath his feet, and each breath of air seemed to bring with it the menace of some hidden danger. His courage was not abashed thereby. More fruitful in resource than his own police, who wasted their time in routine and impotent formalities, his clear-sightedness led him on to important discoveries, and guided his hand to seize the hidden threads of the conspiracy.

Profound was his indignation caused by the odious intrigues to which he was exposed, and by Pitt's answer to those who reproached him with wishing for perpetual war: "We do not want it eternal, but only for a lifetime." A perpetual mental strain seemed from that time forward to disturb the calm and serenity of Napoleon's mind, without, however, changing the kindliness of his nature, if such an expression may be made use of without exaggeration. It was not that he feared for his personal safety. In this respect he possessed an optimism which nothing could shake, and every open or secret precaution was repugnant to him, for he believed in his star, and abandoned himself to his fate with entire confidence. But I had opportunities for noticing that the vexation which he felt used to manifest itself in outbursts of anger, not indeed when in his family, but before witnesses, where such outbursts were not wasted. It was always in public that his displeasure burst out, usually in the form of reprimands, which were often severe, but which were always limited to words. He thought that these scenes were necessary to keep vigilance awake, and to stimulate a zeal which had to increase with the difficulties of the circumstances.

The plots which were brewed in the interior of France were favoured on our frontiers by the machinations concerted between the English Ministers and the French princes who were in refuge in London. The instigators of these conspiracies were the English ambassadors to the smaller Courts, Sir Francis Drake at Munich, and Spencer Smith, brother to the admiral of that name, at Stuttgart. Wickham, the English agent, had returned to Berne where he was playing anew the part of corrupter which, in 1795, 1796, and 1797, he had played towards Pichegru. Taylor was playing the same part at Cassel.

A man whose extreme opinions under the Reign of Terror had brought him into suspicion with the government—Mehée de Latouche was his name—made good his escape from Oléron, to which he had been banished, to England, passing by Guernsey. He passed himself off on Lord Hawkesbury, the Minister, and the exiles who formed the council of the Comte d'Artois, as the envoy of Republican malcontents in Paris, and professed to be anxious to atone for former errors by serving the Bourbons and working towards the overthrow of the First Consul. He won the confidence both of Lord Hawkesbury and the exiles, and was sent on to Sir Francis Drake in Munich, as charged with the execution of a great conspiracy against France. This agent gave him instructions and, supplying him with money, sent him on to Paris to the imaginary Jacobin committee, the existence of which Mehée had asserted, there to contrive the best means of getting rid of Bonaparte. Mehée, on his arrival at Strasburg, being anxious, as he declared, to secure permission to return to France, revealed his business to the Prefect, who listened to his revelations and sent him on to Paris. Here Mehée communicated to the government the instructions and powers he had received from Sir Francis Drake, and gave the information which he had obtained. He was authorized to continue his correspondence, which was favoured by the means in the power of the police. He pretended to have won over the usher of the First Consul's cabinet, and to be able, thanks-to the offices of this man, to obtain documents from the

Emperor's private cabinet at St. Cloud, which he described himself as having communicated to the secretary of the Jacobin committee to be copied. As a matter of fact these documents were manufactured by Méhée himself, and it is needless to say that he had no understanding whatever with the usher of the Consul's cabinet, and that the secretary of the committee, like the committee itself, had never existed. My name had to be mentioned to give an air of truth to M. Méhée's reports. But, as the First Consul did not wish those in whom he confided to be the objects of suspicion, Sir Francis Drake's correspondent was ordered to add that the secretary of the committee was not to be confounded with me, who was the First Consul's secretary, that this secretary was the intimate friend of General Duroc, and that on this account the First Consul gave him the work that I had no time to do. This was the only part which Napoleon would allow his cabinet to play in a hoax which covered the English agents with confusion. Méhée and Captain de Rosey, who was sent in his place to Sir Francis Drake and to Spencer Smith, as the aide-de-camp of a general who was none other than Méhée himself, and who described himself as in a position to raise several departments of France in revolt, obtained from the English agents close upon eight thousand pounds, placed at their disposal by the liberality of the English Ministry. The French Government communicated to the members of the diplomatic corps in residence in Paris the various documents forming the correspondence between Méhée and de Rosey, and the agents in this work of corruption. Their comments were the condemnation of the shameful policy of the British Cabinet. The agents whom he had compromised in this affair were dismissed from the courts to which they were accredited and nothing more was heard of them afterwards.

Two months later another English agent at Hamburg, Rumbold, continued the manœuvres of his colleagues, but, taking a lesson from their disgrace, acted with greater circumspection. During one night in the month of October, 1804, he was seized and removed, together with all his papers, by a detachment of French soldiers. Brought on to Paris, his papers were examined, but this examination led to no discovery. The intervention of the King of Prussia, as director of the Lower Saxony circle, restored him to liberty. A confidential and friendly exchange of letters passed, on this occasion, between the First Consul and the King of Prussia, and it is to be regretted that the letters of the King of Prussia were lost, with the original letters of various sovereigns, which have disappeared from the imperial archives.

A publication which appeared at this time showed the attempts which had been previously made by the princes of the House of Bourbon to establish communications with certain members of the French army, and with residents in the interior of France. An exile —M. de Montgaillard—who had been in the confidence of the French princes, and had been charged by them to negotiate with Pichegru and Moreau, came to offer the Consular Government some very curious revelations on this subject. He was commissioned to write a book showing all the circumstances of Pichegru's treachery, and revealing all the plots which had been set on foot—either with or without the co-operation of the French princes—by the English Government. M. de Montgaillard sent in to the First Consul a series of manuscripts, one of which was a memorandum on Pichegru's treachery in the Years III, IV, and V, with the text of the secret correspondence, the explanation of the ciphers used, and the key to the names. Another of his manuscripts was entitled: "Secret Memoirs of M. J. G. de Montgaillard during the Years of His Exile." These two manuscripts, in which the author confessed that he had played a double part, contained some curious revelations on the intrigues of the exiled princes and of the English agents, and on the illusions of their nomad little court. The First Consul, whose duty it was as the Head of a Government, to lend his ear to traitors, and to turn the scandal of their revelations to profit, ordered that these manuscripts should be printed and published. The peculiar details which they contained, some well-drawn portraits—amongst others the portrait of the Pretender *—helped to enlighten the public mind, and if they did little credit to the author's sense of honour, at least testified to his intelligence.

I was commissioned to correspond with M. de Montgaillard, and to pay over to him the sums which Napoleon allotted to him. During the time that I was in relations with this person, I received from him numerous manuscripts, of which some were printed—such as those which related to the foundation of a fourth dynasty, to the re-establishment of the Kingdom of Italy under the Emperor Napoleon, to the rights of the French Crown over the Duchy of Rome, and so on.

* See note to page 200.

In 1814, Comte de Montgaillard, as was to be expected of him, sang his recantation, and insulted the idol which he had worshipped. I am not aware whether this appeal to the favour of Louis XVIII. stood him in good stead with a prince whose faithless confidant he had been, and whom he had afterwards branded by his revelations under the imperial government.

Since I am speaking of M. de Montgaillard, I must say a few words about his brother's work. M. de Montgaillard had a brother, an abbé, who is the author of a chronological abridgment of the history of France from 1787 to 1818. This book, every page of which is disfigured by injustice and errors, was no doubt written in one of those fits of depression to which its author was subject. It seems to have served him alone as a means to pour out the most vehement invectives on Napoleon and on the most honoured names of the Empire. The chronological abridgment does not justify its title. The author, instead of giving a concise statement of the principal occurrences, is careful to omit all events which do not afford him the opportunity of venting his spleen in sour and interminable diatribes on Napoleon and his acts. Although very incomplete, this book won for its author a letter of congratulation from General Foy, who was pleased with the facilities which books of this kind afford to the student of history, rather than disgusted at the spirit in which it was written.

A voluminous history of France was published after the abbé's death, under his name. This history, which is a prolix amplification of the chronological review of the history of France by the same author, is the work of his brother. The abbé would not have accepted the Comte de Montgaillard as his collaborateur, for it was his habit to answer anybody who asked him for news of his brother: "That is a question which I have refused to answer for the last thirty years."

Another publication which I may mention here, although it only appeared two years later, that is to say in 1806, contained certain revelations on the part which the princes, and notably the Comte d'Artois, had played in our civil wars. It is entitled: "Historical Memoirs to serve for the History of the Vendée War." The author, Comte de Vauban, great-grand-nephew of the Marshal de Vauban, had followed the Comte d'Artois to St. Petersburg as his aide-de-camp, when this prince went to solicit the help of the Empress Catherine in favour of the Bourbons. M. de Vauban, on his return from this journey, after having taken part in the expedition to Quiberon, went to rejoin his prince at the Île Dieu. Then, discouraged at last by the sight of the futilities and the meannesses of which he had been the witness, he took advantage of the amnesty to return to France. Falling under suspicion of the police he was imprisoned in the Temple, and it was in this prison that he wrote his memoirs. He filled them with all the bitterest recollections, and with revelations which were in no way favourable to the party which he had served. The government, having seized these memoirs, thought it advisable to profit by this discovery, and had them published with the author's name.

CHAPTER IV.

Preliminary Reflections on the Affair of the Duc d'Enghien—Universal Anxiety caused in England by the Preparations for Invasion—Participation of the English Government in the Plot Planned by the French Princes—Sinister Rumours and Pamphlets Coming from England—Assembly of Exiles on the Rhine—Judgment on Spies Detained in Prison—Querel's Revelations—General Savary's Mission to the Dieppe Coast—An Unknown Person Received in Paris by Georges—The Mission of an Officer of Gendarmerie to Ettenheim—His Report—Private Council Held at the Tuileries—Fouché's Activity—The First Consul's Hesitation—Instructions given to Generals Caulaincourt and Ordener—Letter from the Minister of Foreign Affairs to the Ambassador at Baden, at Carlsruhe—Scene when the Orders were Despatched—Levee at the Tuileries on the 12th of March—The First Consul's Departure for La Malmaison—Solicitude of the People of Paris—Revelations Contained in Letters Seized on Exiles—Article Published in the *Moniteur*—Arrival of the Duc d'Enghien at Pantin, and Afterwards at Vincennes—Formation of the Military Court-martial—M. Réal Sent to Examine the Duc d'Enghien at Vincennes—His First Examination Before the Head Reporter—The Prince's Request Written at the Foot of His Inquiry—The Same Over-ridden by the Military Commission—Colonel Savary Reports the Execution of the Sentence to the First Consul—M. Réal also Arrives at La Malmaison—The First Consul's Painful Surprise—Irregularities in the Official Report of the Judgment—My own Impressions—Aspect of the Drawing-room at La Malmaison on the Evening of the Execution of the Sentence—Notes Written by Napoleon at St. Helena on the Subject of This Affair—Letter from M. de Talleyrand to the First Consul on March 8th—Letter from M. de Caulaincourt to the Emperor Alexander, and the Latter's Answer, Preceded and Followed by Remarks from the Former—Disadvantageous Position of M. de Caulaincourt at the Imperial Court in Consequence of This Letter—Napoleon's Fairness Towards his Minister—Sensation Created in Europe at the News of the Judgment—Hostile Conduct of the Russian and Swedish Governments—M. de Chateaubriand—He Resigns his Post of *Chargé d'Affaires* in Le Valais—His Letter to the Minister of Foreign Affairs—First Ideas of Heredity—Opinion of the First Consul's Household and Family on This Question—Initiative of the Tribunal—The Council of State is Consulted—A Senatus Consultum Confers the Imperial Dignity on the First Consul—Popular Votes—Presentation of the Senatus Consultum to the Emperor and the Empress—Anecdote—Examination of the Causes of the Foundation of the Empire—The Pretensions of the Senate—Letter from Joseph Bonaparte on the Question of Heredity—The Trial of Georges and of his Accomplices—Acquisition and Distribution of his Estates—Moreau's Punishment Commuted to Exile to the United States—Confiscation and Distribution of his Estates—Mission Entrusted on This Occasion to Bourrienne—The Emperor's Clemency—Formation of the Imperial Court—Creation of the Great Dignities of the Empire and Court Charges—Nomination of Eighteen Marshals of the Empire—Offence Taken by Old Servants at this New Ceremonial—These Events do not Turn the Emperor Away from his Plans of War—The Camp at Compiègne—Octave de Ségur, Sub-prefect at Soissons—His Disappearance and Tragical End—Particulars About the Ségur Family—Inspection of the Fontainebleau Military School—Visit to Marshal Augereau—Re-establishment of the Ministry of Police—Fouché Once More Minister—Fourth Journey to Boulogne—Headquarters at Pont-de-Brique—The Hut at La Tour-d'Ordre—Active Work by the Emperor on the Field and in His Study—Encampment of the Troops—On Fulton's Discovery—The Dutch Flotilla—Admiral Verhuell—Admiral Bruix's Death—He is Replaced by Admiral Villeneuve—Joseph Bonaparte, Colonel of the Fourth Line Regiment—Celebration of the Emperor's Fête at Boulogne—Distribution of Decorations of the Legion of Honour—Banquets—Visits of Prince and Princess Murat, of Princess Louis Bonaparte, and Her Son—M. Chaptal Leaves the Ministry of the Interior—He had Succeeded Lucien Bonaparte—Comparison of Cæsar, Cromwell, and Bonaparte—M. de Fontanes—Lucien's Disgrace—His Embassy to Spain—His Marriage Displeases the First Consul—He Withdraws to Rome—Jérôme Bonaparte—His Marriage with Eliza Paterson—Napoleon Interposes his Authority as Head of the Family—Madame Jérôme Bonaparte Agrees to a Separation—The Emperor's Kindness to This Lady—The Pope Refuses to Annul the Marriage—Jérôme Leaves the Navy for Military Service—Napoleon Leaves Boulogne to Visit the Rhine Departments—The Fête of Charlemagne—*Te Deum*—Lauriston—Mouton—M. de Talleyrand is Compromised in Connection with the Prince of Orange Decrees in Favour of the Rhine Departments—Institution of Decennial Prizes.

THE discovery of the existence of the Royalist conspiracy and the confessions of some of the assassins arrested in Paris, acquainted the First Consul with the fact that the Duc d'Enghien was living at Ettenheim, that Dumouriez had been seen there, and was probably there still. He came to the conclusion that this place was the centre of the various ramifications of the conspiracy. Before relating the circumstances of the forcible seizure and trial of the unfortunate Duc d'Enghien I must go further back in history. I had no desire to recall these sad memories, which have given rise to so many erroneous judgments; but it seems to me to be my duty to render strict justice to the memory of Napoleon, and I believe myself to be acting in obedience to one of his most pressing recommendations, in relating what is my personal knowledge of an affair which party spirit has so strangely transformed.

The occurrence itself is to-day appreciated at its just value. Provoked by the English Government, the death of the last of the Condés has brought forth deplorable fruit. The principal interest attaching to this occurrence is due to the influence which it had on Napoleon's political career, and it is on this account that it occupies so important a place in the history of our times. I propose therefore to give the principal outlines of this story so that the impartial reader, from a consideration of them as a whole, may form an opinion on an act of severity to which Napoleon was impelled by a combination of fatal circumstances and an inflexible interpretation of his duties as the Head of the Government, an act of which this great man accepted the responsibility with the lofty frankness and the pride of his character, and which, as he himself has confessed, was prejudicial rather than useful to his glory.

The English Government, which had at first affected to consider the plan of an invasion of England with contempt, rightly alarmed by the formidable armament which was being prepared in sight of the shores of England, had ended by attaching such great importance to this expedition, that on its side it made the most extraordinary preparations against it. Redouts and entrenchments were multiplied on the southern coast of England, works for inundating the surrounding country were carried out, the Ministers themselves and the principal members of the aristocracy had assumed military uniform and figured in the ranks of the volunteers, and every man able to carry arms had been called out, and was being drilled. The general anxiety was excited and kept alive by a succession of alerts and panics, which carried dismay into the heart of London itself. A large number of families removed from the neighbourhood of the seaboard and took refuge in the interior of the country.

And whilst the government was doing all in its power to avert the storm, it strove to prevent its bursting on British territory. All the resources of the most cunning diplomacy were called into play, and gold was scattered broadcast to induce the powers to declare themselves, and to engage on the continent the enemy which threatened England.

Not considering these means sufficient it had recourse to conspiracies. At the commencement of 1804 the French princes who had retired to London planned a serious attack on the person of the Head of the Consular Government, and were favoured in this by the English Ministers. An order of the King's Privy Council enjoined on the French exiles to betake themselves to the banks of the Rhine, and this under penalty of forfeiting their pensions; and a regulation fixed the amount of pay to be allotted to each officer, and to each soldier. The Duc d'Enghien had previously obtained permission from the Elector of Baden to establish himself at Ettenheim, a small town situated on the right bank of the Rhine, and at a distance of two leagues from this river. At the very time when the exiles, acting under the order of the Privy Council, were assembling on the frontiers of Alsace, some determined royalists, who had fled to London after the pacification of the Vendée, and who were commanded by former Chouan chiefs, secretly landed on the Dieppe coast, and made their way to Paris by roundabout routes, finding shelter on their way in isolated farms and cottages, where they were received by peasants who had been won over to their cause. Georges,

Cadoudal, Rivière, aide-de-camp to the Comte d'Artois, the brothers Polignac, Pichegru, and fifty other conspirators, had in this way secretly arrived in Paris, where they were hiding in places unknown to the police.

The agents of the French police in London reported that some great conspiracy against France was being prepared. The report that the Consular Government was drawing to a close, that the days of its Head were numbered, and that the former reigning family was about to reascend the throne, was generally spread over England and Europe; and, indeed, had even reached our colonies. A pamphlet, entitled "To Kill is not to Murder," which had originally been written against Cromwell, was reprinted in London, in allusion to the First Consul. A newspaper—*L'Ambigu*—written by French exiles, appeared, with a portrait of Bonaparte (with a black mark round his neck) at the head of its columns. Advices received from various sides announced that bodies of exiles would shortly land in the Vendée. The news which the First Consul received from this district induced him to send one of his aides-de-camp, Colonel Savary, to the Vendée. His report confirmed the Consul's suspicions as to the masked agitation which existed there.

The First Consul remembered that there were, in the prisons in Paris, a number of persons who had been arrested on the charge of having been sent from London for the purpose of attempting his life. Their arrest, on the seaboard, in the very act of espionage and corruption, would have sufficiently justified their being tried by court-martial, but as they had been accused of contriving to murder the Head of the State, they had been detained in prison pending the establishment of this charge. The First Consul ordered that some of these persons should be brought before a court-martial, hoping to obtain some revelations as to the object of their journey from some of them. Two were tried and sentenced. The fear of death did not cause them to waver, and they died threatening the government with an approaching catastrophe.

The reports of M. Mehée de Latouche, and of Captain Rosey—whose mission I have related—had revealed the plots which were being hatched on the right bank of the Rhine by the English ambassadors accredited to the Courts of Munich, Stuttgart, and Cassel. The First Consul, whose mind was made up as to the imminence of the danger which threatened the state and his own person, but still to some extent in the dark, had the list of arrested Chouans once more laid before him. The entry in the gaol-book concerning one of these Chouans, who was known to have acted either as servant or as confidant to Georges, during the last insurrection in the West, gave rise to the suspicion that he might know something of the matter. Querel was tried and sentenced without making any confession, but on the night preceding his execution the fear of death prompted him to speak. He related that he had been in Paris six months; that he had come there with Georges and six other conspirators, whom he named; that they had been joined shortly after their arrival by fifteen others; that more were expected to land, and that Paris was the meeting-place generally agreed upon. Querel's declarations, which were rewarded with a pardon, put the authorities on the trace of some important discoveries, leading up to a former emissary of the party, a man called Troché, who was a clockmaker at Eu. The First Consul sent his aide-de-camp, Savary, accompanied by the clockmaker's son, who took the place of his father, who was a very old man, to Dieppe, where a fresh landing of exiles was expected. Colonel Savary, in company with young Troché, on arriving at Dieppe, set out at once for Béville, where the landing was to take place. Owing, however, to bad weather, which lasted several days, and to the fact that in the meanwhile, on information transmitted from Paris, signals had been made to the brig, which cruised for several days in front of the cliffs of Béville, the expected landing, which it is said would have included the Duc de Berri, did not take place.

In the meanwhile the police, under the direction of the Councillor of State, Réal, taking advantage of Querel's revelations, had made active investigations, which had put them on the trace of persons in hiding in Paris. The arrest of Georges and of his accomplices, which rapidly followed, led to the knowledge of the different parts played in the conspiracy by Pichegru and Moreau. Georges had declared, in one of his examinations, that he awaited the arrival of a French prince in Paris, before acting. As new revelations arose, the importance of the conspiracy and its various ramifications were brought to light. From the extent of these ramifications, the magnitude of the danger which menaced the State and the person of the First Consul can be judged. The intrigues of the English diplomatic agents, which were plotted on our frontiers and which extended even to Paris, proved the active co-operation of England, whose government was the soul of the coalitions. The presence of Georges proved that murder was intended; the name of Moreau was a call to insurrection in the army; and a prince of the House of Bourbon was to put himself at the head of the conspiracy, and give the signal for its outbreak.

Amongst other information which was obtained was a detail which attracted attention in the highest degree. A person who was unknown to Georges' gang had had interviews with the latter. He had been received not only by Georges, but by MM. Polignac and de Rivière, with particular marks of deference. This naturally gave rise to the thought—and this would have been the case even if Georges had not declared the fact—that so important a conspiracy must necessarily be under the command of a superior chief, either present or not far distant, invested with extraordinary powers, who could make himself known as soon as the enemy had been struck down. It was concluded from this that the person received by Georges must be this head, and that he was one of the princes of the former royal family. The various members of the royal family were passed in muster. It was known where the Comte de Lille—Louis XVIII.—the Comte d'Artois, the Dukes of Angoulême and Berri, the Prince de Condé, the Duc de Bourbon, and the Princes of Orleans—the latter living peacefully away from all centres of intrigue—were to be found. There remained only the Duc d'Enghien, of whose very existence Napoleon was almost ignorant. The belief was entertained that this prince might well be the mysterious person of whom we have already spoken. Although the description which had been made of him only tallied in a very imperfect way with that of the duke, the most striking differences in the description of a man who was totally unknown in Paris could not put a stop to the conjectures of which he was the object. The presence of the Duc d'Enghien on the banks of the Rhine, his communications with the exiles who were assembling there, the participation of the English Government in the conspiracy, (the fact of which was established by all the informations collected by the police,) the absences of the prince on alleged hunting-expeditions, his excursions on the Rhine, the suspicion that he was in the habit of going to Strasburg, gave new strength to the presumptions, already existing, that he was the chief whose name and rank placed him at the head of the conspiracy. Suppositions excited by suspicion are of rapid growth. It was consequently assumed without hesitation that the Duc d'Enghien might have come to Paris and have stayed there, and have returned to Ettenheim, within the space of eight days. So vivid was this conjecture that the principal houses in the Faubourg St. Germain were searched to see whether the prince was not in hiding there and whether no secret preparations were being made to receive him. It was even supposed that he might have found shelter in the house of the Austrian ambassador. The report to the effect that Dumouriez, the maker of civil wars, and the most active and experienced agent of conspiracies, was at Ettenheim, as the prince's adviser, changed suspicion into practical assurance.

Instructions were sent to M. Shée, at that time Prefect of the Lower-Rhine department. The report which he sent back changed suspicion into certainty. The First Consul had more confidence in his own presentiments and foresight than in the judgment of the police, which, since its suppression as a special department, was lacking in the cohesion and impetus so necessary under the extraordinary circumstances which had arisen. On rising one day, he ordered General Moncey, first officer of gendarmerie, in a confidential way, to send an intelligent officer, under disguise, to Ettenheim, with orders to find out all that was going on there, and to make a list of the people of every rank who were in relations with the Duc d'Enghien. General Moncey handed the report of the officer whom he had entrusted with this mission, direct to the First Consul, without showing it to the police. Amongst the names of the Duke's friends mentioned in this report, were those of Dumouriez and of an English colonel named Smith. It was only later that it was known that the general whom the author of the report had taken for Dumouriez was General Thumery, whose name was mispronounced in German, and that the English colonel Smith was a simple German captain, named Schmidt, who belonged to the prince's staff. This report confirmed the First Consul in the opinion that the Duc d'Enghien presided over the conspiracy of which Paris was the head-quarters. The presence of Dumouriez seemed especially a decisive proof. This general, in his opinion, must be the pivot of the whole conspiracy. Napoleon was at that time in ignorance on what terms Dumouriez might be with the various princes of the former dynasty; his presence at Ettenheim was considered sufficient. He was persuaded that the arrest of this person, and the seizure of his papers, would supply exact information on the organization and the means at the disposal of the conspiracy.

To avoid acting with precipitation, he determined to consult with his wisest advisers. A kind of privy council was called together with this object in view, as soon as he had read General Moncey's report. The two consuls, the Grand Judge, the Minister of Foreign Affairs, the Councillor of State, Réal, and Fouché, although the latter was not a minister, composed this council. Fouché had succeeded in making himself necessary by his extreme activity. He used often to come and tell the First Consul news which he had obtained, thanks to the influence which he had retained over the police-agents, and the confidences which he extracted from them, beating the Grand Judge in his own department.

As no official report was made of the deliberations of this council, the opinions of the various persons who took part in it have been made the subject of conjecture. It appears, however, certain—and this fact will be established or otherwise in the memoirs, which sooner or later, cannot fail to be published— that the two consuls showed themselves little disposed towards immediate severe measures, and that Fouché, on the other hand, did not hide his opinion that it was necessary to make a prompt example, so as to finish with the conspirators.

I will mention later on what influence M. de Talleyrand exercised on the determination of the First Consul. Napoleon hesitated a long time as to how to act in so serious a matter. His first idea had been to have the Duc d'Enghien tried at the same time, and on the same indictment, as Georges. He was loth, however, to couple a prince with a man whom he considered a common murderer. He next thought of giving great importance to the prince's trial, by bringing him before a High Court. Various considerations, and notably the fear of provoking party manifestations, induced him to abandon this plan, which would, perhaps, have been the best. He at last made up his mind to replace the slow and solemn forms of civil proceedings, by the rapid and secret action of a court-martial, a formidable weapon, which would strike terror into the hearts of his enemies. He had always in reserve the right of clemency.

Such was the state of affairs when on the 19th Ventôse, of the Year XII—March 10th, 1804—a day on which I had not dined at the Tuileries, I was sent for at ten o'clock at night by order of the First Consul. I found him, on my arrival, in a room adjoining his study. A number of maps which he had thrown down on the floor—in looking for one of the river Rhine—were at his feet. After helping him to spread this map out on a large mahogany table, which was in the middle of the room, I wrote from his dictation a letter to the Minister of War, Berthier, giving him orders to send off, that night, his aide-de-camp, General Caulaincourt, to Strasburg, and General Ordener, commander of the mounted grenadiers of his guard, to Schelestadt to proceed to the arrest of the Duc d'Enghien. Whilst the First Consul was dictating this letter, General Berthier was announced, and, shortly afterwards, General Caulaincourt. The First Consul dictated the rest of the instructions concerning this expedition to General Berthier, tracing on the map the route to be followed by General Ordener. He then dictated a letter to Minister Talleyrand, prescribing the diplomatic measures to be taken. By the terms of this order the Minister of Foreign Affairs was to hand General Caulaincourt a letter addressed to Baron d'Edelsheim, Minister of the Elector of Baden, which was to be delivered at its address by this officer as soon as he had heard of the arrest of the Duc d'Enghien. It was stated in this letter that "the Minister of Foreign Affairs had previously addressed to the Electoral Government, a note tending to a demand for the arrest of the committee of French exiles, in session at Offenburg, when the First Consul, by the successive arrival of brigands sent into France by the English Government, as well as by the developments and results of the prosecutions instituted in France, had received definite assurance of the part played by the English agents in the terrible conspiracies against his person and the safety of France; that he had moreover learned that the Duc d'Enghien and General Dumouriez were at Ettenheim; and that, as it was impossible that they could be in that town without the permission of His Electoral Highness, the First Consul had not been able to contemplate, without the greatest grief, the sight of a prince—to whom he had been pleased to give the clearest proofs of his sincere friendship—harbouring his most bitter enemies, and allowing the most evident conspiracies to be quietly plotted against him; that under these most unusual circumstances, the First Consul had thought it his duty to give orders to two small detachments to make their way to Offenburg and to Ettenheim, and to seize the persons of the instigators of a crime which, by its very nature, placed those who had palpably taken part in it, outside all human law; that General Caulaincourt was charged with the orders of the First Consul; and that there could be no doubt that in his execution of them he would in no way be wanting in the respect which His Highness might consider due to himself."

The instructions contained in the letter addressed by the First Consul to the Minister of War provided that General Caulaincourt should betake himself to Strasburg, and from there to Offenburg, with two hundred dragoons, to arrest the exiles and the agents of the English Government; that General Ordener should proceed to Schelestadt, where he would take three hundred dragoons, and pass over the Rhine with them to Rheinau, secretly surrounding the castle of Ettenheim and arresting the Duc d'Enghien, and especially Dumouriez, together with all persons found with them. General Caulaincourt was to put himself in communication with General Ordener and, as soon as he had heard of his arrival at Ettenheim, to send Minister Talleyrand's letter to the Minister of the Elector of Baden with apologies for the violation of his territory, which was necessitated by the urgency of the matter and the need of absolute secrecy.

Here is the scene, if I may so express myself, of this memorable evening:—The First Consul, Berthier, the Minister of War, General Caulaincourt, and myself were assembled in the large room in the Tuileries palace, which had been used as a bedroom by Louis XVI., and which afterwards was used for a similar purpose by the Emperor. This room was lighted only by two three-branched candelabra, covered with shades, so that the light of the candles illuminated a circumference of a few feet only. The Minister and I wrote by the light of one of these candelabra, on a corner of the large mahogany table. The First Consul, lighted by the other flambeau, bending over the map, called General Caulaincourt up to his side and, compass in hand, showed him the route from Strasburg to Rheinau, pointing out the exact position of the ferry which joins the two banks of the Rhine, that of the village of Ettenheim and the road which leads to it.

When, on the evening of the day on which the First Consul had sent for me, I arrived at the Tuileries, I did not know what people he had seen in the afternoon. I learned that he had conversed with the consuls, with the Ministers of Justice and of Foreign Affairs, and with Fouché. Two days later, Fouché, as he was coming from the levee, said to me: "General Bonaparte is very indiscreet, he will end by letting the cat out of the bag." He was alluding to the order for the Duc d'Enghien's arrest. The First Consul had spoken at his levee of the matter which exclusively engrossed his thoughts, of the machinations of the exiles, whose proximity he tolerated with too great patience, and had mentioned the names of the Duc d'Enghien and of Dumouriez. Nobody in the consular household, however, not excepting Madame Bonaparte, knew of the orders that had been given. The First Consul remained some days in Paris, and then left the Tuileries for La Malmaison. Although my carriage followed his he gave me an escort of some soldiers, for the greater safety of his papers.

The entire population of Paris showed an interest in the various incidents of this drama, which can hardly be conceived to-day. The arrest of Georges, which had taken place almost simultaneously with the order for the seizure of the Duc d'Enghien, had dispelled all uncertainty as to the existence of a conspiracy, and raised to the highest degree the general solicitude for and sympathy with the Head of the State. It was earnestly prayed that the instigators of the conspiracy might be taken and severely punished.

During his stay at La Malmaison, the First Consul appeared careworn, and indisposed for any occupation. He only received MM. Maret, Talleyrand, Fouché, Réal, the Grand Judge—Régnier—and Cambacérès. On the 25th Ventôse—March 16th—the telegraph announced that the Duc d'Enghien had been arrested in the night at the castle of Ettenheim. Orders were immediately given that he should be brought to Paris, where he arrived on the 29th Ventôse.

The First Consul was fully informed as to the details of the conspiracy. He was aware of the order of the King of England's privy council convoking the exiles of the Condé army to the right bank of the Rhine, under penalty of forfeiting the allowances attached to their rank, an edict which coincided with the presence of the Duc d'Enghien in the same place, and that of Georges and his assassins in Paris. The revelations which were contained in the letters seized on the exiles at Ettenheim, Offenburg, and other points on the right bank of the Rhine, letters which had been sent on to him by special couriers; the reports which he had caused to be drawn up and the information which he had collected on all sides, had dispelled his last doubts. Amongst the papers seized were a note from the Duc d'Enghien in answer to a letter from a certain general, called Vauborel, from which it was gathered that the prince had refused to follow the advice, given him by this general, to absent himself in consequence of the dangers to which under the existing circumstances he was exposed; and a letter from a colonel, named De Lanen, which contained similar advice. "If, as I think," this officer added, " the energetic views of the governments which protect us so particularly, are recognized by the great powers as the only means of restoring tranquillity to Europe by means of peace on equitable conditions, these conditions will naturally be the restoration of the monarchy." These papers proved the plan of hostility which had been conceived against the French Government, the part taken by the Duc d'Enghien in this plan, and his relations with the exiles who were stationed on the right bank of the Rhine. Fouché had declared that a portmanteau full of papers, which would reveal all the ramifications of the conspiracy, would be found at the prince's house, but no such portmanteau was discovered at Ettenheim. Fouché's assertion was only a conjecture, though it may be that the Duc d'Enghien had been persuaded by the advice of his faithful officers, expressing their fears lest a descent might be made on Ettenheim, to remove to a place of safety all papers which might compromise his companions, whilst remaining himself at the post of danger.

The following note which the First Consul sent to the *Moniteur* on the day of the Prince's arrival in Paris, and which appeared in the following day's paper, gives a recapitulation of what he had learned:—

"Paris, 28th Ventsôe, Year XII—March 19th, 1804—

" Whilst England was sending Pichegru, Georges, and the gang of murderers, to Paris, she was assembling and hiring the services of all the exiles, who were to be found in

Germany. A circular from the Prince de Condé summoned them, about three months ago. It is a fact, known to the whole town of Hamburg, that a man named Maillard was entrusted with funds in this town to recruit these wretches, and to send them on to the Rhine. The right bank of the Rhine is filling daily with these new legionaries, whom England summons to be at once the toys and the victims of her cruel Machiavelisms.

"A Bourbon prince, with his staff and certain officers, is fixed at this point and thence directs the movement. The Prince de Guéméné and several officers are expected to arrive on March 25th to complete the organization of the bands.

"The Continental powers make haste to disavow such elements of disorder, and the new attempt of the British Government will not be any more successful than the crime, which it prepared at such great expense, against the First Consul."

The Duc d'Enghien arrived at the Villette barrier of Paris towards three o'clock on the afternoon of March 20th. He was detained there until the order arrived directing his removal to the fort of Vincennes. He entered the Vincennes prison at five o'clock in the evening.

On the same day a decree was issued ordering that the *ci-devant* Duc d'Enghien, accused of having taken up arms against the Republic, of having been and being still in the pay of England, of forming part of the conspiracies fomented by this power against the safety of the Republic at home and abroad, should be brought before a court-martial composed of seven members, nominated by the military governor of Paris, the said court-martial to meet at Vincennes. By the terms of this decree, the five colonels of the infantry and cavalry regiments in the garrison of Paris; the major of the regiment of *gendarmerie d'élite*, acting as reporter, and General Hulin, the city marshal of Paris, were designed by the governor of Paris to form the court-martial. These officers betook themselves separately to Vincennes. Silence having been observed as to the name of the prisoner whom they were to try, it was only there that they learned that it was the Duc d'Enghien. They were all in ignorance of the various circumstances of the conspiracy, but all alike were under the impression of the general indignation which had been excited by the plan of an attack on the person of the First Consul, as well as by the prospect of the chaotic disorder which would have followed on his death. They did not imagine that these plots had been under the direction of a prince of the former dynasty.

The captain reporter, Dautancourt, proceeded to a first examination of the Prince. The duke, deploring the cruel extremity to which he was reduced, expressed the desire to be heard by the First Consul. Dautancourt advised him to write a request for an audience at the foot of the report of his examination. The prince's note was in the following words:

"Before signing this official report of my examination, I earnestly request a private interview with the First Consul. My name, my rank, my way of thinking, and the horror of my situation, lead me to hope that he will not refuse my request.
(Signed) L. A. H. DE BOURBON."

This touching appeal to the clemency of a generous enemy was never to reach the man to whom it was addressed.

The document in question was placed before the members of the military commission. Only one of the judges, namely, General Barrois, expressed the opinion that the request for an audience should be transmitted to the First Consul, but the answers of the Duc d'Enghien, the circumstances with which his arrest was surrounded, the conviction of the members of the court that the Prince was the accomplice and even the leader of the plot that was being hatched in Paris, seemed to officers judging with the rigour of the military penal code, sufficient reasons for applying the law to the Prince, his right of appeal to the First Consul after sentence being reserved. Honourable men, such as the members of the court-martial were, would not have stooped to allow their consciences to waver in the face of a sanguinary order. The First Consul, whose mind was made up, had no doubt that the Prince would be condemned; but there was no doubt that he expected that, should an incident arise, he would be referred to before the execution of the sentence was carried out. The proof of this is that at the same time he ordered his Secretary of State, Maret, who was then staying at La Malmaison, and who returned for this purpose to Paris, to write a letter to the Councillor of State, Réal, ordering him to proceed to Vincennes, and to personally examine the Duc d'Enghien, and then to come and report the result of this examination to him, Napoleon. M. Maret, if I remember rightly, left La Malmaison for Paris towards seven in the evening, and it must have been about ten o'clock when his letter was handed in at M. Réal's house. By the same fatality which seems to have presided over the whole course of events in this affair, Réal, who for the last eight days had not had a moment's rest, and who had passed several nights without going to bed, had that day come in broken down with fatigue. He had forbidden his valet to wake him before five o'clock in the morning, no matter what message might be sent him. A letter coming from the State Secretary's office did not seem of sufficient importance to warrant a disobedience of M. Réal's formal order that he was not to be waked. Amongst the letters which were handed him at his awakening, was that of the Secretary of State. He dressed with all speed, and set out for Vincennes, but on his way there he met Colonel Savary, who informed him that the Duc d'Enghien's execution had taken place. Savary, who was on horseback, continued on his way to La Malmaison, arriving there at eight in the morning. He was at once ushered into the First Consul's study, where I was present. Savary related the sentence and its execution in a few words. On hearing that the Duc d'Enghien had asked to see him, the First Consul, without asking for any of those details of which he was usually so greedy, interrupted Savary to ask what had become of Réal, and to know if he had not gone to Vincennes. Hearing that he had not gone there, Napoleon remained silent, walking up and down his library, with his hands crossed behind his back, until the moment when M. Réal was announced. After listening to the latter's explanation, and having exchanged a few words with him, he fell back into his reverie, and then, without expressing a word either of approval or of blame, he took his hat and said: " It is well," leaving M. Réal surprised, and to some extent disturbed, by his manner. We heard the First Consul slowly ascending the staircase which led to the little apartment which he occupied over his library. He shut himself up here, and did not appear again for a long time.

The official report of the judgment was presented to him during the same day. The perusal of this document was a subject of fresh grief for him. Legal forms had not been respected. The irregularities and the omissions which he noticed in it caused him to order it to be rewritten. Although the First Consul had never doubted that the Duc d'Enghien would be condemned, he must have left the sentence to the discretion of the court-martial. If, as has been said, he had ordered a condemnation, the court-martial would, without fail, have been instructed in advance of the formalities prescribed by the law, formalities which the president, the judges, and even the captain reporter himself, appeared to ignore. It may be said that this judgment was that of a drum-head court-martial. This is another reason for regretting that the president of the commission did not think himself authorized to forward the request for an audience which the Duc d'Enghien had written at the foot of his examination. If General Hulin had had sufficient strength of character to resist the remarks which he alleges were made to him, and had followed the inspirations of his conscience, he would have done himself the greatest possible honour and he would have preserved the First Consul from the redoubling of hostilities of which this act became the pretext; for it can easily be guessed what Napoleon would have done under the circumstances.

These are the only facts which I witnessed. I relate only what I saw or heard. I may add that no verbal or written communication took place between the First Consul and the military commission during the time which elapsed between the examination of the Duc d'Enghien, which preceded his sentence, and the moment of execution. The means which I had of being informed on this point, and the investigations of those who had an interest in discovering any communication of this kind, totally failed to establish its existence.

If I may speak of my private impressions, I do not hesitate to say that the First Consul, justly incensed by the odious plots which were hatched against his person, wished to hurl back on his enemies the thunderbolts which they had launched at his head, and to answer war with war. Was he to allow himself to be quietly murdered, without defending himself? He appeared to me never to have doubted for a single moment that the assembly of exiles on the Rhine had a prince of the House of Bourbon for chief; that this chief was the Duc d'Enghien; that the Duc d'Enghien's mission was to enter France, after the blow had been struck by Georges and his accomplices; and that this mission had devolved upon the Duc d'Enghien, after the Duc de Berri had been prevented from landing in Normandy by the presence at Dieppe of an active and determined officer, who was entirely devoted to the First Consul. Under a deep and just sense of resentment, and clearly foreseeing the sinister future reserved to France, and the bloody revolution which would have been the consequence of his death, he ordered the kidnapping and the trial of the Duc d'Enghien, convinced as he was that sufficient charges to justify a condemnation existed against this prince. What struggles took place in Napoleon's mind are shown by the order given to M. Réal to proceed to Vincennes, and to interrogate the Duc d'Enghien, and by the solitude which he went to seek at La Malmaison, less for the purpose of strengthening his resolution, than with the view of protecting himself against all outside influence, and of calmly reflecting upon his decisions, avoiding Josephine's drawing-room, locking himself up for hours together in his private apartments, and refusing to answer his wife, who frequently came and knocked in vain at his door.

Although the reports received at La Malmaison, together with the letters seized on the exiles, left him no doubt whatever of the Duc d'Enghien's knowledge of the conspiracy, it is my conviction that, satisfied with the humiliation to which he had reduced his enemies, he would have leaned towards clemency if he had been informed in time of the request made by this prince to be brought before him. The evil having become one for which there was no remedy, Napoleon boldly accepted the entire responsibility of this act. He could not disavow the brave and faithful officers who had judged as their consciences had directed them to do. He refused even to enter into an explanation of the causes which had prevented Réal from reaching Vincennes in time; and these would have convinced nobody. His dignity refused to allow him to justify himself from the accusation of seeking to protect himself by false excuses, which would certainly have been brought against him. He therefore resolved to assume the entire responsibility of the affair. He prescribed the strictest secrecy on what had happened, and allowed nobody to be compromised. He imposed silence on himself also—a silence which not even the most violent and the most persistent attacks could induce him to break.

When one looks back to these critical times and reflects on the dangers with which the State was threatened, one is forced to admit that Napoleon fulfilled a painful duty, as Head of the Government, and that instead of charging him with a crime, one should rather pity him for having been placed in the necessity of accepting all the odium of an act, the deplorable consequences of which, in the future, his foresight only too clearly pointed out to him. The position of the sentenced man, and the interested feeling of pity with which the hatred of the enemies of France suddenly covered the Duc d'Enghien, have transformed an act of rigour, which the most imperious circumstances imposed on the Head of a Government, into a crime of savage ferocity. *

Napoleon found compensation for the embarrassments in which his enemies involved him in connection with this matter in the enthusiastic attachment of the people, excited to the highest degree by the imminence of a common danger, and the vigorous

*It has been very authoritatively stated, and was repeated quite recently by M. Henri Rochefort in *L'Intransigeant*, that, before his execution, the unhappy Duc d'Enghien handed his ring, watch, and other trinkets, with a lock of his hair, to the captain in command of the firing party, with the request that they might be given, with his dying love, to his adored Charlotte; that the officer in question consulted Savary after the execution as to whether his request should be complied with; that Savary mentioned the matter to Napoleon, and that Napoleon said with a laugh: "He would be a big fool to give them up. What goes into the ditch (*fosse*) belongs to the soldier." If this be true it adds to the undeniable ferocity of an undeniable crime.—R. H. S.

measures by which it had been averted. But it is true that the first impression produced by this event on the upper classes was a very strong one, the principal and perhaps the only cause of this impression being the mystery and the precipitation with which the Duc d'Enghien had been seized, sentenced, and executed. It was only by reading the *Moniteur* that the Ministers, functionaries, and persons attached to the First Consul's household, learned what had happened. La Malmaison presented a sad spectacle that day. I can still remember the silence which reigned that evening in Madame Bonaparte's drawing-room. The First Consul stood with his back against the mantel-piece whilst Madame de Fontanes read him some book, of which I have forgotten the name. Josephine, with a melancholy look and moist eyes, was seated at the far end of a couch; the persons in attendance, very few in number at that time, had withdrawn into the neighbouring gallery where they conversed in whispers on the topic which absorbed all others. Some people came from Paris, but. struck by the doleful appearance of the room, remained standing at the door. The First Consul, anxious or pre-occupied, or listening attentively to what Madame de Fontanes was reading, did not appear to notice their presence. The Minister of Finance remained standing in the same place for a quarter of an hour without being spoken to by anybody. Not wishing to go away as he had come, he approached the First Consul and asked him if he had any orders to give him; the Consul made a negative gesture in reply.

I think it useful and necessary to reproduce in this place the notes written in pencil by Napoleon on the margins of the work entitled "History of Napoleon in 1815," by M. Fleury de Chaboulon. This book contains a long passage referring to the arrest and trial of the Duc d'Enghien. I have copied these notes from the original without changing a word, and they are as follows:

"Napoleon did not trouble himself about the Duc d'Enghien,* who had been justly tried and punished by a court-martial. Already, in 1797, General Moreau—in his report to the executive Directoire, at the time of the 18th Fructidor—had complained of the intrigues in which this prince was engaged with Pichegru and his agents in the army, from his residence in Offenburg. This prince had a part in Pichegru and Georges's conspiracy. He was in consequence arrested and condemned to death by the competent tribunal. There was only one irregularity, and that was his arrest in the country of Baden, three leagues from the French frontier. But Napoleon was the protector of the House of Baden, and he had ordered Colonel Caulaincourt, his aide-de-camp, to demand the Duke's extradition, whilst Ordener was crossing the Rhine with three hundred dragoons and arresting the prince and his agents in his house at Ettenheim."

To the remark that the death of the Duc d'Enghien settled the question which was agitating France, etc., etc., the Emperor answers:

"The Duc d'Enghien's well-merited death injured Napoleon in public opinion and was of no political use whatever to him."

Answering the statement that Josephine, Queen

* In the second volume of these Memoirs will be found, in the description of a violent attack made by Napoleon on Talleyrand, at the time of the latter's dismissal, a passage which gives the lie to Napoleon's statement that "he did not trouble himself about the Duc d'Enghien." This crime seems, on the contrary, to have weighed heavily on his mind.—R. H. S.

Hortense, Cambacérès, and Berthier had implored him to save the prince's life, the Emperor adds:

"That is false. The Duc d'Enghien, transferred to the castle of Vincennes, was tried and shot before anybody knew that he had been arrested. Besides, everybody at that time was so indignant at the well-known conduct of the Comte d'Artois, who was plotting murders in Paris, that there was a general expression of satisfaction at the news at the Tuileries, and amongst the friends and relations of the Ministers, and of people interested in the State."

It was asserted that the execution had been urged by Murat, who, prompted by a certain number of regicides, at the head of whom was Fouché, thought that he would be serving Napoleon, his family, and France, by the death of a Bourbon. A note in Napoleon's writing denies this assertion:

"That is false. Napoleon knew that if the court-martial found him guilty, his execution would be proceeded to within twenty-four hours."*

I will add that the man who replied to the offer of the smugglers who undertook to hand over to him the princes of the former dynasty, who were retired in England, with the threat that he would have them hanged if a single hair fell from the heads of these princes, was not a man to consider the death of the Bourbons necessary to his fortune. In answer to the reproaches made against M. de Talleyrand on this occasion, Napoleon writes:

"Prince Talleyrand behaved, in these circumstances, like

* Compare this with Méneval's statement on page 262: "Although the First Consul had never doubted that the Duc d'Enghien would be condemned, he must have left the sentence to the discretion of the court-martial."—R. H. S.

a faithful Minister, and the Emperor never had to reproach him on the subject.* If the affair of the Duc d'Enghien had to occur over again, the Emperor would act in exactly the same way. The interests of France, the dignity of the crown, and the law of just reprisals, forced him to act as he did."

It is said, in the passage in the book which was annotated as above by the Emperor, that the arrest of the Duc d'Enghien had been for a long time imputed, and was still imputed by persons who did not know the exact facts, to General Caulaincourt. On the margin is written in the Emperor's writing:

"All this is absurd. Caulaincourt, Napoleon's aide-de-camp, obeyed, and had to obey Talleyrand's order to proceed to Baden, and, at the same time that Ordener arrested the prince, to demand his extradition, accompanying his demand with an apology for the violation of territory. Ordener was forced to obey the order to cross the Rhine with three hundred dragoons and to arrest the prince. The court-martial was forced to condemn him to death, if he was found guilty. Thus, whether innocent or guilty, Caulaincourt and Ordener had to obey. If he was guilty, the court-martial had to condemn him to death, if he had been innocent, it would have been the duty of his judges to acquit him, for no order may sway a judge's conscience. There is no doubt that had Caulaincourt been appointed to try the Duc d'Enghien, he would have declined the nomination; but that, charged with a diplomatic mission, he was forced to carry it out. All that is so simple that it is nonsense to find any fault. It is true also that the Bourbon party, having persisted in calumniating Caulaincourt for the small part he took in this affair, this circumstance was the origin of the favour into which he was taken by the

---

* Attention will be drawn to this passage in the course of the second volume.—R. H. S.

Emperor. The death of the Duc d'Enghien must be attributed to the Comte d'Artois, who directed and commanded, from London, the murder of Napoleon by Pichegru and by Georges, and who had appointed the Duc de Berri to enter France by Béville, and the Duc d'Enghien by Strasburg, after Napoleon's death."

I have spoken of the part played by Talleyrand in the tragical end of the Duc d'Enghien. This is proved by a letter which he wrote to the First Consul under date of Ventôse 17th, Year XII—corresponding to March 8th, 1804. I shall in its place relate that this former Minister, after having removed all personal papers, referring either to the death of the Duc d'Enghien or to the occurrences in Spain, from the imperial archives, in 1814, consigned them to the flames. The letter in question here escaped this fate. Placed for a moment in a writing-table, together with all the documents which had been brought from the imperial archives, this letter had slipped behind the drawer of the writing-table, and had remained there in oblivion. It was not till long afterwards that it was found. I have read and re-read the letter, which, on a double sheet of foolscap paper, is written throughout in M. de Talleyrand's hand, and signed by him. It will certainly be published one day. MM. Molé and Thiers have read it. The person who owns it refused to allow any copy to be taken. I recognized it as soon as it was put into my hands, for I saw it at the time it was addressed to the First Consul. Its contents, in substance, were to the effect that its author —Talleyrand—had reflected on the subject of the conversation which he had the honour of having with the General—which was the title given at that time to the

First Consul—that Frenchmen loved his rule, that they placed all their hopes in him, that if anything could disturb their confidence it would be the fear lest he might play the part of a Monk, that the leaders of the conspiracy which had just been found out were men of Fructidor, that a Bourbon was at their head, and that the safety of the State demanded that all the conspirators without exception should be seized. In a final paragraph M. de Talleyrand added that the First Consul's aide-de-camp, Caulaincourt, was prudent and devoted, and that he would carry out whatever orders might be given him in a proper manner, and in accordance with the Consul's wishes.

This accusing letter appears to have been preserved for the express purpose of giving a striking denial to the assertions of Prince Talleyrand, who has frequently repeated, since the Emperor's fall, that the condemnation of the Duc d'Enghien had been entirely disapproved of by him; whilst, on the contrary, he did all in his power to bring it about.

This deplorable affair had a fatal influence on Napoleon's destiny. It became in the hands of his enemies, who as a matter of fact never on any occasion took any interest in the Bourbons, a weapon with which they served themselves with so much success against him, that those who had taken any part in the affair, being frightened of its consequences, did all in their power to throw off all responsibility in this compromising matter from their shoulders. Amongst these was the Duc de Vicence. The reproach of having been mixed up in this catastrophe filled his life with bitterness. He could not foresee that the execution of the Duc d'Enghien would so speedily follow on his arrest. How many times has he not spoken to me of the disagreeable things which he had had to suffer on account of this affair in his family relations, and of the difficulties he had to overcome for the very same reason, after his arrival in St. Petersburg. His first care, on taking possession of the French embassy in Russia, had been to convince the Emperor Alexander, his Ministers, and the Russian nobility, that he had had no part in this tragic occurrence. This was the subject of the two following letters, which were written without the Emperor Napoleon's knowledge, and which were published in the *Journal des Débats* in 1814.

Copy of a letter from M. DE CAULAINCOURT, *French Ambassador to* H. I. M. THE EMPEROR OF ALL THE RUSSIAS:

"ST. PETERSBURG, $\frac{14}{2}$ APRIL, 1808.

"SIRE,

" The information which Your Majesty has received from the Rhine has cleared me of the odious calumny which has been weighing on me for the last three years. There are particulars which Your Majesty cannot know. I owe it to the confidence with which Your Majesty honours me to lay them before you. They will convince Your Majesty to what a degree I am innocent of the arrest of M. le Duc d'Enghien.

" Sent by the First Consul to Strasburg, at almost the same time as General Ordener, a confusion between these two missions has established itself in the mind of the public. General Ordener was ordered to proceed to Ettenheim, there to seize upon the person of the Duc d'Enghien. The order and the documents which I place before Your Majesty will prove how different was my mission to his, and that, in consequence, I had nothing to do, and could have nothing to do, with this unhappy affair.

"I remain, Your Majesty's etc., etc.

"(Signed) : CAULAINCOURT."

Copy of the answer of H. I. M. THE EMPEROR ALEXANDER *to* GENERAL CAULAINCOURT, *French Ambassador.*

"I knew, General, through my ambassadors in Germany, how innocent you were of the horrible affair of which you speak. The documents which you communicate to me can only add to my conviction. I am pleased to tell you this, and to again assure you of the sincere esteem in which I hold you.

"ALEXANDER."

"ST. PETERSBURG, APRIL 4th, 1808."

These two letters were preceded by an article, communicated to the newspaper, in which it was stated that it was General Ordener who effected the arrest of the Duc d'Enghien, and who conducted him to the Strasburg citadel; that the General started the day before M. de Caulaincourt, and that he had received his orders before he started; that his mission was not one of the kind entrusted to several persons; that even supposing it had been thought necessary to put him under anybody's orders, it would not have been under those of an officer younger both in years and in service, that at this the general was so grieved by what happened that he died of a broken heart at Compiègne; that Caulaincourt could so little foresee the results of this expedition that it was by the telegraph that the order to conduct the prince from Strasburg to Vincennes was transmitted; that when M. de Caulaincourt returned to Paris the death of the Duc d'Enghien had already been deplored for several days; that, like Duroc, Caulaincourt had already filled the posts to which they were definitely nominated when the Consulate was transformed into the Empire; and that, finally, General Caulaincourt's mission had two objects, as is shown by the following copy of the Minister of War's letter:—

"Paris, Ventôse 21st, Year XII (March 12th, 1804.)
"The Minister of War to Citizen Caulaincourt.

"The First Consul commands the Citizen Caulaincourt, his aide-de-camp, to proceed by post to Strasburg. He will accelerate the construction and the launching of the light boats which are being built there for the navy. He will inform himself from the Prefect and Citizen Mehée, of the best steps to be taken to effect the arrest of the agents of the English Government, who are at Offenburg and at Freiburg, and notably that of the Baroness de Reich—unless she has already been arrested.

"Captain Rosey, who is on a mission to the English ambassadors, and who enjoys their entire confidence, will give him the necessary information about the plots which are in progress against the peace of the State and the safety of the First Consul.

"Citizen Caulaincourt will inform the bailiffs of the cities on the right bank that, in giving shelter to people who seek to disturb the peace of France, they are exposing themselves to great dangers; and he will arrange with the general in command of the 5th military division for the services, in case of need, of a sufficient force for carrying out these orders.

"He will make a particular report to the First Consul of Captain Rosey's mission."

[Two paragraphs referring to Captain Rosey are omitted in the copy.]

"The Minister of War,
"ALEX. BERTHIER."

The author of the article added that the falseness of the accusations made against Caulaincourt was known to people at that time near the First Consul, as well as to the residents in the castle of Ettenheim, and to all persons with whom this general officer had to arrange the details of his mission; that his connection with the arrest of the Duc d'Enghien was limited to the grief which he shared with the whole of France and the cruel sorrows which it occasioned him to bear, so that during ten years he could only oppose to this accusation a blameless life; that he was forced on one single occasion to explain the circumstances to a great sovereign, for the purpose rather of returning his confidence than to dissipate doubts which did not exist in that sovereign's mind, as is proved by the two letters mentioned above.

We do not wish to comment in any way on this article. It will suffice us to add that the disadvantageous position in which M. Caulaincourt's susceptibility, which as a matter of principle cannot be blamed, placed him at the court of Alexander, prevented him from serving Napoleon in Russia with the energy and independence which was necessary. His object was to win back public opinion, which was unfavourable to him in St. Petersburg, and to remove the difficulties which this disfavour might throw in the way of the success of his mission. But at the same time he had contracted a tacit obligation towards the Emperor of Russia which had harmful consequences. He had given him an advantage over himself by which this prince knew how to profit. The influence exercised on the mind of our ambassador by the winning and fascinating manners of the Czar, threw the former off his guard, and prevented him from judging rightly the clear-sighted policy of the French Ministry, and from assisting to carry it out. That is the impression which the weak and partial conduct of his ambassador in Russia produced on the mind of Napoleon, who gave him full credit for his devotion and the purity of his intentions. It was owing to this impression that the Emperor consented to Caulaincourt's wish to return to France. The Duc de Vicence was recalled in May, 1811, and replaced by General Lauriston.

The truth is that General Caulaincourt did not know what fate was in store for the Duc d'Enghien. The execution took place whilst the aide-de-camp was still in Strasburg, or whilst he was occupied in the dispersion of the exiles assembled at Offenburg. It was not his mission to arrest the prince, but he could not have been in ignorance that this arrest had been decided upon, seeing that he was present when the orders concerning it were dictated by the First Consul to General Berthier and to myself, and that, together with the First Consul, he looked up on the map the positions of Rheinau and of Ettenheim on the left and right banks of the Rhine, and that he received orders to arrange with General Ordener, and to betake himself to Strasburg with a letter from Talleyrand, which he was to hand to the ambassador of the Elector of Baden, as soon as he had heard the result of General

Ordener's mission; and seeing, finally, that he was entrusted with the use of a sum of twelve thousand francs for paying the expenses of the expedition.

The Emperor, at St. Helena, moved by a feeling of equity and of kindness, such as was the leading trait of his character, wrote most favourably of the Duc de Vicence in the notes in his own hand, which I quoted literally in the first editions of my Memoirs.

In relating the preceding details, I have had no other object in view than to establish the facts as they were, and to define the eagerly discussed part played by the Duc de Vicence in this occurrence, and this in the interests of truth. Far from being animated by any personal feeling, I have always felt as much esteem as respect for the character of this minister.

The sensation produced on the Continent by the arrest and trial of the Duc d'Enghien was great. Two courts, Russia and Sweden, allowed their hostility to break out on this occasion. The one was under the influence of England; the other, whose sovereign carried his hatred for the First Consul to the point of madness, had broken off all relations with the French Government. The Russian Court went into mourning for the Duc d'Enghien, to whom it was in no way related. Protestations were addressed by the Cabinets of St. Petersburg and Stockholm to the Diet of Ratisbon. The Russian ambassador to Paris received orders to make the violation of the Baden territory the subject of an official complaint. Talleyrand answered haughtily to this pretension, on the part of Russia, to interfere in the relations between France and a State to which she was allied. The notes addressed by Russia and Sweden to the Ratisbon Diet were left without answer.

The Elector of Baden declined the intervention of these two powers. Austria, Prussia, and the other continental States took no part in the recriminations which Russia and Sweden were endeavouring to provoke. After replying vigorously to the notes from Russia, the First Consul once more retired into the silence which, during the whole course of this affair, he had imposed upon himself.

Whatever the facts may be, this fatal occurrence has always served Napoleon's enemies as a pretext for attacking him. They have not lost one opportunity of reproaching him with it, seeming to think that all the plots directed against his life, the infernal machine, the conspiracy of Georges, and the isolated attempts to murder him, were perfectly legitimate proceedings, and that he had no right to defend himself against them. These same adversaries, on the other hand, fully absolved the Emperor Alexander for the part he played in the conspiracy which resulted in the dethronement and death of his father.*

It was on this occasion that M. de Chateaubriand began his first attacks upon Napoleon. After the publication of the Concordat, this author had been appointed secretary to the French legation at Rome. His author's pride had been wounded by the indifference with which his "Genius of Christianity" had been received in the capital of the Christian world. There was, moreover, little sympathy between the ambassador—Cardinal Fesch—and the secretary, M. de Chateaubriand, who, unable to content himself with

* All the numerous papers which have been written on the Duc d'Enghien's execution and on the various attempts made by those concerned in it to shift their responsibility to other shoulders have been reprinted in the "*Collection des mémoires sur la Révolution française.*"—R. H. S.

a secondary rank, claimed the right to direct the business of the embassy, and tried on every possible occasion to take the ambassador's place. It was impossible for the Cardinal to allow such an encroachment on his authority. In order to put a stop to this quarrel, which he could no longer appear to tolerate by his silence, the First Consul, yielding to the pressing solicitations of Madame Bacciochi, his sister, recalled M. de Chateaubriand, and appointed him *chargé d'affaires* to the Republic of the Valais. This post appeared a shabby one in the eyes of the person appointed. His ambition was for a post of plenipotentiary minister, and he thought that hierarchical rules might have been dispensed with in his case. The little Republic of the Valais did not play a sufficiently important part in foreign politics to warrant the presence of a plenipotentiary minister there. There was no secretary attached to this post of *chargé d'affaires*, and the salary was only twelve thousand francs. The only consideration which made the prospect of his appointment to the post in the Valais bearable, was that he would not be under the orders of any superior. His friends made him hope that he would soon be called to more important functions, and it was owing to this prospect that he neglected proceeding to his post for some time. He had already received his instructions, when the catastrophe of Vincennes occurred. This occurrence appeared to him to afford an appropriate excuse for refusing a post which he considered beneath him. The letter in which he sent in his resignation to Talleyrand, the Minister of Foreign Affairs, was not, as has been said, offensively brief; nor was it filled with generous anger. M. de Chateaubriand simply said that his wife's health was so bad that the doctors had declared that a change to so pernicious a climate as that of the Valais would be in her case, might prove fatal to her; and that under these circumstances he was forced to resign the post which he owed to the confidence of the government, and that he begged the Minister to persuade the First Consul to accept his resignation, to which he added the homage of his respect. If these were not the exact expressions used in the letter, they at least convey its spirit and its substance. The letter, besides, is to be found in the archives of the Foreign Office. If the motive, namely, the mortal malady with which Madame de Chateaubriand was threatened, which was alleged by its author, was a fallacious pretext, may not this letter be described as a falsehood. If, on the other hand, it was a virtuous indignation which prompted the sick lady's husband, he should, in my opinion, have had the noble frankness to declare it. From whatever point of view one may consider the conduct of the author of "The Genius of Christianity," in this circumstance, it seems to me that it is not too severe to say that he displayed neither delicacy nor true courage.

Napoleon attached but little importance to a step, the motives of which were open to misunderstanding. He treated it with indifference, and ceased to interest himself in M. de Chateaubriand. Later on, in pursuance of his desire of drawing men of talent, with a useful purpose in view, to his side, he thought of employing him on such services as the State was warranted to expect from his talents. M. de Chateaubriand, however, persevering in a weak resistance, he decided to ignore him. This distinguished writer was drawn into this resistance by his own conceit, and by his extreme opinions, which we will at least consider sincere. But it is worthy of notice that a curious eccentricity of mind, or an excessive vanity prompted Viscount de Chateaubriand to imagine himself Napoleon's rival in superiority, establishing constant comparisons between Napoleon and himself, and setting forth their respective characters as the two principles of good and of evil, Oromaze* (Chateaubriand), and Ariman (Napoleon), predestined to eternal antagonism.

I may be allowed to interrupt the chronological order of my narrative to finish what I have to say about M. de Chateaubriand. On his return from his voyage to the Holy Land, he sought on the literary staff of *Le Mercure*, the resources of which he stood in need. The spur of pride which prompted him to revolt against the immense superiority of Napoleon, excited him, whilst forced to admit his own impotence, to commence hostilities against the Head of the Government in the articles which he supplied to *Le Mercure*, a circumstance which brought about the suppression of this paper. M. de Chateaubriand took another opportunity, later on, of defying the Emperor, by putting on mourning, an insulting affectation, for one of his cousins. Charged with a secret mission by the princes of the House of Bourbon, this cousin had been taken in the act and condemned to death. M. de Chateaubriand's publication, in 1811, of the narrative of his journey from Paris to Jerusalem, a work in which,

* Oromaze is an altered form of Ormuzd, the Spirit of sweetness and light, the Being good and pure above all, in the religion of Zoroaster. The etymology of the word Ormuzd is the Zend, *ahoura-mazda* from *ahurô* living, and *mazdáo*, good. Ariman is the spirit of evil.—R. H. S.

better inspired, he nobly praised the Emperor, won back Napoleon's favour to a writer whose talents he esteemed. The preceding year Napoleon had given him a proof of his forbearance, by repairing the omission of "The Genius of Christianity" in the report on the award of the decennial prizes. He further brought the candidature of its author before the Institute. But the obstinacy with which the candidate refused to make any alterations in his reception speech prevented its acceptance. M. de Chateaubriand had been pleased to revive in this speech his hateful memories of the Revolution, and to bring back upon a stage consecrated to literary discussions, *conventionnels* and regicides. A committee of the Institute, to whom this speech was submitted for inspection, decided that it could not be allowed to pass.

The restless and vain mind of M. de Chateaubriand, and his mobile imagination, rendered unbearable the oblivion into which he had fallen, but his pride kept him back. He decided, however, to have the Minister of Police sounded by one of his friends. The Minister of Police had been commissioned by the Emperor to form a kind of literary committee, including such men as Esmenard, Etienne, Jay, Tissot, Michaud, the author of "The History of the Crusades," and others. A chance meeting with the Duc de Rovigo was arranged. The interview passed off to mutual satisfaction. This re-establishment of peace should have been durable if anything could have been lasting with a man like Chateaubriand, for in putting his hand into that of the Minister he had expressed the hope that their reconciliation would not merely be an armistice. An article in *Le Constitutionnel*, which appeared on

August 1st, 1848, and which was written by the clever woman who acted as intermediary in this reconciliation, has revealed details concerning it which were only known to a few people. M. de Chateaubriand, desiring that this reconciliation should be justified in the eyes of the world by a special favour, caused a memorandum to be handed to the Emperor on the subject of the creation of a Ministry of Public Libraries, and asked to be appointed its director. Napoleon did not reject this proposal, but, as by its nature it seemed likely to create difficulties both in men and matters, and because it did not seem very opportune, it was neglected during the time which preceded the rupture of the peace with Russia. The events which followed on this rupture caused both the proposal and its author to be forgotten. M. de Chateaubriand, seeing his powerful adversary abandoned by fortune, had no other thought than to crush him. His instinct of opposition, of resistance and hostility, overflowed in furious attacks against the great and unhappy man. The high opinion which he had of his intellectual value, of the pre-eminence of the race of Chateaubriands, and of the great good fortune which a resuscitation of the ancient monarchy could not fail to bring him, made him lose all self-control and moderation.

The attempts made to effect a revolution in the State by means of the death of the First Consul had given rise to reflections on the inefficacy of a life-long tenure of the supreme post. For many months people had been struck with the necessity of creating a hereditary title, to which the Life Consulate appeared to be a preliminary. The First Consul's household and family took great interest in this important event. In the drawing-room of the ladies and gentlemen in attendance this question had been the subject first of aside and then of general conversations, and the almost general wish expressed was that a hereditary title might be created. Josephine desired this also, although she sometimes expressed to people who were in her confidence that the prospect of the elevation of her husband to a hereditary dignity inspired her with some anxiety for her future. The Senate had given the hint, two months previously, in an address presented to the First Consul; and this example had been followed by the other bodies in the State. The conspiracies and the machinations of the princes, and of the exiles on our frontiers, dispelled many hesitations on this point.

The Tribunate took the initiative in this matter and the Council of State was consulted. Four-fifths of the votes were in favour of heredity. The First Consul was not present at the sitting at which this proposal was discussed. Hearing that the debate had been an animated one, he desired to have the signed opinion of each Councillor of State. He showed no more disfavour to those who had opposed the proposal than to those who had approved it. As a matter of fact he felt respect for those who did not blindly subject their opinions to his own. They had no reason to repent having freely and in good faith expressed their way of thinking. His confidence even was forfeited by those who abdicated their independence before him. Although the vote of the Council of State was not requisite, the First Consul attached importance to the opinion of a body which was justly reputed for its intelligence, and which, though apparently in his hands, was known for its independence.

The wish expressed by the Tribunate, and joined in by such members of the Legislature as were present at the time in Paris, during the vacation of this assembly, was carried to the Senate. On May 18th a senatus consultum was promulgated by which the hereditary imperial dignity was conferred upon Napoleon Bonaparte. The popular vote confirmed that of the great bodies of the State. Out of three millions, five hundred and twenty-four thousand, two hundred and fifty-four electors who registered their votes in the books prepared for this purpose, three millions, five hundred and twenty-one thousand, six hundred and seventy-five voted in favour of the proposal which called Napoleon to the imperial throne. There were only two thousand five hundred and seventy-nine opponents.

At the end of the sitting—during which the First Consul was proclaimed Emperor—the Senate proceeded in a body to St. Cloud to present him with the senatus consultum which they had just passed. The Senate next went to present its congratulations to Josephine. The palace presented that day an aspect of bewilderment and surprise which contrasted with the serenity of the man round whom all this movement centred. An immense crowd covered the steps and approaches to the palace of St. Cloud. I happened to be, after the ceremony was over, in one of the drawing-rooms, conversing with a number of officers and aides-de-camp on the subject which was the one topic of the day. One of the footmen, in full livery, with gold lace on all the seams of his clothes, and dressed in white silk stockings, came to look for me in the midst of a group, and summoned me with the words, spoken in a loud voice: "Sir, the Emperor wishes to see you." These words produced the effect of an electric shock on everybody present. All looked at each other, at first with glances of surprise, but then with smiles, as if to say that it was no dream, but that all were well awake.

There are people who will not hesitate to relate, as though they themselves had been witnesses thereof, the secret communications which, according to them, took place between the First Consul, his colleagues, and their confidants, the good offices performed by these in acting as intermediaries with the influential members of the great bodies in the State, the true or false reasons alleged for necessitating or for justifying this great change, the distribution of offices, and so on. The greatest ingenuity has been displayed in forming more or less erroneous conjectures as to the reasons of Napoleon's elevation. The examples of Cæsar, Augustus, and Cromwell have not been forgotten. According to these Napoleon was only a servile copy of the illustrious men of ambition of antiquity and modern times. It has pleased people to attribute to crooked and crafty ways a solution which the general tendency of public opinion rendered simple and natural. They have tried to spread the belief that he cunningly brought about an event, which pleased him, no doubt, but for the realization of which he had but let himself drift with the tide of public opinion. It has been said that he prepared this transition from the Consulate to the Empire by underhand manœuvres; that he had enshrouded himself in dissimulation and in reticence;

that he had feigned astonishment at the first overtures which were made to him on the subject; that on the reception of the Senate's address he had hidden his joy under the mask of indifference; that he had refused to express any opinion; that in the end he had answered with mock modesty that he desired nothing for himself; whilst as a matter of fact he had forced the army to offer him the Empire; and that, at the same time, he had acted upon the Senate, making it fear lest the initiative should be taken in this matter by the army. The generally accepted opinion that Napoleon was the soul of all these resolutions, and that he was the mainspring of it all, has given credit to these assertions. The character of the Danish monarch, Frederick III., has prompted no historian to look for the determining motive of the resolution taken in 1660 by the States of Denmark, to ascribe absolute power to this prince, in his secret and private promptings.* Neither had Napoleon any need to have recourse to subterfuges and to deceit. His glory and the influence which he had acquired by his victories and his conduct in Italy and in Egypt; success, that magical word which has such an empire over men, had won over almost the entire French nation to his side; whilst at the same time there had sprung up in his mind the conviction that he possessed the strength and the power necessary to raise France to the front rank amongst nations. The efforts and the recent undertakings directed against his power had confirmed him in the opinion that the counter-revolution could

* There are two errors in this statement. In the first place Frederick III. of Denmark conferred the absolute hereditary monarchy upon himself by decree, and secondly this decree was dated and issued November 14th, 1665, not 1660.—R. H. S.

only be prevented by a stable form of government. He had studied the inclinations of the nation. When he was nominated Consul for life, this vote was received with general approbation. He had next been desired to appoint his successor, and this was another step in the same direction. If in the person of this successor there had been recognized a man formed by himself, this successor would scarcely perhaps have been sufficiently strong and sufficiently respected to continue his work without finding obstacles in his path. Had he been a general, rendered famous by his victories, as Moreau for instance, or any other, the first care of the new-comer would probably have been to destroy his predecessor's work. When the fermentation which the questions of lifelong tenure of the supreme post, of the appointment of a successor, had provoked had awakened the idea of a hereditary title, it was found natural that the great bodies of the State should seek out the solution of this question without being driven to do so. France was profoundly impressed with the dreadful excesses of the Reign of Terror and with the flabby regime of the Directoire. As the dangers which Napoleon had incurred were remembered, and the apprehension arose as to what fresh dangers might be menacing him, anxiety was felt as to what would become of France after he had gone. A violent reaction was feared. People were tired of changes, and determined to undergo no fresh vicissitudes. And finally it was the general aspiration to be at last able to rest under the protection of a lasting government.

The opinions on the question of a hereditary title which Napoleon emitted on the day after the 18th

Brumaire, have been quoted against his conduct on this occasion. The march of events, and the constantly increasing inclination of the masses for a hereditary monarchy, had no doubt modified his ideas, and his language, on this subject. At the time when Napoleon pronounced himself opposed to the hereditary idea he declared that Europe must be brought to recognize that a State could exist with the Republican form, that a few years trial would decide this, that the Republic could only be consolidated in France by the perfect harmony of the public powers. Experience had demonstrated the want of such harmony. The opposition which Napoleon had met with in the Assemblies, against his plans of reform, gave him cause to fear a resistance which, as time went on, might become systematic. The Tribunate's opposition was not popular. The nation sympathized with its chief, and applauded the acts of his government. It desired to preserve this government by placing the power of its chief magistrate beyond the uncertainties of hazard, and its government system beyond the reach of the assassin's dagger. To this feeling were due the addresses made by the army and the principal civil functionaries; also the address of the Senate, asking Napoleon to complete his work. This almost unanimous state of public feeling legitimized Napoleon's secret ambition, but he had reason to be surprised at the facility with which people hailed a change towards which he was driven faster than he cared to go. It was therefore unnecessary for him either to abuse or to force public opinion. He guided it in the way in which it was flowing, and occupied himself with regulating its current; proceeding with circumspection, and conciliating the new order of things

with the advantages acquired by the Revolution. The
difficulties which were overlooked by the masses did
not escape Napoleon's far-seeing eye. He had but to
moderate the impatience of the people, and of the army,
and to protect himself against all precipitation. He
had declared that he would only accept the imperial
dignity with the assent of the French nation, an assent
which he was certain of obtaining, but with which he
could have dispensed. The almost unanimous answer
of the votes was in accordance with his expectations
and justified his appeal to the suffrages of the French
people.

He was not obliged, like Cæsar, to fight with a
menacing opposition. The opposition which he met with
in his councils limited itself to the wishes expressed
by certain Republicans of perfect good faith, who
were persuaded that with Napoleon France would be
sufficiently strong to force Europe to live in peace with
her. Napoleon, well aware of the hatred with which
the monarchs regarded the French Revolution, had,
as I have just said, more foresight, and consequently
less confidence in the future of the French Republic.
Had he only considered his personal ambitions he might,
time helping, have come to an understanding with the
foreign Ministries, and have ended by making common
cause with them. His object was a loftier one, his
ambition was more patriotic. Representing the interests
which had sprung from the Revolution, he wished to
definitely assure their victory by making some concessions to the old monarchies, which, as long as France
isolated herself from them, feared for their future existence; a difficult enterprise, which, without being beyond
the power of the genius who had undertaken to carry

it out, demanded as much prudence and dexterity as resolution. Napoleon would have succeeded, in spite of the faults which were less of his doing than the result of circumstances, which he had the strength to master, had time not failed him. The proof that foreigners never ceased to consider him as the champion of liberal ideas and the enemy of privileges, in spite of the purple with which at times he had to cover himself, is that they never compounded with him, convinced as they were that he would never sacrifice the principles of the Revolution to them, and that they could know no rest until they had struck him down. It is, moreover, evident that their suspicion and their ill-will against France have survived the fall of the Empire.

It may be asked to-day what force gave Napoleon the high ambition to assume the crown, and to found a dynasty. The profoundness of the designs of Providence must be recognized here, when one remembers how the haughty Restoration, thinking itself firmly re-established on the ruins of the imperial throne, fell of its own accord, and without glory, by the efforts of some men, prompted by public opinion.* The nation took revenge for the way in which its rights had been ignored by this ancient race, and by the kings who rejected as illegitimate the great man to whom the national gratitude had awarded a crown, because this man was not protected by the prestige of royal birth. In one word, the inauguration of the Empire, in which the privilege of blood was subordinated to the rights and the interests of the nation, weakening as it did the prestige of ancient royalty, founded a new era and made way for the triumph of constitutional ideas in Europe.

* 1830.

The creation of the Empire was a revolution which the Senate wanted to turn to its own advantage, and by which it tried to profit by stipulating for advantages in its favour; amongst others, for the privileges of heredity, and for extraordinary powers. The Tribunate and the Legislative body demanded an increase of pay. A vulgar ambition would not have thought such concessions too high a price to pay for a crown. Napoleon was not dazzled, and saw from a higher eminence. He was not willing, by rendering hereditary the senatorial dignity, to hand over the future of the country to the mercies of an authority which, should it happen to come into conflict with the crown, would impede the onward march of the government, and which, in a time of danger, might render itself independent, and even treat with the enemy if opportunity offered itself. This event, in spite of his foresight, was destined to realization ten years later.

The following extract from a letter by the Comte de Survilliers—Joseph Bonaparte—summarizes, better than I could do, the advantages of the creation of a hereditary title, and answers the reproach addressed to Napoleon of having made himself the heir to the French monarchy:—

"The proclamations of the general of the army of Italy, made it sufficiently clear that if Napoleon came to power, he would establish a government other than the Republic. On the 18th Brumaire, this event was consummated. The Napoleonic monarchy dates from that day. First of all, elective and temporary; next, lifelong; and finally, hereditary; it had to undergo these modifications. The conspiracy of Georges and Moreau decided the declaration of a hereditary title. With Napoleon as Consul for a period, a *coup de main* might overthrow him; as Consul for life, the blow of a murderer would have been required. He assumed hereditary rank as a shield. It would then no longer suffice to kill him; the whole State would have had to be overthrown. The truth is that the nature of things tended towards the hereditary principle: it was a matter of necessity.

"The French monarchy had feudal rights, an exclusive and privileged nobility, a venality in public departments, entail, parliaments, convents, a land-owning clergy, and a confusion of the public treasure with that of the monarch. Did Napoleon re-establish all these things? He consecrated the liberty of the individual and the liberty of property; he rendered public employment accessible to all; he established civil and political liberty in rights and taxation, the liberty of religious beliefs, the jury-system, the system of public registration, the payment of clergymen, distinctions without privileges, and the separation of the public purse from the monarch's privy purse; and enforced the publication of the manner in which the public money was spent. The institution of the Legion of Honour preceded the proclamation of the Empire, but the decoration, instead of being awarded only to special and exclusive classes, was bestowed in return for services of every kind, and was the reward of all kinds of talent. There was a monarch, but he was an emperor, and not a king. It was neither hazard nor caprice, nor a puerile vanity which induced him to take one of these titles in preference to others. The constitutional imperial monarchy was a monarchy, since monarch there was; but it was something very different to the French royal monarchy."

The trial of the Duc d'Enghien was the first act of the great drama which ended in the condemnation of Georges and his accomplices. Hatched by the exiles, at the head of whom the French princes figured, and whose agents were two famous generals—Pichegru and Moreau—the plot was, as I have already said, financed by England, who placed the resources of the State, and the culpable connivance of her diplomatic agents, at the service of the conspirators.

I will not dwell upon the clemency which Napoleon wished to show towards several of the condemned men, who had not blushed to associate with murderers to conspire for his destruction and for the ruin of the State; nor on the assiduity with which his family and his household interceded on their behalf. The execution of Georges caused little regret. Murder, no matter what its object may be, is always odious. Still there was found someone to ask for his pardon. I saw a lady, accompanied by two big daughters, come to La Malmaison one day with this object. They were not received. This lady was not the most respectable agent of the royalist party, which indeed held her in very low esteem. She belonged to a Brittany family, and was the sister of a *conventionnel*. She used to say to her husband's nephew, who was auditor to the Council of State, that, if he accepted the cross of the Legion of Honour, she would never receive him again at her house.

The prosecution of the accused, and the investigation of the charges against them, was proceeded with by the French Government in the full light of day. Not one circumstance, not one detail of the various phases of the conspiracy, not one loophole opened to Moreau and Pichegru, in remembrance of services which they had formerly rendered, was passed over in silence. Nothing was left for the secret historian to glean. Everything bearing upon this vast conspiracy has been published in the *Moniteur*, and a hundred other publications. The murders of Pichegru, and of the English

Captain, Wright, said to have been strangled in prison, are calumnies which are refuted by their very absurdity. It seems to me unnecessary to add a single word to the denials with which this wretched and odious imputation has been met.*

Moreau, after his condemnation, asked and obtained permission to retire to the United States. Napoleon cancelled the sentence of two years' imprisonment to which the general had been condemned, and made no objection to his departure for the United States. It was rumoured that the judges had been secretly pressed to pronounce sentence of death on Moreau, so that Napoleon might have the opportunity of crushing his rival under the weight of his clemency. Napoleon was much too clever to take a false step with people whom he knew to be opposed to him. What has not been said besides? Certain historians have reproduced all these romances with the remarks that there was nothing improbable about these stories. If suppositions were admitted as facts, because they appear probable, might it not be said that Moreau's judges were influenced by his fame, or by the large number of his partisans? For, after all, his guilt was proved, and his name had an immense weight in the conspiracy. Napoleon must have been dissatisfied with the judgment pronounced, because he believed, and probably wrongly, that considerations unfavourable to himself had influenced the members of the tribunal and distorted justice; the resentment was not, however, of long duration. Napoleon had had an idea which was worthy of him;

* The fact remains that Pichegru *was* found strangled in his bed—on April 5th—before his condemnation. See his biography by Gassier, published in 1814, and by Pierret, published in 1826.—R. H. S.

he had had it suggested to Moreau that he should ask him for a private interview. Had the person who was charged with this mission acted with more skill, it is probable that Moreau, in the state of mind in which he was, would have received these overtures favourably. Such a scene would probably have produced the most favourable impression about the new Augustus in the public mind.

Napoleon purchased with the police funds, the estate of Grosbois, and the house in the Rue d'Anjou, which had formerly belonged to Moreau. He gave Grosbois to Marshal Berthier, and the house in Paris to Marshal Bernadotte, whose gratitude for this new favour was as scanty as it had been for previous favours.

It was whilst the Georges trial was in progress before the Seine Court of Assizes that Napoleon remembered Bourrienne. "Do you know," he asked me, "whether Bourrienne is in Paris? You must find out, and write to him to go to the trial. Every evening he must send you a report of what he has heard; he is a very good man for that sort of thing." Bourrienne's reports were regularly sent in to me and transmitted by me to Napoleon. This led to Bourrienne's appointment as plenipotentiary minister to Hamburg, about a year later. Napoleon's return to him is a fresh proof of his remembrance of the services which he had rendered, and of the generosity with which Napoleon forgot the wrong done him. Although the conduct of his old schoolfellow was far from being irreproachable at Hamburg, he tolerated him there. During one of our campaigns in Germany the necessity of being informed of what was going on before and behind our armies made Napoleon desire to receive weekly reports from his ambassadors at Hamburg and Munich. The cross of the Legion of Honour was frequently asked for by M. de Bourrienne in the letters which accompanied his reports. I was ordered not to answer these requests. As they were frequently repeated, I obtained this answer from the Emperor: " Write to him, that, as he worships the golden calf, he shall have money; but that—as to the Legion of Honour—I only give it to those who...."

The Empire had emerged from these storms. All the combinations of corruption, conspiracy and murder had ended only in the elevation of the man whose destruction had been compassed by these infamous means. Like Hercules he strangled the serpents in his cradle. It was the presage of a greatness which will be the subject of the eternal conversation of the world.

The forms of the new court were copied from those of the ancient French monarchy, and the imperial monarchy of Germany, purged of what was servile and Gothic. There were grand charges of the Empire and grand charges of the Court. Napoleon wished to associate his colleagues with his elevation, and one was promoted to the dignity of Archchancellor and the other to that of Archtreasurer of the Empire. The two brothers of the Emperor, Joseph and Louis, were created, the first Grand Elector, and the second Constable. Napoleon created twenty posts of Marshal for his comrades at arms, of which four were bestowed, in reward for former services, on Generals Kellermann, Lefebvre, Perignon and Serrurier. Fourteen places were given to generals on active service, distinguished by the occupation of important commands and likely to be called to render fresh services. These were Generals Berthier, Murat, Moncey, Jourdan, Masséna, Augereau, Bernadotte, Soult, Brune, Lannes, Mortier, Ney, Davout, and Bessières. The other two places were held in reserve.

The Emperor had his chamberlains, equerries, etc. The Empress, on her side, had her ladies in waiting. The prefects of the palace were retained. The chamberlains and the ladies in waiting belonged in part to old families, who desired places at the imperial court, with the exception of some, who remained faithful to their Royalist opinions, or who made it a point of honour to figure in the opposition.

A new ceremonial was established in the services of the court, and was laid down in a code. The Sovereign's person was no longer accessible to the same persons as before. Officers who, till then, had enjoyed the privilege of approaching the Head of the State, and of presenting themselves whenever they pleased, had to yield up this privilege to the chamberlains and to new-comers, who formerly had been obliged to have recourse to the military element. The introduction of this etiquette offended the greater number of these officers. They submitted to it with disgust and grumbling.

Little by little the custom of these changes established itself. Nevertheless, although the army's zeal did not diminish, there remained in the hearts of the soldiers a keen regret for having been deprived of a right by usurpers whom they had never regarded with favour. The object in bringing to the imperial court persons belonging to families which had formerly been attached to the court, was to approach these families to the Sovereign's eyes, to interest them in the new order of things, to remove them from the intrigues of the malcontents, to withdraw them from all harmful influences, and to bring about a fusion of the various classes of society. At the same time, these new servants, more familiar with the usages of polite society, were better fitted for being placed in contact with strangers.

However much Napoleon may have been perplexed by the redoubtable crises through which he had just passed, and in spite of the diversion brought about by his accession to the imperial throne, and by the organization of his court and the imperial State, his attention had never been turned away from the serious war which he was forced to carry on against England. He pushed forward, with the same activity, administrative measures, diplomatic negotiations, and military preparations. He had ordered that several camps should be formed, amongst others one at Compiègne. This camp being nearer to Paris, and within easy reach, the First Consul, who had become Emperor, went to spend some days at the castle of Compiègne, to inspect the camp, which was chiefly composed of dragoon regiments. It was under the command of General Baraguay d'Hilliers, in his capacity of inspector general of troops of this class. At his orders the dragoons went through various exercises before the Emperor's eyes, both on foot and on horse, to show their qualities both as horse and as foot soldiers. The result of these manœuvres was not satisfactory, and the plan was abandoned.

Amongst the authorities of the department who came

to Compiègne to present their respects to the new sovereign, was M. Octave de Ségur, subprefect of Soissons. He was the eldest son of Comte de Ségur, who had been appointed Councillor of State by Napoleon, and who was afterwards made grand master of ceremonies. This young man, who gave the highest promise, and in whose family Napoleon took a special interest, disappeared without leaving any clue that could lead to his discovery, after his return to Soissons, when the camp had been broken up. It was not known for many years what had become of him. Domestic worries, exaggerated by a morbid imagination, had disgusted him both with his home and with society. It was only after the war, in 1809, that Octave de Ségur was heard of. He had enlisted under an assumed name in the 6th regiment of chasseurs, commanded by Colonel Valin and had carefully kept his secret for six years. Taken prisoner, and being invalided, he had been sent to Hungary, where he was living on the estate of the exiled Comte Baschi du Cayla, father-in-law of the Countess du Cayla. The worries of his life as an outlaw, and the privations which he had to undergo, induced him to write to his brother to inform his family of his whereabouts, and to obtain his return to France by means of an exchange. Napoleon had sincerely sympathized with the Comte de Ségur's troubles, and had written him a touching letter at the time of his son's disappearance. He had never ceased to be interested in the mystery which had enveloped his flight. At last, one day, when at Pont-de-Brique, a country house near Boulogne, where his head-quarters were established, he heard that Octave de Ségur was on board one of the ships of the Texel fleet under disguise. Napoleon immediately sent for his brother Philip, who was in service in the palace as captain deputy to the grand marshal of the palace, informed him of what he had learned, and gave him a plausible mission by the help of which he would be able to discover his brother. Philip de Ségur returned from his mission without being able to find any traces of the fugitive, who had either been clever enough to avoid discovery, or who possibly, contrary to what had been reported to Napoleon, had never been on the ship at all.

When Octave returned to France, he had lost precious years for his advancement in the service. The Emperor having asked him if he had the intention of pursuing this career, he answered that he preferred to remain a soldier. Touched by these chivalrous sentiments, but regretting the choice he had made of a career which should only be entered upon by a young man, Napoleon appointed him officer, on the ground of his having been a scholar at the Polytechnic School. His second début in war was unfortunate. Made prisoner near Vilna, at the beginning of the 1812 campaign, he did not return to France until after the fall of the Empire. He then entered the King's military household. A victim to extreme melancholy, he was not able to drive away the sombre fancies which pursued him, and which finally drove him to suicide.

This unhappy man had turned over this fatal design in his mind, long before his death. He used to live in the same rooms as his brother Philip. His son Raymond, who slept in a closet next to his bedroom, heard his father repeatedly getting up in the night and walking about the room, wrapped in thought which was expressed by vague exclamations, the sense of which Raymond was unable to understand. At last, one evening, Octave went to the house of a friend who owed him some money. Finding him out, he tore up the promissory note which this friend had signed in his favour, and threw the scraps of paper before the door. He then went to the St. Michael bridge, carefully filled his pockets with stones, and lying down in the bed of the river, then at low water, crossed his arms with an inflexible resolution, and awaited death. At daybreak on the morrow, he was found in this attitude, and nothing that was done could call him back to life.

Since I have the occasion to speak of this member of the De Ségur family, I will add some details about them. I spent two years as a child at Châtenay, a pretty village in the neighbourhood of Paris. The Comte de Ségur was living there—with his wife, his children, and his aged father, Marshal de Ségur—in a state bordering on destitution. Count and Countess de Ségur's fortune had been exhausted in costly embassies, and the loss of the colony of San Domingo, where they had important properties, had consummated their ruin. M. de Ségur, whose philosophy sustained him against adversity, was living by his pen. He used to write serious books, light comedies, and songs.* He

---

*M. de Ségur d'Aguesseau was born in 1753 and died in 1830. His "Complete Works," published between 1821—1830 comprise thirty-three volumes. His second son, Paul Philip, to whom frequent allusion is made in these memoirs, was born Nov. 4th, 1780, and died in February, 1873. Amongst other works he wrote: "*Campagne du General Macdonald dans les Grisons*" (publ. 1802), "*Histoire de Napoléon et de la grande armée pendant* 1812" (publ. in 2 vols. in 1824), "*Histoire de la Russie et de Pierre le Grand*" (2 vols. 1829), "*Histoire de Charles VIII.*", and "*Histoire et Mémoires*" (8 vols. 1873). His biography by St. René Taillandier was published in 1875.—R. H. S.

composed speeches for the deputies of the *Conseil des Anciens* and the *Conseil des Cinq-Cents*,—amongst others for Baudin des Ardennes. I was present at the marriage of his eldest son, Octave, with his cousin-german, Mademoiselle d' Aguesseau. This union, formed under favourable auspices, was not to be a happy one. The castle of Fresnes, which belonged to the d'Aguesseau family, was close to Châtenay. I can still remember a strange rumour which greatly exercised the peasants in the neighbourhood. It was said that a bull from the Fresnes farm, each time that it was driven out, used to run away from the herd, and force its way to the cemetery where it would dash upon the tomb of an ardent revolutionary who was buried there, and rip up the sods on his grave with its horns, a proceeding which was generally considered a token of divine vengeance.

Napoleon, on his accession to power, called to his side all men of capacity, irrespective of their origin, and of their previous performances and opinions. M. de Ségur's merits could not escape his attention. After the 18th Brumaire, the former ambassador of France to St. Petersburg and Berlin became a member of the Legislative body. He was placed, a year later, in the Council of State, where he rendered useful services. At the time of the foundation of the Empire he was appointed to one of the great charges of the crown, namely that of grand master of ceremonies. Napoleon took this family under his protection and lavished his inexhaustible kindness upon them. The Comte de Ségur's father, former Minister of War and Marshal of France, had lost his pension. Napoleon restored it to him, and when the old mutilated officer came to the Tuileries to thank him, he had the honours paid to him which were formerly attached to his rank. The Comte de Ségur's eldest son, who was thought to have a vocation for the civil service, was appointed, as the reader will remember, subprefect at Soissons; the second son was destined to a military career. He was placed first of all with the so-called Bonaparte hussars, a troop which had been formed as part of the reserve army, which was then being assembled at Dijon. In order to have him near his person, Napoleon afterwards appointed him adjutant of the palace, then quarter-master, and then master of the pages. He married him to Mlle. de Luçay, daughter of one of the prefects of the palace, and endowed him with an income of ten thousand francs charged on the State, and with valuable estates abroad. In 1813 he entrusted him with the command of one of the six regiments of his guard of honour.*

Countess de Ségur, grand-daughter of the celebrated Chancellor d'Aguesseau,† who was distinguished by the loftiness of her character and by most amiable qualities, was nominated vice-president of the Maternity Society, of which, later on, the Empress Marie Louise became president.

The fall of the Empire did not deprive the Comte de Ségur of all the advantages which he owed to the

---

*Philip de Ségur became a general in 1812, a member of the French Academy, peer of France and lieutenant-general in 1830.

† Henri François d'Aguesseau was born at Limoges on Nov. 27th, 1668. Was *Procureur-Général* to the French Parliament from 1700, and Chancellor for various periods, between 1717 and 1750. He died on Feb. 4th, 1751. His works were published in thirteen volumes between 1759 and 1789, and republished in two volumes in 1865. His biography was written by Monnier (second edition published in 1864).—R. H. S.

Emperor's generous patronage. He found himself, at the time, it is true, at Blois, in the suite of the Empress Marie Louise, with three hundred louis as the whole of his possessions, but, some time later, he re-entered the Chamber of Peers as a former senator, and recovered the pension which had been allotted to him in this capacity.

In 1815, he once more fulfilled the functions of Grand Master of Ceremonies during the Hundred Days. It must be said, to Comte de Ségur's honour, that he often used to express his gratitude for the acts of kindness with which the Emperor had loaded his family, and that he religiously respected his memory until the end of his life.

After his stay at Fontainebleau, the Emperor went, by way of Melun, to the castle de la Houssaie, which belonged to Marshal Augereau, who had earnestly begged for the honour of receiving him there. He spent the day there, a splendid fête having been prepared in his honour. Augereau was at that time under the influence of the genius whom fortune abetted. The Emperor expressed the wish that the park should be thrown open to the crowds of people who had come from the surrounding districts to see him.

The events by which Paris and France had been recently disturbed had shown how necessary it was to re-appoint the Ministry of Police, which, before the discovery of the conspiracy, had been annexed to the Ministry of Justice. The inevitable Fouché once more got the portfolio into his hands. In order to minimize the influence of this fatally necessary person, Napoleon associated with the new Minister, four Councillors ot

State, who were charged with the correspondence, and with the carrying out of all instructions in four districts placed under their supervision. The departments of the Empire were divided, with this purpose in view, into three circuits, or zones. The fourth was the prefecture of police of Paris.

The Emperor was always present in spirit at the Boulogne camp. He used to write several letters every day to the Ministers of Marine, War, and the Public Treasury; to Admiral Bruix, commanding the flotilla, and to the generals in command of the troops, to inform them of the plans which he had laid down. He repeated the same orders several times, thinking by these repetitions to keep their vigilance awake. In spite of the short distance from Paris to Boulogne, a distance which had been still further reduced by the creation of a service of couriers, Napoleon felt that his presence on the spot was indispensable to securing a more rapid and more general execution of his orders, the time approaching when there would be a favourable opportunity for setting sail. In consequence he had a house hired in the little village of Pont-de-Brique, situated at about half-a-league from Boulogne, and established his head-quarters there. It was a small country house of but poor appearance, composed of one main building with two wings, and some outhouses. The Emperor took up his abode there with a part of his military and civil households. Almost all his equerries were colonels or generals. Some of the chamberlains also had rank in the army. Napoleon used to leave Pont-de-Brique every day, for Boulogne, at irregular hours, unless detained by some urgent business. He used to return to dinner, inviting two or three generals or superior officers, either military or naval, artillery or engineering, to his table. The Ministers were summoned from Paris when they had some important communication to make. An auditor of the Council of State used to bring him every week the portfolio containing the affairs on which the Council of Ministers had deliberated. Mass was performed every Sunday in a drawing-room, which was fitted for the purpose with a portable altar. Both the military and civil officers of the household were expected to be present.

The position of Pont-de-Brique enabled the Emperor to come to Boulogne in an unexpected manner, to see all with his own eyes, and to provide for unforeseen emergencies. Not considering himself sufficiently near to the scene of his operations, he chose a site on an eminence, which overlooked the sea, and which was called "Tour d'Ordre," from which he could see the English fleet and the various divisions of his flotilla. It is said that Cæsar embarked at this point for the conquest of the British Islands, a favourable omen. Napoleon had a wooden house, composed of several rooms, constructed on this spot and spent several days there. In one of the rooms was a large telescope focussed on the sea, with which one could see distinctly what was going on on the water, and as far as the coast of England. Other huts, for the use of the admiral and the Minister of Marine, were built not far from his. A battery of mortars of unusual calibre had been placed, by his orders, on the Tour d'Ordre. Enormous shells could be fired with these cannons, which had a range of six thousand yards. Ships of the English fleet, which sailed too close to the flotilla, were often struck by these bombs. The detonation of these new mortars was so loud that blood came to the ears of the gunners, and the soil of the Tour d'Ordre trembled beneath their feet. During his stays in his wooden house, Napoleon used to explore the camps and the coast, or, embarked on a flat-bottomed boat, would engage his flotilla in small combats with the English fleet, often pointing a cannon with his own hands.

He superintended the fitting out of the boats, and tested different systems of stowage, being anxious to ship munitions and provisions for twenty days. He considered the stowage of munitions of war and provisions for horses and baggage, and their disposal in the best order, and the least possible space, as a very important part of the campaign. He had the soldiers and sailors drilled, ordered sham embarkations and landings both at day and at night, and spent the best part of his time with the sailors or the soldiers, sharing their labours, urging them on to renewed effort, and inspiring them with the confidence that he felt. He scoured the beach on foot and on horseback, followed by the admiral and the principal naval and military officers. Thanks to this vigilant activity, fresh improvements were every day produced in the details of the armament, whilst the training of both soldiers and sailors gave the best results.

The land forces were encamped in huts, constructed of mud and branches, and were divided into streets. Each regiment, each brigade, and each division had its quarters, separated from the others by broad avenues. Inscriptions expressing patriotic sentiments or testimonials of devotion to the Emperor, some heroic, some comic, could be read on the fronts of these huts.

The gunboats used to leave the various points of

assembly in detachments, coming to the general meeting-place under command of naval officers, replying to the fire of the English cruisers, which were frequently driven back, doubling promontories under the protection of coast batteries, and with the escort of trains of artillery which accompanied them along the coast.

When one thinks of these Homeric times, when the genius of Napoleon was multiplying his gigantic preparations for the invasion of the British Isles, with the determination of striking our eternal enemy to the heart, there comes to one's mind a regret, which is often renewed. This regret is caused by the fact that the Emperor, who had a prescience in things really great, should have thought it necessary to submit the American Fulton's invention, that is to say the application of steam-power to navigation, to the examination of the savants of the Institute. The members of the Institute, after two months deliberation and experiments, declared that this invention was chimerical and impracticable.* Experience has since shown on whose side was the error.

Holland had not made less efforts than France to take part in the expedition against England. Nearly four hundred and fifty vessels were assembled in the ports of the Escaut and the Meuse. It was a dangerous enterprise to bring them up to the French fleet. Napoleon wished that the honour of this undertaking should fall to a Dutch sailor, and Captain Verhuell was chosen by the Dutch Government to be vested with this command. On his refusal, his brother, a simple

* Fulton's invention had not taken a very practical shape at the time, and it was only some years later, namely in 1807, that he was able to realize his conception and launch the first steamship on the Hudson.—R. H. S.

lieutenant who asked for the post, was appointed. Lieutenant Verhuell had been retired from service for some years, but, encouraged by the choice and the instructions of his brother, he accepted this perilous mission. The junction of the two fleets was effected with full success at Ostend, and in spite of the efforts of the English fleet under the command of Sir Sidney Smith. The brilliant way in which Verhuell directed this expedition, bravely attacking the English frigates, won the rank of rear-admiral and the post of aide-de-camp to Napoleon for this able and intrepid officer. Admiral Verhuell, entering the French service was later on rewarded for his talents, with the post of General-inspector of the Northern coasts of France, by his admission to the Senate, and by his naturalization. He was for a long time one of the most distinguished members of the Chamber of Peers.

It was at Boulogne that the Emperor received the news of the death of Admiral Latouche-Tréville, which had occurred on August 19th, 1804, on board the admiral's ship, the Bucentaur, in the roads of Toulon. The Emperor was exceedingly grieved by his loss; he had placed great hopes on the talents and the energy of this general officer, both as regards the Boulogne expedition, and the reorganization of our navy.

To replace Admiral Latouche-Tréville, Napoleon had to choose amongst Admirals Bruix, Villeneuve, and Rosily. Admiral Bruix could not be removed from the command of the Boulogne flotilla, for which he was eminently suited. The Emperor admitted the zeal and ardour of Admiral Rosily, but feared his long absence at sea. Decrés, Minister of Marine, guided his choice to Admiral Villeneuve, who was in command of the Rochefort squadron. Later on Napoleon had reason to bitterly regret his choice of this officer, who, though brave and experienced, was a man of irresolute character.*

During the Emperor's stay at the Boulogne camp, Joseph Bonaparte was nominated colonel of the 4th infantry regiment, and at the same time was appointed Grand Elector. Joseph, after having served under the command of his brother, General Bonaparte, at the commencement of the Italian war, had retired from military service with the rank of major, and, as has been seen at the commencement of this narrative, had taken up a civil career. The Emperor, who reserved for his brother an exalted position, in which military character had to be united to civil character, considered it indispensable that he should resume rank in the army. At the time of the breaking-up of the Boulogne camp, the colonel of the 4th infantry regiment became general of brigade. He was therefore already vested with this rank, when the Emperor appointed him his lieutenant, and entrusted him with the command of the army which was destined to conquer the kingdom of Naples, after the signing of the Peace of Presburg.

The Emperor's fête was celebrated at Boulogne with unusual pomp and ceremony, and afforded those who were present a really magnificent spectacle. Napoleon—raised aloft on a throne, which was canopied by the flags and colours taken from the enemy, surrounded by his Ministers, Marshals, chief officers, senators, deputies, and others present with the army, —towered over the camps and the sea. One hundred

* Defeated at Trafalgar.

thousand armed men, grouped around this throne, were at once the spectators of and the actors in this triumphal feast. The Grand Chancellor of the Legion of Honour presided over the ceremony of the distribution of decorations, which had been placed in the helmets, or on the shields, of Bayard and Duguesclin, which had been brought for the purpose from the museums in which they had been resting. The Emperor handed each man his decoration. The chair which had been prepared for him had not been chosen with the same happy inspiration as the magnificent pieces of armour which served as receptacles for the crosses of the Legion of Honour. It was a chair which was held in some ridicule by the popular mind, it was, namely, the chair of King Dagobert.*

* Compare the verse in the famous popular song "C'est le Roi Dagobert", beginning:
"Le bon Roi Dagobert
"Avait un vieux fauteuil de fer," etc.

The legend relates that St. Éloi, formerly a goldsmith, was commissioned by King Dagobert to make him a chair of gold, that St. Éloi produced two gold chairs out of the materials supplied, and that the King, pleased with his honesty, appointed him his treasurer. The truth is that the chair in question, was not made but simply gilded by St. Éloi. It still exists and is to be seen at the National Library in Paris. This was the chair used at Napoleon's fête at Boulogne. It was repaired and fitted with a back in 1122 by Abbé Suger, of the St. Denis chapter. It may be noted that the song about King Dagobert, alluded to above, was made the vehicle for attacks on Napoleon in 1814, on the eve of his abdication, by the addition of satirical verses. The song was in consequence prohibited, as seditious, by the police. The following are the satirical verses added at that period:

| Le bon roi Dagobert
Se battait à tort, à travers;
  Le grand saint Éloi
  Lui dit : "O mon roi!
  Votre majesté
  Se fera tuer."
  —"C'est vrai," lui dit le roi
"Mets-toi bien vite devant moi." | Le bon roi Dagobert
Voulait conquérir l'univers;
  Le grand saint Éloi
  Lui dit : "O mon roi!
  Voyager si loin
  Donne du tintouin"
  —"C'est vrai," lui dit le roi,
"Il vaudrait mieux rester chez soi." |

During a space of three hours the various regiments marched before the imperial throne to the sound of a hundred thousand cries of "Long Live the Emperor!" to the noise of a thousand drums, and the salutes of three thousand pieces of artillery. In the meanwhile attention was attracted to the sea by the bustle caused by the arrival of a fleet of fifty ships from Havre, in stormy weather, and under the eyes of the English cruisers.

Tables laid for four hundred covers each, had been set up in front of the camps and along the quays. All the members of the Legion of Honour, numbering two thousand, took their places at these tables. A display of fireworks was postponed till the morrow, owing to the violence of the wind.

The preparations for this solemnity, which was remembered for years, had been made during Napoleon's absence on a visit of ten days to the ports of Calais, Dunkirk, Furnes and Ostend. The Emperor had written to Princess Hortense complaining of having received no news of her. This princess, accompanied by the Prince and Princess Murat, came with her son Napoleon, to spend a few days at Boulogne after the Emperor's fête. They lived in a small

Le roi faisait la guerre, Mais il la faisait en hiver ; Le grand saint Éloi Lui dit : " O mon roi ! Votre majesté Se fera geler." —"C'est vrai," lui dit le roi, "Je m'en vais retourner chez moi."	Le bon roi Dagobert Voulait s'embarquer sur la mer; Le grand saint Éloi Lui dit : " O mon roi! Votre majesté Se fera noyer." —"C'est vrai," lui dit le roi, On pourra crier : "Le roi boit !"

The first two verses refer to Napoleon's ambition generally, the third to his Russian campaign, and the last to his proposed invasion of England.—R. H. S.

country house on the banks of the river Liane, quite close to head-quarters. Princess Louis often took her son to see the Emperor, who was very fond of his little nephew.

It was during one of his stays at Calais that Napoleon deprived M. Chaptal of his portfolio as Minister of the Interior. This department was entrusted to M. Portalis, Minister of Public Worship, pending the appointment of a successor to M. Chaptal, an event which took place two days later, M. de Champagny being nominated Minister of the Interior. M. Chaptal entered the Senate. I have heard Napoleon complaining about this Minister on the ground that he did not take any opportunities of speaking to him, that their personal relations were too few and far between, and that he too rarely informed him of the various affairs which were being dealt with in his department. It may be that the Emperor yielded to certain prejudices, which were inspired by his recollections of the failure of the experiment he had tried, in entrusting the same ministry to Laplace, who had had to be replaced by Lucien Bonaparte. He may have thought that savants lost by being diverted from their studies, and were incapable of devoting themselves entirely to the numerous details of a great administration. This was, however, not the case with M. Chaptal, who was a practical savant. As a matter of fact, however, he continued to enjoy Napoleon's favour and esteem. The Emperor took constant opportunities of showing this distinguished savant the high esteem in which he held his talents, and gave him many proofs of his favourable disposition towards him.

M. Chaptal had succeeded Lucien Bonaparte, in November 1800, first of all as 'charged with the portfolio during his absence, and afterwards as his definitive successor. It is known that Lucien's removal was occasioned by the publication of a pamphlet entitled "*Parallèle de César, Cromwell, et Bonaparte*" which, it was thought, was intended to prepare the public mind for the foundation of a new dynasty. On the publication of this book, Fouché, who was Lucien's enemy, came and pointed out that it was producing a bad effect, and offended those who, in the various bodies of the state, in the army, or in different ranks in society, had not abandoned their republican sentiments. It is not probable, as has been reported, that this book was planned out by the two brothers together. Napoleon had no need to sound the hearts of the people, or to prepare the nation for the hereditary idea, since he was very well aware of the existence of a general tendency of the public mind towards these ideas. Fontanes, who lived in the confidence of Lucien and of Madame Bacciochi, was the author of the "*Parallèle.*" He had just returned from exile, and was receiving an allowance from the Ministry, and, being an ambitious man, took this opportunity of showing his zeal to his patrons, and of getting himself known. Lucien adopted Fontanes's work and accepted all responsibility for it, allowing it to be sent out under the stamp of his Ministry, thus giving it official publication in the departments. Excited by the exaggerated reports of the Minister of Police, Napoleon blamed his brother. This circumstance, together with their disagreements on matters of politics and of government, and with Lucien's pretension to be his powerful brother's sole confidant, brought about a coolness between them. Lucien received orders to go to Spain, and to induce the government of that country to unite with France in forcing Portugal to break off her relations with England.

Whether, then, this publication was made by the Minister of the Interior with or without Napoleon's consent, the part which Lucien took in it proves the error of those who have been pleased to attribute to him a spirit of opposition to his brother's plans for the future, or who have considered his alleged resistance to these plans as the reason of their disagreement.

Lucien Bonaparte filled his mission in Spain with brilliant success. He snatched this country away from English influence, and concluded at Madrid numerous diplomatic conventions, which were very favourable to France. On his return to Paris he became first deputy, and then senator, and was endowed with a senatorship on the left bank of the Rhine. He supported the laws presented by the Government, before the Tribunate, with remarkable talent. The Institute admitted him to its membership.

Lucien enjoyed in peace the goods and honours which the First Consul bestowed on his family, and all the respect which his name and talents had won for him. He was called to share the lofty destinies which awaited his brother, when a marriage,* which could not meet with Napoleon's approval, once more disturbed the good understanding which seemed to reign between them. It was in vain that Napoleon

---

*Lucien married twice. His first marriage, a clandestine one, was with Christine Boyer in 1794. Christine Bonaparte died in 1801, when Lucien remarried with Alexandrina de Bleschamp, the widow of a banker, called Jouberton. It is to this union that Méneval refers. Alexandrina died at Sinigaglia in 1855. There were children to both marriages.—R. H. S.

pointed out to his brother what objections there were to his entering upon this marriage. He went so far as to forbid the mayor of the 10th circumscription of Paris to perform the ceremony of the marriage. Lucien left Paris suddenly, went to Plessis-Charmant, a country house which he possessed in the neighbourhood of Senlis, and had the civil and religious ceremony of marriage performed by the village priest, who was at the same time mayor of the commune, before the First Consul could interfere. This open rebellion against the Head of the Government and his family, rendered it necessary for Lucien to leave France. He asked for permission to retire to Italy, and ended by settling down in the Papal States, where he was received with deference by the Pope who, some time afterwards,* conferred on him the title of Prince de Canino. Lucien ceased to wear the insignia of the Legion of Honour. Showing a French general one day, at Rome, the cross of this order, which he had put away in a drawer, and being advised by the general to wear it, he answered: "No, one must not humiliate oneself too much." He took no steps to reconcile himself with his brother, being firmly decided not to submit to the *sine quâ non* of such a reconciliation, namely a separation from his wife. A last attempt was made by the Emperor at the interview which Joseph, King of Naples, had arranged between the two brothers, at Mantua, in 1807, at the end of which they separated not to see each other again till 1815.†

Napoleon's great displeasure at his brother Lucien's marriage was shortly afterwards provoked afresh by

* In 1814, and in exchange for purchase-money.—R. H. S.
† After Napoleon's return from Elba the two brothers met in Paris.

the union which Jérôme Bonaparte, the youngest of his brothers, contracted in the United States. Jérôme, who was at that time serving in the navy as lieutenant, had, towards the end of 1803, married a Miss Eliza Paterson, daughter of a Baltimore merchant. He was nineteen years old at the time. Napoleon, in his double capacity as sovereign and head of the family forbade the transcription of the marriage deed on to the civil registries. Without having recourse to the law-courts, he declared the marriage void, on the grounds that it had been carried out without his consent, without publication of the banns, and whilst the two parties were minors. He asked the ecclesiastical authorities to annul the marriage, but the Pope, who was already for certain reasons antagonistic to the Emperor, taking the interests of a Protestant woman, refused to sever the religious bond which united her to a Roman Catholic.

Recalled to France by the Emperor, Jérôme Bonaparte only returned towards the end of April, 1805. He had arrived at Lisbon on an American vessel, accompanied by his father-in-law and his wife, avoiding the vigilance of the English fleet.* There he was forced to separate from them and, after a sad leave-taking, departed for Madrid. Mr. Paterson and his daughter immediately returned to America.

Jérôme executed to the satisfaction of Napoleon a number of missions with which, as commander and rear-admiral, he was entrusted. He then left the navy for the army, a service for which he had long had an

---

*Some months after the rupture of the Peace of Amiens, the English captured the brig *L'Épervier*, and towed her off in triumph to Spithead, believing that Jérôme Bonaparte, her commander, was on board.

inclination. In 1807, having a body of Bavarians and Würtembergers under his orders, he went through a brilliant campaign in Silesia. One after the other he reduced all the fortresses in a province which had been fortified by Frederick the Great. After the Peace of Tilsit, which by one of the clauses of the treaty raised him to the dignity of King of Westphalia, he married in August, 1807, Catherine, daughter of the King of Würtemberg, a princess whose noble character and admirable conduct under adversity, entitle her to a place in history, and to the praises of all. This marriage having destroyed Madame Eliza Paterson's last hopes, she resigned herself to the annulment of the union which she had contracted in 1803. She addressed herself, in 1808, to General Turreau, who was French ambassador to the United States, and declared to him that she yielded to circumstances which imposed a painful and humiliating sacrifice upon her, and that she placed her own lot and that of her son* in the Emperor's hands. Napoleon, who was at that time in Spain, replied that he would see Madame Paterson's son with pleasure, that he would take him under his protection if she would send him to France, that she could rely on his esteem and his desire to be friendly with her, that in refusing to acknowledge the marriage he had had to yield to political considerations, that he was moreover determined to assure her son's future in a way which would meet her wishes, but that the matter must be treated with prudence and without publicity.

*Jérôme Bonaparte Paterson, born July 7th, 1805 at Camberton. He did not visit France till the reign of Louis Philippe, where he attracted great attention by his remarkable likeness to his great uncle. He died at Baltimore in 1870. A son of his, Jérôme Napoléon Paterson, born in 1832, served in the Crimea.—R. H. S.

Lucien and Jérôme Bonaparte had not been included in the terms of the senatus consultum, referring to the hereditary dignity of the imperial family, because of the marriages which they contracted without the assent, or contrary to the wishes, of the Head of the State. The reasons of this exclusion were well-founded, because it was not possible to separate Napoleon's authority as sovereign from his authority as head of his family. Numerous examples can be cited, if need be, to justify his claim to a right which he believed to be his. In our own days, the Duke of Sussex, son of King George III. of England, having married Lady Murray at Rome, had his marriage annulled, although he had taken the precaution of having it celebrated for a second time after his return to England. His efforts remained without result, and the marriage was declared void because it had been effected without the consent of the English sovereign.

The Emperor went to visit Aix-la-Chapelle, and stayed there eight days. The day after his arrival he received the ambassadors and plenipotentiary ministers who handed him their new letters of credence, and letters of congratulation from their Courts on his accession to the Empire. They were presented at his audience by Minister Talleyrand.

Napoleon went to visit the manufactories of the town and of the little suburb called Borcette, a small manufacturing settlement, about three quarters of a mile from Aix-la-Chapelle, examining all the manufactures exhibited there, and accepting invitations to all fêtes given in his honour. He received in turn the departmental and municipal authorities, the judges, the military, and the clergy, and was present at the singing of a *Te*

Deum which was given in Aix cathedral. The clergy showed him the relics of Charlemagne, who founded this church, and other relics, which formerly had attracted pilgrims to Aix. These relics had been dispersed during the revolutionary period but had been recovered by the Church.

On the eve of August 15th, his fête, the Emperor had taken advantage of his presence at Aix-la-Chapelle with the Empress Josephine, who had preceded him there, to celebrate Charlemagne's fête with all the pomp of military, civil, and religious ceremonies. A pontifical mass was held in the cathedral, in the presence of the Empress, with all her court. It was not to the saint of the legend that this homage was rendered but to the founder of the Western Empire, of which Napoleon considered himself the restorer.

Certain events, more private than public in character, took place during the new Emperor's stay at Aix-la-Chapelle, about which I should like to say a few words.

The indirect part played in the affair of the Duc d'Enghien by General Caulaincourt had been the origin of the favour into which he had been taken. General Lauriston, on his side, had been Napoleon's schoolfellow at the military school, and had become one of his most distinguished, as he was one of his oldest, aides-de-camp. Various positions in the household of the First Consul had been conferred upon him, notably the important post of Master of the Horse. General Lauriston, accordingly, thought that he had a claim to the post of Grand Equerry when the Empire was founded, and was accordingly hurt when this post was given to General Caulaincourt, his junior in service, and his inferior in rank. He complained about the matter to the Emperor, and no doubt made use of expressions which offended Napoleon, for after a most stormy interview with the Emperor at Aix-la-Chapelle, he received orders to start for Toulon to embark on the fleet under the command of Admiral Villeneuve, and to take over the command of an army of seven or eight thousand men in transport. In the course of this expedition, General Lauriston, by a bold stroke, captured a fort in Dominica, the Diamond, which was a source of trouble to the trade and shipping of the island of Martinique. In the end he was present at the fatal battle of Trafalgar, after which he returned to Paris. All remembrance of the unpleasant scene which he had had with Napoleon at Aix-la-Chapelle seemed to have been effaced. The Emperor appeared to have forgotten it, but General Lauriston's attitude in 1814, and since, has shown that he at least remembered it. After his return from his maritime expedition, Lauriston resumed his service, and was employed in the *grande armée* in important commands, which won for him, later on, under the Restoration, his nomination as Marshal of France.*

It was also, I think, at Aix-la-Chapelle, unless it were at Boulogne, that the Emperor caused Colonel Mouton, afterwards Comte de Lobau, to be presented to him. This officer was then commanding the 3rd line regiment. He had opposed Napoleon's elevation

* Alexander James Bernard Law, Marquis de Lauriston, born at Pondichery in 1768, adjutant to Napoleon in 1800, general of division in 1805, accompanied the Emperor to Spain in 1808, fought at Wagram in 1809, commanded the 13th army corps in 1813, was made prisoner at Leipzic, went over to the Restoration, was created a peer in 1815, a marquis in 1817, master of the king's household in 1820, Marshal in 1821, died in Paris in June 1828.—R. H. S.

to the imperial dignity, and had voted against this proposal. The Emperor, satisfied with the discipline which Colonel Mouton maintained in his regiment, and with his knowledge of tactics, was anxious to attach an officer of such merits to his person. He forgot his opposition, and sent for him. The military tribune was converted after a short conversation. Napoleon made him his aide-de-camp, and from thenceforward showed him a confidence which this officer justified by the services he rendered.

Whilst the Emperor was at Aix-la-Chapelle, a fact came to his knowledge which disposed him very unfavourably towards M. de Talleyrand. The matter was in connection with certain territorial advantages which Napoleon wished to bestow on the House of Nassau, in which he was interested. He had reserved to himself to settle this matter with the King of Prussia, with whom he was at that time on the best terms, when he learned that a negotiation, followed up by the French ambassador at the Hague, had been entered upon with a view to obtaining an indemnity of twelve millions from the Dutch Government for the same consideration. The Emperor wrote officially to the Minister of Foreign Affairs to complain that the Dutch Government, already greatly in arrears in carrying out its engagements for the equipment and armament of the flotilla, and whose finances were involved, should be thinking of presenting the Prince of Orange with a sum of money, which was much too great for its resources. Napoleon then spoke in a confidential manner to the Minister about the part which it was alleged had been played in this matter by his ambassador. M. de Talleyrand, however, pretended to be ignorant of it. M. de Sémonville was accordingly ordered to Aix-la-Chapelle to meet the Emperor, and commanded to explain. Our agent at the Hague, thereupon, produced the instructions which he had received from the Minister of Foreign Affairs himself in this matter. The Emperor was most indignant and spoke of nothing less than M. de Talleyrand's dismissal. Armed with the documents which had been handed over to him, he awaited this Minister, who was to come and work with him. He had placed them in the drawer of a little table, and gave me orders not to produce them until I was told to do so. I do not know what happened in the course of this interview, which had threatened to be a stormy one, but M. de Talleyrand went away without the papers being asked for. I heard nothing more about the matter and noticed no apparent difference in the mutual relations of the sovereign and his minister. Doubtless, to make use of Napoleon's own expression, Talleyrand had been so adroitly evasive, that after a long conversation, he had been able to make good his escape, and avoid giving the explanations which the Emperor had promised himself to hear from his lips. Such incidents, however, were so many blows struck at Napoleon's confidence in his minister.

The Emperor continued his journey by way of Cologne, Mayence, and Coblentz, and returned to St. Cloud in the middle of October, after an absence of three months.

Numerous decrees were promulgated on his own initiative, during his visit to the towns of Aix-la-Chapelle, Cologne, Bonn, Coblentz, Mayence, and other places on his route. Others were prompted by reports which he had asked of his various ministers, and which these presented him on his return. These decrees are a proof of the attention with which Napoleon examined all petitions addressed to him, and of the vivacity of conception with which at first sight he saw what improvements were to be made in the towns as well as in the rural districts, and the works of embellishment which might with advantage be carried out in these places. The institution of decennial prizes dates from Aix-la-Chapelle. These prizes were to be distributed every ten years, on the proposal of a committee of the four classes of the Institute, and were to be awarded to the authors of the best works in science, literature, painting, sculpture, and music; to the inventors of the most useful machines for the arts and manufactures; and to the founders of the most advantageous establishments for the furtherance of national agriculture and industries. The disastrous events which occurred in 1814, at the time of the expiration of the first term of ten years, prevented this noble plan, which would have given a salutary impulse to arts and letters, from being carried into execution.

CHAPTER V.

The Pope is Invited to Crown the Emperor in Paris—General Caffarelli's Mission on This Subject—Arrival of the Pope at Fontainebleau, and Afterwards in Paris—Ceremonial of the Coronation—Anecdote—Imperial Protocol—Deposit of the Birth Certificates of the Two Sons of Louis in the Archives of the Senate—The Emperor's Letter to the King of England—Opening of the Session of the Legislative Body—Inauguration of His Statue in the Session Room—Napoleon's Nurse—Proposal by the General of the Jesuits—Its Refusal, and the Supervision of the Members of this Congregation—Project of an Expedition to India—General Desaix's Recollection on This Occasion—Napoleon, King of Italy—Solemn Sitting of the Senate—Death of Admiral Bruix—Departure of the Emperor and Empress for Milan—Departure of the Pope for Rome—Review of His Stay in Paris—Abbés de Pradt and de Broglie—Crossing Mont Cenis—Review Held on the Battlefield of Marengo—Interview Between the Emperor and his Brother Jérôme—Coronation of the King of Italy—The Singer Marchesi—Italian Constitutional Statute—Union of Genoa to the Empire—Departure from Milan—Review of the Montechiaro Camp—Bologna: The Sovereignty of Lucca Given to Princess Eliza—Parma: Moreau de Saint-Méry—Presence of the Emperor and the Empress at Genoa—Magnificent Fêtes Given by the Town—Jérôme Bonaparte's Mission to Algiers—Hasty Return to Fontainebleau—Josephine Refuses to Separate from her Husband—Momentary Estrangement Between the Emperor and Myself—Last Journey to Boulogne—Inexplicable Conduct of Admiral Villeneuve—M. Daru—The Emperor's Letter to M. Dejean—The Plan of Landing in England Quite Serious—Schemes for Using the Boats of the Flotilla for Constantly Menacing the Coasts of England Growing Activity of Napoleon- Night Work—The State of the Army and the Navy—His Memory for Things and Places—His Forgetfulness of Names—Napoleon's Way of Working—His Illegible Writing—His Faulty Spelling—He Obtains Rest through Change of Work—His Power of Concentration—A Sitting of the Council of State—Napoleon Only Leaves Details of Execution to His Ministers—Days of Idleness—Explanation of the Inclination to Superstition which is Attributed to Napoleon—Comte Nowosiltzoff's Mission—Breaking-up of the Camp at Boulogne—Bavaria Invaded by the Austrians Without a Declaration of War—The Emperor Goes to the Senate—The Following Day He Travels to Join the Army—He Stops at Ettlingen and Louisburg—Prince Paul of Würtemberg—Proposal of Armistice Made by Austria—Emperor Alexander at Berlin—The Potsdam Treaty—Battles of Guntzburg, Haslach, and Elchingen—Death of Colonel Lacuée—Napoleon's Stay in Augsburg With the Elector of Treves—Investment of Ulm—Surrender of This Place—Proclamation to the Army—News of the Disaster at Trafalgar—Suicide of Admiral Villeneuve—Battle of Dirnstein—Reflections of Napoleon on the Captivity of King Richard—General Giulay at Saint-Polten—Occupation of Vienna—The Emperor's Short Stay at Schönbrunn—French Flags Found at Innsbruck—Battle of Hollabrunn—Napoleon Extinguishes a Fire There—Arrival at Brünn—M. d'Haugwitz's Mission—General Giulay at Brünn, Accompanied by M. de Stadion, Making Fresh Proposals for an Armistice—General Savary's Mission to the Emperor Alexander—Prince Dolgorouki is Sent to Napoleon—Night Fête Given by the Army to the Emperor—Battle of Austerlitz—Interview of the Emperors of France and Austria at the Sar-Uschitz Mill—Critical Position of Emperor Alexander—Pencil Notes from the Austrian General Meerfeld, and then from Emperor Alexander, to Marshal Davout—Free Retreat Granted to the Russian Army—Success of the Army in Italy—Flags Given to the City of Paris—Decrees—Peace Signed at Presburg—Interview Between Napoleon and Arch-duke Charles—The Emperor's Motives for Signing a Separate Treaty of Peace with Austria—Expulsion of the Bourbons from Naples—Napoleon's Resentment Against Austria—Seizure of Sums Coming from Illegal Taxation—Stay of the Emperor and Empress at Munich—Marriage of Prince Eugène—Re-establishment of the Gregorian Calendar—Return to Paris.

THE question of heredity had been settled by the creation of the Empire. Napoleon's nature was all that was great. The title of Emperor, being the highest title in modern Europe, was the right appellation of the head of a nation which was high above all other nations. This title being admitted, the forms of the courts of neighbouring monarchies, freed from privileges and purged of servility, became a necessity in a new Empire surrounded by ancient European States. If the new Emperor of the French, the chief of a new race, the restorer of religion in France, the most powerful of Catholic sovereigns, stood in need of a religious consecration, he could only receive it at the hands of the Head of the Church and in the metropolis of the Empire. The question of the intervention of the Holy Father in the consecration and coronation of the Emperor, became the subject of the deliberations of the Council of State. Objections were raised in this assembly, where the greatest liberty of discussion was allowed, against a project which seemed likely to prompt the Court of Rome to fresh pretensions. Napoleon's pressing arguments won the day, and Cardinal Fesch, French ambassador at Rome, was charged with the negotiation. After long tergiversations on the part of the Pope and consultations with the most influential cardinals—whose opinions were now favourable, now hostile to the project—the proposals of the ambassador were accepted on conditions which were considered acceptable in Paris. Napoleon, hearing of the Pope's consent, at Mayence, wrote him a dignified and measured letter, *begging him to come and give a religious character to the consecration and coronation of the first Emperor of the French.* This letter was carried by General Caffarelli, one of the Emperor's aides-de-camp, with an invitation to the Pope to come to Paris in the first days of November. Napoleon's letter, which made no allusion to settlement of religious questions which were pending, threw the Pope into a fresh state of perplexity. At last, however, he made up his mind to leave Rome on November 2nd, the day after All Saints Day.

On the 25th the Emperor left the palace of Fontainebleau on the pretext of a hunt in the forest. Informed of the exact time at which the Pope would reach the cross of St. H......, on the Paris road, the Emperor arrived there at the same time. He alighted from his horse and the Pope descended from his carriage. The two embraced, and then entered the Emperor's carriage, Napoleon going first, and placing the Pope on his right. The cardinals, and the Holy Father's suite, entered the other carriages of the court. The procession made its way to the palace, where the two sovereigns were received by Cardinal Caprara, the ministers, and the chief officers of the crown. After resting in his apartment, the Pope paid a visit to the Emperor, and afterwards to the Empress. At four o'clock, Napoleon returned his visit, and remained closeted with His Holiness for half-an-hour. Meanwhile the Ministers and other dignitaries had been presented to the Holy Father. On the morrow, and on the following day the Pope dined with the Emperor. Napoleon kept constantly giving him his hand. I heard Napoleon relate, that in the course of one of their conversations, the Holy Father had pressed him to sign his name at the bottom of a document in which Louis XIV., towards the end of his life, pressed by his confessors, had disavowed the articles of the declaration of the clergy in 1682, which was drawn up by Bossuet as the foundation of the liberties of the Gallican Church. The Pope promised to keep this act of complaisance secret.

On the 28th the Pope went to Paris, accompanied by the Emperor in the same carriage. He was lodged in the Pavillon de Flore where, during his stay in the French capital, he received the bodies of the State, the clergy, the religious corporations, all of whom addressed him, and amongst these addresses the speech of the President of the Legislative Body may be noted. A large number of people belonging to all classes of society solicited the privilege of seeing the Pope, and came to ask him for his blessing. Each day a crowd could be seen under his windows, begging and receiving his blessing on their knees. The Pope used frequently to show himself on the balcony of the Tuileries, sometimes accompanied by Napoleon, and their appearance was always greeted with the loudest cheers.

The ceremony of the coronation took place at Notre Dame on December the 2nd. The Pope went to the cathedral from the Pavillon de Flore, accompanied by a large retinue of priests and prelates, in magnificent robes, preceded by his cross-bearer, who was mounted on a richly-caparisoned donkey. This monk, who wore on his head a broad-brimmed hat of a rounded form, carried a large gilt cross in his hands. Public curiosity was greatly excited by the novelty of a spectacle hitherto unknown to the population of Paris.

It was three hours later that the Emperor followed the Pope from the Tuileries, driving in a state carriage glittering with plate glass and gilding, and laden with pages, who hung on the doors, and before and behind. The pomp of the procession was in harmony with the grandeur of the occasion. I omit the details of the ceremonies, which are to be found everywhere, and content myself with describing the most striking incident in Napoleon's coronation. The Pope, after the usual anointings and blessings, was preparing to take the crown, which was placed on the altar, when suddenly the Emperor seized hold of it, placed it on his head with his own hands, and afterwards crowned Josephine himself. The Pope was reduced to the rôle of a mere spectator. This act, which was a reply to the objections that had been raised through the pretensions of the Court of Rome, provoked a spontaneous movement of surprise amongst all present.

On the eve of the coronation, the Senate had been received in solemn audience by the Emperor, and the result of the voting on the establishment of the Empire was presented to him. Out of a number almost equivalent to that of the citizens who had voted for the Life Consulate, there were only two thousand, or thereabouts, who refused to ratify by their suffrages the elevation of Napoleon to imperial rank. The days which followed on the imperial coronation were taken up with the reception of the bishops, the presidents of the electoral committees, the scientific bodies, and the military deputations. A distribution of the new standards, surmounted by eagles, was made on the Champ de Mars to the regiments of all the forces, and to the national guards of the hundred and eighteen departments of the Empire. On the same day the Emperor and the Pope were present together, at the same table, at a banquet given at the Tuileries. They were attired in their ceremonial robes, and were served by the chief officers of the crown. The event which had just been accomplished was celebrated with fêtes, displays of fireworks, and illuminations.

And as apposite to the Emperor's coronation I will here relate, in its simple truth, an anecdote which Napoleon's biographers have embellished in the most piquant manner. Napoleon lends himself so well to the imagination that it often goes astray when on this subject. But by investing with an air of improbability stories which have no need of any such adornment, the great man is robbed of his originality, and is reduced to a commonplace person. In this way a dénouement has been added to the anecdote to which I am alluding, a dénouement alleged to have taken place at the time of his coronation, but which is a pure invention. Some days before her marriage with General Bonaparte Madame de Beauharnais sent for her notary to talk certain matters of business over with him. When M. Raguideau called he was immediately taken up to Madame de Beauharnais, who was still in bed. The persons who were present in the room withdrew on his entry, with the exception of a young man, who escaped the notary's attention, and who placed himself in the embrasure of the window. After having spoken about certain arrangements in connection with her approaching marriage, Madame de Beauharnais asked to be told what was being said about it. M. de Raguideau did not conceal the fact that her friends regretted to see her marry a penniless soldier younger than herself, whom she would be obliged to support whilst in the army, and who might be killed in war and leave her unprovided for, and with children. Madame de Beauharnais asked him if that was his opinion also. He had no hesitation in answering in the affirmative, adding that with her fortune—she had an income of about 25,000 francs—she could make a very much better match, and that he thought it his duty, both as a matter of conscience and on account of the interest that he took in her, to make these remarks. He concluded by saying, carried away as he was by his zeal, that no doubt this officer was a very respectable man, but that, after all, his sword and his cape were his entire possessions. Madame de Beauharnais thanked him for his advice, and then with a laugh called to the young man who had remained standing before the window, drumming the panes with his fingers and apparently paying no attention to the conversation which had been going on. It is needless to add that this young man was General Bonaparte. "General," said Madame de Beauharnais, "have you heard what M. Raguideau has just been saying?" "Yes," he answered, "he has spoken like an honest man, and what he said makes me respect him. I hope that he will continue to take charge of our affairs, for he has disposed me to give him my confidence." M. Raguideau, learning by what he had heard who this young man (whom he did not know) was, was rather disconcerted. He had, however, no reason to regret his frankness. Napoleon kept General Bonaparte's promises. He appointed him notary of the civil list, always treated him with kindness, and never again alluded to the circumstance by which he had made his acquaintance. This is the little story in all its simplicity; the rest does credit to the imagination of those who invented it. These relate that the Emperor on the day of his coronation, clad in the imperial insignia, and wearing at his side the sword in which the Regent diamond was set, gave himself the pleasure of sending for M. Raguideau to show himself in all the splendour of his rank, and said to him, in a pointed way: "Raguideau, here is the cape, and here is the sword." I regret to be forced to say that this little stroke of revenge, so wittily conceived, never entered the Emperor's mind, occupied as it was with more serious thoughts. The only thing that showed that his thoughts went back to obscurer days was an exclamation which he made to the dearest and most familiar of his brothers: "Joseph," he cried, as he looked at his brother and himself clad in the attributes of power, "if father could see us!" This reflection was inspired less by pride than by a family feeling which in Napoleon's heart towered above the intoxication of glory and the splendours of supreme rank.

The re-establishment of the monarchy rendered the adoption of a protocol or formula of the letters of the cabinet necessary. The Emperor ordered me to look up, at the Foreign Office and at the National Library, documents and traditions by the help of which a protocol was drawn up and adopted by him.

Formerly letters in the Sovereign's handwriting were tied up crossed with two silk ribbons, on the ends of which the royal seal was placed. The colour of the silk was red, or blue, according to the contents of the letter. The Emperor gave up this practice of autograph letters, and the letters were simply placed in sealed envelopes. The height at which the first line might be commenced, the number of times that the words "Your Majesty" might be used, and other minute details were formerly matters of rigorous etiquette. This etiquette was abandoned. Sovereigns of the highest rank used to write to each other as "Sir, my brother;" those of lesser rank were addressed as "My brother," or as "My brother and cousin," the addition of the word "cousin" being a sign of inferiority. The Tuileries Cabinet adopted the use of the formula, "Sir, my Brother," for sovereigns of every degree. The Pope, as in the past, was addressed as "Very Holy Father," or as "Your Holiness," the letters addressed to him ending, as in the past, with the formula: "May God preserve you for long years to come in the government of our Mother the Holy Church." Princes and Princesses, the high dignitaries, the Marshals and their wives, and the cardinals, were addressed as in the past, as "cousins". Letters used to end with the words: "And hereupon, I pray God that He may have you in His holy and worthy keeping," when addressed to the "cousins", and "in His holy keeping" only, when addressed to others; and this formula was retained. Letters addressed by the King, to persons who were not included in these various categories, used formerly to begin on the first line with "Mons. So-and-So." The word "Monsieur", followed by the name and title, was now attributed to everybody without distinction. These modifications, and those which I have mentioned, were the only concessions made to the spirit of the times.

The constitution of the new Empire received its first application on the occasion of the birth of the second son of Prince Louis Bonaparte. A message from the Emperor invited the Senate to register the birth of the eldest son, born under the Consulate, and of his younger brother, and to deposit the deeds of registration in the archives. The Senate, in solemn audience, delivered an official certificate as to the deposit of these deeds of registration, to the Archchancellor, and replied to the Emperor's message with its congratulations.

Napoleon had profited by the circumstance of his accession to the Empire to renew his proposals of peace to the King of England. He never hoped that this proposal would be crowned with entire success, but he was anxious to neglect nothing which might expose the disinclination of the British Government for peace. The letter was addressed to the King, and was answered by Minister Mulgrave in a letter addressed to M. de Talleyrand. Its contents were to the effect that the English sovereign could not reply to the overture which had been made to him in any particular way, without having communicated it to the powers with which he was allied in general, and to Russia in particular; thus refusing to express himself in any way on the Emperor's proposal, and arousing the suspicion that nothing less than a new coalition might be presaged from this new understanding amongst the powers. More formal respect was shown than in preceding communications, but there was not any more sincerity than before in the desire to effect a pacification.

The sessions of the Legislative Corps, which till then had been opened by the Minister of the Interior, were invested with a much more imposing character by the presence of the Emperor, who came to preside over the year XIII—1805—sitting, in person, and with all the pomp of sovereign power.

On this occasion, and in order to perpetuate the memory of the benefits of the Civil Code, a statue of Napoleon was placed in the assembly room of the Legislative Corps. A special sitting, at which the Empress, the princes and princesses of the imperial family, the ladies and gentlemen of their households, the Archchancellor and the Archtreasurer were present, was devoted to the unveiling of this statue. Marshals Murat and Masséna were invited by the President to draw the veil with which it was covered. Immediately after the sitting, which was held at seven o'clock in the evening, a brilliant fête, which the Emperor honoured with his presence, was given in the apartments of the President.

About this time an old Corsican peasant-woman, accompanied by a young woman whom she presented as her niece, was admitted to the Emperor's presence. This woman was Camilla Hari, Napoleon's nurse, who wanted to see him again. He received her with the greatest kindness, and embraced her most affectionately. The poor woman wept tears of joy on seeing her glorious nursling again. I was charged by the Emperor to provide for her wants and her pleasures. She did not speak a word of French. She spent three months in Paris in perpetual enchantment. She was presented to the Pope, who took pleasure in hearing her speak, and was touched by the simplicity of her devotion. The whole Court wished to see her, and she played her part very well indeed. Whilst speaking with tenderness of her foster-child, she did not neglect her interests. She did not seem sorry to return to Corsica, to talk about her journey there, and to show off the presents and the money with which the Emperor and Josephine had loaded her. Napoleon gave her the best part of his paternal inheritance on her return to Corsica. He gave the husband of her niece, whose name was Carboni, a position as tax-collector at Beaucaire.

Whilst the Emperor was occupying himself, not very long after his coronation, with the reform of the religious congregations, only maintaining those which were really useful, he received a letter from the General Superior of the Jesuits, which contained an offer of the services of his Order. The Jesuits were beginning to penetrate into Paris. They had already enlisted a number of young men from the schools, whom they were transforming into emissaries of the opposition against the Imperial Government. The Emperor esteemed this religious Order for the services which it rendered to education, but detested their intrigues. As they were, moreover, the satellites of a foreign government, whose strong pretensions he had reason to fear, Napoleon forbade them to remain in France. They entered the country under different names:*

---

*The invariable custom of the Jesuits to introduce themselves into a new country under the denominations of the clergy of that country. Thus a certain chapel in London was at first ministered to by "gentlemen connected with Stonyhurst College" —R. H. S.

Fathers of the Faith, Paccarists, Ligorists,* Adorers of Jesus, and so on; but his vigilance continued to keep a strict watch on their underhand practices. When, either from reports addressed to him, or from the newspapers, he heard that some new society was establishing itself at any point in the Empire, his instinct did not deceive him. The Emperor then used to make haste to write to the Minister of Police, or to the Minister of the Interior, and blame them for their want of attention, urging them to redouble their vigilance in this matter.

The care bestowed on home and foreign affairs, on fêtes, and solemnities, were only by the way; the great object of Napoleon's solicitude remained his plan of an invasion of England. Some false manœuvres by Admiral Villeneuve, commanding the combined French, Dutch, and Spanish squadrons, made the Emperor dubious of the success of his clever plan, which was to use these fleets to protect the passage of the flotilla. He also conceived the idea of a great expedition to India, and occupied himself, for more than a month, on the means of resolving the difficulties of this great enterprise.

He did not on that account sacrifice the Boulogne expedition; but it seemed to him that an attack directed against England's distant and richest possessions might favour this expedition, by drawing the entire English forces in the wake of our fleets. These, taking advantage of the vastness of the ocean to escape any encounter with the English squadrons, and having landed the

*Members of a sect founded for the propagation of the faith and the amelioration of elementary studies by Alfonzo di Liguori, born in Naples in 1696, and beatified in 1816.—R. H. S.

troops which they were to transport, were to return to our shores and help to cover with their protection the passage across the Channel. However, after having weighed the advantages and the disadvantages of an expedition to India, and taking into consideration the advanced state of the preparations for the Boulogne expedition, Napoleon made up his mind to leave matters as they were, and in no way to complicate his original idea. Judging that it would be asking too much of fortune to attempt such a thing, he decided to postpone the expedition to India to some more favourable time, and impatiently awaited the arrival of the fleets commanded by Admiral Villeneuve. He was much embarrassed as to the choice of a general to direct the invasion of British India. Without doubt he had a high appreciation of the talents of the marshals, and the chief generals who had been formed in his school; but he did not consider them all to possess that combination of good qualities which were necessary for commanding a distant expedition, in which they would have been left to themselves. On this occasion, I heard him regretting General Desaix,* whose high capacity both as a soldier and as a politician he fully appreciated. If General Desaix had still been alive at the time, it is to him that he would have entrusted the execution of his plan of campaign in 1801, which Moreau had not the courage to undertake. The remembrance of Desaix frequently came to Napoleon's mind when he was meditating some great independent military expedition. Perhaps the fact of his being deprived of the assistance of this distinguished commanding officer contributed more than once to a relinquishment of

*Killed at Marengo, June 14, 1800.

his plans. Combined with the Emperor's high esteem for the talents of the regretted general was the superstition of friendship. Desaix's soul responded to his; he would have been the Hephæstion of this second Alexander.

There was another matter in which the Emperor was strongly interested; he was anxious to definitely settle the fate of Italy. In accordance with the wishes of the Italians, he offered the crown of Lombardy to his brother Joseph. Joseph refused it, alleging his desire to preserve his quality as a French prince, and his right of succession to the throne of France; and fearing, so it is said, to alienate his new subjects by paying tribute to France, knowing how much the Italians dislike their money to be carried out of their country. His dominating motive was that he was entirely free from ambition. Napoleon, crossed in his plans, and unwilling to hand over his creation to strange, and possibly hostile hands, decided to join the title of King of Italy to that of Emperor of the French.

During the last days of his stay in Paris Napoleon received, in solemn audience, Vice-president Melzi, accompanied by the members composing the State consultum, and a deputation from the various Italian colleges, who presented him with the address by which the crown of Italy was offered to him.

The next day, so as to dispose of the various matters relating to Italy, and to prepare the future of his further plans concerning this peninsula, at the same time, Napoleon went to the Senate to procure a recognition of Princess Eliza, his sister, as hereditary Princess of Piombino. The title of Prince of Piombino was conferred on her husband, together with the command of the troops charged with the defence of the coasts, and of the communications between the islands, of Elba and Corsica.

At the same sitting of the Senate, the Emperor caused the constitution of the Kingdom of Italy to be laid down in a senatus consultum.

On the same day on which the Emperor was proclaimed King of Italy, Admiral Bruix—who, notwithstanding his shattered health, was struggling, with the energy born of devotion and ambition, with the heavy duties of commander of the Boulogne flotilla—died of consumption in Paris in the prime of life. This admiral had a vigorous mind in the weakliest of bodies. Napoleon, who had watched the struggle of his weakly nature, had had him sounded on the question whether he felt sufficiently strong to resist the fatigues which his command laid upon him. Bruix, either out of devotion to the expedition, or because he was unwilling to appear inferior in capacity to Admiral Latouche-Tréville redoubled his zeal and activity. But soon, his strength spent, he had to be transported to Paris, clinging to his post of commander-in-chief with the tenacity of a drowning man, till the hour when death came to put an end to this painful struggle. He was succeeded by Admiral Lacrosse.

The Emperor having provided for the despatch of business, and having commissioned his brother Joseph to preside over the Senate and the other administrative councils during his absence, which was to last three months, received a farewell visit from the Pope at St. Cloud, and left on the following day, April 1st, for Italy. Four days later His Holiness also left, loaded with costly presents, as were also the members of his suite. Having arrived in Paris in the winter the Holy Father had awaited the spring before returning to Rome. During his stay in the capital of the empire he had been treated with special distinction and honours. He had visited all the public establishments without exception, and a large number of industrial establishments. During his visit to the National Printing-office, Marcel, the director, presented him with a magnificent typographical work: "*L'Oraison Dominicale*," translated into one hundred and fifty languages, and printed in the characters proper to each language. The Pope had performed mass several times at Notre Dame, and at all the parish churches of Paris in turn. Everywhere the greatest respect and deference had been shown him. He left Paris in the first week of April, very much pleased with the religious revival which had been brought about in France by the Concordat, but disappointed in his principal hopes. He had been unable to obtain from the Emperor the concessions which he expected from his gratitude for the step he had taken, and from the influence which he hoped the now firmly established Catholicism of the French nation would have upon Napoleon's purposes. He had failed in various approaches which he had made to the new Emperor on the instigation of his secret council, which was composed of cardinals and bishops imbued with the old notions of the omnipotence of the Holy See, and who only saw in the religious revolution which had taken place in France an opportunity for enforcing their ultramontane ideas. Amongst other concessions, the Pope had demanded the repeal of Bossuet's four propositions, guardians of the liberties of the Gallican Church, and the repeal of the declaration of the French clergy in 1682. He had also asked that the clergy might have the supervision of the schools, and that a public declaration should be made by the Government that the Catholic religion was the dominating religion in France. These pretensions, which were put forward by the Holy Father as points of ecclesiastical discipline, were repelled by Napoleon, with all the respect due to the Head of the Church, but with invincible firmness. Another question, which more closely concerned the Holy See, was the restitution of the legations to the Pontifical States. Napoleon had to show himself inflexible on this point, as on the others. The Pope accordingly quitted Paris regretting to have shown a condescension for which he considered himself very poorly rewarded. His Holiness joined the Emperor at Piedmont, and renewed his leave-taking at the royal castle of Stupinis. Thence he continued his journey to Rome, where he arrived eight months after his departure from the eternal city to crown the new Charlemagne in his capital. It has been noticed that the few sovereigns who were crowned by the Pope went to Rome to receive their consecration at the hands of St. Peter's successor. Pope Leo III. crowned, in Rome,—as Emperor of the Western Empire, —Charlemagne, the benefactor of the Holy See, and the first author of its power.

Napoleon was accompanied, in his journey to Italy, by the Empress Josephine. Cardinal Caprara, Archbishop of Milan, who was to crown the King of Italy, had preceded him. The Emperor had sent the grand master of ceremonies, and part of his court, on in front; the rest escorted him on his journey and Abbés Pradt and de Broglie accompanied him as almoners. These two prelates, restored to reason, appeared to be fully reconciled to the new regime which was established in our country. These two abbés vied with each other in admiration of and devotion to the genius who raised France so high amongst the nations. Their conversations with the Emperor's aides-de-camp during the journey were most secular and gay in tone, and both showed themselves very gallant with the ladies of the palace. They were both men of wit, but Abbé Pradt excelled by his unceasing flow of conversation. Woe to anyone who, in conversation with him, should chance to pause to use his handkerchief, or to take breath; the word was taken from his mouth, and there was no hope of his ever getting a chance to put in another. M. de Pradt was loaded with gifts and honours by Napoleon; but when he saw that the Empire was on its decline, the almoner of the god Mars found out that he had only been serving at the altars of "Jupiter Scapin". He made amends for this aberration in certain writings, which do more credit to his intelligence than to his heart. In one word, his disloyalty can only be described as most scandalous.

M. de Broglie did not act like M. de Pradt, who only insulted the idol when it had been overthrown. Having become first Bishop of Acqui, and then Bishop of Ghent, his attitude and his language changed as soon as the difficulties between the Emperor and the Pope arose. His estrangement from the Imperial Government was as sudden as it was striking. God's elect became, in this prelate's eyes, the enemy of religion and the Antichrist. He took part, resolutely, against the Emperor; and, rejecting with an ardent and obstinate passion, all attempts made by Napoleon to conciliate him, refused even to accept the decoration of the Legion of Honour, wishing to take nothing from the Emperor's hands. His fanaticism reached such a pitch, that his ambition was not for the martyr's palm—the days of martyrdom having passed by—but for that of confessor of the faith. He was confined in Vincennes, and forced to resign his see to gain his liberty. He did not, however, consider himself deprived of his episcopal authority, and continued in secret communication with his clergy, bringing fresh disgrace thereby upon himself. After the fall of the Empire, he was reinstated in his episcopal functions, but lived on no better terms with the Dutch Government. Three years later he was sentenced, *per contumaciam*, to transportation, by the Brussels Court of Assizes, for the crime of disobedience to the laws of the State. At the same time, he was a man of good faith, who was respected for his learning and his irreproachable morals.

The Emperor halted for several days at Lyons and at Turin. Mont Cenis was crossed in the way which was customary at that time. The carriages had to be taken to pieces, and the travellers had to make their way by steep paths, interrupted at each step. Trusty and surefooted men carried the travellers and their luggage on their backs, or in sedan-chairs; other mountaineers, placed in the front of a kind of sledge, and armed with ferruled sticks, guided their rapid course with marvellous dexterity. When we again crossed this mountain, in 1807, a broad and fine road, with a gentle and easy slope, had taken the place of all this chaos. The road was so easy that it was not necessary to put the drag on the post-chaises. On his arrival at Alessandria,* Napoleon visited the immense fortifications which he had ordered, and held a grand review on the battle-field of Marengo. The manœuvres, commanded by Marshal Lannes, were executed on the same plains which, five years previously, had been the scene of the battle. Napoleon had had the coat and the hat which he had worn on that memorable day brought from Paris, and put them on on the day of the review. The sight of this old uniform excited the enthusiasm of the soldiers, most of whom had seen its glitter in the thick of the fire of the great battle, and its dingy embroideries recalled more vividly a memory eminently glorious to French arms, the memory of a victory which had produced such great results.

The Emperor found his brother Jérôme at Alessandria, who had hastened thither, on his return from America, to have an interview with him. He came from Genoa, where he had left the brig *L'Épervier*, which he was commanding. The interview was a stormy one, for the Emperor refused to acknowledge his brother's marriage with Miss Paterson, contracted at a time when the young spouses were under age. The birth of a son, issue of this marriage, had prompted Jérôme to oppose a violent resistance to Napoleon's will. He was forced, however, to yield to the irresistible superiority of his brother's will and returned, immediately after this interview, to Genoa, where he awaited the Emperor's arrival on board his ship.

From Alessandria, Napoleon proceeded to Pavia, where he spent two days. He received there a large

* The fortified town in Piedmont.—R. H. S.

deputation, which had come from Milan to congratulate him, and which helped to swell his procession at the imposing entry which, on May 13th, he made into this capital. The Emperor was received in Milan with enthusiastic demonstrations, rendered more emphatic by the Italian character. The fifteen days which preceded his coronation were employed in completing the preparations for this ceremony. He went to visit the Duomo, the cathedral of Milan, the pride of Lombardy, an immense church, ornamented with a prodigious number of marble statues. He gave orders for the completion of this fine building, which had so long been neglected, a constant subject of regret to the Milanese. It was in this cathedral that, on May 26th, 1805, the coronation of the King of Italy took place with the greatest pomp. The iron crown which had been used for the enthronement of the Lombard Kings had been brought from Monza, where it was preserved as a historical relic. Napoleon placed it on his head with his own hands, as he had done with the imperial crown at Notre Dame, repeating in a loud voice, the words inscribed on the circle of the iron crown: "*Dio mi la diede, guai à chi la tocca.*"

The Empress was not crowned Queen, and watched the ceremony from a gallery on the right of the altar. The coronation was followed by fêtes and popular amusements, amongst others being sports in a circus, constructed after the Roman model, a poor imitation of the antique sports. The Theatre of La Scala displayed all its talent. At the head of the leading singers of Italy figured the celebrated Marchesi, one of the most astonishing eunuchs which the musical conservatories of the country have ever produced.

Marchesi's voice, which had been the object of universal admiration, was heard there for the last time. Enthusiastic about his art he had had himself operated upon, although already in the prime of life. At the time of the coronation he was sixty-three years old. His voice, perfected by the excellence of his method, had remained mellow, pure, and of charming sweetness. He was, moreover, an excellent actor.

The audience granted to the Doge, and to the deputations of the Senate and people of Genoa, afforded an imposing spectacle. The Order of the Crown of Iron was created, and a constitutional statute, settling the organization of the Kingdom of Italy, was presented to the Legislative Corps. Prince Eugène took the oath as viceroy. The constitution provided that the crown of Italy should be hereditary, to the exclusion of women; that adoption could only extend to a Frenchman or an Italian; that as soon as the foreign armies should have evacuated the State of Naples, the Ionian Islands, and the island of Malta, Napoleon would transmit his crown to one of his male children, legitimate, natural, or adopted: and that from that time forward the crown of Italy could no longer be united to the crown of France on the same head, and that Napoleon's successors should constantly reside on the territory of Italy.

After having provided for the general scheme and the most minute details of the constitution of his new kingdom, Napoleon left Milan to visit the different provinces. A large camp had been formed in the plain of Montechiaro, the scene of the battle of Castiglione, and a review was held here before the Emperor; when, as at Marengo, he distributed rewards and decorations. He next visited the fortified towns of Mantua, Peschiera, Verona, and Legnano. The object of these demonstrations was to teach the enemies of France, who were then agitating Germany, to appreciate our military resources, the fine deportment of our troops, their familiarity with war, and the fine spirit with which they were animated.

The union of Genoa to the Empire was accomplished at Milan. The precarious condition of this Republic, a desire to acquire its harbour, and especially the harbour of Spezzia, which was large and safe enough to form the site of a large maritime establishment, and it may also be said the favourable tendencies of the people, decided Napoleon. The Genoese expected a safer future, and the efficacious protection of their commerce, from their incorporation with France. It was this that decided the Senate of Genoa and the Doge himself to go to Milan, and to express their wishes on this subject to the Emperor.

During his stay at Bologna, a deputation from the principality of Lucca, prompted by the same motives, came to ask him to take their country under his protection. There was no need of intimidation on his part to extort the expression of these wishes from these two small states. It was so much to their interest to form integral parts of the great Empire, that they were quite naturally brought to express their desire so to become. Napoleon refused the offer of the Luccans, but he gave them a constitution, and handed over the sovereignty of Lucca to his sister Eliza, who added it to the duchy of Piombino, with which a senatus consultum had three months previously invested her.

The Emperor only stayed twenty-four hours at Parma. He met there with M. Moreau de Saint-Méry, who, owing to the influence of the Empress Josephine, whose compatriot and relation he was, had been appointed Councillor of State and Director-General of the States of Parma, Piacenza, and Guastalla. This director, a man of merit and probity, who, at the beginning of the troubles of the Revolution, had showed firmness as well as moderation, governed these states in a feeble manner, being almost entirely taken up with arts and literature. His way of governing was not in harmony with Napoleon's active and positive processes of administration. He had had a "Treatise on Dancing" printed in a luxurious manner, by Bodoni, and this displeased the Emperor. A mutiny of the militia of the State of Parma severely repressed by Junot—who was sent there with extraordinary powers—was imputed to Moreau de Saint-Méry's weakness. He was recalled, and the States of Parma,—divided into departments, and placed under the French administration—became part of the general organization of the Empire. On his return to France Moreau de Saint-Méry was coldly received by the Emperor. Consigned to oblivion, he received as the reward of his services only a moderate pension, which was increased by the Empress Josephine's liberalities.

Napoleon kept the promises which he had made to the Genoese deputation. He went to Genoa to receive the homage of the new subjects of the Empire, and devoted his attention to the organization of the various departments of the government. The Minister of the Interior had preceded the Emperor to Genoa, and the Archtreasurer, who was commissioned to establish the French regime in this country, was there also. Napoleon was received like a liberator, with effusive demonstrations of gratitude and admiration. Splendid fêtes were given in his honour. The fête in the Roads of Genoa, at which he was present, was fairy-like in splendour. The Emperor, accompanied by the Empress Josephine, and the whole court, crossed the terrace of the Doria palace, which he occupied, and came down the great marble staircase, which goes out into the sea, and from the steps of which Andrea Doria used to embark on board his admiral's galley. Here he got on board an immense rotunda, with columns painted in white and gold, rowed by a hundred oarsmen in rich attire. This rotunda was immediately rowed off towards the harbour, where a regatta was in progress. At the close of the day, numerous floating islands, joined on to this temple as if by enchantment, formed, in the middle of the waves, a garden filled with trees and flowers, and ornamented with statues and springing fountains. As the night grew dark a display of fireworks took place, which lighted up the whole of the Roads, and the numerous buildings built in an amphitheatre around them.

The Emperor met his brother Jérôme again at Genoa. After the reconciliation of the two brothers at Alessandria, Jérôme had been promoted to the rank of commander. He was entrusted with the mission to go with a squadron of vessels to Algiers, and there to summon the Dey to hand over to him the Genoese who had been kidnapped by the Barbary pirates, and who had remained their prisoners. Having become our fellow-citizens the Genoese had a right to the immediate protection of France. The name of Bonaparte, and the commander's firmness, triumphed over the Dey, who had at first refused obedience. Jérôme, within a month after leaving Genoa, brought back to that port all the Genoese and Italians whom he had just rescued from the hardest slavery. This fortunate expedition endeared him to the people of Genoa, who hailed his return with transports of gratitude.

The Emperor, in spite of the eight days spent in Genoa in the midst of rejoicings, did not lose sight of business. Above all, he was constantly preoccupied concerning the war against England, which had been the principal motive of his accepting Genoa. He left this city with the Empress for Turin, where he stayed one day. The extraordinary powers of the Arch-treasurer having lapsed after the union of the Genoese Republic to the Empire, this high dignitary was maintained there in the capacity of Governor-General. The Emperor, on his journey back to Paris, visited the convent of Mont Cenis, where the monks had prepared luncheon for him. This was his only halt till he reached Fontainebleau, towards which he pressed forward with full speed, always accompanied by Josephine, who bore the fatigues and the privations, inseparable from such rapid travelling, with remarkable endurance. It would have been useless for the Emperor to try and spare her; she was indifferent to the length of the journey and the absence of all the comforts to which she was accustomed, so long as she was not separated from Napoleon. In this hurried journey, escorts of under-officers, grenadiers, and chasseurs of the guard, had been formed to accompany the Emperor's carriage, but so fast was the pace that none of them were able to keep up with the carriages to the end. The Emperor thanked them for their zeal, and after that time the experiment was not renewed.

I think it my duty, as a truthful historian, to relate the one occasion, during the many years which I passed near his person, on which he was rather seriously vexed with me. It will also serve to throw a new light on Napoleon's character.

I had been attached to his cabinet for close upon three years. During that time I had received proof of his kindness and his satisfaction with me. No cloud had come to overshadow my relations with him, when their serenity was suddenly troubled by a particular circumstance. Since the rupture of the Peace of Amiens, the work in the cabinet had greatly increased. The hard work to which I was constantly subjected woke in me an irresistible desire for some amusement. Too young, as I was—I was then twenty-seven years old—I was wanting in maturity. I had too little ambition and care for the future not to take advantage of the few hours of leisure which were left me, and which I was able to snatch from the sedentary and monotonous life which I was leading. The Opera masked ball was then at the height of fashion. Napoleon himself used frequently to visit it. I often went there and found some people of my acquaintance, with whom I got accustomed to foregather. That led to our arranging dinner and theatre parties. Once or twice a week we used to dine at the Robert restaurant, there never being more than eight or ten people at the table. The honours were done by one or two ladies of the class it is usual to call "amiable ladies". As fate would have it, most of the men I used to meet at these parties were not in the Emperor's good graces. Amongst them was a former moderate *conventionnel*, his compatriot, and the friend of all his family, whom I had known for a long time,—a keen and clever man, dissatisfied, but incapable of doing any harm. I obtained for him later on a place in the civil service, and he was appointed to a sub-prefecture in Piedmont. He conducted himself with so much skill and loyalty that the Emperor, considering the place he occupied was beneath his merits, put him down for a prefecture. The others were bankers, of whom some had been crossed in their speculations by the general measures of the government, but who, in spite of that, were not hostilely disposed towards it. Although they thought that they had a right to complain, they had sufficient tact not to speak to me of their grievances, to which, in no case, could I have listened. I gave myself up to these innocent pleasures without dreaming of the storm which was gathering over my head. One day when I had been to see the Empress Josephine, she happened to speak to me of the Opera ball, of certain meetings which the Emperor had made there, and which rather excited her jealousy. She added, jestingly, that she knew I was in the habit of seeing a very amiable person there, she complimented me upon my taste, said that she knew her name, and that she was sure that it was because her Christian name was Josephine also that I had chosen her. I denied that I had any such influence with this lady, as she described, and begged her to tell me how she had got to know about these matters. She was good enough to tell me, without a moment's hesitation, that it was Bonaparte who had told her. That gave me cause for reflection. The Emperor's silence towards me, considering how fond he was of joking, surprised me. Then, on thinking the matter over, I felt hurt by this mysterious conduct, and determined to wait until he spoke of the matter to me. Two days later I met him walking with Doctor Corvisart, in a covered alley which led out from the family drawing-room at St. Cloud.

As I passed before them, the Emperor barred the way, and catching me by the arm, looked at me with mocking eyes, and said to Corvisart: " Here, after all, is a man whose usual company is that of my enemies." I was prepared for this sally by what I had heard from Josephine. I was reassured by the rough frankness which the Emperor had used in speaking to me. I ought not to have taken the matter in earnest, but, dissatisfied in my mind with Napoleon's silence towards me, which implied a sort of suspicion, I answered him very seriously that I had had no occasion to see that his accusation was a well-founded one; that if the persons whom I associated with were really his secret enemies, they would find themselves in the wrong box with me; that he could not doubt my loyalty; and that I was not the man to allow anything concerning him to be even hinted at in my presence. He allowed me to speak without interruption, and I withdrew, seeing that he had nothing to add to what he had said. Corvisart, who at first had been surprised at the way in which the Emperor had spoken to me, took my part, and said, with a laugh, that he would willingly go bail for me. The day passed without any allusion being made to what had happened in the morning. Till then my absences had been tolerated, and it sometimes happened that I did not return to the cabinet until the following day. I always managed to get there before the levee, which took place at nine o'clock. When the Emperor crossed his cabinet to go to his levee, I had always taken care, that his papers should be in order, and the letters which had arrived in the morning opened and arranged on the little table which stood by the settee where he usually sat. He used to give a glance at them as he passed, but never stopped unless I told him that there was something important and urgent in the day's letters.

I do not know whether some police reports had put the friendly meetings about which I have spoken, in a false light, but from the moment when I knew that the Emperor had been informed of these meetings, I found that he got to the cabinet before me. I also learned that he had frequently asked for me after dinner, when I was away. It looked as if he was trying to get together as many causes for complaint as possible so as to have all the more right to burst out. The explosion, which took place in the nick of time, was brought about by a parcel which I had sent off by a courier, and which for some reason or other was not punctually delivered at its address. One day, on my arrival at the cabinet, a *huissier* told me that the Emperor had asked for me in an excited tone of voice. Just as the *huissier* was going away, the Emperor made his appearance. He addressed me in a very animated way, and, with an anger which seemed feigned rather than real, reproached me for my neglect of his cabinet, adding that I paid no attention at all, that I was constantly absent, that I absolutely neglected his affairs, and that an important despatch had been lost by my fault. Then, without waiting to hear any explanation from me, he went out to call the courier, and shouted out to him all that his anger could suggest on the subject. Then returning he brusquely opened all the packets which were on his writing-table. He told me that he did not wish me to open his letters in future, and that, without having any doubts of my loyalty, he should not be able in future to trust himself to my vigilance. All this was said and done with so much volubility and precipitation that I was unable to get in a single word. I had never before seen him in such a state of excitement. After this scene he went off to his levee, and thence to breakfast, and did not show himself again. A few minutes before dinner-time I was summoned into the little drawing-room which adjoined his cabinet, where I found him working with the Secretary of State. Napoleon rose on my entrance and approached me with a calm and composed air. In the presence of the Minister he gave me a really paternal lecture, speaking to me of the confidence which he had placed in me, of my duties, of the honour attaching to their right fulfilment, of my future, of all the good he wished me, and so on, speaking to me with so much kindness that, although I had made up my mind to listen to him coldly, I could not help feeling very much touched. He told me that it was necessary that I should cease my absences, because he would have to work all the week. As a matter of fact he came to his cabinet in the evening remaining there a quarter of an hour before calling me. When I came in to his summons, he received me in the most cordial manner possible, calling me his "Dear Ménevalot"—dear little Méneval

— a term of friendship which he often used towards me, made no further allusion to the grievances of the day, and tried to make me forget them. There ended this quarrel, which was never renewed during the long years which Providence destined me still to pass with him. I never ceased to find him good, patient, and indulgent in his treatment of me. I had occasion afterwards, I do not remember in what connection, to allude to this scene. "My dear Méneval," he said, "there are circumstances in which it is necessary for me to put my confidence in quarantine."

The Emperor's attack upon me was without doubt of a nature to hurt my feelings, but to a certain extent it was justifiable. On reflection, I was forced to acknowledge that if sometimes storms arise in the most peaceful minds, and those least exposed to the tempests of life, one cannot be astonished that a keen and ready spirit so susceptible to impressions, so agitated by so many and such various thoughts, should, in circumstances of little importance, have paid its tribute to the imperfections of human nature. The business, the papers which Napoleon entrusted me with, were sufficiently important for him to feel anxiety as to their safety. Besides, although this superior man was not insensible to the pin-pricks of everyday life, under great reverses, he always remained self-controlled, always calm, always serene, and armed with all his presence of mind. So, I bore him no ill-will for what had happened, and neither did he towards me. I may remark, however, that the subjection to which I was constrained seemed to me harder to bear than ever.

On the morrow the Emperor's letters were left unopened on his writing-table. On his entering the cabinet he opened one or two, and handed me the rest, saying, in a tone of some impatience: "Méneval, open these letters!" I touched none of the letters which arrived subsequently. I had often thought that my work was already very heavy, and I did not want to see it increased. I made up my mind to take advantage of the scene which had occurred to get rid of a supervision and a task which, in proportion as business increased, became more and more fatiguing. The duty of opening the sovereign's letters involved their classification according to the Ministers concerned, and the drawing up of a summary on the margin of each communication. Now, very often there was no time for this work. I was constantly being interrupted in it to write at the Emperor's dictation. I will not speak of the responsibility which would have rested on me, to a certain extent, supposing some despatch had been removed or diverted from its destination, or even had simply got lost. Already, in 1803 and 1804, when the English ambassadors, in the residences the least distant from our frontiers, were acting as the agents of disorder and intrigue, and even of corruption, I had suggested to Napoleon how necessary it was that the safety of his despatches should be provided for. He contented himself with giving me a mounted escort. on his journeys between La Malmaison and Paris, which were always made very late in the evening, and this was only done to prevent the carrying off of his portfolio.

In drawing these reflections to a close, I will add that the Emperor gradually accustomed himself to open his letters himself. I helped him in this task, when I had nothing more urgent to do. His devouring cerebral activity, which never could find enough food, and which grew as the demands upon it increased, was all-sufficient. As soon as a letter had been opened he read it, and often answered it at once, putting the others aside to be answered later, and throwing all those which did not need any answer on the floor. Sometimes the Ministers sent to ask me what the Emperor had done with such or such a report. When they heard that he had thrown it aside without an answer they knew what that meant. Napoleon used to call not answering the best part of his work. When he was away, I was charged with opening the letters which might come during his absence, and in case they contained anything urgent to take them to him, wherever he might be, or to hand them to him immediately on his return, even in his private apartments. This custom was established in this way, and was afterwards observed. The little festivities and amusements of which I have spoken to the reader, and which had given offence to Napoleon, were broken off by a series of incidents, and by the absence of the Emperor on a journey in which I had to accompany him.

This episode, which I could not pass over in silence, has interrupted the course of my narrative; may I be allowed to resume it? The Boulogne expedition was ready, and all the vessels were prepared to set sail. Repeated exercises in embarking and landing had trained the troops to precision and speed without confusion, so necessary in this kind of expedition. Each regiment, each brigade, each army corps had its appointed post, and knew on what ships to embark. The most minute instructions had been given to the land forces as well as to the sailors. The winds—which were wanted to blockade the English ships in their ports, and clear the seas—were favourable. Terror reigned in the councils of the Cabinet of London. England, trembling on her island, scattered gold broadcast, and used all the resources of her diplomacy to divert to Austria, or to Russia, the most imminent danger to which she had ever been exposed. The manœuvre, the success of which was to bring together, at the mouth of the Channel, sufficient naval forces to ensure a free passage to the Boulogne flotilla, had succeeded. By skilfully combined manœuvres, Napoleon had succeeded in assembling, in distant waters, the largest part of the fleets of France and of her allies. I must add, in passing, that he did not always find, in his Minister of Marine, the assistance which his ignorance of the element which was the scene of his plans rendered necessary. The responsibility which rested on this Minister on the eve of undertaking so colossal a maritime expedition, rendered him almost constantly negative. This officer, who was so brave at sea, was timid and hesitating in the council. This circumspection might have reacted on the admiral who was charged with the chief command, had not his irresolution and absolute want of strength of character, although he was a brave man, sufficed to paralyse the efficaciousness of the resources at his disposal. The Minister's hesitation and the Admiral's tergiversation provoked the Emperor's impatience in the highest degree. Now discouraged, now regaining confidence, as news came in from the sea, he ended by doubting as to the success of the expedition; and yet, all the preparations had been completed. The Emperor, a prey to all the torments of incertitude, was still clinging to the hope that at any moment he might hear of the appearance of the fleet which he was expecting with such impatience, when he heard that his hopes were shattered by the news of Admiral Villeneuve's entry into Cadiz, where he was blockaded by superior forces. All illusion had then to be abandoned, and Napoleon had nothing else to think of than to prepare for the imminent continental war with which he was threatened by Austria. He determined, in consequence, to break up the camp at Boulogne. Faithful to his custom, to use his own expression, of always doing his work in two ways, he had given secret orders with the object indicated, without, however, making it apparent that he despaired of the success of the expedition, and finally had dictated to M. de Talleyrand directions for the drawing-up of his manifesto.

Some of Napoleon's historians have said that when Admiral Villeneuve's blunders had demonstrated the impossibility of carrying out the plan of an invasion, he sent for M. Daru, general intendant of the army, and dictated to him, in one breath, his plan of campaign against Austria from the different points from which the various regiments should start, up to their arrival at Vienna. That is not like Napoleon. I do not doubt that he would have been able to dictate such an improvised plan, and this was not the first time that he had studied the question of war with Germany. Nor could the plan of campaign have been entrusted to more loyal hands. But it was not his habit to make his secrets known, except where such confidence appeared to him necessary for the success of his plans. Now, in this circumstance, nothing obliged him to take M. Daru into his confidence. The truth is that Napoleon sent for this gentleman and sent him, four days before he himself started for Paris, to General Dejean, Minister of War, with a letter which will be found below, charging him to assist the Minister in carrying out the orders contained therein in the promptest manner possible, so as to avoid letting the office into the secret.

Letter from the EMPEROR *to the* MINISTER OF WAR:

"MONSIEUR DEJEAN,—The Minister of War has no doubt given you various orders to get in readiness for war, armies for Italy and the Rhine. You may consider this war as certain. I have orders for the provision of hoods and boots necessary for the army. Let me know if you have anything at your disposal in Paris. It is necessary that you should give orders to all the cavalry regiments to provide themselves with fresh horses at any price. I see no objection to your supplying them with a million francs for this purpose. I have placed at your disposal an extraordinary sum of two million, two hundred thousand francs, of which one million is for the purchase of horses for the train of artillery, and twelve hundred thousand francs are for the hoods and boots. Look after the carts; have them made at Sampigny. There is a market for transports here; give it greater extension. I presume that you have provided that I be supplied with biscuit at Mayence and Strasburg; I have plenty here. The stock of biscuit made twenty months ago should be used now; there will remain here more than twenty thousand mouths; the biscuit made twelve months ago can be kept. It is possible that matters will be settled after a few battles, and that I shall return to the coast. Hurry on the supply of cloth for Year XIV; it is wanted as soon as possible. You will have, in the whole fifth military division, nine thousand dragoon horses, eight or nine thousand horses of light infantry or hussars, four or five thousand of heavy cavalry, and fifteen hundred of the guards, apart from those of the staff. I wish the service to be carried out by the same administration as far as Boulogne, especially as regards meat and bread. Do not lose a moment in getting supplies of wine and brandy at Landau, Strasburg, and Spires. Landau will be one of the chief points of assembly. I imagine that Vanderberghe is sending the same people to Strasburg as to Boulogne. The first divisions have already started; see him about it. I have asked you for five hundred thousand rations of biscuit at Strasburg, but I have no objection to their being divided thus: two hundred thousand rations at Landau; two hundred thousand at Strasburg, and one hundred thousand at Spires. I expect you to send me two reports, in the first of which you will inform me of the number of horses in each cavalry regiment, fit for service; what funds remain in the treasuries of each regiment; and what horses they are able to provide themselves with. In the second report you will inform me of the state of the clothing of all the regiments of the main army, and at what time they will be in receipt of the clothing for Year XIV. The Minister of War will have sent you the organization of the main army into seven corps. Do not forget the ambulances, and occupy yourself without delay with the details of the organization of this immense army. I may tell you, and you alone, that I expect to cross the Rhine on the 5th Vendémiaire; prepare everything accordingly. I have to add that this letter is intended for your eyes alone, and must not be read by anybody else. Dissemble; say that I am only putting thirty thousand men on the march, to protect our frontiers on the Rhine. Make the various heads of departments, from whom you will not be able to hide the truth, feel the importance of saying the same thing. And, hereupon, I pray God to have you in His holy keeping.

"Napoleon."

"From my Imperial Camp, at Boulogne,
The 18th Fructidor, Year XIII."

I transcribe this despatch as a specimen of thousands of other letters which Napoleon used to write to his Ministers, letters in which, entering into the most minute particulars, he provided for everything. He deemed this necessary for the strict execution of his orders. Often he used to repeat them, to stimulate their zeal.

It has been said that the plan of an invasion of England was only a feint. The reason alleged is that the imminence of a continental war must have made him give up all idea of absenting himself from the Continent with his best army. As a matter of fact, never was there more earnest nor sincerer planning. Napoleon had at first thought of securing the alliance of Prussia, by important concessions, to protect himself against Austria. The conquest of England, with such means as he had prepared, was an expedition which had every chance of success, and which was not to last more than three months. The first victory would have opened the road to London. Communications established in Ireland and Scotland, and a general uprising against the privileged classes of the English lords, would have done the rest. The unfortunate blunder of Admiral Villeneuve, in putting into Cadiz, instead of coming to join the Brest fleet, which was expecting him, and Austria's declaration of war, were the only reasons, first, of the postponement, and then of the abandonment, of this great enterprise.

The necessity of giving up an enterprise which had cost so many efforts, which had given him so much pains, which had involved such enormous expenditure, and which would certainly have succeeded but for the cowardice and incredible irresolution which caused it to fail, filled Napoleon with sorrow and indignation.

Bracing himself, however, to bear up against such a crushing blow, he armed himself with all his resignation under an evil for which there was no remedy. He cast over in his mind the best use that could be made of the flotilla, which could not be maintained in its actual state, but which would always be, in his hands, a powerful weapon for threatening England.

The Emperor's first idea was to form a camp of from sixty to eighty thousand men, and, later on, of one hundred thousand men, on the heights of Boulogne; to reduce the armament of the flotilla to five hundred boats, capable of transporting fifty thousand men and several thousand horses; to embark artillery and material; to form a line of broadsides with these boats, brought up in turn for the purpose of exercise; and to constantly menace the British territory with an imminent descent, which could be carried out immediately after the arrival of the fleet expected at Boulogne.

The advantage of this plan was that it provided for a large camp, placed in a healthy position, and easy to victual, which could be transported to Germany without difficulty, and which compelled England to keep troops on her coasts for her protection, as well as to reserve vessels in the Downs, or on the Thames.

Events and coalitions prevented the execution of this project. In 1811 the Emperor, before starting on his journey to Holland, thought to carry it out. He ordered information on the state of the flotilla at that time to be supplied to him. He desired to spend two millions of francs on the necessary repairs, and to put in order a part of the gun-boats, sloops, and barges, which could be made use of, breaking up such boats as were useless, to use the material for building fresh boats—his object being to form a war flotilla able to embark forty thousand men and two thousand horses. The Emperor had even informed the Minister of Marine of his intention of going to Boulogne to have sail put to the flotilla in his presence, and thus to stimulate the zeal of the crews.

This Boulogne expedition was combined with other armaments which he was preparing at Cherbourg and Antwerp. He considered these the three best points from which to menace the coasts of England and Ireland, and which, according to his plans, were to operate at the same time. The total force of these expeditions would have provided for the transport of one hundred thousand men, and of from six to seven thousand horses.

The English Government, alarmed at the dangers with which the active and resourceful genius of their powerful adversary threatened them, strained every nerve to avert these armaments, by provoking troubles to occupy Napoleon elsewhere. The war with Russia, and the disasters which ensued, caused these enterprises once more to be neglected—enterprises which sooner or later would certainly have eventually succeeded.

The hatred which animated England against France, her perseverance in raising up enemies and difficulties against her everywhere; that policy of hers, which, as the great Frederick used to say, consists in knocking at every door with a purse in one hand, left the Emperor without a moment's peace. But his activity grew in proportion to the obstacles put in his way, and he sorely taxed my strength, which was by no means equal to my zeal. To give an idea of how the gravity of the situation had developed his faculties, and of the increase in work which had resulted therefrom, and that one may judge how his prodigious activity was equal to everything, it is necessary to acquaint the reader with the new order which Napoleon had established in the despatch of his numerous affairs. The Emperor used to have me waked in the night, when—owing either to some plan which he considered ripe for execution, and which had to be carried out, or to the necessity of maturing the preliminaries of some new project, or to having to send off some courier without loss of time—he was obliged to rise himself. It sometimes happened that I would hand him some document to sign in the evening. "I will not sign it now," he would say. "Be here to-night, at one o'clock, or at four in the morning; we will work together." On these occasions I used to have myself waked some minutes before the appointed hour. As, in coming downstairs, I used to pass in front of the door of his small apartment, I used to enter to ask if he had been waked. The invariable answer was: "He has just rung for Constant," and at the same moment, he used to make his appearance, dressed in his white dressing-gown, with a Madras handkerchief round his head. When, by chance, he had got to the study before me, I used to find him walking up and down with his hands behind his back, or helping himself from his snuff-box, less from taste than from pre-occupation, for he only used to smell at his pinches, and his handkerchiefs were never soiled with the snuff. His ideas developed as he dictated, with an abundance and a clearness which showed that his attention was firmly riveted to the subject with which he was dealing; they sprang from his head even as Minerva sprang, fully armed, from the head of Jupiter. When the work was finished, and sometimes in the midst of it, he would send for sherbet and ices. He used to ask me which I preferred, and went so far in his solicitude as to advise me which would be better for my health. Thereupon he would return to bed, if only to sleep an hour, and could resume his slumber, as though it had not been interrupted. The solid *en cas** of food, which used to be brought in at night at the Court, before the Revolution, were not supplied at Napoleon's Court, for the Emperor had not inherited the enormous appetites of the princes of the ancient dynasty. But one of the imperial cooks used to sleep near the larder to serve such refreshments as might be asked for in the night, and which were prepared in advance.

When the Emperor rose in the night, without any special object except to occupy his sleepless moments, he used to forbid my being waked before seven in the morning. On those occasions I used to find my writing-table, in the morning, covered with reports and papers annotated in his writing. On his return from his levee, which was held at nine o'clock, he used to find, on his return to his cabinet, the answers and

* The name "*en cas*" was applied to supplies of all kinds provided "in case" the royal personages should need anything in emergency. The baskets of linen which were placed daily in the bedrooms of the king and the queen, in case their Majesties might want to change without sending to their wardrobes, were called "*en cas*." The term was, however, specially applied to the baskets of provisions placed in the royal bedrooms, "in case" their Majesties might be hungry in the night. The *en cas* basket usually consisted of a large bowl of bouillon, and a cold roast fowl, with wine, lemonade, orgeat, and other drinks. It was the contents of this *en cas* basket that, on a famous occasion, Louis XIV. set before Molière, at his *petit lever*, to show the officers of the bedroom that the King did not share their prejudices against dining with a man who had acted on the stage.—R. H. S.

decisions which he had indicated drawn up and ready to be sent off.

There were on his writing-table reports of the exact state of the land and sea forces. These reports, which were supplied by the Ministers of War and of Marine, were bound in red morocco. They were drawn up on lines which he had laid down, and were renewed on the first of each month. They were divided into columns indicating the number of the infantry and cavalry regiments, the names of the colonels, the number of men composing each battalion, squadron, and company, the departments where they were recruited, and the number of men drafted from the conscriptions, the places where the regiments were garrisoned, the position and the strength of the depots, and the state of their troops and material. If marching regiments had been formed particulars as to their composition, destination, and the dates of their departure and arrival were mentioned in these reports. The marching regiments were composed of conscripts, who were drafted from the depots to the battalions, or squadrons proceeding to the field of battle, when their numbers sufficed to make up a company, a battalion, or a squadron. On arriving at the frontier these various detachments were united into brigades or divisions, commanded by generals, and provided with officers on the way, to take the place of other officers. On their arrival at their destination, these temporary corps were broken up. The officers and the soldiers were distributed amongst the regiments, according to the number that each bore. The corps of engineers, and of artillerymen, and the batteries of artillery, were also described in these reports, which were kept with all the more care that the Emperor had frequent opportunities of testing their correctness. If, during his campaigns, he fell in with isolated soldiers, or small bodies of men, he could tell them at once, from a glance at their regimental number, where to go to, and what stages to pass under way.

The columns of the report referring to the state of the navy contained the names of war-ships of every class, the names of the officers commanding them, the composition and strength of the crews, the names of the departments where sailors and marines were levied, the names of ships which were in docks, and particulars as to what progress had been made in their construction. These latter particulars were ciphered in twenty-fourths.

The Emperor always had a strange pleasure in receiving these reports. He used to read them through with delight, and would say that no work of science or literature ever gave him so much pleasure. His marvellous memory grasped all their details, and retained them so well that, better than the Ministers of War and Marine, he knew what was the composition and the materials of each corps. The spelling and pronunciation of names were less familiar to him, and he never remembered them rightly. But if he forgot proper names, it needed but the mention of them to bring a man or a place most vividly before his eyes. When he had once seen a man, or visited a place, he forgot neither the one nor the other; and anything connected either with the individual or the locality was never effaced from his memory. He knew Gassendi's "Aid to Memory" by heart, and was perfectly acquainted with the use and application of the innumerable details of artillery weapons.

When some lengthy answer was rendered necessary by the reading of a report or despatch; when some spontaneous idea was suggested to him by his observations or comparisons; or when this idea, having sprung up in his mind, elaborated by his meditations, had reached its maturity, and the moment to set it in motion had arrived, Napoleon could not keep still. He could not, like the pythoness, remain attached to his tripod. He collected his thoughts, and concentrated his attention on the subject which was occupying him, taking a strong hold on his mind. He would rise slowly, and begin to walk slowly up and down the whole length of the room in which he found himself. This walk lasted through the whole of his dictation. His tone of voice was grave and accentuated, but was not broken in upon by any time of rest. As he entered upon his subject, the inspiration betrayed itself. It showed itself by a more animated tone of voice, and by a kind of nervous trick which he had of twisting his right arm whilst pulling at the trimmings of his sleeve with his hand. At such times, he did not speak any faster than before, and his walk remained slow and measured.

He had no difficulty in finding words to express his thoughts. Sometimes incorrect, these very errors added to the energy of his language, and always wonderfully expressed what he wished to say. These mistakes were not, moreover, inherent to his composition, but were created rather by the heat of his improvisation. Nor were they frequent, and were only left uncorrected when, the despatch having to be sent off at once, time was short. In his speeches to the Senate and to the Legislative corps; in his proclamations; in his letters to sovereigns; and in the diplomatic notes which he made his Ministers write, his style was polished, and suited to its subject.

Napoleon rarely wrote himself. Writing tired him; his hand could not follow the rapidity of his conceptions, he only took up the pen when by chance he happened to be alone and had to put the first rush of an idea on to paper; but after writing some lines he used to stop and throw away his pen. He would then go out to call his secretary, or, in his absence, either the second secretary or the Secretary of State or General Duroc, or sometimes the aide-de-camp on duty, according to the kind of work in which he was engaged. He made use of the first who answered his call, without irritation, but rather with a visible satisfaction at being relieved from his trouble.

His writing was a collection of letters unconnected with each other, and unreadable. Half the letters to each word were wanting, he could not read his own writing again, or would not take the trouble to do so. If he was asked for some explanation he would take his draft and tear it up, or throw it into the fire, and dictate it over again—the same ideas, it is true, but couched in different language and a different style.

Although he could detect faults in the spelling of others his own orthography left much to be desired. It was negligence which had become a habit, he did not want to break or tangle the thread of his thoughts by paying attention to the details of spelling. Napoleon also used to make mistakes in figures, absolute and positive as arithmetic has to be. He could have worked out the most complicated mathematical problems, and yet he could rarely total up a sum correctly. It is fair to add that these errors were not always made without intention. For example, in calculating the number of men who were to make up his battalions, regiments, or divisions, he always used to increase the sum total. One can hardly believe that in doing so he wanted to deceive himself, but he often thought it useful to exaggerate the strength of his armies. It was no use pointing out any mistake of this kind; he refused to admit it, and obstinately maintained his voluntary arithmetical error. His writing was illegible, and he hated difficult writing. The notes or the few lines that he used to write, and which did not demand any fixed attention, were as a rule free from mistakes of orthography, except in certain words, over which he invariably blundered. He used to write, for instance, the words "cabinet," "Caffarelli" "*gabinet*," "*Gaffarelli*;" "afin que," "*enfin que*," "infanterie," "*enfanterie*." The first two words are evidently reminiscences of his maternal language, the only ones which remained over from his earliest youth. The others, "*enfin que*" and "*enfanterie*" have no analogy with the Italian language. He had a poor knowledge of this language, and avoided speaking it. He could only be brought to speak it with Italians who did not know French, or who had difficulty in expressing themselves in our language. I have sometimes heard him conversing with Italians, and what he said was expressed in Italianized French, with words terminating in *i*, *o*, and *a*.

It is said that Voltaire used to have a number of desks in his room, on one of which was a poem which he had begun, on another a tragedy, on others, a piece of historical writing, and a pamphlet. The author used to pass from one kind of composition to another according as the spirit moved him. Napoleon would deal with in turn, at one sitting, matters relating to war, to diplomacy, to finance, to commerce, to public works, and so on; and rested from one kind of work by engaging in another. Every branch of the government was with him the object of a special, complete and sustained attention; no confusion of ideas, no fatigue, and no desire to shorten the hours of labour, ever making themselves felt.

Napoleon used to explain the clearness of his mind, and his faculty of being able at will to prolong his work to extreme limits, by saying that the various subjects were arranged in his head, as though in a cupboard. "When I want to interrupt one piece of work," he used to say, "I close the drawer in which it is, and I open another. The two pieces of business never get mixed up together, and never trouble or tire me. When I want to go to sleep, I close up all the drawers, and then I am ready to go off to sleep."

The initiative in the drafting of all laws and regulations almost always came from Napoleon. His ideas of amelioration, improvement, and construction kept his ministers sufficiently occupied to need all their time in prescribing and supervising the numerous details of execution. If any regret can be expressed on this subject, it is that the unceasing activity of the highest intellect, which has ever been granted to a human being, should have accustomed his agents to await his inspiration and to distrust themselves; and that in consequence, so many men of talent should have found themselves paralysed and taken by surprise in moments of danger.

Napoleon knew that I did not possess, as he did, the precious gift of being able to go to sleep at will, and that I could not sleep in the daytime. After a piece of work which had occupied a part of the night he would tell me to go and take a bath, and often gave orders himself that it should be got ready for me.

He used sometimes to spend whole days without doing any work, yet without leaving the palace, or even his work-room. In these days of leisure, which was but apparent, for it usually concealed an increase of cerebral activity, Napoleon appeared embarrassed how to spend his time. He would go and spend an hour with the Empress, then he would return and, sitting down on the settee, would sleep, or appear to sleep for a few minutes. He would then come and seat himself on the corner of my writing-table, or on one of the arms of my chair, or sometimes even on my knees. He would then put his arm round my neck, and amuse himself by gently pulling my ear, or by patting me on the shoulder, or on the cheek. He would speak to me of all sorts of disconnected subjects, of himself, of his manias, of his constitution, of me, or of some plan that he had in his head. He was fond of teasing, never bitterly or nastily, but on the contrary with a certain amount of kindness, and accompanied with loud laughter. He would glance through the titles of his books, saying a word of praise or of blame on the authors, and would linger with preference over the tragedies of Corneille, "Zaïre" or Voltaire's "The Death of Cæsar," or "Brutus". He would read tirades from these tragedies, aloud, then would shut up the book and walk up and down reciting verses from "The Death of Cæsar". The passages which he recited with the greatest pleasure, were the following:

"J'ai servi, commandé, vaincu quarante années;
"Du monde, entre mes mains, j'ai vu les destinées;
"Et j'ai toujours connu qu'en chaque événement,
"Le destin des États dépendait d'un moment!"

or again:

"*Caesar:* Qu'oses-tu demander, Cimber?
"*Cimber:* La liberté!
"*Cassius:* Tu nous l'avais promise, et tu juras toi-même
D'abolir pour jamais l'autorité suprême...."

When he was tired of reading or reciting he would begin to sing in a strong, but false voice. When he had nothing to trouble him, or he was pleased with what he was thinking about, it was shown in the choice of his songs. These would be airs from *Le Devin du Village*, or other old operas. One of his favourite songs was about a girl who was cured by her lover of a sting from a winged insect. It was a kind of anacreontic ode, and consisted of one verse only It ended with this line:

" A kiss from his lips was the doctor in this case."

When he was in a more serious frame of mind, he used to sing verses from the Revolutionary hymns and chants, such as the *Chant du Départ,—Veillons au salut de l'Empire*, or he would hum these two lines:

"The man who wishes to bring the world under his sway
"Must begin with his own country."

Was this a piece of self-advice? I believe that he understood his country's happiness otherwise. All the powers of his ambition were strained to render the French nation great and prosperous. He never spoke of France but in terms of affection. France had no rival in his heart, nor in his mind; her greatness was the object of all his thoughts, the opinion that she had of him was his constant preoccupation, although outwardly he seemed to be indifferent to popularity.

I must also speak of that tendency to superstition which has been attributed to Napoleon; for it is a generally accepted idea that he was under the spell of superstitious beliefs. It has even been said that he once consulted the famous Madame Lenormand. Endowed with a vast genius and a vivid imagination, Napoleon may have, at times, taken pleasure in straying into the regions of the world of speculation as a diversion from the realities of life. But so lofty an intellect, so positive a mind, could not admit the prescience of the future, the inversion of the laws of nature, nor let himself be carried away by a sterile love of the marvellous. Like all superior geniuses he had faith in his destiny. His successes, from the very outset of his career, followed by still greater and even unexpected successes, had inspired him with the idea that he was no ordinary man, and that he was called to play a part on the world's stage. "Neither Vendémiaire nor Montenotte,"* he used to say, "led me to believe that I was a superior man. It was not until after Lodi that I began to think that I might

---

* Vendémiaire; when placed in command of the Paris garrison, he successfully repressed the revolt of the Paris sections against the Convention, on Oct. 5th, 1795. Montenotte; scene of his victory over the Austrians, under General Argenteau, April 11th, 1796.—R. H. S.

become a decisive actor on our political stage. Then awoke in me the first spark of a high ambition." His march upwards afterwards confirmed him in this thought. This conviction was a surer oracle to him than the vain predictions of a witch. He drew his confidence from loftier sources. His maxim was: "The future is in the hand of God." He used to say that after he had made the best arrangements, on a day of battle, there came a moment when success no longer depended on him, and that he had to look for it from above.

He could count on his good fortune in the execution of his most daring enterprises. This confidence, inspired by the constancy of his success, was warranted. But he was always prepared in advance for every reverse which he might meet. Luck had no place in the conception of any of his plans. Before finally deciding upon them he would subject them to the minutest scrutiny; every hazard, even the most improbable, being discussed and provided for. I saw Napoleon enjoying prosperity with the keenest pleasure, but I never once saw him betray any surprise. His measures were so well taken, and adverse chances so minimized by his calculations and arrangements that if anything could have surprised him it would have been the failure of plans which he had prepared with so much skill and so much care.

It is difficult to believe that even at a time when no revelation of his future destiny had been made to Bonaparte (still in obscurity) his strong and luminous mind can ever have yielded to the temptation to address himself to the puerile practices of necromancy. It is possible that in the extreme fervour of his love for

Josephine, he may have allowed himself to be drawn into being present at a consultation with a witch, and that he made this sacrifice to the waywardness of the impressionable woman whom he so tenderly loved. However it may be, he did not approve of this weakness of Josephine, and often turned it into ridicule. I was present when he forbade her to go and see Madame Lenormand. He even had this famous juggler arrested. Josephine used to shroud her relations with this woman in the profoundest mystery, and never did the keeper of her privy purse know what sums the Empress had paid for the witch's predictions.

It is a generally accepted belief that great men have been, or must be, superstitious. The vulgar mob, which in that respect is really possessed by the superstitious feeling which it attributes to others, fancies that it is impossible to accomplish great things without supernatural means unknown to the rest of humanity. Others, in short, can only forgive such men their superiority by connecting them in some way with human weaknesses. But, what is the superstition which is attributed to great men? Is it a belief in occult and undefined·powers? Is it, on the contrary, the faith which they have in themselves, or in an intuitive perception of their own value? It is clear that it is in the former of these definitions that superstition lies. This aberration of the human mind cannot be applied to that inner feeling, which led Napoleon, for example, to consider himself a divine instrument charged with a mission on earth, and fated to march onward without fear, and with the certainty of success, under its powerful protection. When Napoleon used to say that the cannon ball that was to kill him had not yet been cast, he did not yield to a feeling of fatalism; he considered that his providential mission had not yet been fulfilled. When he wrote to the Directoire that having seen at the moment of landing in Egypt a sail which he believed to belong to one of the enemy's ships, he had implored Fortune not to desert him, but to grant him five days more, he mentally translated the word "Fortune" by "The Almighty God."

His exceptional situation, the consciousness of the mission which he had to fulfil, suggested to him the best means to secure its success. Thus, when in Egypt he instructed his soldiers to show respect for the religion of Mahomet, for the ministers of this religion, and for its devotees; when he himself attended the religious ceremonies of the Mahomedans, his faith had not changed in the slightest degree. He was acting in the interests of a clever and well-matured policy. His condescension towards the outward signs of Mahomedanism was limited to what was necessary to the success of his plans. His alleged meeting with adepts in the Pyramids, the oath which they exacted from him, and the instructions which they gave him, are so many clumsy inventions, and are not worthy of refutation.

In all the circumstances of his life Napoleon showed that, far from being superstitious, he was penetrated with a profound and mysterious sentiment of the divine omnipotence. His habit of involuntarily signing himself with the cross, on hearing of some great danger; or on the discovery of some important fact, where the interests of France or the success of his plans were concerned, at the news of some great and unexpected good fortune, or of some great disaster, was not only a reminiscence of his early religious education, but also another manifestation of the feeling which led him to attribute these favours or these warnings to the Author of all things. His expectation of help from above at a decisive moment in his battles, his frequent allusions in his conversations, proclamations, and reports to the "only Arbitrator Who holds in His hands all plans and all events;" the religious ideas which the sight of a church, or the sound of church bells awoke in his mind; the re-establishment of the Catholic religion in France; his taking refuge in the consolations of religion during his last moments at St. Helena; do not all these things testify to his faith in Providence?

The storm which had been gathering in the North of Europe, burst forth two months after Napoleon's return from Italy. The Emperor had been watching, for six months previously, the conduct of the Austrian Government, which was trying to deceive him with pretended assurances of friendship, and by the offer of an illusory mediation between France and England, and which replied to all questions as to their armaments either with specious explanations or with formal denials. The friendly demonstrations of this power helped to mask her hostile intentions, and to gain time; she took advantage of this to enter into secret negotiations with Russia and England. The Emperor of Russia had sent one of his chamberlains, Count Nowosiltzoff, to Berlin, and the Prussian Cabinet had asked for his passports in Paris, announcing that this extraordinary envoy was charged with a mission the object of which had not been officially notified. Napoleon, in spite of this reticence, anxious to neglect no means of conciliation, ordered the passports which had been asked for to be sent on at once. The object of this mission, which could not be carried out, was a new proposal of intervention, in conjunction with Austria, between France and England, of which the Russian sovereign took the initiative, and of which he was prepared to assume the responsibility. A mediation of this kind, this understanding between our enemies, the fatal result of which would have been to dictate the law to France, could not be accepted by us. This coalition of three great powers, one of which was making extraordinary preparations for a new war with the French Empire, whilst the others had never ceased to insult our government, was very naturally an object of suspicion in France. Napoleon was waiting to be informed of what was the proposed basis of the negotiation, when the news of the crossing of the Inn by a part of the Austrian army was suddenly received in Paris.

The mission of the Russian chamberlain Nowosiltzoff to Paris was drawing to a close at about the same time, in consequence of the union of the Republic of Genoa with the French Empire. It is well known that peace was not the real object of this mission. The Emperor Alexander, who had just formed the new coalition with Mr. Pitt, had not the least desire to prevent a war in which, with chivalrous ardour, he was only too willing to engage, with the prospect before him of the satisfaction of limiting the power of France. The mission given to his envoy had no other object than to assist the dilatory policy of the Austrian Government, and to help Austria to gain the time which she deemed necessary for the completion of her preparations. When

Austria had thought herself ready, and believed that the right time had come, she had thrown off the mask. In the expectation of taking the Emperor by surprise in the midst of his preparations for his expedition against England, she had marched her troops suddenly into the Bavarian territory. On September 23rd, 1805, the *Moniteur* announced that on the 21st of the same month "the Emperor of Germany, without preliminary negotiations or explanations, and without any declaration of war, had invaded Bavaria."

At the end of the month's journey, which Napoleon had just made on the coast, he had been obliged to renounce, in the presence of the events which we have related, both the plan of an invasion of England and that of breaking up the camp at Boulogne, casting a glance of regret on the prey which had been torn from his grasp. He marched the army which had been collected on the sea-coast to the Rhine, and an official order announced the new destination of the army which from that moment was called "The Great Army." The Emperor's plan was to march his various corps at full speed into the centre of Germany so as to prevent the junction of the Russians and Austrians, and in the hope of giving battle to the allies separately. The expedition to Ireland became out of the question, and Marshal Augereau, who was commanding the corps destined for this expedition, received orders to proceed to the Rhine. This corps, which was only to arrive a fortnight after the others, formed the rearguard. The Emperor wrote to M. Otto, his representative in Bavaria, that the Bavarian troops would have to join the troops commanded by Bernadotte, and to follow his movements. These troops, together with those of Würtemberg, Baden, and several other German principalities who declared in favour of France, added about forty thousand men to the French effective forces. Augereau's army covered the distance which separated it from the scene of war with a rapidity and a precision worthy of the Roman armies.

On the 23rd of September the Emperor proceeded to the Military School, where the Prefect of Paris, with the municipal corporations, handed the keys of the city over to him, which he returned, as though to entrust them to their keeping. He then went to the Senate, there to denounce the triple coalition of Austria, Russia, and England, and announced his departure for the army. As a matter of prudence he had reorganized the national guard, which he charged with the maintenance of order in the interior, and with the defence of our frontiers and coasts, under the command of four senators, former generals. He had moreover summoned to active service a certain class of retired soldiers, who were still fit to carry arms, granting them various advantages.

Prince Joseph was to preside over the Senate, and the other councils of the government, during the absence of Napoleon.

On September 24th the Emperor left Paris, accompanied by the Empress Josephine, whom he left behind at Strasburg, with her court and M. de Talleyrand. He arrived at Ettlingen, a castle belonging to the Elector of Baden, on October 1st. The old Elector, accompanied by his sons and grandsons, had gone there to receive the Emperor, and to seal their alliance with him.

Napoleon was at Louisburg next day. The Elector

of Würtemberg, who was awaiting him there, gave him a brilliant reception. This prince, surrounded by the whole of his court, had at his side his second son, and the Electress, the eldest daughter of George III. He offered his own apartment to the Emperor, and though he was not generally considered a very affectionate father, everything in this home wore a most patriarchal aspect, the stuffs which covered the furniture being in part the work of his children. The Emperor's arrival had put a stop to the Elector's hesitations. He signed a treaty with the French sovereign by which Würtemberg undertook to supply the French army with a corps of troops, with horses, waggons, and artillery. Napoleon spent a week at Louisburg, the object of constant attention and respect. He even accepted an invitation to dine in public with the whole electoral family, to please the Elector. The second son of this prince, Prince Paul, showed himself most attentive to the Emperor, being always at his side, and accompanying him on horseback on all his excursions. Prince Paul had recently married a princess of Saxe-Hildburghausen. This same prince, whose sentiments afterwards changed greatly, for what reason I do not know, at the time of the war with Prussia, in 1806, suddenly left Stuttgart without his father's knowledge, and went to offer his services to the King of Prussia, who gave him a command in his army. He was amongst the number of Prussian officers who were made prisoners at the battle of Jena. The Emperor took no revenge on him for his disloyalty, beyond refusing to see him, and sent him back, out of regard to the King, his father, who had him imprisoned in a fortress. The Elector of Bavaria, who had in vain asked Austria to be allowed to remain neutral, had fled from his capital on the approach of the Austrian army, and took refuge at Würtzburg. Napoleon only saw him at Linz, where the prince came to see him. The Elector returned to Munich, after Bernadotte's army had driven the Austrians out, which took place about a fortnight after the opening of the campaign. The Emperor received the Austrian general Giulay at Linz. He was one of the Austrian generals who had been made prisoner at Ulm, but whom Napoleon had restored to liberty. He came with a request for a suspension of hostilities with a view to opening negotiations for peace. Napoleon asked him if he was vested with sufficient powers to treat for peace then and there. The Austrian general answered that his master could agree to nothing without having first consulted his ally the Emperor of Russia. Such a step could have no other object than to delay the onward march of the French army. Napoleon, in his answer to a letter from the Emperor of Austria— brought by M. de Giulay--said that he was wrong to refer to the Emperor of Russia, who had not the same interest as they had in the war; that this war was only a caprice on the part of the Russian sovereign, whilst for France and Austria it was a struggle which absorbed all their means and all their faculties; that he, Napoleon, was disposed to settle the dispute with the greatest promptitude, but that he could not hide from the Emperor Francis the fear which had arisen from the delays and the intrigues the bitterness of which, considering the past, was still fresh in his memory.

After some hesitation, before the crossing of the Inn

by the Austrians, the Elector of Bavaria had accepted the French alliance, and had added his troops to our army. There remained Prussia which, owing to the personal feelings of the King, was observing neutrality. The passing of Bernadotte's corps through the principality of Anspach gave the war-party in Berlin the desired pretext for persuading the King to assume a menacing attitude. In consequence of this Minister Hardenberg listened with a very bad grace to the explanations which were given him about the march of this corps of the French army. The sudden appearance of the Emperor Alexander in Berlin finally triumphed over the irresolution of the King, and a treaty of alliance was signed between the two monarchs at Potsdam, on November 3rd. It was sealed by oaths taken on the tomb of the great Frederick, a scene which had been prepared by the Queen. The king, however, caused certain reservations which he considered prudent—on account of the success of the French army, and notably by the capitulation of Ulm, a triumph which till then had been unparalleled in the history of our armies—to be inserted in this treaty.

I will mention the fight at Güntzburg, where the Emperor lost a very distinguished officer, who had been his aide-de-camp. This officer, nephew of General Lacuée, had incurred Napoleon's displeasure by his caustic tongue, and by the utterance of certain sarcasms against influential persons who had disposed the Emperor against him. Colonel Lacuée was killed during the attack on the bridge at Güntzburg, fighting bravely at the head of the 59th infantry regiment. Napoleon mourned the loss of this officer and ordered all the troops assembled at Güntzburg to be present at his funeral.

The Emperor removed his headquarters to Augsburg, the centre of his operations, and stopped three days in this city, to await the effect of the movement of the different corps, and to occupy himself with important details in the administration of the army. He had the town protected against any attempt at a surprise, and established a general depot of arms, magazines, and ambulances. He ordered all the Austrian artillery which had been captured at Ulm to be transported there.

The Emperor stayed in the palace of the former Elector of Treves, who did the honours of his episcopal palace, with the princess Cunégonde, his sister. He was a prince of the House of Saxony, who, after the loss of his electorate, which had been suppressed by the Treaty of Lunéville, had retired to the bishopric of Augsburg, amalgamating the title of this see with that of Elector of Treves. The income from this see and various pensions, including one of a hundred thousand florins, enabled him to live at Augsburg in a very honourable manner. He was anxious to show, by the cordial hospitality with which he received the Emperor, how grateful he was to him for the comforts which he enjoyed in his old age—comforts which he owed to the influence which Napoleon had formerly exercised on the secularizations.

The battles which preceded and followed upon the taking of Ulm brought after them results of the highest importance. On October 11th General Dupont, having arrived at the village of Haslach with two regiments of infantry and a brigade of cavalry, attacked one of the corps which were leaving Ulm, and which General Mack was endeavouring to rescue from this place to march them on to the Tyrol and Bohemia. General Dupont sustained, during the whole day of the 11th, an unequal fight of seven thousand men against twenty-five thousand, dispersed the enemy, captured two thousand prisoners, and by audacious tactics prevented the march of the enemy to Bohemia. Who could then have thought that the career of this general, called to so high a military destiny, would have ended three years later in so deplorable a manner?* The other columns which had escaped from Ulm met with a similar fate at Albeck, Neusheim, Nordlingen, and before Ulm itself. The investment of this place began by the seizure of the bridge, and of the abbey of Elchingen. All these feats of arms were carried out in the worst weather imaginable. The soldiers, up to their knees in mud, a prey to privations of all kinds, were re-animated by the sight of the Emperor, himself drenched, harassed and covered with mud. I can remember my stupefaction on looking at the sinuous ramparts of the village of Elchingen, rising in an amphitheatre above the Danube, surrounded by walled gardens and houses rising one above the other. These gardens and houses —filled with troops, and from which constant firing proceeded—were topped by the vast buildings of the fortified abbey which was vigorously defended by formidable artillery. Marshal Ney won his title of Duke of Elchingen there, and fully deserved it.

We spent five days at the abbey of Elchingen in almost absolute starvation. The Emperor used to leave it every morning to go to the camp before Ulm, where he used to spend the day, and sometimes the night.

* Capitulation at Baylen (1808) in consequence of which General Dupont was sentenced to imprisonment. He was set free by Louis XVIII. and appointed Minister of War.—R. H. S.

The French army had become master of the heights which commanded Ulm. The Emperor had some shells fired into the town, and sent a summons to General Mack, commander-in-chief of the Austrian army, who had allowed himself to be shut up in the town with the larger part of his army. This unhappy general found himself reduced to the last extremities. He at first affected great courage and declared that he would eat his last horse before he would surrender. He had so entirely lost his head that he did not notice that in saying this he was confessing that the town was without provisions. He parleyed for several days unsuccessfully, thinking to save his honour and military reputation by proposals which could not stand a moment's examination. He was at last forced to sign a capitulation by the terms of which he agreed to surrender, unless relieved within six days. The Emperor being certain that Munich was in the hands of his troops, that the columns which had come out of Ulm were being pursued and beaten in every direction, that the Russians had not crossed the Inn, and that Mack had no chance of being rescued, consented to give him this satisfaction. Mack, however, shortened the term which he himself had asked for. On the 20th of October, from noon till six in the evening, the Austrian army shut up in Ulm, numbering thirty-three thousand men, and under the commander-in-chief, eight field-marshals, and seven lieutenant-generals, marched past the Emperor. Arms were laid down, and the army was transported to France. The officers were allowed to remain in Austria on parole not to serve against France until they had been exchanged. The first column of prisoners left the next day for

France. The Emperor treated the general officers well, and deported himself towards the commander-in-chief with the respect due to misfortune. He severely repressed certain humiliating remarks of which the vanquished had been the subject.

On the 21st a proclamation to the soldiers of the Great Army, congratulating them, and announcing the immense successes of this fortnight's campaign was followed by a decree which ordered that the month which had just elapsed—from September 22nd to October 24th—would count as a campaign for the whole of the army.

On the morrow of the day on which this glorious feat of arms was accomplished at Ulm, our navy met with a great disaster. Whilst our Great Army, led by the Emperor, routing his enemies on the continent, was forcing its triumphal way on to Vienna, the splendid combined fleet, which, in protecting the passage of the flotilla across the Channel at Boulogne, was to realize such lofty hopes, met its doom at Trafalgar. It needed the glorious victory of Ulm, and the prospect of the successful issue of the further operations which Napoleon had prepared, to console him for a catastrophe which postponed, indefinitely, all hope of ruining the English fleet. The Emperor felt that the only resource left to him was the execution of a vast continental blockade, and the extraordinary measures which would complete its effectiveness.

The unhappy Villeneuve, the responsible author of the ruin of the expedition, and author of the disaster of Trafalgar, having fallen into the hands of the English, and having been released by them, put an end to his life in a moment of despair.

Of all the battles which preceded the entry of the French into Vienna, the one which took place at Dirnstein was the most remarkable, because of the critical situation in which Marshal Mortier found himself, and from which he was fortunate enough to escape. The Marshal, who was skirting the left bank of the Danube, engaged in the pursuit of the enemy in the narrow defile which, at this place, is formed by the river and the mountains had only half his *corps d'armée* with him, the rest of his troops being disposed in echelons at one or two marches distance. Mortier easily drove the enemy before him, but these were soon reinforced by superior troops. In the meanwhile a Russian division had come down from the mountains behind him, and had placed itself between his feeble corps and the Dupont division, which was following him. Mortier, thus shut in between two hostile forces, had no other alternative than to cut his way through them or to perish. In this extremity he turned against the weaker enemy, and charged the Russian division, which was pressing on in his rear, and was followed by the enemy which he had previously attacked from the front. But at this moment the scene changed. The Dupont division which at the sound of the cannon had hurried up, came behind the Russian division, which was now caught between two fires from the French troops. This hostile division had only just time to make good its escape by the ravine which they had followed in coming down the mountain—a retreat which would have been closed to them if the Dupont division had been able to reach this ravine before they did. Marshal Mortier, having rallied this division, was now in a position to drive back the other Russian corps which he previously had to resist in front. This corps of the French army owed its safety to the Marshal's coolness and to the promptness of Dupont, and the intrepidity of the officers and men. The Emperor had halted at St. Polten, a village situated almost opposite Dirnstein, alarmed by the loud cannonade which echoed through the rocks. He did not leave St. Polten until he had received reassuring news of Marshal Mortier and of the corps under his command.

The castle of Dirnstein, which overlooked this scene, and which recalls the memory of the captivity of Richard Cœur de Lion, added to the moral effect produced by the combat which had just ended in so happy a way. The sight of these old towers inspired Napoleon with reflections which are thus reported by General Pelet in his "History of the Campaign of 1809":—

"The Emperor was riding between Berthier and Lannes, when a guide pointed out to him, between Moelk and St. Polten, the towers of the castle of Dirnstein, which could be seen far off. The Emperor halted and spent some time in looking at these ruins. Continuing his ride he said to Berthier and Lannes: 'He also had been to fight in Palestine. He had been more fortunate than we were at Acre, but not braver than you, my good Lannes. He had defeated the great Saladin. And in spite of that hardly had he returned to the shores of Europe than he fell into the hands of people who were certainly not his equals. He was sold by an Austrian Duke to an Emperor of Germany, who shut him up, and who is only remembered by this act of felony... The last of all his court, Blondel alone, remained faithful to him, but his people made great sacrifices for his deliverance....' Napoleon seemed unable to turn his eyes away from these towers. He added: 'Such, indeed, were those barbaric times which people are foolish enough to depict as so grand, when the father sacrificed his children, the wife her husband, the subject his sovereign, the soldier his general; when everything was done without shame, and even without disguise, for the lust for gold or power.... How times have changed since then ! What progress our civilization has made! You have seen emperors and kings in my power, besides their capitals and their States, and I have exacted from them neither ransom nor any sacrifice of honour. And this successor of Leopold and of Henry, who is already more than half in our power, no more harm will be done to him than last time, in spite of his somewhat treacherous attack....' Abandoning himself gradually to profound reflections the Emperor fell into a sad melancholy, to which we all remained foreign; for who could follow the master of Europe, the giver of crowns, in his mighty thoughts. What things must have risen before his eyes. He alone knew the fury of his enemies, and all that they would dare, if ever they had the power over him which he so often might have used against them. Who could foresee, at that time, that this new Cœur de Lion would have to envy the fate of him of the eleventh century?"

Whilst the Emperor was at St. Polten, he received a second visit from General Giulay, coming on behalf of the Emperor of Austria to renew his proposals of an armistice. This application was as unsuccessful as the first. Its result was rather to accelerate than to retard the onward march of the French army.

The Grand Army entered Vienna the next day, the Austrians having decided not to defend their capital. They had thought of disputing the crossing of the Danube, in spite of the fact that the bridges had not been broken down, and inflammable material had been prepared to blow them up on the approach of the French. The taking of these bridges, and of the big Tabor bridge by surprise, carried out by an audacious ruse by Marshals Ney and Murat, rendered the French masters of these most valuable approaches.

The Emperor went and established himself in the castle of Schönbrunn, where he spent two days, using this short time to advantage in organizing the Vienna police. Napoleon appointed General Clarke governor of the city, and ordered him to maintain the most rigid discipline, and to protect the citizens. At the same time he prescribed military arrangements for protecting his rear. He thereupon left Schönbrunn to pursue the Russian army, which, after having joined in with the remnants of the Austrian army, was retreating upon Moravia.

Before leaving Schönbrunn the Emperor received the news of the submission of the Tyrol, which Marshal Ney had been ordered to occupy. A touching scene took place at Innsbruck, after the Marshal's entry into this town. An officer of the 76th infantry regiment discovered in the arsenal two flags which had fallen into the hands of the enemy during the preceding war, and whose loss had been deplored by the whole regiment. The sight of these glorious insignia, riddled with bullets, and so gloriously recovered, brought tears to the eyes of the old soldiers. It was a real family feast when Marshal Ney handed these flags back to the regiment. The Emperor ordered the memory of this scene to be perpetuated by a picture and a medal.

Crossing through Vienna only, the French army, accordingly, continued its march in pursuit of the Russian army. The rear-guard of the army was caught up at Hollabrunn, a village situated half-way between Vienna and Brünn. The meeting gave rise to a sanguinary battle, from which the baggage corps was only able to make good its escape through the darkness of the night, leaving behind them a goodly number of prisoners in our hands and a battle-field covered with their dead. The Russians set fire to all that they passed, and destroyed the most beautiful villages in Moravia. The Emperor, on his way to Hollabrunn, was delayed on his journey by the burning of one of these villages. He spent more than an hour in the midst of the frantic inhabitants, using his escort to help them save their houses and to arrest the progress of the flames.

The French army was so fatigued that, in spite of Napoleon's wish not to grant the Russian army a moment's respite, he thought it necessary to give his soldiers a day's rest. His first columns entered into Brünn the next day, where they found abundant provisions of all kinds. During Napoleon's stay at Brünn, before the battle of Austerlitz, he had received M. d'Haugwitz, the Prussian envoy, who had come to his audience-chamber by means of a secret staircase. The persons in attendance were sent out and it was I who was charged to introduce him. This was on the eve of the Emperor's departure, Napoleon wishing to make all speed to join his bivouac between Brünn and Austerlitz, where he spent the week which preceded the great battle. He refused to listen to any communication from the King of Prussia's envoy, postponing all explanations until after the battle which, according to all appearances, was about to be fought. When he returned victorious to Vienna, he gave audience to M.

d'Haugwitz, on the very evening of his arrival in Schönbrunn. The minister took good care not to show the Potsdam treaty which he had brought with him. He complimented the Emperor on his victory, and Napoleon replied, "That is a compliment whose destination has been changed by fortune." Indeed, the past ten days had totally changed the situation for everybody, and the Prussian envoy was inspired with very different sentiments from those with which he had come. He decided, and rightly so, that the time for threats had passed by, that he had to get himself out of a scrape, and thought of nothing but how to get Napoleon to forget the hostile attitude which the government of his King had taken up.

The Emperor received M. d'Haugwitz with kindness, the envoy's attitude not being hostile to France; but he was not chary in blaming the Prussian Cabinet for the perfidy of its conduct. He dictated the terms of a treaty to M. d'Haugwitz, which the latter accepted, and by which Napoleon offered Prussia, in the form of an alliance which it was his desire to make lasting, a chance of safety of which Prussia was foolish enough not to take advantage.

The Austrian general, Giulay, presented himself for the third time to the Emperor at Brünn, accompanied by M. de Stadion. These two envoys came to renew the offer which the first of them had already made twice—at Linz and at St. Polten,—to come to an understanding as to the conditions of peace. Napoleon consented to treat then and there, and to decide upon the preliminaries of peace. But he could not commit the mistake of accepting a simple armistice, without taking advantage of his position. The Austrian envoys did not think fit to accept the conditions which he imposed. The Russians, before the battle of Austerlitz, had asked for nothing less than the return of the French army to the Rhine, and had proposed several other unacceptable conditions, which were in harmony with those which later on they tried to impose on the Emperor at Prague.

The Emperor had sent General Savary from his bivouac to present his compliments to the Emperor Alexander, and at the same time to take notice of what was going on around him. Savary brought back with him Prince Dolgorouki, one of the most influential of the Emperor's young counsellors. This officer considered the French army in jeopardy, and did not doubt that Napoleon would be glad to escape an imminent disaster. The retreat which the Emperor had ordered for the purpose of choosing his battle-field and the position of his camp had confirmed Prince Dolgorouki in this opinion. He addressed the Emperor with assurance, and argued on political questions with a presumption which revealed his inexperience in these matters. He undertook to demonstrate to his master's redoubtable adversary, the necessity of abandoning his conquests, and of giving up possession of Italy, and even of Belgium, in the interests of a durable peace. Napoleon listened to this strange talk, and these unseasonable insinuations, which were simple braggadocio, with great patience and coolness. The only answer he gave was by making his final arrangements for the battles which he was going to fight.

In the night which preceded this memorable day, the Emperor visited the bivouacs of his troops on foot. He was soon recognized, in spite of his incognito, and was received with an enthusiasm difficult to describe. By a concerted movement the camp was suddenly illuminated by thousands of straw torches, which each bivouac raised aloft to salute the Emperor, and to celebrate the anniversary of his coronation. Napoleon, deeply touched by this improvised act of homage, expressed his regret, on returning to his bivouac, at having on the morrow to fight a battle which would rob him of a large number of these good fellows, and added that he considered this the best evening of his life. The sun shone the next morning on the battle of Austerlitz. The Emperor, on horseback from the break of day, surrounded by his marshals kept them by his side, until the mist, which in that season betokens a fine morning, had been entirely dispelled. Then, on a signal which he gave, each galloped off to his corps. I saw General Junot, who was rather late, rush up and throw himself into the saddle with an air of resolution which showed that he had no intention of sparing himself. It was not long before the sound of the cannon was heard. The Emperors of Austria and Russia witnessed, from the heights on which they were placed, the complete routing of their armies. This battle—which was one of the greatest which Napoleon ever won, and the issue of which, thanks to his skilful tactics and the madness of his adversaries, was never in doubt for an instant—ended this campaign, which had lasted two months.

Prince John of Lichtenstein presented himself in the morning of the next day at our outposts. He came to ask the Emperor Napoleon to grant an interview to the Emperor of Austria. Napoléon consented, after some hesitation, and could not help saying, after he had taken leave of the prince: "This man makes me commit a great mistake. It is not after battles that conferences can be held. I ought to-day to be nothing but a soldier. As such I ought to follow up my victory, and not listen to words of peace." The interview was fixed for the morrow at a bivouac near the Sar-Uschitz Mill, about three leagues from Austerlitz.

On December 4th the Emperor Napoleon set out on horseback, at nine o'clock in the morning, accompanied by Marshal Berthier, the chief officers of his military household, and a part of his guard, for the meeting which had been agreed upon. He arrived there before the Emperor of Austria, who drove up shortly after his arrival in an open carriage, accompanied by Prince John of Lichtenstein, several field-marshals and generals of his army, and escorted by a squadron of Hungarian cavalry. The Emperor went to meet the Emperor of Austria, and embraced him. They drew up to the fire, whilst their suites withdrew to fires which had been lighted within view, but sufficiently far off to prevent what the two sovereigns were saying from being heard. The conference lasted about two hours, and the two monarchs agreed upon an armistice and the principal conditions of peace. The Emperor Francis asked that a truce might be granted to the Russian army. Napoleon consented on condition that the Russians should evacuate Germany, and Prussian and Austrian Poland, and return to Russia. In the movement caused by the separation of the two Emperors their officers approached them, and overheard the Austrian monarch saying to Napoleon, apparently in answer to some remark of his: "I promise not to fight you any more."

The Russian army was surrounded on all sides, and

had no chance of escape. The Russian troops were fleeing in such disorder that the Emperor Alexander, separated from his followers, was in danger of falling into the enemy's hands. He sent flag of truce after flag of truce to Marshal Davout, to obtain a suspension of arms; but the Marshal pursued his onward march.

General Meerfeld, whose vanguard had been routed by Marshal Davout's soldiers, sent the Marshal the following note, written in pencil:

"Colonel Count Walmoden will go with a bugler to the French general in command of the third division of the corps d'armée and will inform him that there is an armistice lasting from six o'clock this morning till six o'clock to-morrow morning, H.M. the Emperor of Germany being in conference with the Emperor of the French at Uschitz. By order of H.M. the Emperor of Russia,

(Signed) MEERFELD, Lieutenant General."

Marshal Davout, having answered M. de Meerfeld that his note did not seem to him a sufficient guarantee, he having very naturally to be on his guard against these little ruses, and quoting to him, amongst examples, that of Steyer, declared that he required a written assurance from the Emperor Alexander. M. de Meerfeld assured the Marshal that he should shortly receive satisfaction in this respect, and that all his doubts would be dispelled. Colonel Walmoden immediately set out to search for the Emperor of Russia, but did not know, in the extreme confusion which reigned in the Russian army, where to look for him. At last, after numerous comings and goings, he saw afar off some mounted guards, whom he recognized by the height and the shape of their helmets. He rode in this direction and found the Emperor Alexander with Prince Czartoryski, his Minister of Foreign Affairs. The Russian sovereign, on hearing what was demanded of him by Marshal Davout, declared that he could not write this note, and ordered Prince Czartoryski to write it in his name. Colonel Walmoden having pointed out to him that Marshal Davout would not stop his movement unless an assurance was given him in the Emperor's own writing, Alexander, in order to avoid being taken prisoner by the French troops, who were approaching, consented to write the letter. It was written in the following words, and in pencil, pen and ink not being procurable:

"General Meerfeld is authorized to tell Marshal Davout from me that a truce of twenty-four hours has been agreed upon for the interview which the two supreme chiefs of their nations will hold together to-day at Uschitz.

"(Signed) ALEXANDER."

One of the Russian Emperor's aides-de-camp, accompanying Colonel Walmoden, carried this note to Marshal Davout. The Marshal was forced to believe this formal assurance of the suspension of hostilities, and the meeting of the two Emperors. He accordingly halted and took up his position at Josephsdorf, where he happened to be, sending word to the Russian commander-in-chief Kutusoff, who had also written to him, that hostilities would be suspended until six o'clock on the following morning, and that in order to avoid all error or surprise notice of the end of the truce would be given one hour previously. The Emperor Alexander, delivered from the extreme perplexity and the great anxieties which had beset him, took refuge at Holitch, on the left bank of the March. The confusion of the various scattered corps of the Russian army was so complete, that the Emperor Alexander remained separated from his servants for nearly a week, and that Prince Czartoryski, his Minister, had, so to speak, to act as his valet.

It should be added, in the interests of truth, that the assurances given by the Russian monarch to Marshal Davout were not strictly true. An armistice between the Austrian and French armies had certainly been agreed upon by the Emperor Napoleon and the Emperor of Austria, but the truce, as far as the Russian army was concerned, though consented to in principle, had not yet been notified. Another hour's march and Davout would have made the Czar his prisoner. The Marshal, to clear himself, sent the note on to the Emperor, who ordered me to preserve it in his portfolio as one of the most important documents of the history of this war.

The Emperor showed himself generous towards the Emperor Alexander. He ordered his aide-de-camp Savary to go and tell him that if he would consent to return with his army, he would suspend the onward march of the French troops and leave the Russians a free retreat. He sent also back, without any ransom, Colonel Repnin, and all the prisoners of the Russian Imperial guard, with a flattering message about their bravery.

The French army in Italy, commanded by Marshal Masséna, had rivalled the *Grande Armée* in ardour and devotion. Opposed to the French army was an Austrian army, of almost equal strength, under the command of Arch-duke Charles. After a series of bloody fights, and a great battle, in which the Archduke had heavy losses, and on receipt of the news of the capitulation of Ulm, and the march of the French on Vienna, the Austrian commander-in-chief ordered a retreat. Closely pursued by the French army, and driven from all the strongholds in which he halted to protect his retreat, in turn, he arrived at Laybach to hear that his brother, the Arch-duke John, had had no better fortune than himself, and had evacuated the Tyrol, seeking to make his way to Hungary with the remnants of his troops.

On his return to Schönbrunn, the Emperor granted an audience to the deputation of mayors which had been sent him from Paris, and commissioned them to carry back to Notre Dame the enemy's flags taken at Austerlitz, and which he intended for this cathedral. He had published a series of decrees in which he awarded pensions to the widows and children of soldiers of all ranks, generals, officers, or privates, who had perished at Austerlitz, granting them further the permission to add Napoleon to their names. He further ordered that a triumphal column should be erected on the Place Vendôme, the metal to be taken from the Russian and Austrian cannon captured at Austerlitz.

The peace conference was opened at Brünn, but the negotiators removed shortly afterwards to Presburg, where the treaty of peace was signed on December 26th, 1805. This celebrated treaty confirmed all our conquests, and put us in possession of the whole of Italy. Bavaria received the Tyrol. The electorates of Bavaria and Würtemberg, enlarged with territories ceded by Austria, were elevated to the rank of monarchies. The electorate of Baden, which in spite of its increase of territory, was not of sufficient importance to be made a monarchy, was raised to a grand-duchy. Austria received Salzburg, and Arch-duke Ferdinand, former Grand-duke of Tuscany, to whom Salzburg had been attached by the Treaty of Lunéville, was transferred to Würzburg, this principality being raised, in his favour, to a grand-duchy. The war indemnity, which Napoleon had at first fixed at one hundred millions, was reduced, by his consent, to forty millions of francs.

The day on which peace was signed at Presburg, the Emperor met Arch-duke Charles at the castle of Stammersdorf. This interview was brought about by a mutual feeling of esteem. On taking leave of the Arch-duke, Napoleon presented him with a sword.

After the great disaster inflicted on the Russian and Austrian armies at Austerlitz, the Emperor regretted the necessity which he could not avoid, of having to sign a separate peace with Austria without forcing Russia to join in the treaty, thus depriving himself of the fruits of his victory; but a whole Russian army remained intact in the hands of his enemies. The Austrian army from Italy, which was in Hungary, united with the débris of the armies which had escaped Austerlitz, and strongly reinforced, could have been formed into a formidable army, and have prolonged the war. The enmity of Prussia, the vacillating and timid character of the King, who might easily be led away to make common cause with our enemies, aggravated the danger to which Napoleon would have been exposed, and made him fear lest his rear might be seriously menaced. He accordingly contented himself with exacting that the Russian troops should evacuate Germany and Poland, and should withdraw to Russia. In the bottom of his heart he had a strong feeling of resentment for the perfidious conduct of the Prussian Ministry which, after avoiding any alliance whatever with the French Empire had, by its equivocal attitude, foiled all Napoleon's good intentions for increasing the strength and power of Prussia. This government, without directly encouraging Austria to attack us, had allowed this power to hope that, in case of a war with France, she would easily be able to draw over to her side an irresolute prince under the influence of a hostile cabinet. Exposed by this dangerous uncertainty to a menacing peril, forced to postpone the accomplishment of his designs, and his dream of general pacification, to an indefinite epoch, Napoleon had already had occasion to witness the full ingratitude and hostility of the Berlin Cabinet, on the specious pretext of a violation of territory, on the occasion, namely, of the marching of French troops through Anspach, which before then had been crossed by the Austrians and the Bavarians. He had, from that time on, no feeling for the pusillanimous character of the King of Prussia but one of contempt and disdain. His irritation against this monarch was constantly manifesting itself, and this irritation only increased after he had made his personal acquaintance. Napoleon considered the King to be fated, from the circumstances of his unfortunate birth, to moral and physical clumsiness. He gave up his plan of making him his ally. In the place of his favourable feelings toward Prussia, and his ardent desire to unite himself to her by strong ties, there arose in the Emperor's mind the determination to regard as an enemy the power whose alliance he had not been able to win.

Whilst the French army was following up its

successes in Austria, the Court of Naples, struck with blindness, was violating its promises of neutrality, and opening its ports to the naval and military forces of our enemies.

Napoleon, hearing of this imprudent act of disloyalty after the victory of Austerlitz sent orders to his brother Joseph, who was then at the head of affairs in Paris, to proceed to the army in Italy, which was under the command of Marshal Masséna, to take over the command of it, with the grade of general of division, and the title of lieutenant to the Emperor, and to march on Naples, where a crown awaited him.

It was reported to the Emperor that extortions and abuses had been committed in this army, which his brother Joseph was leading to Naples. He gave orders for their repression. A fund of eight hundred thousand francs, produced by illegal requisitions, had been fraudulently appropriated and deposited in a Milan banking-house. The heads of this house, having denied that any such deposit had taken place, and evaded the restitution of the amount, the Emperor had the bank's paper seized and boycotted in every market. This interdiction was only raised after the entire sum had been restored.

Immediately after the ratification of the treaty of peace, the Emperor left for Munich. He wrote a long letter from this town to the major general, containing a general order for the execution of the provisions of the treaty. This order summarized with the foresight and precision which characterized all Napoleon's purposes, all arrangements concerning the army, the successive evacuations of the various parts of the enemy's territory, the occupation of the provinces which had been ceded, the cantonment of the troops, the transport of the wounded, the putting the sovereigns of Bavaria and Würtemberg in possession of the territories to which they were entitled by the treaty, the payment of the war indemnities, all matters concerning the military administration, what the engineer and artillery regiments had to do, the return of the armies of General Marmont and Marshal Masséna into Italy, and so on.

The Empress Josephine had preceded the Emperor to Munich. The marriage of Prince Eugène with Princess Augusta, eldest daughter of the King of Bavaria, was celebrated there, and formed, as one of Napoleon's best historians—Thibaudeau*—has said, the first link in the chain which was to unite for ever the new Napoleonic dynasty to the ancient dynasties of Europe. This Bavarian princess had previously been betrothed to the hereditary prince of Baden. Politics decided it otherwise. In this case, interests of state did not disturb the reciprocity of sentiments which this union awoke in the two spouses.

The Emperor informed the Senate of this marriage by a message in which he associated this body with his family joys with a paternal feeling. He informed them, at the same time, that he had adopted Prince Eugène as his son, and that he had appointed him his successor, in default of direct successors, to the hereditary throne of Italy.

The 10th Nivôse of year XIV of the Republic—corresponding to December 31st, 1805—was the last day of the Republican calendar. The Gregorian ca-

* *Mémoires sur le Consulat et l'Empire*" (1835, 10 vols.) and "*Histoire de Napoléon*" (1827—1828, 5 vols.) by Antoine Claire Thibaudeau—(1765—1854.)—R. H. S.

lendar had the advantage of being used by almost all the peoples of Europe and America, whilst the Republican calendar, apart from its inconvenience for our relations with foreigners and the isolation which resulted therefrom, had the further disadvantage of deriving its origin from a period which was remembered with as great disfavour in France as in the rest of Europe.

The great corporations of the State and the people of Paris prepared to receive the victor of Austerlitz with solemnity. The Senate on the initiative of the Tribunate, which went in a body to the Luxembourg Palace, to carry the flags which the Emperor destined for it there, decreed, in the name of the French people, that a triumphal monument should be erected to Napoleon the Great, that the Senate should go to meet him in a body, and that the letter by which the Sovereign entrusted the care of the flags captured from the enemy to the high assembly, should be engraved on a marble tablet and placed in the sessions-chamber.

The Paris municipality handed over to the metropolitan clergy with great pomp and ceremony the flags which the Emperor had destined to be hung up in Notre Dame.

Napoleon and Josephine, received with general enthusiasm, re-entered Paris on January 26th, 1806.

INDEX

OF NAMES OF PERSONS MENTIONED IN THIS VOLUME. *

A.

Abercromby (General), 62, 83.
Abrantès, Duchess of (Mme. Junot), 110.
Abrial, 141.
Addington, 76, 208.
Aguesseau (Chancellor d'), 304.
Aguesseau (Mlle. d'), 303.
Alembert (d'), 3.
Alexander I. (Emperor of Russia), 61, 161, 162, 200, 215, 272, 273, 275, 276, 278, 382, 383, 387, 388, 399, 400, 402, 403, 404.
Alexander the Great, 340.
Almeida (Don João d'), 167, 168, 169.
Andréossy (General), 9, 184, 214, 217.
Andrieux, 55, 58.
Angoulême (Duke of), 248.
Antoine (M., *Architect*), 6.
Ariman, 281.
Arnault (M., *Poet*), 55.
Arras, Bishop of, 149.
Artois (Count d'), 149, 235, 240, 245, 248, 268, 270.
Audenarde (M., *Equerry to the Empress*), 87.
Augereau (Marshal), 222, 298, 305, 384, 385.
Augusta of Bavaria (Princess), 409.

Augustus, 286.
Aumale (Duc d'), 114.
Austria (Emperor Francis of), 200, 384, 387, 395, 400, 401, 402, 404.
Azzara (Chevalier d', *Spanish Ambassador*), 28, 84.

B.

Bacciochi (M.), *see* Piombino, Prince of.
Bacciochi (Mme.), *see* Bonaparte, Princess Elisa.
Baculard-Arnauld, 21.
Baden (Elector of), *see* Baden, Grand-duke of.
Baden (Grand-duke of), 181, 197, 244, 253, 254, 276, 278, 385.
Baden (Hereditary Prince of), 409.
Baden (Margrave of), *see* Baden, Grand-duke of.
Badia, 174.
Baraguay-d'Hilliers, 299.
Barbé-Marbois, 141, 142, 205.
Barberi, 8, 9, 10.
Barbier, 114, 115.
Barras, 15, 16, 18, 20.
Barrois (General), 260.
Barthélemy, 197.
Bassano, Duke of (M. Maret), 79, 142, 143, 196, 256, 260.
Basseville, 28.

* Napoleon Bonaparte, being mentioned on almost every page is not referred to in this Index. His first wife, whether mentioned as Mme. de Beauharnais, Mme. Bonaparte, or the Empress, is indexed under "Josephine."

INDEX

Baudin des Ardennes, 303.
Bavaria (Elector-King of), 386, 387, 388, 409.
Bayard, 312.
Beauclerc (General), 93.
Beauharnais (Mlle. E. de), 92, 93.
Beauharnais (Mme. Fanny de), 180.
Beauharnais (Prince Eugène de), 123, 348, 409.
Beauharnais (Queen Hortense de), 59, 92, 93, 98, 123, 152, 213, 268, 313, 314.
Beauharnais (Josephine de), *see* Josephine.
Beauharnais (Grand-duchess Stéphanie de), 181.
Bellegarde (General), 45.
Belleville, 18.
Belliard (General), 62.
Bénévent (Prince de), *see* Talleyrand.
Béranger (*Poet*), 125.
Berlier, 144.
Bernadotte (General), 71, 72, 93, 97, 192, 232, 296, 298, 384, 387, 388.
Bernadotte (Mme.), 28.
Bernadotte (Oscar), 192.
Bernardin de Saint-Pierre, 124.
Bernier (Abbé, Bishop of Orleans), 65, 66.
Berri (Duc de), 247, 248, 263, 270.
Berthier (Marshal), 9, 58, 127, 130, 252, 254, 268, 275, 276, 296, 298, 394, 401.
Bertrand (General), 14.
Bessières (General), 117, 231, 298.
Beugnot (Count), 204.
Bichat (Doctor), 158.
Biennais, 113.
Binau (M. de, *Saxon Ambassador*), 171.
Blacas (M. de), 202.
Blondel, 394.
Bodoni, 350.
Bonaparte (Charles, Father of Napoleon), 23, 110, 111.
Bonaparte (Mme., Mother of Napoleon), 110.
Bonaparte (Princess Caroline, Mme. Murat), 30, 54, 58, 94, 313.

Bonaparte (Princess Elisa, Mme. Lacciochi), 54, 58, 59, 75, 279, 315, 341, 350.
Bonaparte (Prince Jerome, King of Westphalia), 318, 319, 320, 346, 351, 352.
Bonaparte (Prince Joseph, Comte de Survilliers), 14, 19, 27, 28, 30, 35, 36, 43, 45, 46, 49, 52, 54, 55, 57, 59, 65, 72, 83, 88, 96, 97, 101, 111, 167, 173, 187, 192, 232, 292, 297, 311, 317, 333, 340, 341, 385, 408.
Bonaparte (Princess Joseph), 35, 56, 192.
Bonaparte (Empress Josephine), *see* Josephine.
Bonaparte (Prince Louis, Comte du Saint Leu, King of Holland), 7, 8, 20, 21, 25, 26, 27, 92, 93, 111, 297, 335.
Bonaparte (Princess Louis), *see* Beauharnais, Queen Hortense.
Bonaparte (Archdeacon Lucien), 110, 111, 112.
Bonaparte (Prince Lucien), 54, 59, 75, 314, 315, 316, 317, 320.
Bonaparte (Mme. Lucien), *see* Boyer, Christine.
Bonaparte (Princess Pauline, Mme. Leclerc), 30, 54, 58, 191, 193, 195, 232.
Bon-Saint-André (M. Jean), 175.
Borghese (Prince Camille), 232, 233.
Bossuet, 329, 343.
Boucher (*Artist*), 179.
Boufflers (M. de), 55.
Boufflers (Mme. de), 55.
Boulay de la Meurthe, 144.
Bourbaki, 14.
Bourbon (Duc de), 248.
Bourgoin (Mlle.), 6, 7.
Bourrienne (M. de), 12, 96, 103, 116, 123, 128, 129, 130, 131, 132, 133, 134, 135, 200, 296, 297.
Bourrienne (Mme. de), 129.
Boyer (Christine, Mme. Lucien Bonaparte), 59.
Breteuil (Baron de), 147, 148.

INDEX. 413

Bretenil (M. de), 147, 148.
Broglie (Abbé de), 344, 345.
Brome (Lord), 91.
Bruix (Admiral), 12, 15, 16, 17, 18, 19, 20, 306, 310, 341.
Brulart de Sillery (Count), 50.
Brune (General), 45, 298.
Bry (Jean de), 212.
Buhler (de), 53.

C.

Cacault (*Chargé d'Affaires*), 75.
Cadoudal, *see* Georges.
Cæsar, 177, 286, 290, 307, 377.
Caffarelli (General), 117, 328, 374.
Calonne (M. de), 148.
Cambacérès (*Second Consul*), 136, 140, 143, 153, 227, 256, 268.
Cambry (*Prefect of Oise*), 33.
Campan (Mme.), 92.
Canino (Prince de), *see* Bonaparte, Prince Lucien.
Canova, 178, 179, 180.
Caprara (Cardinal), 71, 74, 94, 230, 328, 343.
Carboni, 337.
Caselli (Father), 65, 72.
Cassius, 377.
Casti (*Poet*), 54, 57, 58.
Catherine II. (Empress of Russia), 240.
Caulaincourt (Duc de Vicence), 117, 185, 252, 253, 254, 255, 267, 269, 271, 272, 273, 274, 275, 276, 277, 321.
Cayla (Count Baschi du), 300.
Cayla (Countess du), 300.
Cellerier (*Architect*), 157.
Champagny (M. de), 167, 314.
Champcenetz (Mme. de), 149.
Chaptal (Court), 140, 314.
Charlemagne, 321, 343.
Charles (Arch-duke), 43, 404, 406.
Charles (Prince, of Baden), 181.
Charles IV. (King of Spain), 182, 183.
Charles XII., 177.
Chatham (Lord), 208.
Chateaubriand (M. de), 54, 75, 278, 279, 280, 281, 282, 283.
Chateaubriand (Mme. de), 280.
Chauvelin, 55.
Chénier (Marie-Joseph), 4, 5, 150.
Chevigny (Mlle., Mme. Cellerier), 156, 157.
Choiseul (Duc de), 3, 4.
Cicero, 74.
Cimber, 377.
Clarke (General), 47, 49, 114, 396.
Cobenzl (Count Louis de), 35, 41, 43, 45, 46, 50, 52, 54, 55, 56, 57.
Condé (Prince de), 248, 258.
Consalvi (Cardinal), 65, 66, 72.
Constant, 368.
Contat (Mlle. Louise), 6, 32.
Corneille, 6, 376.
Cornwallis (Lord), 84, 87, 88, 90, 91, 159.
Corvisart (Doctor), 103, 104, 158, 355.
Coston (Baron), 110.
Coulon (the brothers), 129, 130.
Cramayel (M.), 118.
Cretet (*Councillor of State*), 65.
Cromwell, 286.
Cunégonde (Princess), 389.
Cuvillier-Fleury, 114.
Czartoryski (Prince), 403, 404.

D.

Dagobert, 312.
Dalberg (Duc), 197.
Damas (Mme. de), 149.
Dante, 99.
Daru, 362, 363.
Daunau, 25.
Dautancourt, 259.
Davout (General), 98, 117, 200, 298, 402, 403, 404.
Davy (*American Diplomatist*), 28.
Dazincourt (*Actor*), 32.
Debray, 92.
Decrès (Admiral), 140, 174, 310.
Defermon, 144.
Dejean (General), 363.
Delille, 31.
Denina (Abbé), 114.
Denon, 123.

INDEX.

Desaix (General), 339, 340.
Desault (Doctor), 158.
Desmazis (the brothers), 117.
Desmeuniers, 197.
Destaing (General), 157, 158.
Devienne (Mlle.), 32.
Dey of Algiers, 351, 352.
Didelot (M.), 117.
Diderot, 3, 4.
Diogenes, 4.
Doge of Venice, 348, 349.
Dolgorouki (Prince), 399.
Domergue (Urbain), 7.
Doria (Andrea), 351.
Drake (Sir Francis), 234, 235, 236.
Ducis, 124, 125.
Dufresne, 141.
Duguesclin, 312.
Dumas (Mathieu), 39, 41.
Dumont (*Author*), 159.
Dumouriez (General), 242, 249, 250, 253, 254, 255.
Dumoustier (General), 161.
Dundas, 76.
Dupaty, 156.
Duphot (General), 28.
Dupont (General), 374, 389, 390, 393.
Dupuis (*Librarian*), 116.
Dupuy, 86, 88.
Durand, 51.
Duroc (Marshal), 61, 97, 103, 117, 131, 231, 236, 274, 373.
Dutheil, 149.
Duval (Alexandre), 155.

E.

Écouchard, *see* Lebrun (*Poet*).
Edelsheim (Baron d'), 253.
Edgeworth (Abbé), 201.
Elchingen (Duke of), *see* Ney.
Ellsworth (*American Diplomatist*), 28.
Enghien (Duc d'), 150, 242, 244, 248, 249, 250, 251, 252, 253, 254, 255, 256, 257, 258, 259, 260, 261, 262, 263, 264, 265, 266, 267, 268, 269, 270, 271, 272, 273, 274, 275, 276, 277, 278, 293, 321.
England (King of), *see* George III.
Esmenard, 282.
Etienne, 282.
Etruria (King of, Infant of Parma), 62, 182, 183.
Eugène (Prince), *see* Beauharnais (Prince Eugène).

F.

Fain (Baron), 135.
Fariau, 5.
Ferdinand (Archduke), 406.
Fesch (Captain), 74.
Fesch (Cardinal, Archbishop of Lyons), 74, 109, 110, 278, 328.
Fitzgerald (Lord), 167.
Flahaut (Mme. de), *see* Souza (Mme. de).
Fleurieu (Councillor of State), 28.
Fleuriot (Abbé), 202.
Fleury (*Actor*), 32.
Fleury de Chaboulon, 135, 267.
Folleville (M. de), 91.
Folleville (Mme. de), 91.
Fontanelli (General), 117.
Fontanes (M. de), 55, 59, 75, 315.
Fontanes (Mme. de), 266.
Fouché (Duke of Otranto), 119, 129, 137, 138, 186, 190, 197, 212, 251, 255, 256, 257, 268, 305, 315.
Fox, 159, 160.
Foy (General), 239.
Francis (Emperor), *see* Austria, Emperor of.
Frederick II. (Frederick the Great), 113, 114, 319, 367, 388.
Frederick III. (King of Denmark), 287.
Frederick William III. (King of Prussia), *see* Prussia, King of.
Fréron, 193.
Fresnel (M. de), 48.
Frotté, 26, 27.
Fulton, 309.

INDEX.

G.

Gabrielli (Prince), 59.
Ganteaume (Admiral), 10, 174, 175.
Garat, 31, 32, 33.
Gassendi, 371.
Gaudin (Duke of Gaëte), 102, 138, 139, 149.
Genlis (Mme. de), 50.
George III. (King of England), 76, 220, 256, 320, 335, 386.
Georges Cadoudal, 119, 132, 160, 233, 244, 245, 246, 247, 248, 251, 255, 256, 257, 263, 267, 270, 278, 292, 293, 294, 296.
Gérard (*Engineer*), 186.
Germany (Emperor of), see Austria (Emperor Francis).
Girardin (Stanislas), 22, 54.
Giulay (General), 387, 395, 398.
Gourgaud (General), 25.
Granville, 76, 80.
Grenville (Lord), 39, 40, 82, 89.
Gresset (*Poet*), 92.
Guéméné (Prince de), 258.
Guidal (General), 27.
Gustavus Adolphus, 177.

H.

Hancucourt (d'), 58.
Hannibal, 177.
Hardenberg, 388.
Hari (Camilla), 336, 337.
Harville (General d'), 185.
Haugwitz (M. d'), 397, 398.
Hauté, 116.
Hawkesbury (Lord), 40, 76, 77, 235.
Hédouville (General), 65, 218.
Heine, 221.
Henri III., 205.
Henri IV., 184, 203, 205.
Hephæstion, 340.
Hercules, 297.
Hoppé, 35, 56.
Hortense (Queen), see Beauharnais (Queen Hortense de).
Hugo (Abel), 49.
Hugo (General), 49.
Hugo (Victor), 49.
Hulin (General), 162, 259, 262.
Hulot (Mme.), 160.
Hyde, 149.

I.

Ideville (Lelorgne d'), 115, 116.

J.

Jacqueminot, 51.
James II., 205.
Jaubert (Amédée), 10, 12, 115, 126, 195, 196.
Jaucourt (M. de), 55.
Jay, 282.
John (Archduke), 43, 405.
Josephine (Empress), 32, 59, 94, 97, 98, 101, 117, 118, 121, 122, 123, 126, 135, 155, 160, 163, 171, 172, 177, 180, 181, 183, 184, 185, 186, 213, 223, 227, 255, 264, 266, 267, 284, 285, 298, 321, 329, 331, 332, 336, 337, 343, 347, 350, 351, 352, 354, 355, 376, 380, 385, 409, 410.
Jourdan (General), 182, 298.
Junot (General, Duke d'Abrantès), 350, 400.
Junot (Mme.), see Abrantès, Duchess of.
Jupiter Scapin, 344.

K.

Keith (Admiral), 231.
Kellermann (General), 297.
Kléber (General), 61, 75, 83, 114, 157.
Kutusoff (General), 403.

L.

Lacroix (Charles), 79.
Lacrosse (Admiral Count), 341.
Lacuée (Colonel), 388.
Lacuée (General), 388.
Lafayette (M. de), 30, 33, 34, 35.

INDEX

Lafond (*Actor*), 59.
Laforêt (M. de), 47, 53, 188.
Lagarde, 16, 17.
Laharpe, 149.
Lahorie* (General), 42.
Lalande, 4.
Lanen (Colonel de), 257.
Lannes (Marshal), 104, 117, 166, 167, 168, 169, 170, 171, 172, 298, 346, 394.
Lansdowne (Marquis of), 159.
Laplace, 314.
Laréveillère-Lepeaux, 12, 16.
Las-Cases (M. de), 24.
Latouche-Tréville (Admiral), 224, 310, 341.
Lauriston (Marshal de), 116, 117, 123, 195, 208, 276, 321, 322.
Lauriston (Mme. de), 118.
Lavalette, 93, 189.
Lawoestyne (General Anatole de), 49, 50, 51.
Leblanc (Abbé), 4, 5.
Lebrun (Captain), 117.
Lebrun (*Poet*), 5, 7.
Lebrun (*Third Consul*), 136, 154.
Leclerc (Dermide), 192, 195, 232.
Leclerc (General), 191, 192, 193, 194, 232.
Leclerc (Mme.), *see* Bonaparte (Princess Pauline).
Lecourbe (General), 14, 15.
Lefebvre (Marshal), 297.
Legouvé, 6.
Leissègues (Admiral), 162.
Lekain (*Actor*), 6.
Lemarrois (Colonel), 117.
Lemercier (Népomucène), 124, 125.
Lenormand (Mme.), 378, 380.
Leo III. (Pope), 343.
Lepelletier (Félix), 120.
Lesueur, 178.
Letourneur, 79.
Lichtenstein (Prince John of), 400, 401.
Liébaut (General), 48.
Lille (Comte de), *see* Louis XVIII.
Limoëlan, 149.
Livingstone (*American Envoy*), 206.

Lobau (Marshal Count), 322, 323.
Lombard (M.), 228, 229, 230.
Louis XIV., 134, 329.
Louis XV., 23, 57, 71, 179, 191, 228.
Louis XVI., 99, 254.
Louis XVIII., (*Comte de Lille*), 47, 124, 133, 200, 201, 202, 203, 204, 205, 239, 248.
Luçay (M. de), 117, 156, 157.
Luçay (Mlle. de), 304.
Luçay (Mme. de), 118.

M.

Mack (General), 389, 391.
Mackintosh (*M. P.*), 210.
Mahomet, 381.
Maillard, 258.
Mallet, 27.
Malmesbury (Lord), 79, 143.
Marat, 138.
Marcel, 342.
Marchesi, 348.
Marcoff (Count), 217.
Maret, *see* Bassano, Duke of.
Marie Louise (Empress), 156, 179, 181, 304, 305.
Marmont (Marshal), 55, 222, 223, 409.
Massa (Duke of), 141, 186, 256.
Massaredo (Admiral), 17.
Masséna (Duc de Rivoli), 298, 336, 404, 408, 409.
Maupeou (Chancellor de), 136.
Mazarin (Cardinal), 134.
Meerfeld (General), 402, 403.
Mehée de Latouche, 235, 236, 246, 274.
Melzi, 340.
Méneval (Baron de), 129, 358, 359.
Menou (General), 61, 62, 157, 158, 182.
Mercy d'Argenteau (Count de), 56.
Merlin de Donai (*Director*), 12, 16, 17.
Merlin (General Engène), 12.
Merry (*English Secretary of Legation*), 87, 159.
Metastasio, 57.

INDEX. 417

Meyer (M.), 201.
Mézeray (Mlle.), 32.
Michaud, 282.
Michot (*Actor*), 123.
Miot, 55.
Mirabeau, 159.
Molé, 270.
Mollien (Count), 54.
Moncey (General), 250, 251, 298.
Moncrieff (General), 127.
Monk, 271.
Monroe (*American Envoy*), 205.
Montcabrié (M. de), 185.
Montgaillard (Abbé de), 239.
Montgaillard (Count de), 204, 237, 238, 239, 240.
Montmorency (Mathieu de), 55.
Moore (Rev.—), 127.
Moreau (General), 15, 41, 42, 43, 49, 132, 160, 237, 247, 248, 267, 288, 292, 293, 294, 295, 296, 339.
Moreau de Saint-Méry, 183, 350.
Morny (Duc de), 171.
Mortier (Marshal), 220, 221, 232, 298, 393, 394.
Mounier, 23.
Moustache (*Courier*), 46.
Moustier (M. de), 47.
Mouton (Colonel), *see* Lobau (Count).
Mulgrave, 335.
Murat (Prince Joachim), 9, 94, 202, 268, 298, 313, 336, 396.
Murat (Mme.), *see* Bonaparte (Princess Caroline).
Murray (*American Diplomatist*), 28.
Murray (Lady), 320.
Musnier (General), 91.

N.

Naigeon, 4.
Naples (King of), 86.
Napoleon (Son of Queen Hortense), 313, 335.
Nassau-Orange (Prince of), 161.
Neuf-Château (François de), 5.
Ney (Marshal, Duke of Elchingen), 298, 390, 396.

Nightingale (Captain), 90, 91.
Nodier (Charles), 210, 211, 212, 213.
Nogaret (Felix), 5.
Nowosiltzoff (Count), 382, 383.

O.

Orange (Prince of), 323.
Ordener (General), 252, 254, 267, 269, 272, 273, 276, 277.
Orleans (Duke of), 71.
Orleans (Princes of), 248.
Oromaze, 281.
Orsay (Comte d'), 127, 128.
Ossian, 192.
Otranto (Duke of), *see* Fouché.
Otto (M.), 36, 40, 76, 77, 78, 134, 384.

P.

Paisiello, 177, 178.
Palissot, 3, 4, 5, 6, 7, 57, 98.
Parma (Infant of), *see* Etruria (King of).
Paterson (Miss Eliza), 318, 319, 346.
Paterson (Mr.), 318.
Paul I. (Emperor of Russia), 60, 61, 161, 203, 278.
Pelet (General), 394.
Peltier, 210.
Pergolesi, 178.
Perignon (General), 297.
Permon (Mme. de), 110.
Petty (Lord Henry), 159.
Pichegru, 235, 237, 238, 245, 247, 257, 267, 270, 293, 294.
Pichon (*Councillor of State*), 29.
Piombino (Prince of), 341.
Pitt, 40, 76, 79, 82, 159, 208, 234, 383.
Pius VII., *see* Pope (The).
Plato, 109.
Polignac (the brothers), 245, 248.
Pompadour (Mme. de), 4.
Pope (Alexander), 4.
Pope (The), 64, 65, 66, 68, 318,

327, 328, 329, 330, 331, 337, 342, 343, 344.
Portalis, 45, 74, 87, 142, 314.
Portugal (Prince Regent of), 167, 169, 170.
Poter (M.), 149.
Pradt (Abbé), 227, 344.
Prussia (King of), 161, 162, 199, 200, 201, 203, 228, 229, 230, 237, 323, 386, 388, 397, 406, 407.
Prussia (Queen of), 161, 388.

Q.

Querel, 246, 247.
Quinette (M.), 92.

R.

Raguideau (M.), 331, 332, 333.
Rapp (General), 117.
Raynal (Abbé), 23.
Rayneval (M. de), 218.
Réal, 188, 247, 251, 256, 260, 261, 264.
Reding (Aloys), 197, 198.
Regnauld de Saint-Jean-d'Angély, 55, 144.
Regnier, *see* Massa (Duke of).
Reich (Baroness de), 274.
Rémusat (M. de), 117.
Rémusat (Mme. de), 118.
Repnin (Colonel), 404.
Reynier (General), 157, 158.
Rheims (Archbishop of), 201.
Richard Cœur-de-Lion, 394, 395.
Richelieu (Duke of), 155.
Ripault, 114.
Rivière (M. de), 245, 248.
Robert (*Restaurateur*), 353.
Rochambeau (General), 194.
Rochefoucauld-Liancourt (M. de la), 30.
Roederer, 28, 46, 55, 148, 197.
Roll (Baron de), 149.
Romulus, 71.
Roquelaure (M. de), 227, 228.
Rosey (Captain de), 236, 246, 274, 275.

Rosily (Admiral), 310.
Rousseau (Jean-Jacques), 22, 23.
Rovigo (Duc de), *see* Savary.
Rumbold, 237.
Russia (Emperor of), *see* Alexander I., *and* Paul I.

S.

Sabran (Mme. de), *see* Boufflers.
Saint-Ange, 5.
Saint-Leu (Comte du), *see* Bonaparte (Prince Louis).
Saladin, 394.
Sanson, 175.
Santa-Cruz (Marquise de), 59.
Savary (M., Duc de Rovigo), 117, 245, 247, 261, 265, 282, 399, 404.
Saxe-Hildburghausen (Princess of), 386.
Schimmelpenninck (M.), 84, 90.
Schimmelpenninck (Mme.), 90.
Schmidt (Captain), 250.
Scipio, 177.
Sébastiani (General), 90, 195.
Ségur (Comte de), 300, 302, 303, 304, 305.
Ségur (Comtesse de), 302, 304.
Ségur (Marshal de), 302, 303.
Ségur (Octave de), 300, 301, 302, 303, 304.
Ségur (Philip de), 301, 304.
Ségur (Raymond de), 301, 302.
Sémonville (M. de), 324.
Serrurier (Marshal), 297.
Shee (M.), 249.
Sièyès, 18.
Siméon (Comte), 46, 52, 228.
Simon (General), 71.
Singleton (Colonel), 91.
Smith (Admiral Sir Sidney), 310.
Smith (Colonel), 250.
Smith (Spencer), 234, 236.
Soult (Marshal), 117, 298.
Souwaroff, 48.
Souza (M. de), 171, 172.
Souza (Mme. de), 171, 172.
Spina (Mgr., Archbishop of Corinth), 64, 65, 66, 72, 74.

Stadion (M. de), 398.
Staël (Mme. de), 54, 55, 56.
Stuart (Lord Dudley), 59.
Survilliers (Comte de), *see* Bonaparte (Prince Joseph).
Sussex (Duke of), 320.

T.

Talhouet (Mme. de), 118.
Talleyrand (Charles Maurice de, Prince de Bénévent), 15, 17, 18, 19, 20, 24, 35, 53, 137, 168, 201, 251, 252, 254, 256, 267, 268, 269, 270, 271, 276, 277, 279, 320, 323, 324, 335, 362, 385.
Talma, 6.
Taylor, 235.
Thainville, 175.
Theilhard, 16.
Thibaudeau, 409.
Thiers (M.), 150, 151, 270.
Thumery (General), 250.
Tissot (Doctor), 111.
Tissot (M.), 282.
Toussaint L'Ouverture, 193, 194.
Treves (Elector of), 389
Troché, 247.
Turreau (General), 319.
Tuscany (Grand-duke of), 44, 45.

V.

V―― (Professor), 24.

Valin (Colonel), 300.
Vanderberghe, 364.
Vauban (Comte de), 240.
Vauborel (General), 256.
Vaudreuil (M. de), 149.
Vauguyon (Duc de la), 204.
Verhuell (Admiral), 310.
Verhuell (Captain), 309.
Vicence (Duc de), *see* Caulaincourt.
Vigogne (*Equerry*), 126.
Villeneuve (Admiral), 310, 311, 322, 338, 339, 362, 365, 382.
Voltaire, 3, 22, 58, 374.

W.

Walmoden (General Count), 402, 403.
Wellington (Duke of), 127, 179, 180.
Whitworth (Lord), 209, 214, 215, 216.
Wickham, 234.
Willot, 149.
Woronzoff (*Russian Chancellor*), 217.
Wright, 295.
Wurtemberg (Princess Catherine of), 319.
Wurtemberg (Elector-King of), 319, 386, 409.
Wurtemberg (Electress-Queen of), 386.
Wurtemberg (Prince Paul of), 386.

INDEX

OF BOOKS, PERIODICALS, PLAYS, HYMNS, SONGS, ETC., REFERRED TO IN THIS VOLUME.

Aid to Memory, by Gassendi, 371.
Ambigu (L'), Newspaper edited by Peltier, 210, 245.
Animaux (Les) Parlants, Poem by Casti, 54, 57, 58.
Antichambre (L'), Play by Dupaty, 155.
Archives of the Lyons Academy, 25.
Atala, by M. de Chateaubriand, 54.
Biography of the First Years of Napoleon Bonaparte, by Baron Coston, 110.
Brutus, Tragedy by Voltaire, 376.
Bulle (La) d'Alexandre VI., Tale by Casti, 58.
Chant du Départ, by Chénier and Méhul, 377.
Chronological Abridgment of the History of France from 1787 to 1818, by Abbé de Montgaillard, 239.
Constitutionnel (Le), 282.
Courrier (Le) des États-Unis, American Newspaper, 23.
Cours de Littérature, by Lemercier, 125.
Death of Cæsar, Tragedy by Voltaire, 108, 376, 377.
Devin (Le) du Village, Opera by Rousseau, 22, 377.
Dictionnaire des Anonymes, by Barbier, 115.
Don Sancho of Aragon, by Corneille, 6.
Dunciad, Satire by Pope, 4, 5.

Edward in Scotland, Tragedy by Alexandre Duval, 155, 156.
Épreuves du Sentiment, by Arnauld Bacculard, 21.
Genius (The) of Christianity, by M. de Chateaubriand, 75, 278, 280, 282.
Historical Memoirs to Serve for the History of the Vendée War, by the Comte de Vauban, 240.
History of France, by the Comte de Montgaillard, 239.
History of Napoleon in 1815, by Fleury de Chaboulon, 267.
History of the Campaign of 1809, by General Pelet, 394.
History of the Crusades, by Michaud, 282.
Hours (The), Ballet by Dupaty, 156.
Journal (Le) des Débats, 272.
Manco-Capac, Tragedy by Abbé Leblanc, 4.
Mémoires de Napoléon à Ste-Hélène, by Gourgaud and Montholon, 25.
Mémoires du Règne de Napoléon en 1815, by Fleury de Chaboulon, 135.
Memoirs of Bourrienne, 12.
Memoirs of General Hugo, 49.
Memoirs of Laréveillière-Lepeaux, 12.
Memoirs of Stanislas Girardin, 22.
Memorial of St. Helena, by Las Cases, 24.

INDEX.

Mercure (Le), 281.
Metamorphoses of Ovid, translated by Saint-Ange, 5.
Moïna, Story by Joseph Bonaparte, 28.
Moniteur (Le), 61, 142, 176, 195, 196, 202, 209, 227, 257, 266, 294, 384.
Napoléone (La), Ode by Charles Nodier, 210, 211.
Nouvelle (La) Heloïse, by Rousseau, 22.
Parallèle de César, Cromwell, et Bonaparte, by M. de Fontanes, 315.
Philosophes (Les), Comedy by Palissot, 3, 4.
Précis des Événements Militaires, by Mathieu Dumas, 39.

Proserpine, Opera by Paisiello, 178.
Réné, by M. de Chateaubriand, 54.
Revolutions in Italy, by Abbé Denina, 114.
Revue des Deux Mondes, 109.
Secret Memoirs of M. J. G. de Montgaillard during the Years of his Exile, 238.
Spectateur (Le) Militaire, Newspaper, 11.
Stabat Mater, composed by Pergolesi, 178.
To Kill is not to Murder, pamphlet, 245.
Veillons au Salut de l'Empire, Patriotic Hymn, 377.
Vert-vert, Poem by Gresset, 92.
Zaïre, Tragedy by Corneille, 376.

END OF VOL. I.

D. APPLETON & CO.'S PUBLICATIONS.

A FRIEND OF THE QUEEN. (Marie Antoinette —Count de Fersen.) By PAUL GAULOT. With Two Portraits. 12mo. Cloth, $2.00.

"M. Gaulot deserves thanks for presenting the personal history of Count Fersen in a manner so evidently candid and unbiased."—*Philadelphia Bulletin.*

"There are some characters in history of whom we never seem to grow tired. Of no one is this so much the case as of the beautiful Marie Antoinette, and of that life which is at once so eventful and so tragic. . . . In this work we have much that up to the present time has been only vaguely known."—*Philadelphia Press.*

"A historical volume that will be eagerly read."—*New York Observer.*

"One of those captivating recitals of the romance of truth which are the gilding of the pill of history."—*London Daily News.*

"It tells with new and authentic details the romantic story of Count Fersen's (the friend of the Queen) devotion to Marie Antoinette, of his share in the celebrated flight to Varennes, and in many other well-known episodes of the unhappy Queen's life."—*London Times.*

"If the book had no more recommendation than the mere fact that Marie Antoinette and Count Fersen are rescued at last from the voluminous and contradictory representations with which the literature of that period abounds, it would be enough compensation to any reader to become acquainted with the true delineations of two of the most romantically tragic personalities."—*Boston Globe.*

"One of the most interesting volumes of recent publication, and sure to find its place among the most noteworthy of historical novels."—*Bos on Times.*

THE ROMANCE OF AN EMPRESS. Catherine II, of Russia. By K. WALISZEWSKI. With Portrait. 12mo. Cloth, $2.00.

"Of Catharine's marvelous career we have in this volume a sympathetic, learned, and picturesque narrative. No royal career, not even of some of the Roman or papal ones, has better shown us how truth can be stranger than fiction."—*New York Times.*

"A striking and able work, deserving of the highest praise."—*Philadelphia Ledger.*

"The book is well called a romance, for, although no legends are admitted in it, and the author has been at pains to present nothing but verified facts, the actual career of the subject was so abnormal and sensational as to seem to belong to fiction."—*New York Sun.*

"A dignified, handsome, indeed superb volume, and well worth careful reading."—*Chicago Herald.*

"It is a most wonderful story, charmingly told, with new material to sustain it, and a breadth and temperance and consideration that go far to soften one's estimate of one of the most extraordinary women of history."—*New York Commercial Advertiser.*

"A romance in which fiction finds no place; a charming narrative wherein the author fearlessly presents the results of what has been obviously a thorough and impartial investigation."—*Philadelphia Press.*

"The book makes the best of reading, because it is written without fear or favor. . . . The volume is exceedingly suggestive, and gives to the general reader a plain, blunt, strong, and somewhat prejudiced but still healthy view of one of the greatest women of whom history bears record."—*New York Herald.*

"The perusal of such a book can not fail to add to that breadth of view which is so essential to the student of universal history."—*Philadelphia Bulletin.*

New York: D. APPLETON & CO., 72 Fifth Avenue.

D. APPLETON & CO.'S PUBLICATIONS.

THE GILDED MAN (EL DORADO), and other Pictures of the Spanish Occupancy of America. By A. F. BANDELIER. 12mo. Cloth, $1.50.

"Every paper in this volume is wonderfully interesting, and the collection is of such historical value as to make it a necessary part of every library in which American history is represented."—*Boston Herald.*

"One of the most entertaining of recent historical works, and, besides its novelty and freshness has the great merit of being original historical research."—*Philadelphia Times.*

"Mr. Bandelier's work under the auspices of the Archæological Institute of America and on the Hemenway Survey entitles him to rank as the leading documentary historian of the Southwest. . . . The book possesses genuine historical value, and is a necessary part of the annals of our country."—*Philadelphia Ledger.*

"Just such a work as Mr. Bandelier has done has long been needed. . . . A contribution of the first order of value to a part of American history that deserves to be more fully studied."—*Literary World.*

WARRIORS OF THE CRESCENT. By W. H. DAVENPORT ADAMS, author of "Battle Stories from English History," etc. 12mo. Cloth, $1.50.

"A work without a rival in its particular field. . . . All the gorgeousness of the barbaric East invests this glowing pageant of kings and conquerors. . . . This is a remarkably able book in thought and in manner of presentation."—*Philadelphia Ledger.*

"A lively, carefully prepared chronicle of the careers of quite a number of the Mohammedan rulers in Asian regions who made their marks, one way or another, in the development of the peculiar civilization of the East. . . . This author has selected from the long chronicle the salients likely to be most interesting, and has obviously taken much pains to sift the fact carefully out of the rather confused mass of fact and fable in the Moslem chronicles."—*New York Commercial Advertiser.*

"Nowhere in history are there to be found such records of conquest, such frightful tales of blood, such overwhelming defeats or victories, as in the lives of the Asiatic sovereigns. . . . The author is a historian who tells his story and stops. He has done his work faithfully and well."—*Cincinnati Commercial Gazette.*

PICTURES FROM ROMAN LIFE AND STORY. By Professor A. J. CHURCH, author of "Stories from Homer," "Stories from Virgil," etc. Illustrated. 12mo. Cloth, $1.50.

"Prof. Church is a tried and approved master of the art of interesting young people in historical themes. The present work, while too thoughtful to be called strictly juvenile, treats of the great emperors and families of Rome in a simple narrative style certain to captivate youth and older people fond of historic lore."—*The Chautauquan.*

"The material for these sketches is drawn partly from the inexhaustible riches of Plutarch, partly from contemporaneous history, and partly from letters, edicts, etc.; and, well chosen and briefly related, are interesting, whetting the appetite of the studiously inclined. . . . Various illustrations add to the interest of the work."—*Springfield Republican.*

"Each of the chapters presents some striking scene or personality in the period from Augustus to Marcus Aurelius. . . . Several of the chapters are thrown into the form of contemporary letters. The plan of the book is well conceived, and the subjects are those of general human interest."—*New York Critic.*

New York · D. APPLETON & CO., 72 Fifth Avenue.

D. APPLETON & CO.'S PUBLICATIONS.

LOUISA MÜHLBACH'S HISTORICAL NOVELS. New edition, 18 vols. Illustrated. 12mo. Cloth, per volume, $1.00. Set, in box, $18.00.

In offering to the public our *new and illustrated 12mo edition* of Louisa Mühlbach's celebrated historical romances we wish to call attention to the continued and increasing popularity of these books for over thirty years. These romances are as well known in England and America as in the author's native country, Germany, and it has been the unanimous verdict that no other romances reproduce so vividly the spirit and social life of the times which are described. In the vividness of style, abundance of dramatic incidents, and the distinctness of the characters portrayed, these books offer exceptional entertainment, while at the same time they familiarize the reader with the events and personages of great historical epochs.

The titles are as follows:

Napoleon and the Queen of Prussia.
The Empress Josephine.
Napoleon and Blucher.
Queen Hortense.
Marie Antoinette and her Son.
Prince Eugene and his Times.
The Daughter of an Empress.
Joseph II and his Court.
Frederick the Great and his Court.
Frederick the Great and his Family.
Berlin and Sans-Souci.
Goethe and Schiller.
The Merchant of Berlin, and Maria Theresa and her Fireman.
Louisa of Prussia and her Times.
Old Fritz and the New Era.
Andreas Hofer.
Mohammed Ali and his House.
Henry VIII and Catherine Parr.

New York: D. APPLETON & CO., 72 Fifth Avenue.

D. APPLETON & CO.'S PUBLICATIONS.

THE UNITED STATES OF AMERICA. A Study of the American Commonwealth, its Natural Resources, People, Industries, Manufactures, Commerce, and its Work in Literature, Science, Education, and Self-Government. Edited by NATHANIEL S. SHALER, S. D., Professor of Geology in Harvard University. In two volumes, royal 8vo. With Maps, and 150 full-page Illustrations. Cloth, $10.00.

In this work the publishers offer something which is not furnished by histories or encyclopædias, namely, a succinct but comprehensive expert account of our country at the present day. The very extent of America and American industries renders it difficult to appreciate the true meaning of the United States of America. In this work the American citizen can survey the land upon which he lives, and the industrial, social, political, and other environments of himself and his fellow-citizens. The best knowledge and the best efforts of experts, editor, and publishers have gone to the preparation of a standard book dedicated to the America of the present day ; and the publishers believe that these efforts will be appreciated by those who desire to inform themselves regarding the America of the end of the century.

LIST OF CONTRIBUTORS.

HON. WILLIAM L. WILSON, Chairman of the Ways and Means Committee, Fifty-third Congress.
HON. J. R. SOLEY, formerly Assistant Secretary of the Navy.
EDWARD ATKINSON, LL. D, PH. D.
COL. T. A. DODGE, U. S. A.
COL. GEORGE E. WARING, JR.
J. B. McMASTER, Professor of History in the University of Pennsylvania.
CHARLES DUDLEY WARNER, LL D.
MAJOR J. W. POWELL, Director of the U. S. Geological Survey and the Bureau of Ethnology.
WILLIAM T. HARRIS, LL. D.; U. S. Commissioner of Education.
LYMAN ABBOTT, D. D.
H. H. BANCROFT, author of "Native Races of the Pacific Coast."
HARRY PRATT JUDSON, Head Dean of the Colleges, University of Chicago.
JUDGE THOMAS M. COOLEY, formerly Chairman of the Interstate Commerce Commission.
CHARLES FRANCIS ADAMS.
D. A. SARGENT, M. D., Director of the Hemenway Gymnasium, Harvard University.
CHARLES HORTON COOLEY.
A. E. KENNELLY, Assistant to Thomas A. Edison.
D. C. GILMAN, LL.D , President of Johns Hopkins University.
H. G. PROUT, Editor of the Railroad Gazette.
F. D. MILLET, formerly Vice-President of the National Academy of Design.
F. W. TAUSSIG, Professor of Political Economy in Harvard University.
HENRY VAN BRUNT.
H. P. FAIRFIELD.
SAMUEL W. ABBOTT, M. D., Secretary of the State Board of Health, Massachusetts.
N. S. SHALER.

Sold only by subscription. Prospectus, giving detailed chapter-titles and specimen illustrations, mailed free on request.

New York: D. APPLETON & CO., 72 Fifth Avenue.

www.ingramcontent.com/pod-product-compliance
Lightning Source LLC
Chambersburg PA
CBHW022141300426
44115CB00006B/291